ROYAL NAVY SHIPBOARD AIRCRAFT DEVELOPMENTS 1912 - 1931

DICK CRONIN

Some aspects of early naval aviation at sea

"The Navy is our Father (in the strictly legal sense)
That binds an obligation just of shillings, pounds and pence.
A parent so neglectful of us children of the Air,
That had not hope maintained us we'd have died of sheer despair.
For Our Father didn't want us and he didn't want to know
What it was we wanted or the way, the why or wherefore."

Sqdn Cdr Douglas Hyde-Thomson RNAS, 1917

An Air-Britain Publication

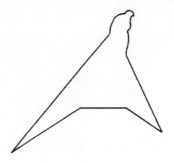

Published in the United Kingdom
by Air-Britain (Historians) Ltd
1 East Street, Tonbridge, Kent

ISBN 0 85130 165 7

Typeset by Arioma Editorial Services
Gloucester House, High Street,
Borth, Dyfed, SY24 5HZ

Printed by Halstan Limited,
Plantation Road, Amersham,
Bucks, HP6 6HJ

Cover drawings by George Burn

Front cover:

Sopwith Pup N6453 in which on 1st October, 1917,
Flt Cdr F.J. Rutland took off from B turret ramp on
board HMS *Repulse* to pioneer this type of
launching.

Back cover:

Baby 8188 was operated by HMS *Ben-my-Chree*
with the EI &ESS from May 1916 until the ship
was lost at Castelorizo in January 1917.

FOREWORD

Dick Cronin has invited me to write a foreword to this book, which I have seen grow from small beginnings. I feel privileged to be able to do so.

As a hardworking Leicestershire farmer, Dick has had to fit in his researches between harvesting, cattle feeding and other demanding tasks. He comes from a naval family and served with the Royal Navy himself during the Second World War. He has memories of Murray Sueter, the father of British naval aviation, being entertained at the family dinner table.

His naval background, and a long-standing interest in the earlier years of aviation in general and British naval aviation in particular, drew him in the early eighties to the self-imposed task of writing down for posterity an account of the work of some of the pioneers in this field. He sought my help and guidance from time to time, but the main inspiration and the great depth of research were entirely his own.

Dick felt that there were a number of aspects of early British naval aviation which had been given little attention and were in danger of being lost in the mists of antiquity. These he refers to as the sideshows and, in terms of the whole, this is probably an apt phrase to use. However, a lot of hard work went into developing these peripheral aspects of the use of air power at sea, and some of the results were impressive by any standards. Notable examples were the involvement in the sinking of the German cruiser *Königsberg* and the destruction of the Zeppelin L53.

A surprising quantity of material relating to these varied activities still survives, mainly at the Public Record Office, but also in various other national archives. Over the years, Dick has ferreted these out, extracted everything he could find of relevance, and turned the resulting mound of paper into a very readable account. In addition he has interspersed his narrative with comprehensive lists showing exactly which individual ships and aircraft were involved in each activity, the whole illustrated with many hundreds of photographs in addition to a number of very useful line drawings. The book therefore provides for future researchers a wealth of reference material which has hitherto not been readily available.

Ray Sturtivant, I.S.O.

PREFACE

History should be fun, and the task of a historian should be to see yesterday with the eyes of yesterday. One hopes that some of the fun is here, and if the two-edged sword of hindsight is not entirely absent, then perhaps some allowance may be made for human nature.

The narrative is based upon unpublished sources which are listed separately, and is an attempt, occupying parts of eight years, to trace the development of aeroplanes and seaplanes for use in ships of the Royal Navy, the thinking behind the uses to which these aircraft might be put and finally their operational employment from 1912 to 1919.

With the exceptions of the service of H.M.Ships *Ben-my-Chree* and *Empress* with the East Indies and Egypt Seaplane Squadron, the story of the other eight specialised seaplane carriers and of the two aircraft carriers has been purposely omitted. Instead the opportunity has been taken to record the lesser known aspects of the early use of air power at sea by the Royal Navy - in the ''sideshows'' in fact. As a consequence of a long-standing interest in 20th Century naval history, attention has been given to the ships from which the aircraft operated.

Of prime importance to the compilation has been the very generous help received from many people and organisations in this country and abroad. Two people have made the book possible. My daughter Nicola Driver's typing of what was euphemistically known as ''the manuscript'' has succeeded in making it legible and getting it airborne. And Ray Sturtivant, besides ensuring that the project suffered no engine failure, provided invaluable items from his own researches into RNAS serials. The author just had all the fun, having merely to kick the tyre and light the fire. Thank you both.

Over the past eight years Joe Barr (Australia), Anne Bell, Jack Bruce, Ian Burns (Canada), John Cross, Jean-Pierre Dubois (France), Mike Goodall, Dick Layman (USA), Stuart Leslie, Len Lovell, Graham Mottram and Bob Todd have all provided me with specialised information and shown me some of my mistakes. The errors and omissions that remain are therefore all mine.

I have been fortunate in enlisting the talent of George Burn who has designed an excellent cover. Mike Keep's unrivalled skills as a draughtsman have depicted several of the lesser known types of heavier than air craft employed by the RNAS and RAN. Mick Davis has transformed my crude attempts at map making, and my attempts to illustrate platforms in HMS Ships, into something worthy of an Air-Britain publication. I am indebted to all three. The line drawings of the five seaplane carriers comprising the East Indies and Egypt Seaplane Squadron are based on drawings by the late C.E.Hughes in his excellent book ''Above and Beyond Palestine, published in 1930.

I acknowledge also the help and encouragement received from R.C.B.Ashworth, R.F.Barker, P.J.Kemp, E.Ledger, K.Macpherson (Canada), R.Mack, J.W.Mitchley, L.Morareau (France), P.G.Murton, R.H.Nailer, H.P.Playford, Mrs J.Porter, S.Pulfrey, Professor Sir A.Robinson, V.Sheppard, Dr P.Thwaites, A.K.Vicary and M.Willis.

All of those named above are associated with one or more Societies or Museums which deserve recognition for the knowledge they share and which is there for the seeking. These organisations are Air-Britain, Cross and Cockade International, Australian War Memorial, Fleet Air Arm Museum, Imperial War Museum, Maritime Photo Library, Museum of Army Flying, National Maritime Museum, Port of Lowestoft Preservation Society, Royal Marines Museum, Royal Air Force Museum, World Ship Society and World Ship Society Photo Library.

I hope that everyone who has helped me will recognise, as I do, their individual contributions, and trust I have let down none of them.

Writing this account of early naval aviation has been a kind of love affair. Any fool can start one, but ending it is harder. Fortunately I was told to stop.

Dick Cronin
Shornhill Farm, Twycross
January 1990

INTRODUCTION

The early days of naval aviation at sea, with the exception of the diligently researched histories published in Cross and Cockade Journals, have received little attention.

The methods employed in operating aeroplanes and seaplanes from HM Ships now seem primitive, and they were, because flying in war had no precedent. However, the first attempts by the RNAS to employ airpower at sea provided a model upon which future exponents could base their policy.

Although aeroplanes flown from platforms in cruisers and capital ships had few opportunities for action, their use paved the way for and spurred the development of a warship with a landing deck - the Aircraft Carrier. Had the war lasted beyond November 1918, aeroplanes operating from the Royal Navy's first time Aircraft Carriers would have attacked the German High Seas Fleet in its harbours.

Seaplanes were operated extensively in the North Sea between 1914-1916 from cruisers, from the specialised Seaplane Carriers, and from trawlers and paddle steamers on anti-Zeppelin patrols, but to very little effect. A combination of adverse weather conditions and the poor performance of the seaplanes tipped the scales heavily in favour of the Zeppelins.

However seaplanes found their true niche under better flying conditions in the Eastern Mediterranean, Red Sea and off East Africa in support of land operations. The possibilities of seaplanes for reconnaissance, and spotting for ships' gunfire, at the Dardanelles in 1915 were realised by the men who flew them, but not then by the Admiralty.

The whole Mediterranean from 1914-1917 was a backwater of the war at sea, with constant disagreement between the Allies and ineffective use of the very limited resources in ships and aircraft at their disposal.

But in the Eastern Mediterranean the East Indies and Egypt Seaplane Squadron demonstrated the proper use of sea-borne airpower, and showed that effective co-operation with the French Navy brought dividends.

The purpose of the narrative has been to highlight some of the lesser known aspects of the Royal Navy's early use of aircraft launched from ships in war and peace.

*For Anne
and Eileen*

MAPS AND DIAGRAMS

	Page
Patent for ship catapult by Sueter etc Feb 1911	17
Parent ship for aircraft, Beardmore Dec 1912	17
HMS *Hibernia* fixed forecastle ramp 2.5.1912	18
HMS *Aurora* fixed forecastle ramp 1915	18
HMAS *Sydney* revolving platform 1917	42
HMS *Delhi* revolving platform 1919	42
HMS *Royalist* fixed platform 1918	43
The lighter side of turret operations (Vic Sheppard)	47
HMS *Caledon/Cassandra* fixed forecastle ramp 1917	64
HMS *Lion* turret ramp 1918	68
HMS *Barham* turret ramp 1918	68
Mafia Island 11.14 - 7.15	130
Attack on *Königsberg* 6.7.15	136
Rufiji Delta 6-11.7.15	140
Seaplane ops against Zeppelins and their bases 1915-1916	158
Aegean - RNAS seaplane ops 1915 - 1918	171
EI&ESS against Turkish railway communications 1915-1917	181
EI&ESS ops off Turkish coast 1915-1917	188
HMS *Raven II*	196
HMS *Anne*	200
HMS *Ben-my-Chree*	204
EI&ESS ops against Turkish forces in Hejaz and Yemen 1915-1918	206
EI&ESS attack against El Afule railway junction 25.8.16	221
EI&ESS ops against Turkish forces in Hejaz 1915-1918	227
Red Sea: EI&ESS 1915-1917	239
Beirut harbour - Short 184 targets 13.5.17 & 17.8.17	248
HMS *Empress*	253
Short 184 ops 3rd Battle of Gaza 10.17-11.17	256
HMS *City of Oxford*	265
Short 827 ops HMS *Himalaya, Manica, Laconia* 1916-1917	267
Short 184 operations in Caspian Sea 1919	288
Side view drawings of RNAS shipboard aircraft	352

CONTENTS PART I

I   Early Days, Home Waters 1912-1917   **Page 11**

Trials with fixed forecastle ramps 1912-1915. Beardmore and Lanchester projected designs for ''aircraft carrying ships'' 1914. Trials in *Hermes* 1913. Final development and eventual abandonment of fixed forecastle and quarterdeck ramps 1915-1917. Grand Fleet Aeronautical Committee 1917. First installation of fixed platforms in cruisers 1917. Policy for use of airpower at sea 1917.

II   Operational uses of platforms in cruisers, Home Waters 1917-1918   **Page 30**

Flt Sub Lt B.A. Smart's destruction of L23 from *Yarmouth*'s fixed platform 1917. Flt Lt A.C. Sharwood's 1918 flight from *Sydney*'s revolving platform. Final development of fixed platforms combined with bridge hangars and their eventual abandonment 1917-1918. Projected flying off platforms in destroyers 1918. Operation of 2F.1 Camels from towed lighters and Samson's trial 1918. Lt S.D. Culley's destruction of L53 in 1918. Installation and trials of revolving platforms 1917. Tables of cruisers fitted with platforms and examples of aeroplanes embarked 1917-1918. Post-war trials of revolving platforms.

III   Turret ramps in capital ships, Home Waters 1917-1918   **Page 57**

Sqdn Cdr F.J. Rutland's first flight from *Repulse* 1917. Development and trials of Tail Guide Trestle and Quick Release Stop. Flt Cdr D.G. Donald's first flight from *Australia* in a Ship Strutter 1918. Tables of capital ships fitted with turret ramps with examples of aeroplanes embarked 1917-1918.

IV   Turret ramps in capital ships 1924-1931. Catapult trials 1911-1927   **Page 70**

Postwar use of turret ramps. Gravity operated catapults. RAE catapult trials 1917. Catapult trials in *Slinger* 1917. RAE. 1921 Target and gravity operated catapult trials 1923- 1924. Catapult trials in *Vindictive* 1925. RAE Larynx drone 1927.

APPENDIX IA   Examples of aeroplanes embarked in ships of the Grand Fleet 1917-1918 with their serial numbers for cross reference purposes.   **Page 88**

APPENDIX IB   Examples of aircrew borne in ships of the Grand Fleet on 2 September 1918.   **Page 94**

CONTENTS PART II

V   Seaplane operations East Mediterranean 1914 and East Africa 1915   **Page 123**

Operational limitations of seaplanes. Reconnaissance by *Doris*'s seaplane over Syria and Palestine 1914-1915. Nieuport seaplanes embarked in *Diana* and *Minerva* in Gulf of Akaba 1914. *Roberts* operates a Short 166 at Dardanelles 1915. Seaplanes employed in attack on SMS *Königsberg* in Rufiji Delta 1915.

VI   Anti-Zeppelin operations by seaplanes in Home Waters 1915- 1916   **Page 153**

Seaplanes embarked in trawlers for anti-Zeppelin patrols 1915. Patrols augmented by paddle steamers carrying seaplanes 1916. Abortive attempts to bomb Zeppelin bases by seaplanes operated from cruisers of the Harwich Force 1915- 1916.

VII   Early operations by *Anne*'s and *Raven II*'s seaplanes, East Mediterranean January-April 1915   **Page 170**

Aenne Rickmers and *Rabenfels* converted to seaplane carriers December 1914. Flights by seaplanes from *Anne* and *Raven II* over Egypt and Palestine January-March 1915. *Anne* ordered to Gulf of Smyrna March 1915. *Anne* torpedoed by *Demir Hissar* off Chustan Island 11 March 1915. *Anne* dry docked at Alexandria for repairs May 1915.

VIII   Operations by *Raven II*'s seaplanes April-July 1915   Page 180

Raven II's seaplanes spot for fire of French warships April 1915. Rendezvous with French warships off Asia Minor April 1915. Reconnaissances over Palestine May 1915. Reconnaissances by Nieuport seaplanes from French cruiser *Montcalm* off Akaba May 1915. Reconnaissances by Nieuport seaplanes from *Hardinge* in Red Sea June 1915. Further cruises by *Raven II* off Syria to land Agents July 1915.

IX   *Anne*, returns to service, June-December 1915   Page 189

Anne's seaplanes operate off Asia Minor July 1915. Combined operations with *Raven II* in Gulf of Alexandretta to bomb Chicaldere bridge August 1915. *Anne*'s seaplanes fly reconnaissances over Palestine and Syria August-September 1915. Further flights over Palestine and Syria and landing Agents October-November 1915. Attacks by *Anne*'s seaplanes on railway at Mersina December 1915.

X   Operations by *Anne* and *Raven II* January-May 1916, and *Ben- my-Chree* February 1916   Page 197

Ben-my-Chree's first operations with EI and ESS. *Anne*'s last sorties with Nieuport seaplanes March 1916. *Anne* at Castelorizo for reconnaissance of suspected U-Boat base at Marmarice April 1916. French Nieuport seaplanes leave EI and ESS May 1916. Operations by Nieuport seaplanes from *Campinas* March 1916 at Castelorizo.

XI   Operations by the three seaplane carriers of EI and ESS April-August 1916   Page 205

Cdr C.R. Samson assumes command of EI and ESS May 1916. *Raven II*'s seaplanes bomb Turkish forces near Aden April 1916. *Ben-my-Chree*'s seaplanes renew this attack in June 1916. *Anne* in Red Sea June-July 1916. *Ben-my-Chree*'s seaplanes attack El Afule junction July 1916. *Anne*'s seaplanes spot for French warships bombarding Mersina August 1916. *Raven II* to Gulf of Akaba for photo reconnaissance by her seaplanes, and then to Red Sea August 1916. *Ben-my- Chree*'s seaplanes reconnoitre Palestine coastline and attack El Afule August 1916.

XII   Further operations by the three seaplane carriers of EI and ESS August 1916-January 1917   Page 220

Seaplanes from *Anne, Raven II* and *Ben-my-Chree* bomb El Afule junction August 1916. Methods employed in launching and recovering seaplanes. Duties of observers. *Raven II* bombed at Port Said August 1916. *Anne*'s seaplanes active in Red Sea September 1916. *Northbrook* embarks a Schneider from *Anne* September 1916. *Anne* returns to Syrian coast October 1916. *Ben-my-Chree* seaplanes in action off El Arish September 1916. Joint attack by seaplanes from *Ben-my-Chree* and *Raven II* on Chicaldere Bridge December 1916. *Ben-my-Chree* lost at Castelorizo January 1917.

XIII   Operations by *Anne* and *Raven II* Red Sea and Indian Ocean January-June 1917   Page 238

Anne proceeds to Red Sea where her seaplanes spot for bombardment of Wej, January 1917. Seaplanes from *Anne* make reconnaissance flights off Haifa February 1917. *Anne* paid off in August 1917. *Raven II*'s seaplanes search for German raider *Wolf* in Indian Ocean March-April 1917, and are again in action off Aden in June 1917.

XIV   Operations by *Empress*, East Mediterranean May-October 1917   Page 245

Empress replaces *Ben-my-Chree* in EI and ESS April 1917. Seaplanes from *Empress* attack Beirut May 1917. Samson succeeded in command of EI and ESS by Wg. Cdr. C. E. Risk in June 1917. Seaplanes from *Empress* bomb railway at Tul Keram June 1917. *Empress*'s seaplanes attack Adana July 1917, and Beirut in August and September 1917. Adana and Chicaldere bridge bombed by seaplanes from *Empress* in October 1917.

XV   Operations by seaplanes of EI and ESS off Palestine, October-November 1917   Page 255

City of Oxford joins EI and ESS August 1917. Operations in support of Allenby's advance in Palestine by seaplanes from *Raglan, City of Oxford, Empress* and *Raven II* October-November 1917. *Raglan*'s seaplane spots for her fire off Gaza November 1917. *Raven II* pays off December 1917.

XVI   Operations by *City of Oxford*, Red Sea February-March 1918   Page 262

Sortie by *Goeben* and *Breslau* and attacks on *Goeben* by seaplanes from *Empress* in January 1918. Operations by *City of Oxford*'s seaplanes in Red Sea February-March 1918. Absorption of RNAS into RAF April 1918.

XVII   Seaplane operations from *Laconia, Himalaya* and *Manica*, East Africa April 1916-May 1917   Page 266

Seaplane base established at Chukwani Bay March 1916. Operations commence to support land operations against Germans April 1916. New seaplanes received November 1916. *Laconia* and *Himalaya* leave the station by early 1917. *Manica* returns to Suez May 1917 and is decommissioned August 1917.

XVIII   Seaplanes embarked briefly in ships on anti-submarine and anti-Zeppelin duties 1915-1918   Page 277

Seaplanes embarked in cruisers 1915-1917. Use of seaplanes from AMC's on convoy escort duties 1918. Seaplanes engaged on anti-submarine patrols on board *Peony* and *Halcyon* during 1917. Intention to equip *Albion III, Beryl, Angora* and *Lordship* with seaplanes in Home Waters 1917.

XIX   Seaplane operations from *Alader Youssanoff* and *Orlionoch*, Caspian Sea 1919   Page 287

266 Squadron's Short 184s leave Mudros February 1919. Seaplane base constructed at Petrovsk March 1919. *Alader Youssanoff's* seaplanes take part in attack on Fort Alexandrovsk May 1919. *Orlionoch's* seaplanes engaged in attacking Bolshevik shipping July 1919. Both carriers turned over to Russian Volunteer Navy in August 1919.

XX   Tables of H.M.Ships operating or transporting seaplanes 1913-1920   Page 298

Brief particulars of each ship and its history, together with examples of seaplanes embarked.

APPENDIX IIA   Examples of seaplanes embarked in ships of EI and ESS 1915-1918 with their serial numbers for cross reference purposes.   Page 316

APPENDIX IIB   Aircrew of EI and ESS December 1914-January 1918, with Ships in which they served and dates on which they flew operationally from those ships.   Page 319

APPENDIX IIC   Summary of operations by the five seaplane carriers of EI and ESS from January 1915 to February 1918.   Page 325

APPENDIX IID   Extracts from the diary of Flt Lt G.B. Dacre between January and August 1916.   Page 330

APPENDIX IIE   Administration of HM Ships *Anne* and *Raven II* from June 1915.   Page 335

APPENDIX IIF   Brief details of French warships operating with EI and ESS 1915-1917.   Page 336

APPENDIX IIG   Brief details of H.M.Ships comprising Caspian Flotilla 1919   Page 338

APPENDIX IIH   Summary of seaplanes and pilots embarked in HM Ships engaged in anti-Zeppelin patrols in North Sea June 1915 - July 1917   Page 339

Sources   Page 341

Drawings of representative aircraft   Page 352

Additional illustrations   Page 354

Abbreviations   Page 370

Indices   Page 371

CHAPTER I

Early Days, Home Waters 1912-1917

From the start of the war of 1914-1918, the value of aerial reconnaissance in any naval engagement had been appreciated in some quarters, as had also the use of air power at sea as a means of frustrating the Germans' use of Zeppelins for reconnaissance. The practical application of this new factor in naval warfare was, however, beset by difficulties.

In the early years of the war, such ships of the Royal Navy as were capable of operating aircraft suffered from having a very slow speed at sea, well below the speeds of ships of the Fleet with which they had to operate. Additionally, because they had no decks on which aeroplanes could land, they were restricted to the use of seaplanes, which again imposed a severe penalty upon performance.

Although between 1914 and 1916 some ships operating seaplanes were equipped forward with flying-off decks, they were rarely used in practice. Instead the ship, having steamed to her launching position, stopped to hoist out her seaplanes, which might then take off if sea conditions allowed. Except under ideal conditions - rare in the North Sea - this was hardly an effective substitute for the light cruiser screen (the A to K line) operating in line abreast ahead of the Fleet, and acting as a reconnaissance force. A substitute was sought, and the decision was taken in 1917 to instal aircraft platforms on the forecastles of cruisers and, later, turret ramps mounted upon the turrets of capital ships' main armaments.

This decision was based upon the results of trials conducted with aircraft launched from fixed forecastle ramps in HM Ships between 1912 and 1915. On 9 January 1912 erection of a wooden launching ramp commenced on the forecastle of HMS *Africa* at Sheerness.

The first flight was scheduled for the following morning, but thick fog shrouded the harbour until noon. At 1300 however Lt C.R. Samson, flying a Short S38, T2, appeared over the harbour and landed at Grain. Here the Short was hauled over the sea wall and down onto the hard whence it was manhandled up two ramps onto a lighter and towed out to *Africa* by a steam pinnace from HMS *Actaeon*.

Once the Short had been hoisted on to *Africa*'s fixed forecastle ramp, contemporary accounts state that

Lt C.R. Samson making the first take-off from one of HM Ships at 1420 on 10th January 1912 in Short S.38 T2. The Short was airborne after a take-off run of 100ft from HMS Africa's fixed forecastle ramp while she lay at anchor.
(FAAM)

Samson ran down the starboard launching trough and jumped upon it to test its stability!

Satisfied that all was well Samson climbed to his seat and when the 50 hp Gnôme engine was started gave the order "Let go all" at 1420. Although *Africa* was at anchor the Short was airborne in 100 feet well before the end of the ramp was reached, and after circling the harbour Samson flew on to Eastchurch and landed.

By April of that year *Africa*'s fixed forecastle ramp had been installed in HMS *Hibernia*, and on 30 April/1 May at Sheerness dockyard she embarked two aircraft. These were the Short S38, T2 now re-engined with a 70 hp Gnôme, and the Short S41, H1, powered by a 100 hp Gnôme. At 1100 on 1 May *Hibernia* sailed for Portland, and Samson's log book for 2 May states

"6.a.m. Flew from forecastle of Hibernia steaming $10^1/_2$ knots in Weymouth Bay on T2, (70 hp Gnôme) 3 miles off breakwater. Flew to Lodmore and landed. 6 miles, 9 minutes - rather bumpy. Felt no gusts when leaving ship. T2 got off in 60 feet I should calculate. First time from ship steaming."

Elated by his success, Samson took up three of *Hibernia*'s officers for short flights in T2 on 3 May, and at 1000 that day he took off from Portland harbour in the Short S41, H1, and

"flew round Fleet in harbour, 3 miles in 4 minutes, landed on water. First time I have been off water and landed on water."

Hopes of continuing these trials in *Hibernia* were extinguished when the ship was designated to become flagship of Rear Admiral Sir C. Cradock. *Hibernia*'s fixed forecastle ramp was transferred to HMS *London*, from which on 4 July Lt Malone flew T2, airborne in 25 feet, into a Force 3 wind.

The accepted date for the first flight of an aircraft from one of HM Ships under way has long been 9 May 1912, but in fact *Hibernia*'s log records no flying from the ship on that date. However, her log for 2 May states that at 0427 she was making five knots off Portland and steering N73W. At 0430 she altered course to N56W which brought the ship into the Force 2 wind blowing from the west. By 0540 she had stopped, and at 0555 her log entry states

"Aeroplane T2 left ship, Cdr. Samson as pilot and flew to Lodmoor".

Although the ship's log does not say whether *Hibernia* was under way at the time, Samson's flying logbook leaves no doubt that this was the case.

These experiments had proved that it was possible to launch an aeroplane from a fighting ship, but because the ramp obstructed the ship's forward guns they did not lead directly to any practical scheme for launching aeroplanes. However, the experiments did arouse enthusiasm in the Royal Navy for the use of aeroplanes at sea, and a number of proposals were made for ships specially designed to carry aircraft at sea.

Of these the most practical was a design for a "Parent Ship for naval aeroplanes and TBD's" drawn up by William Beardmore & Company, and probably based on the ideas of Capt Murray Sueter (as he then was).

The design was submitted to the Admiralty by the Air Department in December 1912, and envisaged a ship of 15000 tons, 430 feet in length and with a beam of 82 feet at the waterline increasing to 110 feet overall. (see sketch)

Two parallel port and starboard superstructures each measuring approximately 220 feet long and 30 feet wide were to accommodate three aircraft with wings stretching fore and aft in each superstructure. These twin hangars were separated by a clear central deck 50 feet wide and joined above it by a navigating bridge forward of the parallel single funnels and mainmasts. This central deck was to be provided with a hinged windbreak at its forward end. The quarterdeck of approximately 70 feet in length and the forecastle of approximately 140 feet in length were to be unobstructed decks used for landing on and taking off respectively.

Correspondence in February 1913 between Winston Churchill, then First Lord of the Admiralty, and Admiral of the Fleet Sir Arthur Wilson in February 1913 reveals further details of the proposed Beardmore design. Churchill wrote:-

"The Third Sea Lord has under consideration a design of depot ship for destroyers and submarines that will carry 6 aeroplanes ready for service and 4 to 6 spares. Her chief features are:

Oil storage 5500 tons
6 x 4 inch AA guns
Powerful W/T equipment
Large supplies of ammunition, spare torpedoes, stores, etc

A ship is badly required for developing aeroplanes for ship work".

The "4 to 6 spares" were probably seaplanes with wings detached stowed in a forward hold and handled by cranes mounted on the forward ends of the twin superstructures. A similar pair of cranes was mounted aft. The AA armament was to be in single mounts on top of the twin superstructures. It was envisaged that aeroplanes would begin their take-off run from the deck between the twin superstructures. This 50 feet wide deck also allowed the movement of aircraft between take-off and landing decks.

Some 75 years later one can perceive the difficulties in operating aircraft from such a ship, but in 1913 the concept was several years ahead of its time, and its apparent merit convinced the Admiralty that a conference should be held to discuss one great drawback in the design. The drawback was the wasted space entailed in the stowage on board of aircraft with fixed wings, a problem to be solved the next year with the design of folding wings.

The conference was never held, and the ship was never built because it was considered uneconomical to build a new specialised ship before experience had been gained in operating aircraft from an existing vessel. And so failed the first formal proposal for an aircraft carrier for the Royal Navy.

Others whose thinking ran on similar lines included Dr F.W. Lanchester, whose outline specification for a "pontoon ship" for carrying aeroplanes with the Fleet appeared in November 1914. His proposed vessel of c.20,000 tons with a speed of 20 knots was to carry 50 to 60 aircraft, with hangars and workshops, and armed with guns sufficient to repel light cruiser attacks. The flight deck was to be an unrestricted space of 500 feet by 90 feet.

The exploitation of the uses to which aircraft at sea could be put had, however, to wait until 7 May 1913 when the cruiser HMS *Hermes* recommissioned at the Nore as parent ship for the Aeroplane and Airship Section of the Naval Wing of the Royal Flying Corps.

Hermes, in addition to provision for stowage and handling facilities for two seaplanes on her quarterdeck, was also fitted with a 100 feet long forecastle ramp for the operation of a Caudron G.II amphibian, serial No 55. This ship took part in the Naval Manoeuvres of July 1913, off the East coast, and although much of the flying was done by her Short Folder, the Caudron G.II was successfully launched at sea on 28 July from her fixed forecastle ramp for a flight to Yarmouth. Trials with the Caudron continued in *Hermes* during September, and at 1430 on 3 September, Lt Ross, RN took off from Invergordon in a Maurice Farman Seaplane, serial No 117, and sighted *Hermes* about 6 miles out to sea. Every available seaplane then took off from Invergordon and flew over *Hermes* while she launched her Caudron, into a wind of about 20 mph, to land back at Invergordon. The Caudron attempted

Caudron G.II 55 at Great Yarmouth in July 1913 prior to embarkation in HMS Hermes for the Naval Manoeuvres. (IWM Q90147)

another take off on the 6th but could not rise owing to a flat calm. Another attempt on the 8th was successful, however, and after a short flight it returned to *Hermes* and was hoisted in. The possibilities of aerial reconnaissance at sea had been demonstrated but, after a period of 9 months, and the inevitable approach of war with Germany, *Hermes*'s fixed forecastle ramp was removed and she reverted to her rôle as cruiser. Unfortunately, while transporting two Short Folders to France on her quarterdeck, *Hermes* was torpedoed by a U-boat and sank in the Straits of Dover on 31 October 1914. The final developments of the wooden fixed forecastle ramps of 1912/13 were fitted to four cruisers of the Harwich Force in May 1915 - HM Ships *Arethusa, Aurora, Penelope* and *Undaunted. Aurora* embarked Deperdussin Monoplane 1378, whilst the other three ships operated Schneiders in floatplane form, their fixed forecastle ramps probably never being used for launching aircraft. It is likely that the North Sea inflicted more damage on these frail aircraft than anything the enemy could hand out. By August 1915 the fixed forecastle ramps had been removed from all four ships, no operational success having been recorded from their use.

The original fixed forecastle ramps had all consisted of three wooden troughs to accommodate the aeroplane's two main undercarriage wheels and tailskid, the whole structure sloping downwards from forward of the conning tower to the stem. It is noteworthy that after this abandonment of the fixed forecastle ramp a modified form appeared in HMS *Renown* in November 1917, mounted on the forecastle, this being horizontal and with only twin troughs, for launching a Beardmore W.B.III (N6115) and a Pup (N6443).

As the fitting of this form of take off ramp in *Renown* was contrary to the opinion of the pilots in HMS *Furious*, the Commander in Chief requested that the pilots, on whose advice the Admiralty had decided to fit troughs, should be loaned to the Grand Fleet to make the first flights. Two pilots were selected to carry out the trials, but the first flight was a failure and the aircraft, a Pup, N6443, crashed over the bows on 1 December 1917. A fresh type of platform giving freedom of track to the aircraft was then substituted.

Apparently, on the evidence of two members of *Australia*'s crew, a type of fixed take off ramp similar to that installed in *Renown* had also been fitted on the quarter deck of HMAS *Australia*. The first flight from this ramp was made on 18 December 1917 by Flt Lt F. M. Fox in a Pup while *Australia* was at anchor at Rosyth. A second flight from the quarterdeck was made on 30 January, but this method of launching an aeroplane was not proceeded with, for the ship's log for 5 February 1918 records that at 0930 working parties were "rigging Q aeroplane platform" - ie on Q turret -

and that evening *Australia*'s first 2F.1 Camel was hoisted on board.

At a conference in August 1917, Admiral Sir David Beatty, by then Commander in Chief Grand Fleet, and the Third Sea Lord Rear Admiral L. Halsey discussed fitting "flying off decks" (i.e. fixed and revolving platforms) in cruisers, and turret ramps in HMS *Glorious* and HMS *Courageous*.

The possibility of taking aircraft to sea in *Courageous*, and also *Furious,* both then fitting out at W. G. Armstrong's yard at High Walker, had been considered a year previously.

A letter from the Director of Navy Contracts to Armstrongs of 29 June 1916 proposed that *Courageous*'s shelter deck be cut away, the forward 4-inch guns raised and a new shelter deck built with watertight doors to be fitted in the screen bulkhead. A portable platform 60 feet x 12 feet was to be installed on each side of the forecastle deck abaft of the breakwater, each to accommodate one seaplane, and capable of being raised when required. However these modifications were never carried out.

Those platforms to be fitted to light cruisers were reported to weigh only two tons. Accordingly the Commander-in-Chief requested that one ship in each of the light cruiser squadrons comprising the A-K line be fitted with fixed platforms, namely HMS *Caledon* (1st Cruiser Squadron), HMS *Dublin* (2nd Cruiser Squadron), HMS *Yarmouth* (3rd Cruiser Squadron) and HMS *Cassandra* (6th Cruiser Squadron). By this date both *Yarmouth* and *Cassandra* had already been so fitted.

The fixed platforms consisted of a raised deck 36 feet in length mounted on the forecastle, and extending forward from the foremast to a point just above the forward 6-inch gun mounting in cruisers and light cruisers. Twenty-two of these ships had been fitted with fixed platforms by the end of the war, and most had a canvas hangar at the after end of the platform to protect the aeroplane before launch. Of these 22 ships, 7 were later converted to have revolving platforms mounted immediately forward of the bridge, or just forward of the searchlight platform and abaft the funnels. A further five D-class cruisers had revolving platforms fitted in the latter position when they were completed between 1919 and 1922.

It must be said that fixed or revolving platforms in cruisers were used only by single seaters, e.g. Pups, 2F.1 Camels and later by Flycatchers. The deck of the platform was parallel to the deck, i.e. not inclined.

A new disadvantage, of course, was that launching an aeroplane from a platform implied a ditching upon return, with at best the loss of airframe and engine, and at worst the loss also of the pilot. That it spurred the development of landing decks in carriers was a bonus,

Detail of HMS Hibernia's wooden twin-trough launching ramp May 1912. (FAAM)

but that is a quite separate subject.

The conference of August 1917, referred to above, was vital to the future of airpower at sea, because no air policy for the Fleet existed until then. The conference went on to discuss the question of carriers with the Fleet and, although not entirely relevant to the subject of aircraft platforms and turret ramps, the Memo of 30 August 1917 by Wing Capt. A. V. Vyvyan, RNAS which stems from the conference, is worth quoting in full. Addressed to the 5th Sea Lord, and headed "secret", it read

"In submitting a policy for aircraft and carriers for the Grand Fleet, it is imperative to state certain fundamental axioms which must define the basis upon which any policy can be built up".

These axioms are as follows:

1. "Hostile aerial reconnaissance may, if developed, become the greatest menace to our sea power".

2. "The reply, or antidote, to hostile aircraft, is better aircraft on our side. There is no other reply whatsoever".

3. "To have the better aircraft we must have the best possible performance from our aircraft".

4. "To get the best possible performance we must reduce weight carried, and this means we must discard every ounce of weight which can be spared, particularly, where possible, excessive weight of petrol, and we must have aeroplanes rather than seaplanes".

5. "If we are to have aeroplanes, and if we have to reduce petrol and so the length of time in the air, in order to get the best possible performance, we must have flying off decks and alighting decks".

6. "The only carriers which can reasonably be expected to work with the Grand Fleet at the present moment are *Yarmouth* and *Cassandra*. There is no

question at all that *Riviera, Engadine, Empress, Vindex, Manxman, Nairana, Pegasus, Ark Royal* and *Campania* are unsuitable for work with the Grand Fleet. They are not fast enough''.

These six axioms were to have very far reaching effects in forming future policy. Some are beyond the scope of the story of platforms and turret ramps but from them sprang the immediate recommendation that fighters, initially Pups and later 2F.1 Camels, be carried

in HMS *Dublin* and HMS *Courageous,* in addition to *Yarmouth* and *Cassandra* mentioned above. Their duties would be to destroy or deter any aerial reconnaissance of the Fleet by the Germans. These recommendations had the benefit of some hindsight, for in June 1917 Flt Cdr F.J. Rutland had successfully flown a Pup from a fixed platform 36 feet in length mounted above *Yarmouth*'s forward 6-inch gun mounting. The ship steamed into wind to produce a wind speed of 20 knots over the platform.

Flying log book entry for Lt C.R. Samson for 2nd May 1912 (via IWM)

Patent no. 3333, for a gravity operated shipborne aircraft catapult, taken out February 1911, by M.F. Sueter F.L.M. Boothby and H.G. Paterson.

1 - aircraft   2 - trunnions   3 - rails   4 - trolley   5 - arms   6 - struts   7 - weight   8 - cable

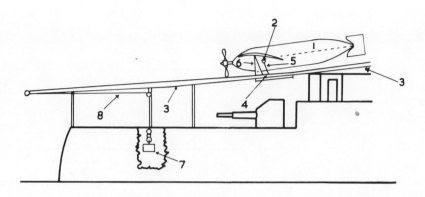

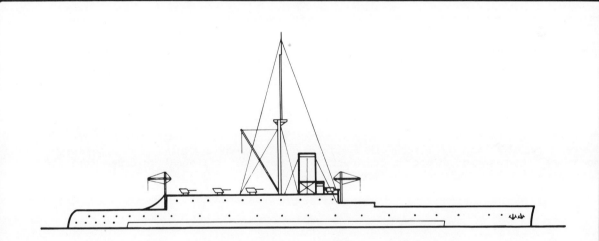

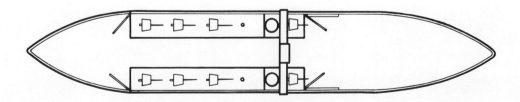

"Parent ship for naval aeroplanes and T.B.Ds". Wm. Beardmore design project, December 1912.

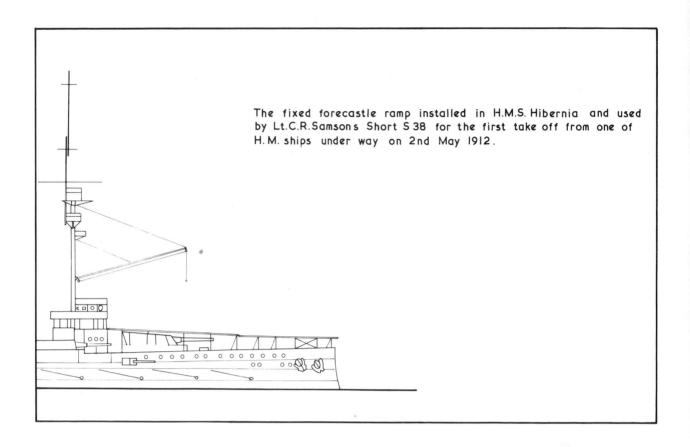

The fixed forecastle ramp installed in H.M.S. Hibernia and used by Lt.C.R.Samsons Short S 38 for the first take off from one of H.M. ships under way on 2nd May 1912.

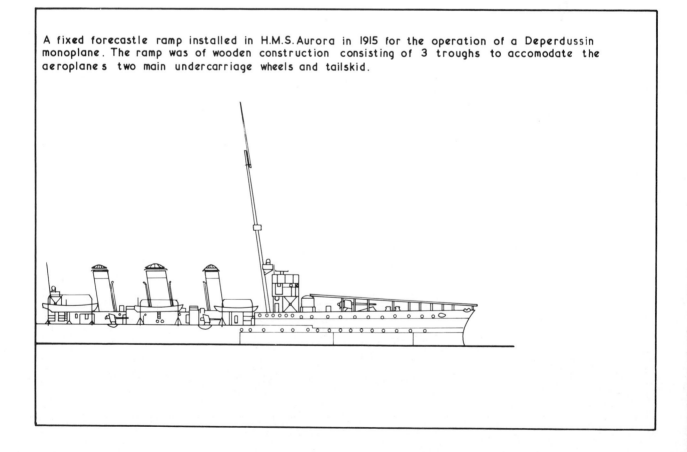

A fixed forecastle ramp installed in H.M.S.Aurora in 1915 for the operation of a Deperdussin monoplane. The ramp was of wooden construction consisting of 3 troughs to accomodate the aeroplanes two main undercarriage wheels and tailskid.

Three views of Short S.38 T2 being loaded on to a lighter and being towed out to HMS Africa by a steam pinnace from HMS Actaeon at Sheerness on 10th January, 1912. (G.S. Leslie / J.M. Bruce collection)

Two views of Short S.38 T2 being hoisted on board HMS Hibernia in Weymouth Bay during May 1912. (R.D. Layman via G.S. Leslie)

Short S.38 T2 installed on HMS Hibernia's fixed forecastle ramp in May 1912. (A.K. Vicary)

Short S.38 T2 on HMS Hibernia's fixed forecastle ramp, and Short S.41 H1 being hoisted on board at Sheerness Dockyard, 1st May, 1912. H1 was hoisted out in Portland harbour on 3rd May and flown by Samson. (RAFM)

A spare fuselage with wheeled undercarriage for Short S.41 H1 being hoisted on board HMS Hibernia, May 1912. This was not used for a take-off from the fixed forecastle ramp. (FAAM)

Close-up of HMS Hibernia showing the launching ramp above her forward 12-inch turret and the Short S.38 being readied for take-off, May 1912. (MAP)

0600 on 2nd May, 1912, and Samson takes off in Short S.38 T2 from HMS Hibernia's fixed forecastle ramp in Weymouth Bay while the ship steamed at 10½ knots. (FAAM)

0609 on 2nd May, and Samson strides away from T2 after landing at Lodmoor following the first take-off from one of HM ships under way. (FAAM)

The original caption states ''Short S.38 landing after flying off warship, possibly at Eastney.'' Would that it could be confirmed that the date was 2nd May, 1912, and the place Lodmoor! (G.S. Leslie / J.M. Bruce collection)

Short S.38 T2 at Portsmouth after being flown off the fixed forecastle ramp of HMS London by Lt C.J.L'Estrange Malone on 4th July 1912.
(G.S. Leslie / J.M.Bruce collection)

HMS Hermes, parent ship for the Aeroplane and Airship Section of the Naval Wing of the Royal Flying Corps c. May 1913. The canvas hangar on the fixed forecastle ramp protected her Caudron G.II amphibian, and the canvas hangar on her quarterdeck housed her Short Folder seaplane.
(A.K. Vicary)

HMS Hermes c. July 1913 with canvas hangar rigged on her forecastle.
(IWM SP1926)

Two views of Caudron G.II 55 taking off from the fixed forecastle ramp of HMS Hermes on 28th July, 1913, piloted by Lt R.P. Ross. The installation of the wooden forecastle ramp necessitated the removal of the cruiser's forward 6-inch gun.
(Dr. A. Hewlett via M.H. Goodall)

Short Folder 81 being hoisted by HMS Hermes's derrick c. July 1913.
(Dr. A. Hewlett via M.H. Goodall)

Short Folder 81 operating from HMS Hermes during July 1913. The pilot in the rear cockpit is Lt C.R. Samson.
(G.S. Leslie/ J.M. Bruce collection)

Borel Seaplane 48 being hoisted by HMS Hermes's derrick c. July 1913. (Dr. A. Hewlett via M.H. Goodall)

Three views of Deperdussin Monoplane 1378 on the fixed forecastle ramp of HMS Aurora prior to Flt Lt R.J.J. Hope-Vere's successful take-off on 4th November, 1915.   (SP1199, NMM N22555 to N22557)

Beardmore WB.III N6115, stowed on the fixed forecastle ramp of HMS Renown c. November 1917. (FAAM)

A close-up view of HMS Renown's forecastle ramp, which was removed by early 1918. (FAAM)

Four views of Pup N6443 attempting to take off from HMS Renown's fixed forecastle ramp in the Firth of Forth on 1st December, 1917. The trial was unsuccessful! (FAAM)

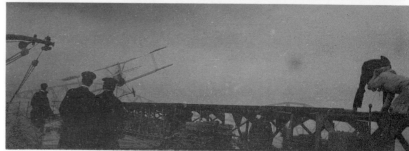

Three views of 2F.1 Camel, N6779, on the fixed platform of HMS Calliope c. 1918. The Aeroplane is firmly lashed down for proceeding to sea, and locks are fitted to rudder, elevators a and ailerons. (RAFM)

CHAPTER II

Operational uses of platforms in cruisers, Home Waters 1917-1918

The only operational success against Zeppelins resulting from the use of aeroplanes launched from the platforms of HM Ships in the war of 1914-1918 resulted in the destruction of L23 (Oberleutnant Zur See Bernhard Dinter), operating from Tondern, by HMS *Yarmouth*'s Pup N6430 piloted by Flt Sub Lt B.A. Smart, RN off the Danish coast on 21 August 1917.

On 18 August 1917 *Yarmouth* (Capt. Grace, RN) lay moored to H4 buoy at Rosyth. At 0640 the collier *Cedar Tree* secured alongside and *Yarmouth*'s ship's company spent the forenoon coaling ship. After cleaning ship a well-earned "Hands to make and mend clothes" was piped at 1400. In the gathering darkness of the evening of the 18th, *Yarmouth* slipped at 2128 and proceeded to sea, in company with the 1st Light Cruiser Squadron, for a minelaying operation off the German coast during the night of the 19th/20th.

On 20 August, with a good sea running, Smart made a brave attempt to eat some nice fat, greasy beef. At 1300 a surfaced U-Boat was sighted and, after she had dived, was depth charged by the destroyer escort. By 2154 that evening the Doggerbank Noord Light bore South West by South at a distance of two miles. *Yarmouth* was due the next morning to traverse the course taken by known Zeppelin patrols, and conversation in the wardroom that night naturally turned to the chances of a successful interception. Knowing he had an early call, Smart soon turned in.

Smart was called at 0230 on Tuesday 21 August. By the time he had dressed and climbed up to the platform, dawn was just breaking, and his two mechanics were stripping the tarpaulins from N6430's engine and cockpit. He climbed into the cockpit for an engine test, then having run it up to full revs, he shut off and took out the Lewis gun. After testing the weight of the spring and firing 12 rounds he replaced the gun on its centre section mounting. By this time it was quite light, and the Captain called down to Smart from the bridge, to turn in below until he was needed. However, after only 30 minutes Smart was summoned to the bridge. It was now 0500, and *Yarmouth* was steering N12 degrees east after taking station astern of HMS *Caledon*. The furthest destroyer of the screen had reported increased German W/T traffic and the sighting of an aircraft. The latter, a German seaplane, was soon sighted from *Yarmouth* bearing ESE. This was

Friedrichshafen FF33E, No. 874, from List Naval Air Station, which at about this time reported back to List by W/T that she had sighted a force of enemy cruisers 50 miles North of List, and steering towards the North at full speed. A few rounds of 4-inch in the seaplane's direction were sufficient to make her turn for home.

Yarmouth now increased engine revolutions from 217 rpm to 276 rpm, with the wind south-west by west Force 2. Smart once more went below, but at 0530 a Zeppelin was sighted from *Yarmouth*, bearing south-west and steering to the North, and he quickly returned on deck to order his mechanics to take off all lashings from N6430, with the exception of the quick release strop. The colours of the Pup's roundels and rudder stripes looked especially glaring on this morning in particular, so Smart gave orders for them to be toned down with "pusser's" grey paint, to give him a better chance to close the Zeppelin unobserved. Smart reported to Captain Grace that everything was ready. The Zeppelin closed to within seven or eight miles of *Yarmouth* and then altered to a parallel course, signalling back to base all the while what she could see from that distance. When it was evident that she would approach no closer, Capt. Grace signalled to the Commodore for permission to turn *Yarmouth* into wind for launching her Pup.

Flt Sub Lt B.A. Smart DSO, RNAS. (via FAAM)

Flt Sub Lt B.A. Smart's Pup, N6430, ditched off the Danish Coast on 21st August, 1917. After taking off from Yarmouth's platform, Smart intercepted and shot down Zeppelin L23. Here a whaler from HMS Prince, which rescued Smart, stands by the ditched Pup. Note that N6430's rudder and elevator stripes have been overpainted with grey to create a low visibility effect. N6430 was not salved. (FAAM)

Smart put on his helmet and goggles, and having provided himself with a flask of brandy and two lifebelts against the almost inevitable ditching, climbed into his cockpit and strapped himself in. The Pup was now ready for launching, with a take off run of 16 feet before the end of the platform was reached. N6430, with 19 gallons of petrol and fully armed with a single Lewis gun firing upward through the centre section, weighed about 1,300 lbs and took 12-15 minutes to climb to 10,000 feet, at which altitude its maximum speed was about 100 mph. The Zeppelin, L23, was powered by four Maybach 280 hp engines giving a maximum speed of 58 mph. Her length was 585 feet and her diameter 61 feet.

As *Yarmouth* turned out of line and into wind it brought her onto a converging course with L23. The Pup's rigging wires started to sing, but with only a moderate wind, nothing registered on the ASI, so Smart requested Capt. Grace for more speed. The Commander lay down under the Pup to operate the quick release strop, and when Smart had run up his engine he raised his arm to indicate to the Captain on the bridge behind him that he was ready for take-off, Capt Grace signalled the Commander to pull the release cord, and the Pup rose like a bird well before reaching the end of the platform. It was a glorious morning, and Smart climbed hard to gain a bit of cover from friendly clouds to

starboard. By now L23 was flying at around 6,000 feet, about 9 miles away to the south-west, also taking advantage of some cloud cover. Smart took a compass bearing on L23, to use if he lost sight of her. At about this time L23 sent the last signal Tondern ever received from her - "Am pursued by enemy forces".

Smart's airspeed had fallen to 60 mph during the climb, but levelling off at 9,000 feet as he emerged from cloud cover, he found he had a considerable height advantage over L23, which had now turned and was heading for Germany. Easing his stick forward, he dived at 110 mph to 8,000 feet, with the silver L23 growing larger every moment. He found that with his height advantage he could outmanoeuvre L23 to keep the Zeppelin end on, and so blind the gunners in the gondola beneath her. At 7,000 feet L23 was still 1,000 feet below him and at an angle of 45 degrees Smart then pushed the joystick forward and dived at 150 mph for her stern, aiming to cut underneath a few yards astern. At 250 yards range and at L23's altitude he flattened out and fired. His incendiaries passed over the top of L23 so he dived to gain speed and came round again. He pressed home his second attack to within 100 feet and saw about 6 incendiary bullets enter L23's stern, before he dived to avoid a collision.

Levelling out at 3,000 feet, Smart looked back at L23. Her after section was now a mass of flame and had dropped so that the nose section was pointing upwards at an angle of 45 degrees. Her engines were still turning, and one parachute was seen to descend before the Zeppelin hit the sea off Lodbjerg, continuing to burn for another three or four minutes. There were no survivors from her crew.

By now there was no sight of the light cruiser squadron, but Smart turned his Pup until his compass was in the opposite direction from that of his outward flight. He edged to port to get a better sight of the ships between himself and the sun, expecting to have them in sight to starboard after 45 minutes flying. The sea was still empty however, and he had almost decided to land in Denmark when he sighted them about 7 or 8 miles away to port. They had altered course on sighting the smoke from L23, which they had taken for the High Seas Fleet. Smart selected two destroyers near which to ditch, switched off his engine and glided down to land ahead of them. He undid his straps and put a plug in the tube, which acted as a valve to the air bags in the tail. At 15 feet above the sea he pulled back the stick gradually until all flying speed was lost. N6430 dropped on an even keel into the waves, and within a very short time only the tail was above the water, to which Smart clung until rescued by a boat from HMS *Prince*.

After Smart was safely aboard HMS *Prince*, a signal was sent to *Yarmouth* at 0740 to report that Smart had been recovered, and that he had destroyed the Zeppelin. It was not long before the following signal was received in *Prince* -

"Commodore HMS *Caledon* to Flight Sub Lt
Smart, HMS *Prince*. You have done most
splendidly and I am sure your reward will be
prompt".

When radio contact was lost between L23 and
Tondern, the Germans sent out a large number of
seaplanes to make a search. One of these found a large
patch of oil and petrol 500 miles north-west of List, and
on landing at the spot recovered the blade of an airship
propeller, charred at the boss.

The light cruiser squadron turned for home, and at
0150 on 22 August *Caledon* signalled to *Prince* -

"F/S/L Smart is to be returned to *Yarmouth* on
anchoring. Commodore wishes to see him at
1000 BST today Wednesday. Boat will be sent
to *Yarmouth*. Acknowledge and repeat back
time".

At 0345 *Yarmouth* secured to H4 buoy at Rosyth
once more, and at 0400 Smart rejoined the ship from
Prince.

Not much chance occurred for *Yarmouth*'s ship's
company to get their heads down, for by 0705 the collier
Agnes Duncan was secured alongside, and at 0755
coaling ship was commenced ready for the next sortie
into the North Sea. A hard life, and typical routine for
the light forces of the Grand Fleet and Harwich Force
throughout the war.

N6430's replacement Pup was taken on board
Yarmouth at 1130 on 23 August, probably being
lightered out to the ship. Flt Sub Lt Williams joined the
ship as pilot at 1830 on the 25th, and at 2145 that
evening Smart left the ship - suitably fortified one hopes
- to go on leave before joining HMS *Furious*. The
award of a DSO to F/S/L Smart, RN was gazetted on 14
September 1917.

To sit in an open cockpit, on a platform, that would
be both rolling and pitching, with only 80 hp of not
always reliable engine in front to pull one into the air
after a take-off run of only 16 feet, took courage. The
Royal Naval Air Service, and its successor the Fleet Air
Arm, never lacked it.

One other action deserving mention, and involving
the use of aeroplanes launched from cruisers' platforms,
took place on 1 June 1918. Admiral Beatty decided to
launch an attack upon German naval forces giving
protection to their minesweepers in the Heligoland
Bight. His plan was to commit four separate forces,
converging on the enemy by separate routes. These four
consisted of the Harwich Force of nine light cruisers
and 28 destroyers - three of the latter ships, *Redgauntlet*,

Stork and *Sybille*, each towing Felixstowe F2A flying
boats on lighters; the 2nd Light Cruiser Squadron with
four destroyers; the battle cruisers *Courageous* and
Glorious with their destroyer escort; and finally the
battle cruiser *Lion* and light cruiser *Champion* with nine
destroyers.

Heligoland Bight was patrolled by both Zeppelins
and seaplanes to give the German Navy early warning
of the approach of our forces - the Royal Navy had
made many sorties into the Bight since August 1914.

Beatty hoped that German air patrols would sight
only one of his four squadrons, and so tempt the
German Navy to engage an apparently inferior force, in
this case the ships of the Harwich Force which sailed in
advance of the main force from Rosyth.

To counter the enemy's aerial reconnaissance,
Beatty's force embarked at least seven 2F.1 Camels.
Courageous, Glorious and *Lion* each carried one (and
probably two) 2F.1 Camels on their turret ramps. And
the 2nd Light Cruiser Squadron consisting of
Birmingham, Dublin and *Southampton* and HM
Australian Ships *Melbourne* and *Sydney* carried a total
of four 2F.1 Camels. *Birmingham,* flying the flag of
Rear Admiral J. A. Fergusson, did not embark a Camel
because the Admiral's quarters meant there was no
room for the installation of a platform.

The 2nd Light Cruiser Squadron sailed at 1400 on
31 May from Rosyth. 1 June dawned cloudy but the sea
smooth, and each of the four forces proceeded
independently until entering the Bight.

Sydney was commanded by Captain J.S. Dumaresq,
who had supervised the installation of her revolving
platform during her Chatham refit in late 1917.
Dumaresq was one of a band of senior officers in the
Service who since 1916 had pressed for the carrying of
aeroplanes in cruisers and capital ships. His foresight
was shortly to be rewarded.

As the Squadron entered enemy controlled waters,
two German seaplanes were observed from *Sydney* at
0933 diving out of a cloud bank and heading westwards.
Melbourne's log recorded that both seaplanes dropped
bombs as they passed over the cruisers at 0940, but no
hits were scored.

By this time Flt Lt A.C. Sharwood RAF, was
already seated in the cockpit of *Sydney*'s 2F.1 Camel,
N6783, and the revolving platform was turned into the
mean wind at 20 degrees to the centreline of the ship.

Under the command of *Sydney*'s First Lieutenant, Lt
Cdr Garcia RAN, Sharwood's launching party (Birch
the engine fitter, Radcliffe rigger, and Graffy joiner/
mechanic) now took up their positions. After running up
his engine to full power, Sharwood dropped his raised
arm and Garcia pulled the Quick Release Strop at 0955.
As the Camel's whitewashed tyres passed the two white
squares at the forward corners of the platform Sharwood

HMAS Melbourne at speed with a 2F.1 Camel on her forward revolving platform. (IWM SP718)

eased his stick back, and having done so put the nose down to the sea to gain flying speed for the climb.

At 1000 on board *Melbourne* also, Flt Lt L.B. Gibson in his 2F.1 Camel, N6756, was airborne in pursuit of the seaplanes. These were the only two aeroplanes launched during the action. In June 1918 a ship's Camel was just another of that ship's weapons, and was launched on the orders of her Captain. But by October 1918, when Sharwood had become the 2nd Light Cruiser Squadron's Flight Commander, the chain of command was changed. Henceforth Sharwood's orders to operate all four Camels in his Flight would be given by Admiral Fergusson in *Birmingham*.

However, while Sharwood and Gibson were climbing for altitude, the two German seaplanes were sighted returning from the west. Gibson, who had climbed through a cloud bank, failed to locate the enemy seaplanes and returned to circle the cruiser squadron. His return deterred the Captain of *Courageous* from launching her aeroplanes, thinking the seaplanes had been driven off. *Melbourne*'s log records *Sydney* reported that Gibson had put down N6756 near the cruiser *Centaur* at 1122, and that he had then been rescued by the destroyer HMS *Osiris*. *Osiris* later reported that she had also recovered N6756 and returned both pilot and Camel to Harwich.

Sharwood meanwhile had climbed to 10,000 feet, and having sighted the German seaplanes, pursued them for 60 miles before he was able to dive on the tail of one of them and fire several bursts into it. Official accounts mention only two seaplanes, but Sharwood's Log Book says "Flight from *Sydney* after three Hun seaplanes (two two-seaters and single-seater)".

Evidently it was the single seater which he had hit. It shuddered and started spinning towards the sea, and Sharwood followed it down, but as he passed through a cloud he sighted another German seaplane on his tail. He banked sharply to bring the Camel round behind the German's tail, but only managed to fire one short burst from his Vickers gun before it ran out of ammunition. He turned to attack once more, but his Lewis gun jammed, so he broke off the action to try to find *Sydney* again. The pursuit had taken Sharwood 70 miles from the Squadron and increasing cloud reduced his visibility. He had just decided to land in Denmark - for which eventuality five gold sovereigns were sewn into the lining of his coat - when he sighted a Harwich Force destroyer. It was in company with another towing home one with a damaged stern. Several rounds of AA fire greeted Sharwood as he circled the ships at 7,000 feet, fortunately ceasing as he lost height prior to ditching.

Sharwood had previous experience of ditching a Camel seven months previously which now stood him in good stead. There was a sea with about four foot waves. Sharwood brought the Camel down to about five feet above the wavetops, having previously released his safety belt, and held off until it stalled. Undercarriage and tailskid touched the water at 40-45 knots, the rear fuselage filled with air bags shot upwards and the nose of the Camel plunged into the sea. Just before the cockpit submerged, Sharwood was catapulted out through the cutout in the upper centre section, landing head first in the sea some 20 yards head of the Camel. The Camel's cut-out had been specially enlarged by his riggers to avoid a repetition of Sharwood's previous ditching, when his exit through the cut-out had removed

Sydney's 2F.1 Camel airborne from her platform in May 1918. The hand held flag on the bridge indicates to the pilot that the Quick Release Strop lanyard is about to be pulled. Sydney's commanding officer, Capt J.S. Dumaresq, stands just to the left of the range clock, and the accompanying cruiser is HMAS Melbourne. (AWM EN224)

most of the skin from his face. The rigger had also fitted hand grips to the rear fuselage for the pilot to hang onto after swimming back to the Camel.

The ditching had taken place 500 or 600 yards on the starboard bow of the destroyer *Sharpshooter*. One of her boats soon picked up Sharwood, and the cruiser *Canterbury* later salved the Camel.

When Sharwood was eventually back on board *Sydney*, his joiner/mechanic Graffy was there and seeing that no skin was missing from Sharwood's face greeted him with "Well Sir, I see that we did make the cutaway big enough after all!"

The 2nd Light Cruiser Squadron returned to Rosyth on 2 June, and the expected naval engagement did not take place. German forces covering their minesweeping operations had not been sighted by nightfall, and Beatty ordered the whole force to retire.

Sharwood's claim of one enemy seaplane forced down onto the sea was never recognised by the Admiralty, and his gallantry was never rewarded. But his interception of the reconnaissance seaplanes prevented them from reporting the composition of the British force, confirming Captain Dumaresq's belief in the rôle of naval aircraft.

The ultimate development of the fixed platform in cruisers resulted from the weather damage to

aeroplanes, and to their flimsy canvas hangars, on ships' platforms at sea. While still fitting out in 1917, HMS *Cassandra* had a permanent hangar built into the starboard side of the bridge and, initially, a 45 feet fixed forecastle ramp, positioned on the forecastle forward of No.1 six-inch mounting. The hangar was only wide enough to house an aeroplane with folding wings, the Beardmore W.B.III being selected. A fixed platform was substituted for the outdated fixed forecastle ramp, but the combined weight of hangar and fixed platform was 15 tons, which had the handicap of considerably reducing the ship's stability. HMS *Caledon* was similarly equipped.

Although the Beardmore W.B.III was a derivative of the Pup, fitted with the same power plant, its performance was well below that of the Pup, and it was not a success. In consequence hangars and platforms were removed from both *Cassandra* and *Caledon*, and revolving platforms were fitted aft in both ships, just forward of the after control.

In 1918 a design was prepared for a hangar, to house a fixed wing aeroplane, incorporated into the bridge structure of C and D class cruisers. The hangar was a large T shaped structure, open at the back and closed at the front by a roller blind shutter. The aeroplane was intended to take off from within the hangar, completing its take-off run from a fixed platform extending over the mounting of No 2 gun. The outboard end of the platform was hinged to fold upwards when no flying was taking place, to allow a full arc of fire for No 2 gun.

The design proved unsatisfactory because the closed front of the hangar created considerable wind resistance, and the added top weight affected the ship's stability. Only *Carlisle, Dragon* and *Dauntless* ever had bridge hangars fitted and, with the end of the war in November 1918, aeroplanes were no longer operated from cruisers' platforms, except for a short period in North Russia in 1919.

Carlisle did briefly embark a 2F.1 Camel, but her bridge hangar and platform were removed in 1920. Although *Dragon* and *Dauntless* retained their bridge hangars for a short time, it is doubtful if they ever operated aeroplanes from them. When their bridge hangars and fixed platforms were removed, these two ships were both fitted with revolving platforms aft, as were five other ships of the D class. *Delhi* at least operated a 2F.1 Camel from her revolving platform.

An unusual, and as it transpired quite impractical, attempt was made to see if single seater aeroplanes - i.e. Pups or Camels - might be operated from destroyers. In June 1918 the destroyer *Senator* was fitted with a flying off platform on her quarterdeck. The theory was that with the ship going full astern the aeroplane would be able to take off over the stern. However, with the ship going astern at 16 knots the stern wave produced was well above the level of the quarterdeck. The trial - one hopes without the aeroplane embarked -was never repeated, and the platform was removed.

A slightly more practical proposal for destroyers of the Harwich Force to carry their own aeroplanes was submitted by Capt (D) of the destroyer leader *Spencer* during July 1918. His proposal was that destroyers be fitted with a forecastle platform for flying off a 2F.1 Camel. His suggestion was supported by Admiral Harwich Force, who stated that he had no objection, provided the gun masked by the platform could be brought into action after the Camel had been launched. Accordingly Major F. J. Rutland RAF was instructed to proceed on board *Spencer* on 14 August to discuss the feasibility of the project with Capt (D), who stated that they had lately had as many as eight Zeppelins in sight at any one time.

Rutland next visited the destroyer *Redoubt,* whose captain Cdr Holt had experience in towing lighters with a 2F.1 Camel on board. His view was that, provided his ship's stability was not adversely affected, a Camel could be flown from a forecastle platform. But he added the proviso that the use of a towing lighter was preferable.

The proposal to use towing lighters, initially for extending the radius of action of flying boats, was the brainchild of Cdr. Porte in 1916. Their first operational use was on 19 March 1918, when three Felixstowe flying boats on lighters were towed by destroyers for a reconnaissance of the Heligoland Bight.

The success of this operation prompted Col. C. R. Samson RAF, on 3 May 1918, to request from the Admiralty the loan of a lighter for trials with a 2F.1 Camel. Characteristically Samson himself undertook to conduct these trials.

A flying-off deck was fitted to lighter H3, and 2F.1 Camel N6623's wheeled undercarriage was replaced by a twin skid undercarriage to run in troughs mounted on the lighter's deck, to maintain directional stability.

The first trial took place off Orfordness on 30 May, with the destroyer *Truculent* towing H3 with N6623 and Samson on board. However, at a towing speed of 30 knots the lighter assumed a stern down attitude, and since the deck was built parallel to the lighter's hull, the Camel had an uphill task to become airborne.

This reduced N6623's take-off speed, the skids jumped out of the troughs, and the aeroplane stalled over the bows of the lighter, which then ran over the Camel and Samson. The Camel was a write-off, but not so Samson who was fortunately rescued.

As a result of this trial, upon the recommendation of Capt G.W.R. Fane RAF, the flying off deck was raised at its after end so that when the lighter was towed at speed the deck was horizontal, and a normal wheeled undercarriage was fitted to the Camel.

A Tail Guide Trestle was provided, and a Quick Release Strop employed exactly as in launches from platforms and turret ramps in HM Ships. The first successful take-off was achieved on 31 July 1918 by Lt S.D. Culley in 2F.1 Camel N6812 from lighter H3, again towed by *Truculent*.

On 2 August 1918 Col C.R. Samson wrote a Memorandum entitled ''Uses of Camel Aeroplanes flown from Towing Lighters'', of which the following are extracts.

> ''The latest Zeppelins in commission have a ceiling of 20,000-22,000 feet. The service ceiling of a BRI Camel is about 18,000 feet. Therefore, on occasions the Zeppelins may escape, but it is extremely likely that surprise attacks may be made. Zeppelins in daytime in the North Sea fly about 10,000-13,000 feet when on patrol near the Doggerbank Lightships.
>
> If on days when the weather conditions are good, a destroyer could tow a lighter with a Camel aboard, arriving at the South Doggerbank Light Vessel at dawn, and remain cruising in the vicinity, sending up the Camel when the Zeppelin was sighted, it is certain that the Zeppelin will not see the Camel until the

This photograph on board the Lighter H3, probably taken just prior to his attempt of 30th May, 1918, epitomises the spirit of Samson (standing in the foreground) - brave and buccaneering. (FAAM)

Zeppelin has got within 10 miles of the destroyer. The Camel would be given orders to climb to a higher altitude than the Zeppelin, keeping outside visual range from the Zeppelin, i.e. about seven miles or more for certainty and at the same time keeping to windward of the Zeppelin.

The Camel would take about 22-23 minutes to get to 15,000 feet and would then attack. The first warning the Zeppelin would get would be when the Camel was within 1-2 miles of it, as the Camel coming with the wind would be flying at 100 plus say, 20 miles for wind = 120 miles per hour. Therefore it's approach would be at the rate of two miles a minute. Provided average shooting and no jams, the Zeppelins would have in my opinion, little chance to escape, especially so if the Camel kept its height until the last moment.

The Camel would then return to the destroyer, come down into the sea, and the pilot would be picked up by the destroyer. The average time a Camel floats from experience is 3-5 minutes. On occasions, with fairly empty tanks and a very good landing it would float longer.

Although I have fitted the lighter with a powerful derrick I doubt if the Camel could be salved; but on occasions this would be possible.

A second destroyer would be required to follow the towing destroyer. The whole operation would take about one hour."

To this Memorandum Samson added in his own hand

"To Lieut. Culley. The part I have marked with pencil lines refers to the method of carrying out the attack, you must strictly carry out this otherwise there is a chance of the Zeppelin outclimbing you. If you follow the rules you are certain to bring her down. 5 August 1918".

Attached to the above, also in Samson's hand were more detailed instructions.

"The positions to avoid in a Zeppelin are (A) directly below or (B) behind it's tail and below, unless in position (B) you can get in a blind spot. The best attack is a dive on top of it and then passing along just on its beam so as to avoid the flames. You should bag him in the first burst of shooting especially if he puts his nose up to climb.

If you fail from this method dive from behind at him but on his quarter, but you will then be under heavy fire. Don't use all your ammunition in the first attack. Remember according to our information that the gun on top of the envelope is not used. Get close to the Zeppelin but keep out of danger of his flames, which will burst up pretty high; but mostly to leeward of the Zeppelin so you are alright if you keep ahead and on the bow''.

Samson's instructions were soon put to good effect.

Since June the Harwich Force had been taking Coastal Motor Boats embarked in cruisers, to attack German minesweepers in the Heligoland Bight. At 2100 on 10 August a force consisting of the cruisers *Curacoa, Coventry, Concord* and *Danae* (each carrying two CMB's) with eight escorting destroyers sailed from Harwich with the same objective. Accompanying them were the destroyers *Retriever, Thisbe* and *Teazer* each towing a flying boat lighter with a flying boat on board and finally the destroyer *Redoubt* towing a lighter with 2F.1 Camel N6812 embarked. While proceeding to the rendezvous 25 miles north-west of Vlieland, *Redoubt* with the wind on her bow was taking spray over her forebridge, whereas the towed lighter was comparatively dry. The rendezvous was reached at 0600 on the 11th, but owing to very light winds and a long swell, the three flying boats were unable to take off. They returned to their lighters and the six CMB's were sent in toward the Ems estuary without air cover. Three flying boats from Great Yarmouth now joined the Harwich Force at 0700 and shortly after being ordered by visual signal to follow the CMB's, one of these flying boats sighted a Zeppelin north-east of the flotilla and steering west at 0830. Knowing that Lt Culley and his Camel were with the flotilla, the flying boats turned back, and signalled their sighting of the Zeppelin to *Curacoa*.

Admiral Tyrwhitt then ordered the flying boats back to Yarmouth and turned his force away 16 points to try and persuade the Zeppelin to follow seawards. The Zeppelin was in fact L53 commanded by Korvettenkapitän Proells, who now altered course towards the flotilla.

At 0815 *Curacoa* signalled to *Redoubt* that L53 was in sight, and Culley climbed into the cockpit of N6812 and ran up his engine. *Redoubt* worked up to 30 knots and turned into wind. At 0858 the Quick Release Strop was slipped and after a take-off run of only five feet N6812 was airborne and climbing for L53's altitude at 52 mph with the sun behind it.

While we leave Culley climbing for height, the fate

S.D. Culley when still a Flt Sub Lt c. early 1918.
(FAAM)

(for such it was) should be considered of the six CMB's. Briefly they came under heavy attack by Hansa Brandenburg W19 seaplanes, and all were either sunk or driven ashore without achieving any of their objectives. The Royal Navy had only to wait another 22 years to painfully relearn the lesson that inshore operations without air cover against land based airpower are costly.

Now to return to Culley. By 0930 he had reached 18,000 feet, but L53 was still 1,000 feet higher and broadside on to Culley. Shortly afterwards, while still struggling to gain more altitude he saw L53 turn head on towards him and at 0958 L53 was only 300 feet immediately above him. With the Camel now almost at stalling speed Culley wasted no more time. He pulled hard back on the stick and opened fire with his two Lewis guns.

The port gun jammed after 15 rounds but the starboard gun emptied its full tray of 97 rounds into the underside of L53. The Zeppelin appeared to be undamaged, so diving away to starboard he looked back over his shoulder to see bursts of flame issuing from the envelope. Within a few minutes L53 was burning. The bow section broke away, and standing vertically, she plunged blazing into the sea 10 miles south-west of Borkum Riff Light Vessel. Of L53's crew there was only one survivor.

Culley then made for the Dutch coast, turned south as far as the Texel, and made for the rendezvous at Terschelling Bank. From 6,000 feet patchy clouds obscured his vision and no destroyers were visible. His pressure tank now ran dry and switching to the gravity tank, he decided to ditch close to a Dutch fishing vessel. But at the last moment he sighted the destroyers and, firing a Very light, landed just ahead of *Redoubt*. Culley was picked up and the Camel salved and taken back to Harwich aboard the lighter. N6812 is now exhibited at the Imperial War Museum. Culley was recommended for the VC, but his eventual award for gallantry was the DSO.

Clearly the lighter-borne Camel had proved its advantage over the proposed flying off platform on a destroyer's forecastle. The captains of destroyers stated that towing a lighter at 30 knots made about half a knot difference in speed, and did not affect rapid alterations in course. *Redoubt* steaming at 25 knots used 25 degrees of helm all the time.

The only apparent disadvantage was that the destroyer could not carry out screening duties, which she could do if the aeroplane was carried on board. However, by this stage in the war the shortage of destroyers, experienced only a year before, was not a problem. And so the proposal to fit destroyers with forecastle platforms was never proceeded with.

Fixed platforms were successful, but they had their limitations. A ship steaming in line ahead in company with others must always turn out of line and into wind to launch her aeroplane. The effect this would have upon the doctrine of battle of a fleet, nurtured in a policy of line of battle and exchange of shot with the opposing battle line, may be imagined.

It was only just over 100 years since Trafalgar, and "crossing the T" of an enemy's battle line was to remain effective until the Battle of Surigao Strait in October 1944. The answer lay initially in the almost simultaneous adoption of turret ramps upon turrets of main armament of capital ships and the introduction of revolving platforms in cruisers. In both cases the turret ramp or revolving platform could be traversed to face into wind, while the ship maintained her course and position in the line of battle.

Reference will be made to the trials involving the launching of aeroplanes from turret ramps in HMS *Repulse* commanded by Capt J.S. Dumaresq RN. On the successful conclusion of those trials, Capt Dumaresq suggested the installation of revolving platforms on the forecastle of cruisers. The first installation of a revolving platform, in HMAS *Sydney*, was completed by Chatham Dockyard in November 1917.

The deck of the platform measured 16 feet from the aeroplane's wheels to the leading edge of the deck. Steel side sheeting was fitted to the sides of the platform to afford some protection from spray and blast from the guns. In addition canvas webbing blast shields were rigged on frames in front of the aeroplane, and prior to take-off the frames were lowered forward.

The blast shields were devised by *Sydney*'s three RNAS ratings responsible for her aeroplane's maintenance. The first time the guns were fired without the blast shields being rigged all four wingtips were smashed.

On 30 November 1917, with her new platform installed, *Sydney* put in to Rosyth on her way back to Scapa Flow, where her platform was inspected "with a view to forming proposals for flying arrangements on other light cruisers".

But *Sydney* was still without an aeroplane. To remedy this ludicrous situation Dumaresq, on returning to Scapa, borrowed a Pup which was then operating from the cruiser *Dublin*'s fixed platform. A first trial was carried out on 8 December 1917 when the Pup took off with the platform in the fixed position, followed by a second launching on 17 December when the platform was turned into wind.

The pilot for both these trials is unknown, but on 3 January 1918 Flt Sub Lt A.C. Sharwood RNAS, by then *Sydney*'s pilot, flew from the ship to Donibristle probably in Pup N6446. Dumaresq however wanted the loaned Pup to be replaced by the more modern 2F.1 Camel, and to this effect a signal had been sent to RNAS Smoogroo requesting that "*Campania* may be asked to supply a pilot and Camel complete with two mechanics to *Sydney*".

Two days later a reply was received stating "Does Camel refer to part of equipment or to a particular type of aeroplane?"

A further signal from *Sydney* dispelled any misconception the staff at Smoogroo may have harboured concerning the unusual eating habits of the wild colonials, for an aeroplane - 2F.1 Camel, N6635 - was lightered out to *Sydney* in the Flow during February 1918. And Sharwood's first take-off in N6635 from the ship to Donibristle took place on 27 February.

This arrangement was satisfactory for cruisers with only one gun mounted on the centre line on the forecastle - i.e. forward of the revolving platform. However in cruisers with two guns mounted on the centre line forward, one superimposed over the other, a forward revolving platform was not practicable. In these ships the platform was fitted abaft the funnels, and sited to allow as much training before and abaft the beam as possible. It was thought at first that the ship might still have to turn out of line to ensure that the "felt wind" was along the centre line of the platform. After trials in *Sydney*, however, it was found that an aeroplane could safely take off from her platform when the "felt wind" was as much as 20 degrees off the centre line of the platform.

A standard design of revolving platform was evolved and these platforms were prefabricated ashore, so that when a cruiser entered dockyard hands for any reason a platform could very quickly be installed.

Official listings of cruisers and light cruisers show that it was the intention to fit platforms in 33 ships for the operation of aeroplanes. But to date the evidence,

documentary and pictorial, shows that only 28 ships were so fitted between 1915-1919. Of these 28 ships it seems unlikely that six of them ever operated aeroplanes from their platforms.

The following 22 cruisers and light cruisers are known to have operated aeroplanes from fixed forecastle ramps (FFR), or fixed platforms (FP) or revolving platforms forward (RP[F]) and revolving platforms aft (RP[A]) between 1915-1919.

SHIP	TYPE(S) EMBARKED	EXAMPLE(S)	PLATFORM TYPE
AURORA	Deperdussin 2F.1 Camel	1378 N6756, N6770, N6816	FFR 1915 FP 1918
BIRKENHEAD	2F.1 Camel	N6753, N6759, N6833, N6844, N7110, N7111	FP 1917
CALEDON	Pup 2F.1 Camel	N6602	FP c. 1917 RP(A) c. 1918
CALLIOPE	2F.1 Camel	N6636, N6637, N6768, N6775, N6779	FP 1918
CARLISLE	2F.1 Camel		FP and BH 1918
CAROLINE	2F.1 Camel	N6602, N6617, N6637 N6766, N6768, N6831 N7108, N7121	FP 1918
CASSANDRA	W.B.III Pup 2F.1 Camel	N6100, N6128 N6200 N6794, N7122	FFR 1917 FP 1917 RP(A) 1918
CHATHAM	2F.1 Camel Pup	N6616, N6773, N6848 N6449	FP 1918 RP(F) 1918
COMUS	2F.1 Camel	N6614, N6629, N6632, N6642, N6760, N6768, N6775, N6780, N6790, N6793, N6810, N6811, N6846	FP 1918
CORDELIA	Pup 2F.1 Camel	N6757, N6767	FP 1917
DELHI	2F.1 Camel		RP(A) 1918
DUBLIN	Pup 2F.1 Camel W.B.III	9931, N6431, N6449 N6828, N7138 N6123	FP 1917 RP(F) 1918

GALATEA	2F.1 Camel	N6616, N6625, N6755, N6756, N6766, N6770, N6772, N6829, N7116, N7126, N7136	FP 1918
INCONSTANT	2F.1 Camel	N6631, N6640, N7100, N7116, N7119, N7123	FP 1918
MELBOURNE	2F.1 Camel	N6603, N6756, N6785, N6794, N6820, N6821, N6822, N7104	RP(F) 1918
PENELOPE	2F.1 Camel	N6646, N6768, N6778, N6799, N6824, N6845, N7109, N7110, N7117	FP 1918
PHAETON	2F.1 Camel	N6631, N6644, N6649, N6758, N6774, N6787, N6789, N6800	FP 1918
	W.B.III	N6127	
ROYALIST	2F.1 Camel	N6611, N6639, N6751, N6754, N6762, N6782, N6795, N6831, N7113	FP 1918
	W.B.III	N6686	
SOUTHAMPTON	2F.1 Camel	N6607, N6752, N6784, N6787, N6842, N7107, N7112	RP(F) 1918
SYDNEY	Pup	9931, 9932, N6431 N6446, N6449	RP(F) 1917
	2F.1 Camel	N6629, N6631, N6635, N6638, N6783, N6789, N6797, N6798, N6820, N6822, N6838, N7101	
UNDAUNTED	2F.1 Camel	N6603, N6773, N6824, N6847, N7107, N7119, N7139	FP 1918
YARMOUTH	Pup	9901, 9932, 9944, N6430, N6431, N6443	FP 1917
	2F.1 Camel	N6600	RP(F) 1918
	W.B.III	N6129	

FFR	Fixed Forecastle Ramp
FP	Fixed Platform
FP and BH	Fixed Platform and Bridge Hangar
RP(F)	Revolving Platform (Forward)
RP(A)	Revolving Platform (Aft)

The light cruiser and cruisers below were all fitted with platforms during 1918 and 1919, but probably never operated aeroplanes:

CONSTANCE	FP 1918
COVENTRY	RP(A) 1918
DAUNTLESS	FP and BH 1918
DRAGON	FP and BH 1918, RP(A) 1919
DUNEDIN	RP(A) 1919
WEYMOUTH	FP 1918, RP(F) 1918

It may be safely said that the withdrawal of the 2F.1 Camel from service in about 1919 marked the temporary end of the operation of aeroplanes from revolving platforms in HM Ships.

With the introduction of the Flycatcher into service with the Fleet Air Arm in 1924, however, a renewed interest in revolving platforms -in the complete absence of any further progress with catapult operations - was now shown. Accordingly during 1925 experiments were carried out in a 7-foot wind tunnel at the National Physical Laboratory, using a wooden model of the revolving platform in HMS *Caledon* to investigate the airflow over the platform. The platform could be trained into the relative wind for flying off operations, the possible range of yaw, ie variation, of the wind to the ship, being 30 degrees to 90 degrees port and starboard.

A small model aerofoil was used during the wind tunnel tests, held in positions which would be occupied by the wings of a Flycatcher on the platform during its take-off run, to measure the lift for a number of angles of yaw of the relative wind. These experiments found that at the start of its take-off run, the aircraft was subjected to a tilting effect by the airflow, and it was concluded that a launch should not be attempted when windspeed over the platform exceeded 30 knots. However, with a take off run of only 23 feet to the end of the platform, it was estimated that a Flycatcher would need a relative wind over the platform of at least 35 knots to reach sufficient flying speed for a safe take-off.

The problem was to prevent the aircraft overturning before release. The recommendation was that this be achieved either by use of the ailerons, or by "external stops at the wing tips". No evidence of the latter method has yet come to light, so presumably use of the ailerons was found to be the practical solution.

Other findings from the wind tunnel tests were that there was a large updraught over the end of the platform, the airstream becoming horizontal over the middle line of the ship. The superstructure immediately abaft the platform also caused the airflow to be unsymmetrical in relation to the aircraft on the platform, causing the seaward, or sternward, wing to tilt upwards.

Full-scale trials in launching a Flycatcher from *Caledon*'s platform were also conducted in Home and Tropical waters. Tropical trials showed that with higher temperatures, engine revolutions were higher and the thrust of the airscrew increased. Acceleration of the aircraft was increased, but only in proportion to the density of the air. The increased take-off speed attained was therefore cancelled out by the increased take-off run required.

The operation of aircraft from revolving platforms must have required great skill, and not a little luck. The Flycatcher trials in HMS *Argus* had shown that the aircraft could be airborne in a 28 knot wind after a take-off run of 20 feet. On a platform the aircraft had a maximum run of 23 feet. A variation in wind speed of plus or minus 20 per cent at launching, or prior to launching, might have disastrous results, since the requirements of adequate flying speed and safety when stationary on the platform undoubtedly conflicted.

Caledon certainly operated Flycatchers from her revolving platform during the 1920s, and possibly *Cassandra* also. *Emerald* and *Enterprise* on the East Indies Station carried one Flycatcher each of 406 Flight on their revolving platforms until 1934, but in every photograph of these two ships during this period, their Flycatchers were always fitted with floats. It is a fair assumption therefore that their aircraft were only stowed on their platforms, and were always hoisted outboard to take off from the water. There is no evidence that the five cruisers of the D class ever operated Flycatchers from their revolving platforms. The following cruisers were equipped to operate aeroplanes or seaplanes from their revolving platforms between 1924 and 1934:

SHIP	TYPES EMBARKED	EXAMPLES	LAUNCHED FROM
CALEDON	Flycatcher	N9679, N9902	RP(A)
EMERALD	Flycatcher (Seaplane)	N9670, N9894, S1063	RP(A) 1926
ENTERPRISE	Flycatcher (Seaplane)	N9894, N9902, N9917, N9940	RP(A) 1926
DELHI	) Although revolving platforms were retained		
DESPATCH	) in these five "D" Class cruisers until about		
DIOMEDE	) 1927, it is doubtful if any aeroplanes were		
DUNEDIN	) operated from them after the withdrawal		
DURBAN	) from service of 2F.1 Camels.		

A revolving platform (forward), installed in H.M.A.S. Sydney in 1917 for the operation of a Pup or 2F1 Camel. The platform was of a standard pattern similar to those fitted to all cruisers with revolving platforms (forward).

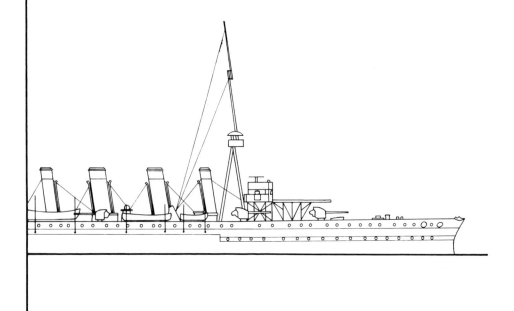

A revolving platform (aft) installed in H.M.S. Delhi in 1919 for the operation of a 2F1 Camel. The platform was of a standard pattern, similar to those fitted to all cruisers with revolving platforms (aft).

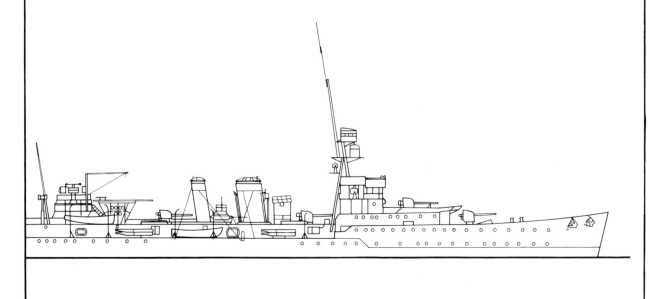

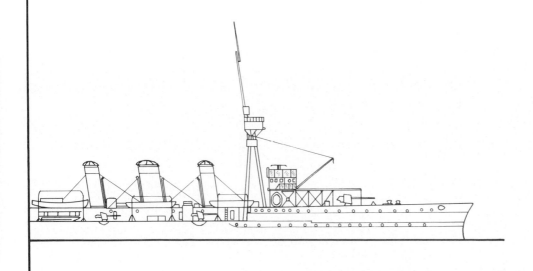

A fixed platform installed in H.M.S. Royalist in 1918 for the operation of a 2F1 Camel. The platform was of a standard pattern similar to those fitted to all cruisers with fixed platforms.

Flt Cdr F.J. Rutland's first flight from HMS Yarmouth's fixed platform in Pup 9901. This trial took place off the Firth of Forth on 28th June, 1917, and the platform was the prototype for all the fixed platform installations in cruisers.
(G.S. Leslie/J.M.Bruce collection)

HMS Yarmouth proceeding to sea with a Pup on her fixed platform. (IWM SP1388)

2F.1 Camel on Melbourne's revolving platform 1918. (A.K. Vicary)

HMAS Sydney's 2F.1 Camel protected from the elements on her forward revolving platform. (IWM SP1261)

HMAS Sydney's 2F.1 Camel on her forward revolving platform. The white rectangles on the outboard corners of the platform were used by the pilot in conjunction with the Camel's whitewashed tyre "treads" to indicate to him that he had run out of deck when taking off. The white line down the centre was an aid to avoid the rotary engine's tendency to swing the aircraft to port. (RAFM)

Two views of Sydney's 2F.1 Camel on her revolving platform trained fore and aft, and into wind to starboard. The canvas lattice windbreaks were easily removed before take-off, but the steel side sheeting was left in place. (RAFM)

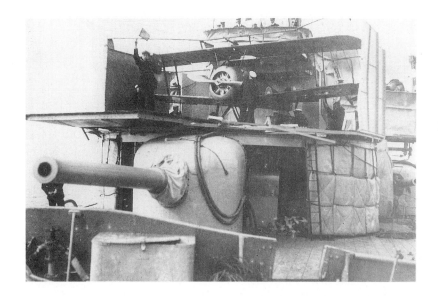

The officer holding the flag indicates that Sydney's platform is turned to face into wind, and the Camel's launching crew are assembled. (RAFM)

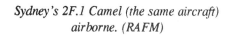

Sydney's 2F.1 Camel (the same aircraft) airborne. (RAFM)

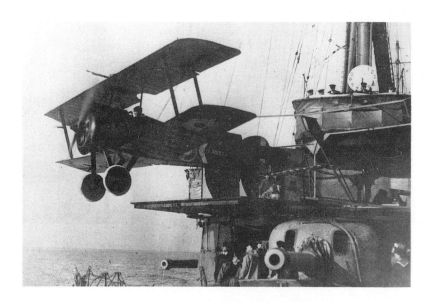

2F.1 Camel N6822 leaving Sydney's forward revolving platform. The Camel's whitewashed tyres used in conjunction with white painted marks in the outboard corners of the platform indicated to the pilot that his take-off had reached the end of the platform. (RAFM PO15831)

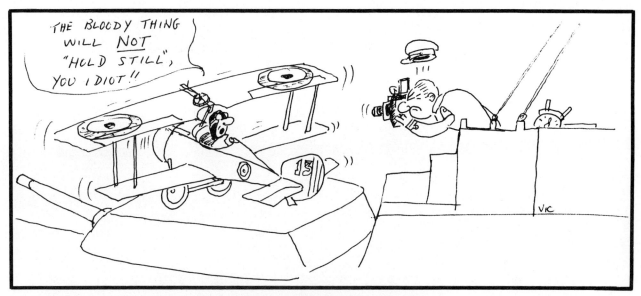

The lighter side of turret operations (Vic Sheppard)

A photograph taken on board HMAS Sydney at Rosyth on 2nd July, 1918. The pilot at the front is Flt Sub Lt T. Brewen, and the three Air Mechanics behind him are C. Graffy, R.H. Radcliffe and E. Birch who were responsible for the maintenance of the 2F.1 Camel N6783 in which Flt Lt A.C. Sharwood forced down a German seaplane in Heligoland Bight on 1st June, 1918. (AWM A2676)

HMS Delhi with a 2F.1 Camel on her aft revolving platform c. 1919. (FAAM)

Beardmore WB III, N6100, which HMS Cassandra operated from her fixed platform c. late 1917/early 1918.
(via R.C.B. Ashworth)

HMS Carlisle c. 1919 showing the arrangements of her fixed platform and bridge hangar. The outward end of the
platform extending over No.2 gun was hinged to fold upwards when no flying was taking place to allow a full arc of fire
for that gun. (NMM BJL.1)

*2F.1 Camel N6623 on the Lighter
H3 at Felixtowe on 29th May,
1918, prior to Cdr Samson's
attempted take-off on 30th May.
(G.S. Leslie/J.M. Bruce collection
and R.C.B. Ashworth)*

Two views of Cdr Samson's near fatal attempt to fly 2F.1 Camel N6623 from the horizontal deck of Lighter H3 towed by HMS Truculent off Orfordness on 30th May, 1918.
(G.S. Leslie/J.M. Bruce collection)

HMS Springbok towing a Lighter with inclined deck carrying a 2F.1 Camel, 1918. (A.K. Vicary)

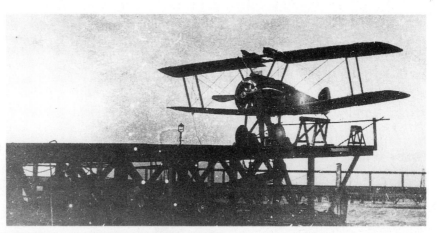

2F.1 Camel N6812 on a Lighter at Felixtowe prior to Lt S.D. Culley's destruction of the Zeppelin L53 in the Heligoland Bight on 11th August, 1918. The twin Lewis guns can be seen mounted above the upper centre section. (via R.C.B. Ashworth)

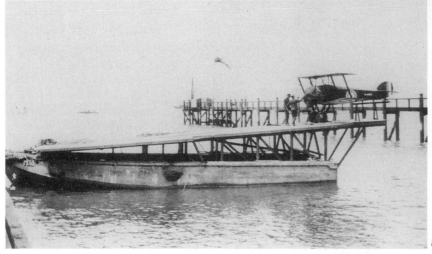

Two views of 2F.1 Camel N6812 on the Lighter H3 with inclined deck prior to the successful take-off by Lt S.D. Culley on 31st July, 1918. (G.S. Leslie/J.M. Bruce collection)

HMS Redoubt, here towing a Lighter with a Felixtowe F3 on board, was the destroyer which towed Culley's lighter borne Camel N6812 into action on 11th August, 1918. (G.S. Leslie/J.M. Bruce collection)

A 2F.1 Camel on HMS Caledon's aft revolving platform. (FAAM)

Caledon's 2F.1 Camel, probably N6602, taking off from her aft revolving platform in the Baltic early 1919, possibly in support of White Russian forces. (via V. Sheppard)

Two views of a wooden model (scale ⅛″ to 1′) of the aft revolving platform mounted in HMS Caledon. The model was used in the wind tunnel tests to assess the feasibility of operating a Flycatcher from the platform prior to full scale trials in September 1925. (RAFM B1479)

A Flycatcher on Caledon's aft revolving platform. (FAAM)

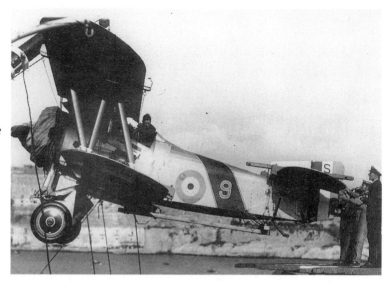

A Flycatcher being lowered onto Caledon's revolving platform. The ship's pentagonal badge is visible on the original print on the side of the aeroplane's engine cowling. (RAFM P11796)

A Flycatcher on Caledon's aft revolving platform, 1930. (N.H. Hemming via R.C. Sturtivant)

Flycatcher N9679/13 taking off from Caledon's aft revolving platform, May 1929. (N.C. McKinnon via R.C. Sturtivant)

Flycatcher S1063 of 406 Flight on the aft revolving platform of HMS Emerald on 15th September, 1928.
(NMM N8129)

Flycatcher of 406 Flight, possibly N9670, on Emerald's aft revolving platform at Karachi in 1933.
(RAFM PC 72/200/8)

HMS Enterprise with a Flycatcher of 406 Flight, possibly N9894, on her aft revolving platform c. 1927. (A.K. Vicary)

HMS Enterprise in dockyard hands with Flycatcher N9902 on her aft platform. (via RCC)

CHAPTER III
Turret ramps in capital ships, Home Waters 1917-1918

In spite of the limited endurance and lack of W/T in single seaters embarked in cruisers, it was at first envisaged that reconnaissance would be their main rôle. This being so, it was felt in 1917 that battle cruisers also would need to embark single seaters to act as what would now be known as "air superiority fighters" to clear the skies above the Fleet of enemy aircraft and Zeppelins. Lt Cdr C. H. B. Green, RN, who had been concerned with the fixed platform trials in *Yarmouth* during the summer of 1917, together with Cdr Gowan, RN, was responsible for initiating the experiment of mounting turret ramps in capital ships.

It was more important that a capital ship should not have to leave the battle line, compared with a cruiser, in order to launch an aeroplane. By mounting a ramp upon the turrets of a capital ship, this objection was overcome. The ship could turn her turret so that the aeroplane to be launched from it faced into wind, while she maintained her course and position in the line of battle.

On 1 October 1917, Sqdn Cdr F.J. Rutland flew a Pup from B turret of *Repulse*. The result of this trial is contained in a Report by Capt J. S. Dumaresq, commanding *Repulse*, No 5/2356 to Rear Admiral commanding 1st Battle Cruiser Squadron entitled "Airplane (sic) Flight from roof of B turret".

1. "I have the honour to report as follows on the flight from a platform on top of B turret of HMS *Repulse* made by Sqdn. Cdr. Rutland of HMS *Furious* at 10 am today the 1 October 1917."

2. "The object of Sqdn. Cdr. Rutland's trial was to test flying off from a training platform into the "wind felt", i.e. relative wind, thereby avoiding turning the ship through the full amount required to get the wind right ahead."

3. "The position of the ship was 4 miles east by north from Inchkeith: course 145 degrees; speed 24 knots. The observed direction of the true wind was about 230 degrees, force about 17 mph. The turret was trained 24 degrees on the starboard bow. The strength of the "wind felt", as measured on the anemometer on the flying platform was $31\frac{1}{2}$ mph."

4. "The turret was trained through the left training periscope under the directions of the pilot, and both the pilot and the trainer could see a hollow bunting windvane, which was fixed to the muzzle of the left gun, on a line from the trainer's eye parallel to the axis, but the pilot trained the turret finally by a flag held in front of him."

5. "The original course of the ship was altered towards the wind twice by one point, in order to strengthen

Flt Cdr F.J.Rutland in the cockpit of Pup N6453 on B turret ramp of HMS Repulse 1st October 1917. (FAAM)

Rutland commences his historic take-off from HMS Repulse's B turret ramp at 1000 on 1st October 1917 in Pup N6453.
(FAAM)

the 'wind felt': the pilot did not seem to have any difficulty in flying off, and immediately rose into the air with about 6 feet of the platform untouched.''

6. ''The platform was constructed of 2-inch deals supported on steel angle bars, and was sloped slightly in the direction of flight: at the inboard end was a frame to guide the tail, and the outboard end of the platform projected beyond the end of the turret, so that any upward rush of air would pass under the platform.''

7. ''The turret officer's sighting hood, etc, was obstructed by the platform, but the turret was being used merely as a means of easily obtaining a training platform.''

The 2-inch deals referred to in paragraph 6 of the Report comprised that part of the turret ramp extending over the gun barrels. The deals would be removed before the turret's guns were fired, and stowed upon that part of the turret ramp above the turret. This part of the turret ramp was constructed of perforated sheet steel and, because it did not interfere with the firing of the turret's guns, remained a fixture.

Also in paragraph 6, the ''frame to guide the tail'' was the Tail Guide Trestle. With only a very limited take off run from the platform, the Trestle held the aeroplane in a flying attitude. It consisted of a grooved horizontal member 7 feet long, in whose groove was inserted the aeroplane's tailskid which terminated in a ball fitting. This both helped to counteract the torque of

the rotary engine and provided directional stability during the first 7 feet of the take-off run, until there was sufficient wind over the rudder for it to become effective. A Tail Guide Trestle had been used as far back as 3 November 1915, when Bristol Scout C, 1255, became the first aeroplane with wheeled undercarriage to take off from the forward flying off deck of HMS *Vindex*.

Many of the innovations in early naval aviation were associated with Lt Cdr G.R.A. Holmes, RNVR. Formerly a naval architect in the Cunard Company, he served in the DNC's Department and played a considerable part in the design of early seaplane carriers in 1915, and the following year in connection with arrester hooks and arrester wires in the proposed new aircraft carriers. As a member of the Admiralty Committee on Deck Landing in November 1917, he was also involved with the development of the ''Ball Tailskid Fitting'' and the ''Quick Release Gear''.

Both these two latter devices had undergone extensive trials in HMS *Campania* with a Fairey Campania seaplane in June 1916. The Tail Guide Trestle used in *Campania* was actually designed by Holmes. It was constructed of 9-inch x 3-inch deal, height above the deck was 34-inch forward and 50-inch aft. The length was 24 feet, of which it was noted that 19 feet 7'' was not required!

The report on the Rubery Owen quick release device in *Campania* states that it was secured to the foremost leg of the tail guide by a steel clip, which held a wire cable span of 7/16-inch cable wire, secured to the

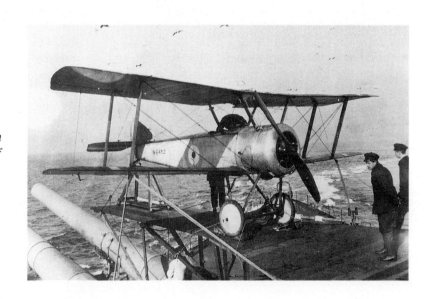

Three views of Pup N6453, in which on 8th October 1917, Flt Cdr F.J.Rutland took off from HMS Repulse's Y turret ramp. (FAAM)

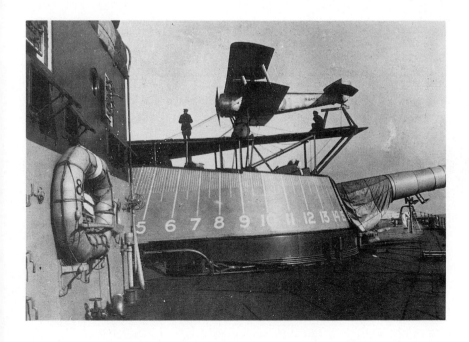

HMS Repulse with a Ship Strutter on B turret ramp and a Pup on Y turret ramp. (RMM 14/2/2 (316))

rear float axles. A long release wire with two toggles on it allowed the operator to stand clear of the slipstream. It was concluded that an external release device was superior to any which had to be operated by the pilot.

By the time of Rutland's historic flight in October 1917, both the Tail Guide Trestle and Quick Release Strop had been modified and tested. With the aeroplane's tail skid fitted to the Trestle, the engine was run up to full power. In the absence of any wheel brakes the aeroplane was held to the platform by the Quick Release Strop. The upper end of the Strop terminated in a slip hook attached to a cross wire stretched between the rear undercarriage struts. The strop ran aft at an angle of 45 degrees, and the lower end was anchored to an eyebolt in the deck of the turret ramp. The Quick Release Strop was operated from the turret ramp by a smart pull on a lanyard attached to the slip hook, on a signal from the pilot. The launching procedure was exactly the same on cruisers' platforms.

Following the trial of 1 October 1917, Flt Cdr Rutland successfully flew a Pup, N6453, from a ramp mounted on *Repulse*'s Y turret on 8 October, the turret being trained 30 degrees before the beam, and the aeroplane taking off over the back of the turret. It was thought that this latter arrangement for turret ramps on the after turrets of capital ships would reduce the training of those turrets to a minimum to enable the aeroplane to take off into wind. Experience showed, however, that this form of turret ramp for the after turrets was not necessary. Only five battle cruisers - *Renown, Repulse, Lion, Tiger* and *Princess Royal* launched their aeroplanes over the backs of their turrets. All remaining battle cruisers and all battleships were fitted with turret ramps which extended over the gun barrels.

On 4 March 1918 Flt Cdr D.G. Donald attempted to fly a Ship Strutter, 9744, from an extended ramp constructed of flexible wire rope on Repulse's B turret.

HMS Repulse with a Ship Strutter on B turret ramp and a 2F.1 Camel on Y turret ramp. (IWM SP720)

Donald's flying logbook describes this as:

"an experimental flight from a "spring mattress" on B turret. Rather a failure as my prop hit the "mattress" and broke. I just managed to clear the forecastle and dived into the ditch. Picked up five minutes later by *Rival*. Really had a lucky escape, only slightly bruised".

The "mattress" was then removed from B turret and this dangerous contraption was never used again.

Undaunted by his experience, Donald's logbook records that three days later on 7 March he flew Ship Strutter, N5644, from *Australia*'s Q turret ramp, extended in more orthodox manner.

"Wind about 20 mph. Got off straight and dropped very little, although engine only giving 1050 revs." It has been presumed that the first successful take-off in a Ship Strutter from a turret ramp was achieved by Flt Cdr F.M. Fox from *Australia*'s Q turret on 4 April 1918, but Donald's flight predates this by four weeks.

No capital ship so equipped carried more than two turret ramps, and these ships, with seven exceptions, had the turrets of their main armament mounted on the centre line. Of these seven exceptions, only four - HMAS *Australia*, HMS *New Zealand*, HMS *Indomitable* and HMS *Inflexible* - had ramps mounted upon turrets not on the centre line. Their ramps were on P turret which was mounted on the port side abaft the second funnel, and on Q turret which was on the starboard side forward of the third funnel. HMS *Bellerophon*, HMS *Collingwood* and HMS *Neptune* all had P and Q turrets, but their turret ramps were mounted respectively on A + Y, B + X, and A only.

There were exceptions to the rôles of aeroplanes embarked in capital ships, but in general it would be one fighter - Pup or 2F.1 Camel, and one reconnaissance aeroplane - Ship Strutter. Most aeroplanes, unless the ship lay alongside in harbour, had to be transferred from shore to ship by lighter or drifter. From the deck of a lighter to the ramp on top of a superimposed turret would be a height of 35-40 feet. Various methods of hoisting an aeroplane inboard and up to its turret ramp

were employed, including an adjacent derrick, the guns of another turret elevated to act as a crane, or sheer manpower to haul the aeroplane, suspended from the $4^1/_2$'' steel wire rope fore stay which stretched from the stem at deck level to a point, some 80 feet above deck level, on the foremast. This of course passed directly over the centre of the turret ramp and 25 feet above it. If we take *Repulse* as a typical example, B turret carried a ramp of 57 feet in length and was used by the Ship Strutter. The Pup or 2F.1 Camel, because of their smaller dimensions and lighter weight, used the 47-foot ramp on Y turret.

Protection for the embarked aeroplanes, again taking *Repulse* as an example, could be provided by portable hangars constructed of oiled canvas stretched over an iron framework. B turret's aeroplane hangar was sited on deck forward of A turret, and Y turret's hangar between the mainmast and the two aftermost 4-inch gun mounts. With the low freeboard of *Repulse*, and the other battle cruisers, one suspects that these hangars were never rigged while at sea. Contemporary photographs of capital ships at sea always show their aeroplanes stowed on their turret ramps.

All official lists of battleships and battlecruisers agree that 44 ships were fitted with turret ramps for the operation of aeroplanes between late 1917 and early 1919. However, from documentary and photographic evidence, it appears that in fact only 36 of these 44 ships were ever actually fitted with turret ramps, and that of these 36 ships only 26 ever embarked aeroplanes.

So far, there is no evidence at all that the remaining 8 ships of the total of 44 were ever fitted with turret ramps. It is likely that the official lists contained all those capital ships which it was the intention to equip with turret ramps. Had the war continued beyond November 1918 it is probable that all 44 ships would have operated aeroplanes from their turret ramps. The following 26 battleships and battlecruisers therefore are known to have operated aeroplanes from their turret ramps between 1917 and 1919:

SHIP	TURRET(S)	TYPE(S)	EXAMPLE(S)
AJAX	B and Q	2F.1 Camel	N6834
AUSTRALIA	P and Q	Pup	N6446
		2F.1 Camel	N6786, N6790, N6820, N6822, N6826, N6828
		Ship Strutter	N5606, N5644, A6968, A5985, F7562
BARHAM	B and X	2F.1 Camel	N6750, N6762, N7103, N7136
		Ship Strutter	A5988, A6006, F2228 F2225
BELLEROPHON	A and Y	Ship Strutter	A5984, A5985

SHIP	TURRET(S)	TYPE(S)	EXAMPLE(S)
CANADA	B and X	2F.1 Camel	N7116
COURAGEOUS	A and Y	2F.1 Camel	N6619, N6645, N6751, N6752, N6763, N6773, N6775, N6793, N6842, N7128
		Ship Strutter	A5994, A5998, F2210, F2222, F2227
EMPEROR OF INDIA	B and Q	2F.1 Camel	N7129
		Ship Strutter	F7561
GLORIOUS	A and Y	2F.1 Camel	N6604, N6605, N6614, N6776, N6778, N6788, N6835, N7117, N7121
		Ship Strutter	N5644, A5990, A6905, B744
INDOMITABLE	P and Q	2F.1 Camel	N6614, N6647, N6759, N6790, N6791, N6792, N6813
		Ship Strutter	A5988, A6952, A6966, A8277, F2216
INFLEXIBLE	P and Q	2F.1 Camel	N6759, N6786, N6787, N6792, N6817
		Ship Strutter	A6010, A6980, A8224
IRON DUKE	B and Q	2F.1 Camel	N6751, N6757, N6791, N6799, N7125
LION	Q and Y	Pup	N6455
		2F.1 Camel	N6600, N6602, N6604, N6607, N6629, N6631, N6647, N6764, N6769, N6773, N6776, N6819, N7120, N7126
MALAYA	B and X	2F.1 Camel	N6789, N7146, N7148,
		Ship Strutter	A6967, A8277, F2221
NEW ZEALAND	P and Q	Pup	N6440
		2F.1 Camel	N6617, N6832, N6833, N7109, N7134, N7140
		Ship Strutter	N5644, A6981, F2220
ORION	B only	2F.1 Camel	N6819, N7119
PRINCESS ROYAL	Q and Y	Pup	N6440, N6443, N6445, N6633
		2F.1 Camel	N6604, N6633, N6642, N6758, N6768, N6770, N6830, N6839, N6849, N7114
		WBIII	N6115
QUEEN ELIZABETH	B and X	2F.1 Camel	N7120
		Ship Strutter	A6006

SHIP	TURRET(S)	TYPE(S)	EXAMPLE(S)
RENOWN	B and Y	WB.III	N6109, N6115, N6116
		Pup	9944, N6434, N6444, N6448, N6456
		2F.1 Camel	N6606, N6611, N6617, N6619, N6630, N6633, N6638, N6641, N6751, N7101
		Ship Strutter	A5981, A5987, A5993, A5995, F2215, F2225, F2228, F2229
REPULSE	B and Y	Pup	9944 , 9945, N6438, N6443, N6446, N6453, N6455, N6456
		2F.1 Camel	N6605, N6606, N6637, N6638, N7105, N7106,
		Ship Strutter	A5982, A5988, A6967, A8300, F2224, F2228, 9744, N5644
		Panther	N92, N7468
RAMILLIES	B and X	2F.1 Camel	
REVENGE	B and X	Pup	
		2F.1 Camel	
		Panther	
ROYAL OAK	B and X	2F.1 Camel	N6819
ROYAL SOVEREIGN	B and X	2F.1 Camel	N6752, N7103, N7108
		Ship Strutter	
TIGER	Y only (1917)	Pup	9934, 9944, N6438, N6443, N6455, N6456
	B and Q	2F.1 Camel	N6601, N6603, N6606, N6648, N6750, N6797, N6835, N7103
		F.1 Camel	D9523
VALIANT	B and X	2F.1 Camel	N6795, N6838
		Ship Strutter	A6952
WARSPITE	B and X	2F.1 Camel	N7120
		Ship Strutter	A5987

The following ten battleships are known to have been fitted with turret ramps, but it is unlikely that any of them operated aeroplanes:

BENBOW	B and Q	MARLBOROUGH	B and Q
COLLINGWOOD	A only	MONARCH	B only
CONQUEROR	B and X	NEPTUNE	A only
ERIN	B and Q	RESOLUTION	B and X
KING GEORGE V	B and Q	CENTURION	B and Q

It was probably the intention to fit a further eight battleships with turret-ramps, but it is unlikely that this was ever carried out. These eight ships were:

AGINCOURT   ST VINCENT
COLOSSUS   SUPERB
DREADNOUGHT   TEMERAIRE
HERCULES   THUNDERER

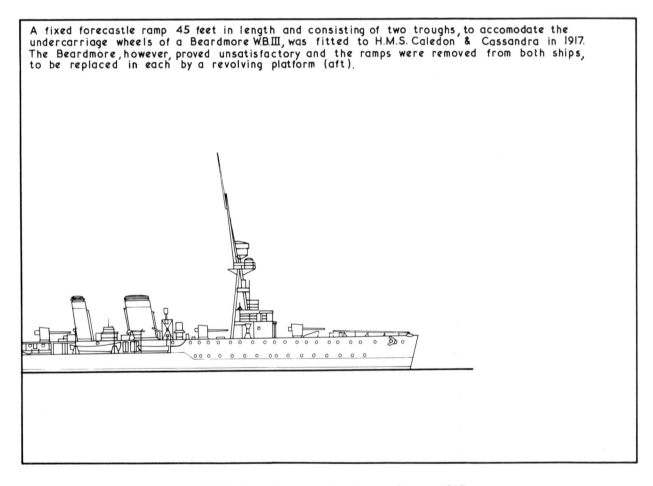

A fixed forecastle ramp 45 feet in length and consisting of two troughs, to accomodate the undercarriage wheels of a Beardmore W.B.III, was fitted to H.M.S. Caledon & Cassandra in 1917. The Beardmore, however, proved unsatisfactory and the ramps were removed from both ships, to be replaced in each by a revolving platform (aft).

HMS Caledon/Cassandra fixed forecastle ramp 1917

HMAS Australia with a Ship Strutter on P turret ramp. (RCC)

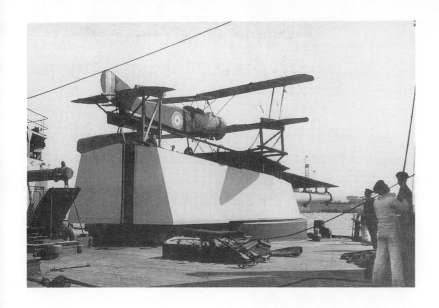

Ship Strutter, probably N6968, on HMAS Australia's P turret ramp. (RAFM)

Flt Sub Lt Simonson taking off in Ship Strutter N5644 from HMAS Australia's Q turret ramp, Firth of Forth 8th March 1918. An example of an incorrectly marked serial with the N prefix omitted. (IWM Q18729)

Ships Strutter N5644 (incorrectly marked 5644) is hoisted from a lighter on to HMAS Australia's Q turret ramp around March 1918 (RAN Photographic Section 4209, via J.P.Barr)

Ship Strutter F7562 on HMAS Australia's P turret ramp on 12th December 1918. (AWM EN11)

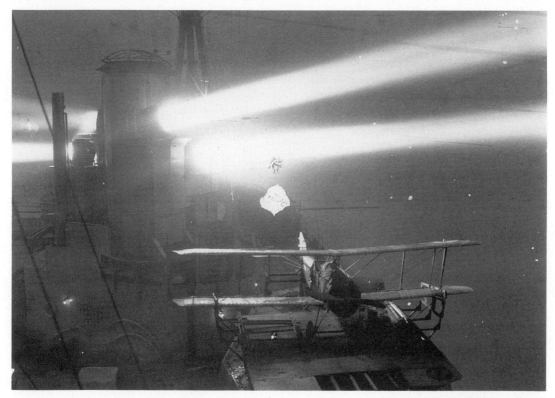

Also taken in December 1918 looking aft, this spectacular night scene in the Firth of Forth shows HMAS Australia's Ship Strutter F7562 on P turret ramp, and her 2F.1 Camel on Q turret ramp. (AWM EN17)

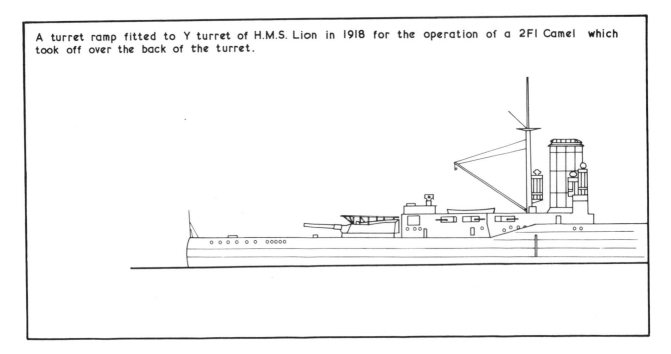

A turret ramp fitted to Y turret of H.M.S. Lion in 1918 for the operation of a 2Fl Camel which took off over the back of the turret.

HMS Lion turret ramp 1918

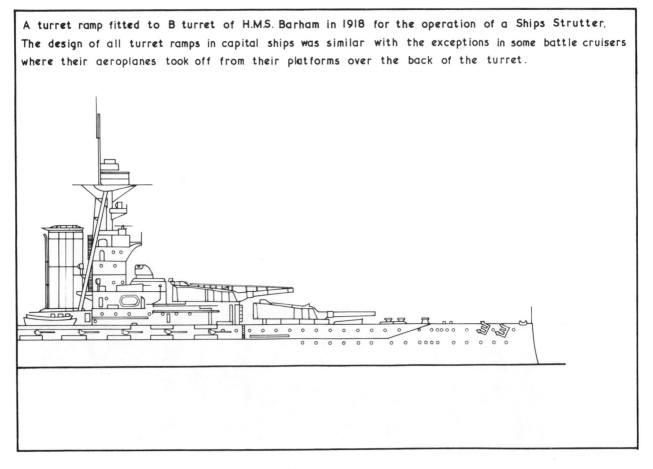

A turret ramp fitted to B turret of H.M.S. Barham in 1918 for the operation of a Ships Strutter. The design of all turret ramps in capital ships was similar with the exceptions in some battle cruisers where their aeroplanes took off from their platforms over the back of the turret.

HMS Barham turret ramp 1918

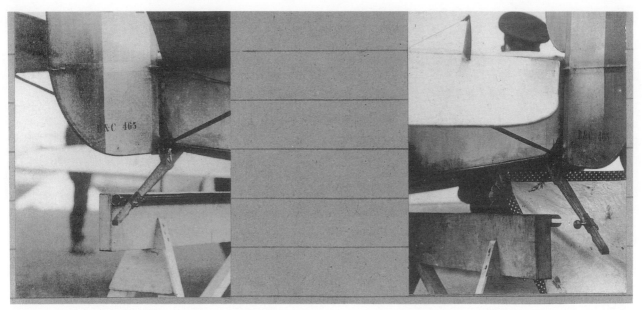

Details of the Tail Guide Trestle and Quick Release Strop tested on Bristol Scout C 1246. Both devices became standard equipment for launching aeroplanes from platforms and turret ramps in H.M.Ships. (FAAM)

CHAPTER IV

Turret ramps in capital ships 1924-1931.
Catapult trials 1911-1927

F ollowing the Armistice of November 1918, the only capital ship to be completed until the late 1920s was HMS *Hood*, and she was fitted with turret ramps on B and X turrets, although that on X turret was soon removed. In common with all HM Ships still fitted to operate aeroplanes from platforms or turret ramps

during the early 1920's, she had no suitable aeroplane until the entry of the Flycatcher into service during 1923. *Hood* operated a Flycatcher from B turret ramp in the mid 1920's, and in fact B turret's ramp was retained until at least July 1932, though it is doubtful if it was then still used. An illustration of the continued use of aeroplanes launched from turret ramps may be given by the trials involving the use of Siskin IIIA, J8390, from *Repulse*'s B turret and Y turret ramps in the summer of 1928. *Repulse* was unique in retaining a ramp on Y turret at this time, and operated two aeroplanes, a Siskin and a Flycatcher.

The following battleships and battle cruisers operated aeroplanes from turret ramps from 1924 to around 1931.

SHIP	TYPE(S)	EXAMPLES EMBARKED	TURRET RAMPS FITTED
BARHAM	Flycatcher	N9670	B
HOOD	Flycatcher		B
MALAYA	Flycatcher	N9675	B
RAMILLIES	Flycatcher	N9894, N9913 S1070, S1280	B
RENOWN	Flycatcher		B
REPULSE	Flycatcher Siskin IIIA	J8390	B and Y
REVENGE	Flycatcher	S1277	B
ROYAL OAK	Flycatcher	N9894	B
ROYAL SOVEREIGN	Flycatcher	N9895	B

The relationship between wing loading and stalling speed lay behind the fact that every increase in performance of an aircraft rendered it less suitable for operation by ships, and more effective for operating against them. Thus the simple expedient of launching aircraft, with increasingly powerful engines and higher wing loadings, from turret ramps could not be retained, and catapults had to be introduced for the purpose.

Aeronautically, the catapult can be defined as a device capable of launching an aircraft into wind at more than minimum flying speed.

Nautically the catapult and its aircraft take up much

valuable deck space, both drip oil on the decks, the aircraft is liable to blast damage from the guns, and if not launched before a gun action the aircraft becomes a fire hazard.

The continuance of the outdated method of launching aeroplanes from platforms into the 1930s retarded the development of catapults for launching aircraft from warships.

In this country a patent was taken out as early as 1911 by Sueter, Boothby and Paterson for a gravity-operated catapult. The operation of the device, as depicted in the accompanying sketch, was described as

HMS Hood with a Flycatcher on B turret ramp c. mid 1920's. (J.Hartley via R.C.Sturtivant)

HMS Repulse with a Siskin on B turret ramp in 1926. At this date HMS Repulse was the only ship in the Royal Navy operating aeroplanes from two turret ramps. (NMM.N7099)

follows:

"Starting - to start an aeroplane in a confined space, such, for instance, as from a ship, it is supported by trunnions (2) upon arms (5) carried by a trolley (4) adapted to run upon widely separated inclined rails (3). The trolley may be propelled by a falling weight (7) and cable (8). The weight may instead be suspended from the mast of the ship. Outwardly extending struts (6) may be provided on the trolley for supporting the wings of the machine".

Perhaps fortunately, this design was not proceeded with, although the designers' foresight at the birth of naval aviation is remarkable.

Experiments with catapults were meanwhile being conducted by the US Navy. These catapults were operated by compressed air and consisted of a trolley mounted on a 50 foot runway fixed to the ship's deck. The trolley was connected by a system of wire ropes to a ram which moved in a cylinder. In the first designs the trolley went overboard with the aircraft, but in later models buffers or brakes were fitted to absorb the energy of the system after launch, in order to bring the trolley to rest at the end of the runway. In late 1912 the U.S.Navy successfully launched a Curtiss A-3 flying boat from a compressed air catapult on shore. And on 5 November 1916 Lt Cdr H.C. Mustin USN in a Curtiss AB-2 was catapulted from the deck of USS *North Carolina* while under way.

In Britain, as the potential of airpower at sea came to be realised, the first experiments with catapults at the Marine Aircraft Experimental Station at Grain began in 1917, using a railway truck as the launching carriage, following a 1916 Admiralty invitation for tenders for hydraulic, electric and compressed air catapults. Specifications called for the launching of a $2^1/_2$-ton aircraft at 60 mph and with an acceleration of not more than 2.5g.

The hydraulic and electric types were not proceeded with, but by July 1916 a provisional specification for a compressed air or powder operated catapult was received in the Munitions Department, and by 1917 two compressed air catapults were ready for testing.

Concern was expressed about the amount of acceleration that a pilot could endure,

so before the tests on human guinea pigs were conducted a series of diverting catapult trials was initiated at the RAE Farnborough, which nowadays would draw some attention from animal rights "activists".

On the edge of Farnborough aerodrome stood the prototype of the R.A.E. catapult designed by P.Salmon. It was intended to launch aircraft weighing 7,000 lb up to a speed of 45 knots after a run of 34 feet. It consisted of a girder structure in which was mounted a cylinder containing a number of telescopic tubes. The cylinder was mounted so that three or four tubes could slide out of each other in a forward direction. The innermost tube was attached at its forward end to the launching trolley, which ran on wheels joined by rails on top of the catapult. Each tube was made smaller than the one into which it telescoped, and the annular space formed between them had a piston fitted at the rear end of the smaller tube and a bush at the front end of the larger. The resulting space was filled with fluid and the annular area made equal to the bore of the smaller tube. Ports were formed in the circumference of the inner tube at the rear end. The propelling force was compressed air which acted on the first ram's piston. The motion of this ram was transmitted to the other rams by the fluid and the resulting motion of the final ram was that of the first multiplied by the number of rams. To bring the trolley to rest at the end of the track, the rams were designed to act as buffers for the last part of their stroke. To return the rams and trolley after launching, use was made during the launching stroke of the kinetic energy of the fluid issuing from the final ram to charge up a cylinder of compressed air attached to this ram. When the residual pressure in the firing cylinder was released, the

Siskin IIIA J8390 on Y turret ramp of HMS Repulse for trials during 1928. The type was not adopted for use in HM Ships. (Via RCC)

HMS Barham with a Flycatcher on B turret ramp c. 1927. (FAAM)

trolley automatically returned and its rate of return was controlled by the release valve on the firing cylinder.

So the R.A.E. catapult was arranged to discharge its missile into a kind of slide. The missile was the fuselage of an aircraft, and strapped into the cockpit, in an intrepid and professional attitude, was a large sheep - because that was the nearest approach to a naval pilot that the RAE scientists could think of, or that the Admiralty would permit.

Early catapults had their propulsive ram (no relation to the above) operated by compressed air, which made the catapult very heavy. These were supplanted by types powered by cordite, the weight of which could be varied to suit different conditions of launch, and the violence controlled by the use of large diameter sticks of explosive to yield slow burning.

But to revert to the human side of catapult launches from the first two compressed air catapults ready for testing by 1917.

One, designed by R.F. Carey and built by Waygood-Otis, was installed at Hendon, and from it was launched an Avro 504H - a strengthened 504B with catapult spool and neck support for the pilot, Flt Cdr R.E. Penny. Three such conversions were in use at Hendon in May 1918, these being N5261, N5269 and N5270.

The second catapult, built by Armstrong Whitworth,

was installed in HMS *Slinger* - a former steam hopper of 875 tons, specially commissioned for catapult trials by the Marine Aircraft Experimental Depot at Grain. *Slinger*'s catapult was a steel box girder 60 feet in length and slightly inclined downward toward the ship's bows. The aircraft was mounted on a trolley which was propelled along the central of three parallel rails by a compressed air system operating a series of wires.

The first launch from *Slinger*'s catapult was made on 1 October 1917 in the Tyne using a Short 184 whose fuselage, but not wings, was stripped of fabric and whose engine was replaced by ballast of equivalent weight. The overall weight was 5,000 lbs and the launching speed 30 mph. This was followed by the launching of a pair of Short 184 floats, sand-loaded to a weight of two tons, at a speed of 40 mph.

HMS *Slinger* now went to the MAED at Grain for full scale tests with a piloted seaplane, in this case Fairey F.127 N9. The first successful launching of N9 piloted by Lt Col H.R. Busteed took place on 14 May 1918.

These trials were finally abandoned because the catapult was considered too cumbersome for installation in fighting ships and, as previously mentioned, the operation of aeroplanes from platforms in HM Ships appeared to satisfy the Royal Navy's requirements for airpower at sea - at least pro tem.

A further seven years was to elapse before a Service aircraft was to be launched from one of HM Ship's catapults - a Fairey IIID from HMS *Vindictive* in October 1925 from a Carey catapult. Preparatory to this, experiments were carried out in September 1924 to examine the airflow over the forward superstructure of HMS *Vindictive* upon which the catapult was to be mounted, to obtain information for the launching of a seaplane from the catapult. The tests were made in the 4-foot wind tunnel at the National Physical Laboratory, the flow being examined by means of smoke jets and by the NPL Velocity and Direction Meter. A double model - i.e. model and image - to a scale of $1/_8$" to one foot of the forward part of *Vindictive* was used so that the model might be yawed in the wind tunnel.

It was found that in high winds, at a considerable angle to the fore and aft line of the ship, the catapult being trained into the relative wind, there was a dead air region on the after side of the catapult and a strong up current on the forward side which would result in considerable tilting of the seaplane on the catapult. At the end of the catapult there was an updraught which became very large at big angles of yaw of the relative wind. A drop in relative wind speed at 30-50 feet in front of the catapult was also noticed.

From these observations it was calculated that with wind velocities at the end of the catapult varying from between 20-40 mph, the minimum speed of projection for the safe launching of a Fairey IIID seaplane from the catapult should be between 47 mph and $32^1/_2$ mph, provided the angle of yaw of 45 degrees was not exceeded. Full scale trials with a Fairey IIID on *Vindictive*'s Carey catapult were carried out between 14-21 October 1925, largely confirming the conclusions derived from the wind tunnel tests of the previous year. The Carey catapult was designed to launch an aircraft up to 7,000 lb in weight at a mean acceleration of 2g,

attaining a speed of 45 knots at the outboard end of the catapult.

The mechanism was similar to that on the early U.S.Navy catapults, except that retardation of the trolley was achieved hydraulically. A mixture of glycerine and distilled water in equal parts was displaced during the acceleration stroke into a receiver cylinder fitted to the side of the catapult. Propulsion was transmitted by means of wire ropes and pulleys at a three to one multiplication ratio to the launching trolley. After launch, air was admitted into the receiver cylinder and the liquid was forced back into the power cylinder, returning the system to its pre-launch position.

Although catapult development had some way to go, the Carey catapult in *Vindictive* proved to be effective, and similar types were installed in *Resolution* in 1926 and the submarine M 2 in 1927.

Concurrent with the completion of the two E-Class cruisers, wind tunnel tests with a double model, to a scale of $1/_4$-inch to one foot, of HMS *Emerald* were conducted during April 1926 to assess the airflow over a catapult installed on a turntable abaft the third funnel for launching a Fairey IIID seaplane. One of the features limiting the range of angle of the catapult was the close proximity of the third funnel forward of it. The catapult could be trained from 33 degrees before the beam to 30 degrees abaft the beam on the port side, and from 33 degrees before the beam to 15 degrees abaft the beam (owing to installation of a crane) on the starboard side. With the catapult trained into wind, the conclusions at the end of the wind tunnel tests were that the minimum relative wind speed at the end of the catapult should be 24 mph with the flaps straight for a successful launch, or 15 mph with 12 degrees flap angle, and that the seaplane should always be launched at the catapult's maximum speed.

In practice, before sailing for duty with the East

HMS Revenge with a Flycatcher on B turret ramp on 25th August 1927. (NMM.N7509)

Flycatcher S1277/1 of 406 Flight with control locks on rudder, elevators and ailerons on HMS Revenge's B turret ramp, Mediterranean 1931. (RAFM P020093)

Two further views of S1277 being readied for flight and taking off from Revenge's B turret ramp in 1931. (RAFM P020094/5)

Indies Squadron, *Emerald* was fitted with a revolving platform mounted in the same position proposed for a catapult. She was to wait until her refit of 1935/36 for the installation of her first catapult, designed to launch much heavier seaplanes than were in service 10 years earlier.

Before the last aircraft platforms were removed in 1935/36 from *Emerald* and *Enterprise,* work continued slowly on catapult design and operation. Between 1922 and 1927 two destroyers, *Stronghold* and *Thanet,* were fitted to launch radio controlled missiles from a launching track angled sharply upwards and mounted in the bows. For security reasons these flying bombs were known as Aircraft Targets and were based upon Royal Aircraft Factory designs produced by H.P. Folland in 1916-17. Three launches were made during June and July 1917 and all ended in failure. The Armistice of November 1918 meant that further trials were abandoned and work did not restart until 1920 when four airframes left from 1917 were re-engined with 45 hp Armstrong-Siddeley Ounce engines, and six more airframes were built at Farnborough. These six were known as the RAE 1921 Target and were capable of delivering a 200-lb warhead under radio control.

By mid-1922 attempts to launch the 1921 Target were restarted. A single channel radio was fitted to be switched on when the aircraft had reached operating height. Direction was controlled by a gyroscopic rudder control and height by an aneroid operating the elevator. Two launches from horizontal rails laid on the flight deck of *Argus* on 13 July and 31 August 1922 ended in failure, and both Targets were written off after crashing into the sea. It was considered that the transition from the horizontal rails to climbing flight with fixed elevator was a cause of the problem, and so it was decided to launch into the climb from an inclined catapult mounted in the bows of *Stronghold*. The missile was accelerated up the catapult's track by a large bag of water which was allowed to fall into the sea.

The first two launches from *Stronghold* on 13 and 17 September 1923 were satisfactory, but on the third flight the Target collided on 22 February with a camera carrying Fairey IIID seaplane and dived into the sea. The seaplane survived the collision which was probably caused by the gyro toppling. The fourth launch from *Stronghold* on 6 June was a successful programmed flight and for the fifth flight radio control was installed and the Target responded to commands transmitted from

a Fairey IIID on 3 September. Two further flights were made on 12 September and 16 October 1924 using two transmitters, one each in *Stronghold* and a Fairey IIID, but both Targets crashed and were written off. The last launch from *Stronghold* made on 26 February 1925 was controlled by a standard transmitter in the cruiser *Castor*. Forty-three commands were transmitted and obeyed, and the Target made a successful 39 minute flight. The trials demonstrated that remotely-controlled flight had been successfully tested, limited only by the unreliability of the engine. It was also apparent that for some applications radio control was unnecessary, and that a missile could be guided by autopilot alone.

This led to the design and production by the RAE of the Larynx in September 1925. Larger than the 1921 Target, and powered by a 200 hp Armstrong-Siddeley Lynx, it had a range of 300 miles carrying a 250 lb warhead - the first successful surface to surface missile. Guidance accuracy was achieved by the use of a magnetic compass to monitor the rudder gyro and an air log to measure the distance flown, basically the same instrumentation used by German flying bombs in 1944. Successful trials using cordite operated catapults in *Stronghold* and *Thanet* were conducted with the Larynx in 1926-27 before trials were moved to the Iraq desert on security grounds. Development eventually ceased because it was thought the weapon would be of greater importance to an aggressor than to ourselves!

By 1930 the replacement of platforms by catapults as a means of launching aircraft of ever increasing weights from fighting ships was becoming an urgent necessity. Intensive catapult trials took place in HMS *Ark Royal* between 1930-32, involving the use of all the main types of catapult (with the exception of the fixed athwartship type) which were to be installed in cruisers and capital ships for the next thirteen years. However, that is another story, as is the adverse effect that overlong dependence on catapult-operated aircraft had upon the development of deck landing techniques in carriers in the 1930's.

Let us allow Cdr Peter Bethell RN a last word on catapult launches:

"Personal experience of being catapulted seems too dull to relate. It seemed prudent to hold the control column in a normal position and to hope for the best, not forgetting a brief prayer to St Lawrence, Deacon of Rome, who was broiled on a gridiron in AD 258".

*Flycatcher S1292/3 of 406 Flight on B turret ramp of
HMS Royal Sovereign c.1931. (FAAM)*

*Flycatcher on HMS Royal Sovereign's B turret ramp.
(FAAM)*

*HMS Slinger in 1917. A former steam hopper she became an experimental catapult ship with the installation of an
Armstrong Whitworth catapult. (IWM SP1265)*

Flycatcher S1280 on B turret ramp of HMS Ramillies, Mediterranean c. 1931. (FAAM)

A Short 184 catapult dummy on Slinger's catapult prior to the first launch on 1st October 1917. (G.S.Leslie/J.M.Bruce collection)

HMS Slinger in the Tyne with the wreckage of the Short 184 catapult dummy on deck after the launch of 1st October 1917. (FAAM)

HMS Slinger's catapult. The trolley was propelled along the central rail by a compressed air system operating a system of wires. (FAAM)

HMS Thanet with a gravity operated catapult on her forecastle for launching a radio controlled missile with 200-lb warhead - the RAE 1921 Target. (NMM CQV2)

Four views of Fairey F127 N9 on and airborne from Slinger's catapult at the Isle of Grain on 14th May 1918. (G.S.Leslie/J.M.Bruce collection)

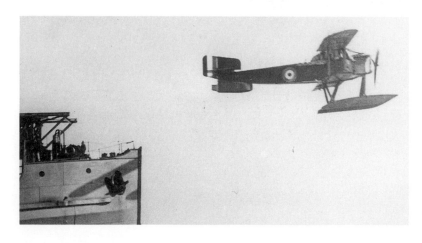

Wooden model (model and image) of the forward section of HMS Vindictive used in wind tunnel experiments at the National Physical Laboratory during September 1924 to examine the airflow over the Carey catapult to be mounted on the forward superstructure. (RAFM)

HMS Vindictive c. February 1926 showing arrangement of catapult, crane and hatch to hangar. (FAAM)

The Carey catapult installed in HMS Vindictive. This view shows Fairey IIID N9469 of 444 Flight being hoisted by the ship's crane at Wei-Hai-Wei in July 1926 (FAAM)

The old and the new. The turret ramp on HMS Resolution's X turret installed in 1918 is still in place. Fairey IIID S1089/30 of 443 Flight is launched from the quarterdeck Carey catapult c.1929. (via R.C.Sturtivant)

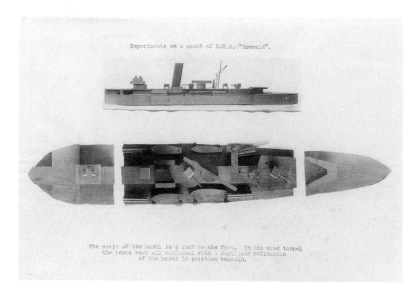

Wooden model (model and image) of the midships section of HMS Emerald used in wind tunnel experiments at the National Physical Laboratory during April 1926. The experiments were to examine the windflow over the S.IIL catapult which it was proposed to instal abaft the third funnel.(RAFM)

Upon completion in 1926 Emerald was fitted with a revolving platform abaft the third funnel. The installation of her S.IIL catapult was not undertaken until 1935, as shown in this view. (NMM B23/463)

HMS Stronghold with a cordite operated catapult on her forecastle for launching a radio controlled missile with 250-lb warhead - the RAE 1927 Larynx Drone. (NMM CQ04)

HMS Renown's Pup, possibly N6444 safely installed on Y turret ramp. The Quick Release Strop is visible anchored to the deck of the turret ramp. (FAAM)

These were the sort of conditions often endured by aeroplanes on turret ramps. Here a Ship Strutter is seen on a battleship's B turret ramp in the North Sea. (FAAM)

Pup N6444 is hoisted on board HMS Renown from the drifter alongside.
(G.S.Leslie/J.M.Bruce Collection)

2F.1 Camel N6611 on HMS Renown's Y turret ramp, Firth of Forth. (FAAM)

2F.1 Camel N6611 on HMS Renown's Y turret ramp, Firth of Forth, HMAS Australia astern. (FAAM)

HMS Renown with a Ship Strutter on B turret ramp and a 2F.1 Camel on Y turret ramp. (IWM SP1777)

2F.1 Camel N6611 taking off from HMS Renown's Y turret ramp. (FAAM)

A 2F.1 Camel taking off from Renown's B turret ramp 17th January 1918. (FAAM)

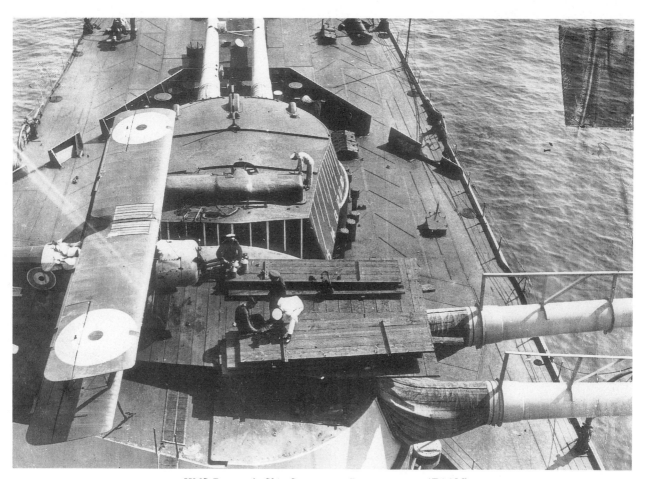

HMS Renown's Ship Strutter on B turret ramp. (FAAM)

Ship Strutter A5987 airborne from HMS Renown's B turret ramp 1918. (FAAM)

The guns of HMS Renown's B turret used to hoist Ship Strutter A599-on board, possibly A5995. (FAAM)

Battleships of the Grand Fleet in line ahead, North Sea 1918. The second ship in line has turned B turret to starboard, ready to launch her Ship Strutter into wind. (FAAM)

The wreckage of a 2F.1 Camel, blown from Y turret ramp in HMS Repulse or HMS Renown, lies on deck. (FAAM)

APPENDIX IA

Aeroplanes flown from platforms and turret ramps in cruisers and capital ships 1917-1919,

SOPWITH 2F.1 CAMEL	N6600	LION 3.18, YARMOUTH 1.18
	N6601	TIGER 2.18 - 3.18
	N6602	LION 1.18, CAROLINE 9.18 - 10.18, CALEDON 11.18 - 1.19
	N6603	UNDAUNTED 9.18; TIGER 9.18 & 12.18, MELBOURNE 11.18 & 1.19
	N6604	LION 12.17, PRINCESS ROYAL 4.18, GLORIOUS 5.18
	N6605	GLORIOUS 5.18, REPULSE 2.18
	N6606	REPULSE 2.18, RENOWN 2.18, TIGER 4.18 - 5.18
	N6607	SOUTHAMPTON 3.18 & 5.18, LION 11.18 - 12.18
	N6611	ROYALIST 3.18 - 4.18, 9.18 -10.18, RENOWN 4.18 - 6.18
	N6614	COMUS 5.18, GLORIOUS 5.18, INDOMITABLE 9.18, 10.18, 1.19
	N6616	GALATEA 4.18, CHATHAM 4.18 - 6.18
	N6617	RENOWN 1.18 - 3.18, 5.18, CAROLINE 6.18 - 7.18, NEW ZEALAND 7.18 - 8.18
	N6619	RENOWN 2.18, COURAGEOUS 8.18
	N6623	LIGHTER H3/TRUCULENT 5.18
	N6625	GALATEA 5.18
	N6629	SYDNEY 2.18, LION 2.18 - 3.18, 5.18, COMUS 6.18
	N6630	RENOWN 7.18 - 8.18
	N6631	LION 2.18, SYDNEY 2.18, PHAETON 8.18 - 9.18, INCONSTANT 1.19
	N6632	COMUS 3.18, 5.18
	N6633	PRINCESS ROYAL 2.18 - 3.18, RENOWN 4.18 - 5.18
	N6635	SYDNEY 2.18 - 5.18
	N6636	CALLIOPE 3.18, 5.18
	N6637	CAROLINE 3.18, 5.18, REPULSE 6.18 - 9.18
	N6638	REPULSE 2.18 - 3.18, SYDNEY 11.18 - 1.19
	N6639	ROYALIST 3.18 - 4.18
	N6640	INCONSTANT 7.18 - 8.18
	N6641	RENOWN 4.18
	N6642	PRINCESS ROYAL 5.18 - 6.18 COMUS 7.18
	N6644	PHAETON 3.18
	N6645	COURAGEOUS 4.18 - 6.18
	N6646	PENELOPE 11.18
	N6647	LION 3.18 - 4.18, 8.18 INDOMITABLE 12.18 - 1.19
	N6648	TIGER 6.18 - 8.18
	N6649	PHAETON 6.18 - 10.18
	N6750	BARHAM 1918, TIGER 1.19
	N6751	ROYALIST 5.18, RENOWN 5.18, COURAGEOUS 8.18 - 10.18, IRON DUKE 1918

N6752	COURAGEOUS 5.18, SOUTHAMPTON 5.18 - 6.18, ROYAL SOVEREIGN 1918
N6753	BIRKENHEAD 5.18 - 6.18
N6754	ROYALIST 5.18
N6755	GALATEA 4.18 - 5.18, SOUTHAMPTON 5.18
N6756	MELBOURNE 4.18 - 5.18, GALATEA 6.18, AURORA 7.18 - 8.18
N6757	CORDELIA 6.18, IRON DUKE 10.18
N6758	PHAETON 4.18, PRINCESS ROYAL 8.18 - 10.18
N6759	BIRKENHEAD 4.18 - 5.18, INDOMITABLE, 8.18 - 9.18 INFLEXIBLE 12.18
N6760	COMUS 5.18
N6762	ROYALIST 4.18 - 5.18, BARHAM 1918
N6763	COURAGEOUS 5.18 - 6.18
N6764	LION 4.18 - 5.18
N6766	CAROLINE 4.18, GALATEA 5.18
N6767	CORDELIA 6.18
N6768	CALLIOPE 5.18, COMUS 5.18, CAROLINE 6.18, PENELOPE 1918, PRINCESS ROYAL 10.18 - 11.18, 1.19
N6769	LION 5.18 VALIANT 1.19
N6770	PRINCESS ROYAL 6.18 - 7.18 GALATEA 9.18 - 10.18, AURORA 12.18 - 1.19
N6772	GALATEA 5.18
N6773	COURAGEOUS 5.18, CHATHAM 7.18 - 8.18, UNDAUNTED 10.18, LION 1.19
N6774	PHAETON 5.18 - 6.18
N6775	COMUS 4.18 - 5.18, COURAGEOUS 5.18, CALLIOPE 1918
N6776	GLORIOUS 1918, LION 12.18 - 1.19
N6778	GLORIOUS 5.18, PENELOPE 1918
N6779	CALLIOPE 4.18 - 5.18
N6780	COMUS 4.18 - 5.18
N6782	ROYALIST 5.18 - 6.18
N6783	SYDNEY 5.18 - 6.18
N6784	SOUTHAMPTON 5.18, 7.18
N6785	MELBOURNE 5.18
N6786	INFLEXIBLE 5.18, AUSTRALIA 10.18
N6787	PHAETON 7.18, SOUTHAMPTON 11.18, INFLEXIBLE 12.18 - 1.19
N6788	GLORIOUS 5.18
N6789	MALAYA 1918, SYDNEY 5.18, PHAETON 11.18

N6790	COMUS 7.18, AUSTRALIA 8.18 -10.18, INDOMITABLE 12.18
N6791	INDOMITABLE 5.18, IRON DUKE 10.18
N6792	INDOMITABLE 5.18, INFLEXIBLE 10.18, 1.19
N6793	COURAGEOUS 10.18, COMUS 12.18
N6794	CASSANDRA 12.18, MELBOURNE 1918
N6795	ROYALIST 10.18, VALIANT 1.19
N6797	SYDNEY 5.18, TIGER 6.18 - 7.18
N6798	SYDNEY 5.18
N6799	PENELOPE 10.18, IRON DUKE 12.18 - 1.19
N6800	PHAETON 5.18
N6810	COMUS 10.18
N6811	COMUS 9.18 - 11.18
N6812	LIGHTER H3/TRUCULENT 7.18, LIGHTER H3/REDOUBT 8.18
N6813	INDOMITABLE 7.18 - 8.18
N6816	AURORA 9.18 - 1.19
N6817	INFLEXIBLE 8.18 - 10.18
N6819	LION 10.18, ORION 12.18, ROYAL OAK 1918
N6820	MELBOURNE 1918, SYDNEY 1918
N6821	MELBOURNE 9.18
N6822	AUSTRALIA 1918, MELBOURNE 1918, SYDNEY 10.18
N6824	PENELOPE 10.18, UNDAUNTED 1918
N6826	AUSTRALIA 1918
N6828	DUBLIN 8.18 - 10.18, AUSTRALIA 12.18 - 1.19
N6829	GALATEA 8.18
N6830	PRINCESS ROYAL 8.18
N6831	CAROLINE 8.18 - 10.18, ROYALIST 10.18
N6832	NEW ZEALAND 1918
N6833	BIRKENHEAD 8.18, NEW ZEALAND 9.18 - 11.18
N6834	LION 8.18, AJAX 12.18
N6835	GLORIOUS 7.18 - 8.18, TIGER 10.18 - 1.19
N6838	RENOWN 9.18 - 10.18, SYDNEY 1918, VALIANT 12.18 - 1.19
N6839	PRINCESS ROYAL 8.18
N6842	SOUTHAMPTON 8.18, COURAGEOUS 9.19 - 10.18
N6844	BIRKENHEAD 8.18
N6845	PENELOPE 8.18
N6846	COMUS 9.18
N6847	UNDAUNTED 8.18, BIRKENHEAD 9.18
N6848	CHATHAM 9.18 - 1.19
N6849	PRINCESS ROYAL 9.18 - 10.18
N7100	INCONSTANT 9.18, 12.18 - 1.19

	N7101	RENOWN 9.19 - 10.18, 11.18 -1.19, SYDNEY 10.18
	N7103	TIGER 9.18, BARHAM 1918, ROYAL SOVEREIGN 1918
	N7104	MELBOURNE 10.18
	N7105	REPULSE 10.18 - 11.18
	N7106	REPULSE 10.18, 12.18
	N7107	UNDAUNTED 9.18 - 10.18, SOUTHAMPTON 10.18
	N7108	CAROLINE 10.18, ROYAL SOVEREIGN 1.19
	N7109	NEW ZEALAND 10.18, PENELOPE 1918
	N7110	BIRKENHEAD 11.18 - 1.10, PENELOPE 10.18
	N7111	BIRKENHEAD 9.18 - 10.18
	N7112	SOUTHAMPTON 9.18 - 10.18, 1.19
	N7113	ROYALIST 10.18 - 1.19
	N7114	PRINCESS ROYAL 10.18 - 11.18, 1.19
	N7116	INCONSTANT 9.18, GALATEA 10.18, CANADA 12.18 - 1.19
	N7117	GLORIOUS 10.18, PENELOPE 12.18
	N7119	INCONSTANT 10.18, UNDAUNTED 10.18, ORION 12.18
	N7120	LION 10.18, WARSPITE 12.18 -1.19, QUEEN ELIZABETH 1918
	N7121	CAROLINE 10.18, GLORIOUS 10.18 - 12.18
	N7122	CASSANDRA 10.18 - 11.18
	N7123	INCONSTANT 10.18 - 11.18
	N7125	IRON DUKE 10.18 - 1.19
	N7126	GALATEA 10.18, LION 11.18 -1.19
	N7128	COURAGEOUS 10.18 - 12.18
	N7129	EMPEROR OF INDIA 12.18
	N7134	NEW ZEALAND 12.18
	N7136	BARHAM 1918, GALATEA 12.18
	N7138	DUBLIN 12.18 - 1.19
	N7139	UNDAUNTED 12.18 - 1.19
	N7140	NEW ZEALAND 1918
	N7146	MALAYA 1918
	N7148	MALAYA 1918
SOPWITH SHIP STRUTTER	N5606	AUSTRALIA 2.18
	N5644	AUSTRALIA 3.18, REPULSE 3.18, GLORIOUS 11.18 - 12.18
	A5982	REPULSE 5.18 - 7.18
	A5984	BELLEROPHON
	A5985	AUSTRALIA 3.18, 5.18 - 6.18, BELLEROPHON 1.19
	A5987	RENOWN 5.18 - 8.18, WARSPITE 1.19
	A5988	INDOMITABLE 4.18, 5.18, 6.18, REPULSE 5.18, BARHAM 9.18 -10.18
	A5990	GLORIOUS 7.18
	A5993	RENOWN 7.18

	A5994	COURAGEOUS 8.18
	A5995	RENOWN
	A5998	COURAGEOUS 10.18
	A6006	BARHAM 8.18, QUEEN ELIZABETH
	A6010	INFLEXIBLE 8.18
	A6905	GLORIOUS 8.18 - 10.18
	A6952	INDOMITABLE 8.18,
		VALIANT 12.18 - 1.19
	A6966	INDOMITABLE 9.18 - 12.18
	A6967	REPULSE 9.18, 11.19,
		MALAYA 12.18
	A6968	AUSTRALIA 8.18 - 10.18
	A6980	INFLEXIBLE 9.18 - 10.18, 1.19
	A6981	NEW ZEALAND 8.18
	A8224	INFLEXIBLE 8.18
	A8277	MALAYA, INDOMITABLE 8.18
	A8300	REPULSE 8.18
	B744	GLORIOUS 12.18
	F2210	COURAGEOUS 11.18 - 12.18
	F2215	RENOWN 10.18 - 12.18
	F2216	INDOMITABLE 12.18 - 1.19
	F2220	NEW ZEALAND 9.18 - 10.18
	F2221	MALAYA 1.19
	F2222	COURAGEOUS 9.18 - 10.18
	F2224	REPULSE 10.18
	F2225	RENOWN 9.18 - 10.18, BARHAM 11.18
	F2227	COURAGEOUS 12.18
	F2228	REPULSE 10.18, BARHAM 10.18 -11.18,
		RENOWN 1.19
	F2229	RENOWN 9.18 - 10.18
	F7561	EMPEROR OF INDIA 12.18 - 1.19
	F7562	AUSTRALIA 11.18 - 1.19
SOPWITH PUP	9901	YARMOUTH 6.17
	9931	SYDNEY 12.17 - 1.18,
		DUBLIN 2.18 - 3.18
	9932	YARMOUTH 11.17 - 12.17,
		SYDNEY 12.17
	9934	TIGER 5.18
	9944	YARMOUTH 7.17, REPULSE 12.17,
		TIGER 1.18 - 3.18
	9945	REPULSE 11.17
	9964	REPULSE 12.17
	N6200	CASSANDRA 12.17
	N6430	YARMOUTH 8.17
	N6431	YARMOUTH 9.17 - 10.17, SYDNEY 12.17,
		DUBLIN 12.17 - 1.18
	N6434	RENOWN
	N6438	REPULSE 12.17, TIGER 12.17 - 1.18
	N6440	PRINCESS ROYAL 12.17,
		NEW ZEALAND
	N6443	TIGER 1917, REPULSE 11.17,
		RENOWN 12.17, YARMOUTH 12.17,
		PRINCESS ROYAL 2.18
	N6444	RENOWN 11.17

N6445	PRINCESS ROYAL 12.17
N6446	SYDNEY, AUSTRALIA 12.17, REPULSE 1.18
N6448	RENOWN 11.17 - 12.17
N6449	SYDNEY, DUBLIN 11.17 - 2.18, CHATHAM 3.18
N6453	REPULSE 2.18
N6455	LION 11.17, TIGER 12.17, REPULSE 1.18
N6456	REPULSE 12.17, TIGER 1.18

BEARDMORE W.B.III		
	N6100	CASSANDRA 11.17 - 3.18
	N6109	RENOWN 12.17
	N6115	RENOWN 11.17 - 12.17, PRINCESS ROYAL 1.18
	N6116	RENOWN 12.17
	N6123	DUBLIN 2.18
	N6127	PHAETON 12.17
	N6128	CASSANDRA 3.18, 5.18 - 6.18
	N6129	YARMOUTH 1.18 - 3.18, 5.18
	N6686	ROYALIST 2.18 - 3.18, 5.18

PARNALL PANTHER		
	N92	REPULSE 10.18
	N7468	REPULSE

Ship Strutter on HMS Warspite's B turret ramp, probably in the summer of 1919 if the frocks are any guide. (FAAM)

APPENDIX IB

At PRO Kew, under Air1/2111/207/49/1 to 9, Disposition of Officers, are listed those officers comprising the aircrews of aeroplanes operated by ships of the Grand Fleet. These weekly listings are useful in determining which ships actually operated aeroplanes from their platforms or turret ramps.

The listings have been used also as an indication of those ships which did NOT operate aeroplanes between October 1917 and the Armistice of November 1918.

As an example, the following list shows the aircrews embarked in cruisers and capital ships of the Grand Fleet on 2 September 1918. The date following each name is the date on which that officer joined his ship.

AURORA	F/S/L H. H. S. Eaton
AUSTRALIA	Flt Cdr E. R. Pritchard
	F/S/L V. F. Symondson. 4 March 1918
	Obs Lt F. A. Whippey
BIRKENHEAD	F/S/L G. W. J. G. J. Dunn. May 1918
CALEDON	Flt Cdr J. C. Brooke DSC
CAROLINE	Flt Lt G. G. Simpson DSO. 17 January 1918
CHATHAM	Flt Lt H. M. Morris DSC. April 1918
COMUS	Flt Cdr R. T. Kirkland F/S/L P. R. Musson
COURAGEOUS	Flt Cdr E. G. Hopcraft. May 1918
	F/S/L A. E. Murrell. May 1918
	F/S/L F. H. Pratchett
GALATEA	Flt Lt J. A. Robb
	F/S/L M. H. W. Trendall. 7 February 1918
GLORIOUS	F/S/L J. F. T. Fenn. May 1918
	F/S/L A. V. Britnell
INCONSTANT	F/S/L F. F. Garraway
INDOMITABLE	F/S/L P. A. H. Lalouette
	F/S/L R. A. McCance
	F/S/L F. C. F. Walwin
INFLEXIBLE	Flt Lt M. M. McMaster. 20 February 1918
	F/S/L J. C. Leggett. 7 June 1918
	F/S/L R. Ritterdon
	Obs Lt R. H. S. Calver
LION	Sqdn Cdr R. D. G. Sibley. 5 March 1918
	F/S/L H. R. G. Whates. May 1918
MELBOURNE	F/S/L L. B. Gibson. 5 March 1918
NEW ZEALAND	Flt Cdr A. W. Mylne. 20 December 1918
	F/S/L V. S. Grigg. 17 May 1918
	Wt Off A. Neeson (O). 17 May 1918
PHAETON	F/S/L E. B. Jones. 26 January 1918
PRINCESS ROYAL	F/S/L J. E. Pugh. 20 November 1917
RENOWN	F/S/L N. T. Thorneloe. 1 February 1918
	Obs Lt J. A. Small. April 1918
REPULSE	Flt Cdr D. G. Donald. 5 March 1918
	Flt Lt G. M. Clark. 1 January 1918
	Wt Off G. E. Durrance (O). 27 April 1918
ROYALIST	F/S/L G. M. Bryer
SOUTHAMPTON	F/S/L J. W. G. Price. 1 January 1918
SYDNEY	F/S/L T. Brewen. 22 April 1918
TIGER	F/S/L J. A. Rossington-Barrett. February 1918

If Air 1/2111/207/49/9 were used in conjunction with Air 1/670/17/124 a complete ''Order of Battle'' for aeroplanes in ships of the Grand Fleet could probably be compiled for any week of 1918.

HMS Weymouth showing her forward revolving platform upon which is the framework of the canvas protection for the aircraft. (IWM SP113)

HMS Cassandra at Libau in 1918 with a 2F.1 Camel on her aft revolving platform. (IWM.Q19378)

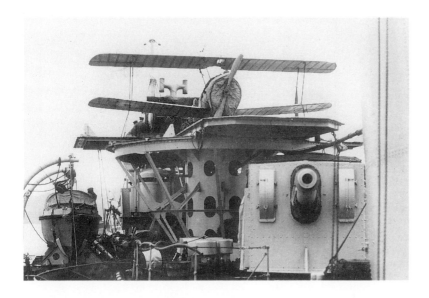

Three views of HMS Cassandra's 2F.1 Camel on her aft revolving platform. It is likely that the diamond marking on the white outboard end of the platform's deck is both a reference point visible to the pilot on take-off, and to enable him to ditch close to his parent ship on return. (RAFM)

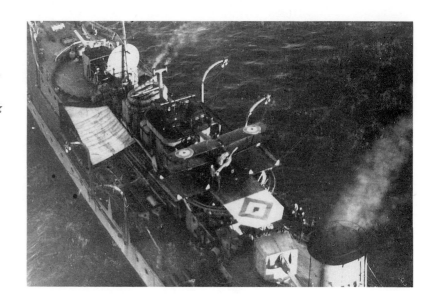

Two views of Chatham's 2F.1 Camel on her fixed platform. The roundel painted at the outboard end of the very narrow platform is probably a visual guide to the pilot that he was about to ''run out of deck''! (RAFM)

HMS Chatham with a 2F.1 Camel on her fixed platform. (IWM SP1034)

Probably HMS Dublin with a 2F.1 Camel on her forward revolving platform. (RAFM)

Two views of a 2F.1 Camel on the forward revolving platform probably in HMS Dublin. The contrast in the width of this platform compared to the fixed platform installed in HMS Chatham is noteworthy. (RAFM)

HMS Southampton at Murmansk in July 1918 with a 2F.1 Camel on her forward revolving platform.
(IWM Q16950)

A 2F.1 Camel on the forward revolving platform of a Chatham class cruiser, possibly HMS Southampton. (RAFM)

HMS Galatea's 2F.1 Camel on her fixed platform. (IWM SP715)

HMS Birkenhead in 1917 with a 2F.1 Camel on her fixed platform. (IWM SP847)

HMS Birkenhead in 1918 with a 2F.1 Camel on her forward revolving platform. (IWM SP165)

A 2F.1 Camel on HMS Penelope's fixed platform. (IWM SP1806)

An aerial view of HMS Royalist
with a 2F.1 Camel on her fixed
platform. This photograph
illustrates an early example of
the use of 'deck letters' - RO in
white on the quarterdeck.
(G.S.Leslie/J.M.Bruce
collection)

Two views of a 2F.1 Camel on the
fixed platform of an 'Arethusa' class
cruiser, probably HMS Royalist.
(RAFM)

HMS Undaunted with a 2F.1 Camel on her fixed platform. In action the two forward supports of the platform were removed to allow the forward 6'' gun to be trained port and starboard. (IWM SP1804)

2F.1 Camel, probably N6649, on HMS Phaeton's fixed platform. (via G.S.Leslie)

HMS New Zealand with a 2F.1 Camel on P turret ramp and a Ship Strutter on Q turret ramp. (IWM. SP484)

HMS New Zealand's Pup N6440 taking off from Q turret ramp.(RAFM)

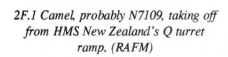

2F.1 Camel, probably N7109, taking off from HMS New Zealand's Q turret ramp. (RAFM)

***HMS Emperor of India** with a Ship Strutter on B turret ramp and a 2F.1 Camel on Q turret ramp. (IWM SP1896)*

***HMS Emperor of India's** Ship Strutter begins to take-off from B turret ramp. The Quick Release Strop, operated by the officer standing behind the turret's sighting hood, may be seen lying on the ramp's deck. (FAAM)*

With chocks in place and with the aircraft firmly secured, Flt Sub Lt Fenn runs up his 2F.1 Camel's engine to full power on Y turret ramp of HMS Glorious. (FAAM)

Another view of Flt Sub Lt Fenn's Camel on HMS Glorious Y turret ramp. (FAAM)

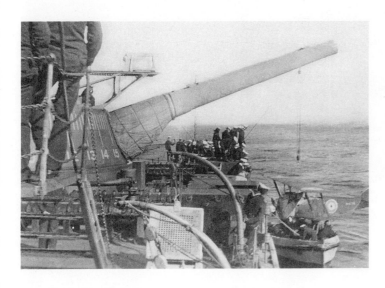

2F.1 Camel N6776 is hoisted on board the quarterdeck of HMS Glorious using one of Y turret's guns as a crane (FAAM)

HMS Iron Duke with 2F.1 Camels on B and Q turret ramps. (IWM SP1736)

HMS Courageous with a 2F.1 Camel on Y turret ramp. (RMM 14/2/2 (315))

HMS Courageous with a Ship Strutter on A turret ramp and a 2F.1 Camel on Y turret ramp. (RMM 14/2/2 (317))

2F.1 Camel on A turret ramp of either HMS Courageous or HMS Glorious.(RAFM)

2F.1 Camel N6643 on Y turret ramp of either HMS Courageous or HMS Glorious. (RAFM)

*HMS Tiger with a 2F.1 Camel on Q turret ramp.
(RMM 14/2/2 (48))*

*2F.1 Camel on HMS Tiger's Q turret
ramp and stowed in its detachable
canvas hangar. The letters TI painted
on the side of the turret are probably
an early example of 'deck letters' to
enable the pilot to ditch his aircraft
close to his parent ship. (G.S.Leslie/
J.M.Bruce collection)*

*2F.1 Camel N6797 on
Tiger's Q turret ramp.
(IWM SP374)*

2F.1 Camel on X turret ramp of HMS Ramillies. HMS Royal Sovereign and HMS Royal Oak lie astern. (via R.C.B.Ashworth)

2F.1 Camel in 6819 on Royal Oak's B turret ramp in 1919. (via M.H.Goodall)

HMS Royal Oak in 1919 with a 2F.1 Camel on X turret ramp. (IWM SP1005)

HMS Revenge in 1919 with a Panther on B turret ramp and a Pup on X turret ramp. (IWM SP1003)

HMS Royal Sovereign in 1919 with a Ship Strutter on B turret ramp and a 2F.1 Camel on X turret ramp. (IWM SP1004)

HMS Royal Sovereign's Ship Strutter about to take-off from B turret ramp. (FAAM)

Two views of 2F.1 Camel N6752 on Royal Sovereign's X turret ramp. (FAAM)

*HMS Lion with a 2F.1 Camel
on Y turret ramp. (IWM
SP1791)*

*2F.1 Camel N6764 on HMS Lion's Q
turret ramp. (RAFM)*

*Aerial view of HMS Lion's
2F.1 Camel on Q turret ramp.
This shape of turret ramp was
designed for flying aeroplanes
off the back of the turret, yet
this ramp is positioned the
opposite way round, and not
even facing along the centre
line of the turret. The author
would welcome information on
this apparent anomaly. (RAFM)*

HMS Princess Royal with a 2F.1 Camel on Q turret ramp, and a canvas hangar housing another 2F.1 Camel on Y turret ramp. (IWM Q19280)

2F.1 Camel on HMS Ajax's B turret ramp. (FAAM)

HMS Canada with turret ramps on B and X turrets. It is known that HMS Canada embarked at least one 2F.1 Camel. (WSS Photo Library)

HMS Indomitable's Ship Strutter A5988, piloted by Flt Sub Lt R.A.McCance is airborne from Q turret ramp. (FAAM)

HMS Indomitable with a 2F.1 Camel on P turret ramp and a Ship Strutter on Q turret ramp, 1918. (IWM SP656)

Although HMS Centurion was fitted with turret ramps on B and Q turrets it is unlikely that she ever embarked any aircraft. (FAAM)

HMS Monarch's B turret was fitted with a turret ramp but it unlikely that she ever embarked any aircraft. (WSS Photo Library)

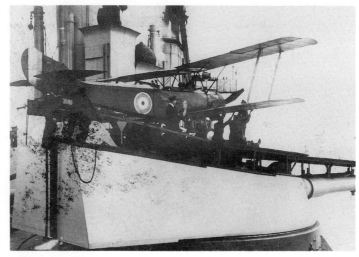

HMS Inflexible's Ship Strutter, probably A6980, on Q turret ramp. (RAFM)

2F.1 Camel taking off from HMS Inflexible's Q turret ramp. (IWM Q71274)

*HMS Valiant with a Ship
Strutter on B turret ramp
and a 2F.1 Camel on X
turret ramp c. 1918.
(A.K.Vicary)*

*HMS Valiant's Ship
Strutter taking off from
B turret ramp. (FAAM)*

*HMS Warspite with a Ship
Strutter on B turret ramp and
a 2F.1 Camel on X turret
ramp. (IWM SP1062)*

*Ship Strutter on HMS
Warspite's B turret
ramp 1918.
(A.K.Vicary)*

HMS Queen Elizabeth's Ship Strutter taking off from B turret ramp with full right rudder applied to counteract the torque of the 130 hp Clerget. (FAAM)

Queen Elizabeth's 2F.1 Camel N7120 on X turret ramp. (G.S.Leslie/J.M.Bruce collection)

Pup N6458 on B turret ramp of probably a Queen Elizabeth class battleship. This may have been an early take-off trial using a Pup since a Ship Strutter or 2F.1 Camel usually occupied B turret ramps in capital ships. (RCC via M.H.Goodall)

Ship Strutter A6006 on Queen Elizabeth's B turret ramp. (G.S.Leslie/J.M.Bruce collection)

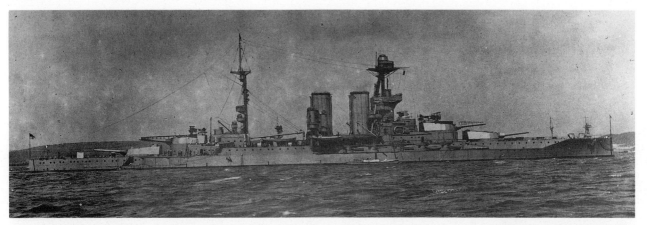

HMS Malaya with a Ship Strutter on B turret ramp and a 2F.1 Camel on X turret ramp. (RMM 14/2/2 (283))

HMS Malaya's Ship Strutter A8277 is hoisted on board using B turret's 15'' gun barrel as a crane. After hoisting onto the roof of A turret the Strutter would have been hauled manually onto B turret ramp. On the lighter alongside may be seen 2F.1 Camel N7148, to be hoisted onto X turret ramp (FAAM)

HMS Malaya's 2F.1 Camel on X turret ramp. (FAAM)

HMS Barham with a Ship Strutter on B turret ramp. (RMM 14/2/2 (43))

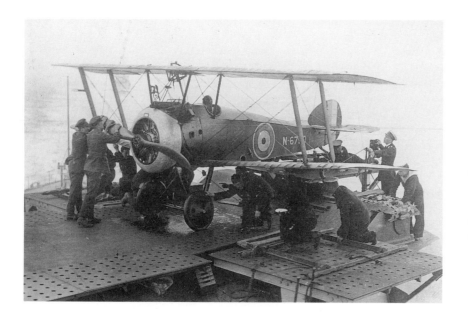

HMS Barham's 2F.1 Camel N6750 is readied for take-off on X turret ramp. The Quick Release Strop is clearly visible beneath the aircraft, and the Royal Marine officer holds the lanyard operating it in his left hand. The presence of so many R.M. personnel is because the Marines always manned X turret in capital ships. The Camel's toolkit can be seen on top of the turret's sighting hood. The aircraft is being rolled forward to take up any slack in the Quick Release Strop before the propeller is swung. (FAAM)

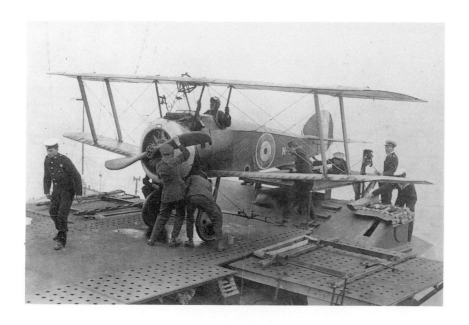

Flt Lt Remnitz taking off in 2F.1 Camel N6789, from HMS Malaya's B turret ramp. (FAAM)

Preparations for launching HMS Barham's 2F.1 Camel N6750, from X turret ramp. The flag held at the outboard end of the ramp indicates that the turret is turned to face into wind. Next left, the pilot holds up an anemometer to measure the wind speed over the turret ramp. (FAAM)

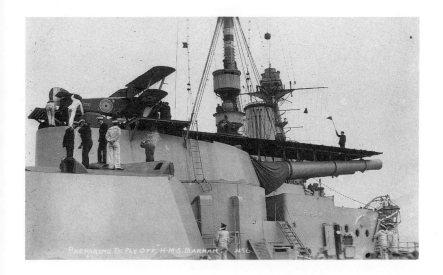

On Barham's B turret ramp the Ship Strutter's pilot holds an anemometer to measure the wind speed over the turret ramp. (FAAM)

Swinging the Ship Strutter's propeller on Barham's B turret ramp. (FAAM)

Barham's Ship Strutter is launched from B turret ramp. The pilot has either failed to apply sufficient right rudder to counteract the torque of the engine, or possibly the turret was not trained directly into wind. (FAAM)

PART II

"Always wind in the aerial before alighting. Nothing looks more unseamanlike
than to alight with your aerial dragging in the water".

Cdr. C. R. Samson, 1916

CHAPTER V

Seaplane operations East Mediterranean 1914 and East Africa 1915

Air operations at sea by the Royal Navy in the period 1914-1919 fell broadly into four main categories. Firstly were those aircraft which operated from fighting ships. Secondly there were those which flew from the ten "recognised" Seaplane Carriers (HM Ships *Ark Royal, Ben-my-Chree, Campania, Empress, Engadine, Manxman, Nairana, Pegasus, Riviera,* and *Vindex*). Thirdly, there were those flying from the two Aircraft Carriers (HM Ships *Furious,* and *Vindictive*). Finally, there was another important aspect of the Royal Navy's use of airpower at sea in this period.

During the First World War, seaplanes of the Royal Naval Air Service and later the Royal Air Force were operated from the decks of many different classes of ships. They carried out a variety of tasks, spotting for the gunfire of warships against targets ashore, bombing, strafing and photographing those same targets, and carrying out anti-Zeppelin and anti-U-boat patrols. From late 1914 until August 1919 these seaplanes saw action in the North Sea, Aegean, Eastern Mediterranean, Red Sea, Indian Ocean, South Atlantic and Caspian Sea. There can have been few months between these dates when they were not in action in one or more of these theatres of war.

Many of the seaplanes issued to these ships, designed in the early years of flying to operate under European climatic conditions, presented problems when flown in the higher temperatures of the Eastern Mediterranean and in theatres East from there. Water cooled engines overheated, limitations were imposed on service ceilings, and the effects of hot sun and sea water on wood and fabric were destructive. There was a

HMS Doris in the Mediterranean c.1914/15 with derrick mounted aft for handling a seaplane on her quarterdeck.
(G.S.Leslie/J.M.Bruce collection)

HMS Minerva in January 1915. During 1914/15 she operated in turn a Schneider and a Sopwith 807 in the E.Mediterranean and Gulf of Akaba. (A.K.Vicary)

constant shortage of spares for engines and airframes - cannibalisation was frequent - and during the early years of the war the only issue of ''new'' equipment was of those types of aircraft long considered obsolete on the Western Front and in Home Waters.

There was a severe shortage of anti-aircraft guns in all the ships - never wholly rectified - for countering growing German and Turkish air attacks. Conditions below decks in such temperatures, in ships never designed for the purposes to which they were put, were extremely testing. Only the leadership of men like L'Estrange Malone and Samson, and the offensive spirit of their pilots and observers, overcame these difficulties, which were not at all lessened by the early failure of the Admiralty to understand the potential of the Navy's air arm in support of land operations against the Central Powers in these areas.

Indeed official histories of the war at sea between 1914 and 1918 deem that events taking place above masthead height were hardly worthy of mention.

From August 1914 the command of the

Mediterranean became a French responsibility. Upon the outbreak of hostilities with Turkey, and the subsequent threat to the Suez Canal, however, the French agreed to the withdrawal of the Dardanelles and Egyptian areas from their control. Accordingly the C. in C. East Indies Squadron at Bombay shifted his HQ to the Canal, and hoisted his flag in HMS *Swiftsure* at Suez in December 1914.

Until the Dardanelles campaign opened in February 1915 the Royal Navy bore responsibility for patrolling the coast between El Arish and Mersina, with the French Navy responsible for the coastline between Mersina and Smyrna.

From February 1915, however, control of the coast of Syria and of Palestine as far south as Jaffa reverted to the French, and the C. in C. Vice Admiral Sir Richard Peirse was instructed to act upon orders from the admiral commanding the Syrian Division of the French Navy for operations along the Syrian coast.

By late 1914 the Turkish threat to the Suez Canal had assumed alarming proportions. No aeroplanes of the RFC based in Egypt had sufficient range to fly a reconnaissance as far as the forward Turkish positions in south Palestine and Sinai, so HMS *Doris* embarked a Nieuport VI seaplane of L'Aviation Maritime Française, from the seaplane carrier *Foudre*, at Port Said on 10 December to undertake this task. The pilot was Lt Destrem and the observer Capt J.R. Herbert, and flights were carried out over El Arish and Beersheba before *Doris* returned to Port Said on the 13th. On 15 December *Doris* launched her Nieuport Seaplane again for a reconnaissance of Beersheba and El Arish, and while awaiting its return shelled a Turkish coastal fortification at Askalon and put a landing party ashore. *Doris*'s seaplane made flights over Jaffa on the 16th, and off Haifa on the 17th over the area round Mount Carmel, neither reconnaissance revealing troop concentrations.

Doris had proceeded north to a position just south of Sidon on the 18th, where Capt Larken sent a landing party ashore which sawed down several miles of telegraph poles and cut up the wires.

On the 19th *Doris* intercepted and boarded the Italian steamer *Porto Di Smyrne*, which had just left Alexandretta. Her captain told Larken that the port was full of troop trains and war material. The section of railway from the north to Aleppo was not completed, so that all troops moving south towards the Suez Canal must detrain at Alexandretta and march to rejoin the railway at Aleppo.

At last *Doris* had located the advancing Turkish army, and at 2300 on the 19th Larken took his ship into the bay two miles to the north of Jonah's Pillar, under cover of darkness. All watertight doors were closed and a reserve of coal piled on the stokehold floor plates to

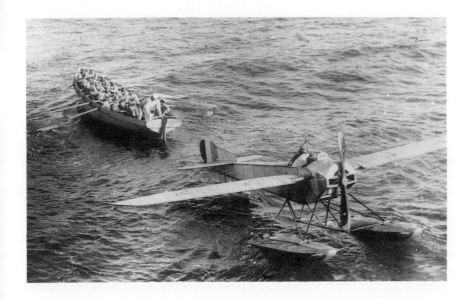

*Nieuport VI seaplane of
L'Aviation Maritime
Française after launching
from HMS Doris in the
Gulf of Smyrna in 1915.
The ship's cutter is towing
the seaplane clear of the
ship's side prior to
take-off. (G.S.Leslie/
J.M.Bruce collection)*

*HMS Doris's Nieuport on her
quarterdeck at the entrance to the
Suez Canal 1915.
(G.S.Leslie/J.M.Bruce collection)*

*The Nieuport VI is hoisted
back on the quarterdeck of
HMS Doris in the Gulf of
Smyrna in 1915. (G.S.Leslie/
J.M.Bruce collection)*

avoid having to open the bunkers.

A landing party, with blackened faces and muffled oars, under Lt H. Goodier, was then despatched to wreck a section of the railway north of the town, where it ran close to the coast.

After the landing party's return *Doris* lay off the coast to await results. At 0230 the sound of an approaching train was heard. The engine jumped the gap and steamed on, but the train of 35 trucks loaded with camels was derailed and the line effectively blocked.

When at 0600 a second train approached and stopped at the wreckage, Capt Larken put a few 12-pounder shells into the second engine, and then steamed north to cut off the train's retreat over the bridge at Deurt Yol near Payas. Several rounds of lyddite and common shell put the bridge out of action, and he then shelled two culverts and three more bridges on the line.

Doris now returned to Alexandretta, with a white flag hoisted at the foremast, and lowered a cutter, bearing a letter addressed to the Military Governor. The letter demanded the surrender to him of all British and Allied subjects and the surrender of all munitions and locomotives for destruction. Failure to comply with these conditions by 0900 on the 20th would render the town liable to bombardment.

Doris lay off the town during the night of 19/20 December, and in the beams of her searchlights columns of troops could be seen evacuating the town.

The Governor's reply next morning rejected the British ultimatum, and in return threatened the execution of British hostages on the orders of the military C in C, Djemal Pasha. Larken immediately let it be known that any officer giving such orders would be handed over "to the justice of His Britannic Majesty", and gave the Governor a further 24 hours to reconsider his decision.

Meanwhile another engine had crossed the supposedly damaged bridge at Deurt Yol, hitched onto the stranded train, and towed it away.

Doris weighed and proceeded towards Jonah's Pillar again, where she lay with all guns manned to cover a landing party of 70 men in the steam pinnace and two cutters. Five minutes' bombardment from *Doris* sufficed to dislodge the enemy defenders, and with bluejackets in extended order preceeding them, the demolition party advanced with their charges of guncotton across a mile of marshy ground to the bridge. One column and the

span above it were wrecked, and the party safely withdrew to the ship.

Doris returned to Alexandretta where at 0900 the Turkish reply to the effect that they would shoot no hostages was received. Another demolition party was landed, and after Turkish delaying tactics, the two locomotives in the town were finally blown up by nightfall. At 0645 on 22 December *Doris* sailed to destroy a road bridge near Jonah's Pillar by shellfire, and thence to Mortalik Bay where she destroyed the German SS *Odessa* with her guns.

The buccaneering attacks by HMS *Doris* on Turkish communications in the Gulf of Smyrna and off the Syrian coast continued until March 1915, always with a seaplane embarked to spot for her guns - in turn a Nieuport VI, a Sopwith 807 and a Schneider.

These operations provided a classic example of the correct use of seapower on an enemy's exposed seaward

Sopwith 807 922 seen here hoisted aboard HMT Yarmouth (BL 9) in Kephalo Bay in 1915 while operating from HMS Ark Royal. This seaplane was later operated by HM Ships Minerva and Doris. (G.S.Leslie/J.M.Bruce collection)

flank, and above all, aerial reconnaissance provided the forces defending the Suez Canal with information on Turkish troop movements.

While operations proceeded on our left flank defending the Suez Canal, our right flank resting on the Gulf of Akaba was patrolled by the cruisers *Diana* and *Minerva*, each with a Nieuport seaplane embarked for reconnaissance duties. Both these seaplanes had been transferred from the French seaplane carrier *Foudre* at Port Said, and were operated by French pilots with British observers.

Between 9-17 December 1914 *Minerva*'s seaplane made four reconnaissance flights to check on Turkish troop movements, but these were unsatisfactory due to

Two views of Short 166, 164, transferred from HMS Ark Royal, stowed on the deck of HMS Roberts at the Dardanelles in September 1915. (A.K. Vicary)

the seaplane's inability to gain sufficient height to fly over the high ground which rises steeply from both shores of the Gulf.

On 22 December *Minerva* returned to Suez where a second Nieuport VI and another pilot joined the ship. On 29 December *Minerva* was again off Akaba, and at 0600 she hoisted out her seaplane for a reconnaissance of the town. The seaplane was hoisted aboard again at 0845. Shortly after, *Minerva* opened fire on a concentration of Turkish troops to the east of the town, and a Royal Marines Light Infantry landing party was put ashore to disrupt communications.

On the last day of 1914 *Minerva*'s seaplane, crewed

by Chief Petty Officer Grall and Capt F. Stirling of the Dublin Fusiliers was hoisted out at 0945 for a reconnaissance flight to Ma'an. At 0950 a RMLI landing party from *Minerva* was put ashore to examine a beach in the NW corner of the Gulf. A relief party then had to be despatched from the ship to assist in the withdrawal of the landing party, now under heavy fire from Turkish troops in the hills, and fire from *Minerva*'s 6-inch guns covered the withdrawal.

The Nieuport seaplane meanwhile had force landed with engine trouble at Wadi Araban some 29 miles from the sea. Both men were badly shaken, but having set fire to the seaplane, crawled a good distance away and hid in the scrub. Grall was too weak to move, so Stirling set off for the coast on foot to get help from the ship, leaving Grall his waterbottle and chocolate.

Stirling reached the coast in a state of exhaustion at 2000 that evening, and once back on board reported the position where he had left Grall. An armed party of 200 men landed and marched to the spot, but found no trace of the pilot, and after a long search returned on board.

Minerva returned to the head of the Gulf again after dark and a searchlight revealed Grall on the shore. He had mistaken the search party for Turkish troops and hidden himself until they had gone, then struggled to the coast where he was safely returned to the ship. Grall was to make many flights in Nieuport seaplanes from *Anne* and *Raven II* in the months to come.

During late December 1914 *Diana* joined *Minerva* in the Gulf of Akaba to see what possibilities Akaba offered as a base for operations northwards towards Palestine, up the Wadi Akaba. Once again it was found that *Diana*'s Nieuport VI seaplanes were unable to gain sufficient altitude to cross the mountains between Akaba and Ma'an; they were however able to carry out reconnaissances at the head of the Gulf to find a suitable

landing place. A detachment under Captain J.W. Snepp, RMLI was landed, and advanced through the town of Akaba without opposition. On 31 December Capt Snepp's detachment had to be withdrawn under heavy fire after a reconnaissance of the Wadi Akaba.

With the start of the Dardanelles campaign in 1915 many Turkish troops were withdrawn from Sinai in February, but the significance of the Royal Navy's aerial reconnaissance was not lost upon the Germans who despatched a force of Rumpler C.Is to Beersheba to counter it.

The Navy's main part in the Dardanelles Campaign was the bombardment of Turkish forts and troops on the Gallipoli Peninsula. To augment the firepower of the Allied warships, the monitors *Abercrombie*, *Raglan* and *Roberts*, later joined by the Lord Clive class monitor *Sir Thomas Picton*, were despatched to the Dardanelles in the summer of 1915 to form the 1st Division Special Squadron.

All ships of the *Abercrombie* class were designed to carry a seaplane, which had to be hoisted over the side before guns were fired to avoid blast damage. Indeed all the monitors of the *Abercrombie* class were the first

Kinfauns Castle in pre-war Union Castle livery. Hired as an A.M.C she transported two Sopwith 807's to Niororo Island in February 1915 for operations against SMS Königsberg, where she was employed as a seaplane depot ship. (FAAM)

Two Short Folders, 119 and 122, being erected on the Durban dockside in early April 1915. They and 121 were shipped from the U.K. in packing cases aboard HMS Laconia. Based at Niororo Island they were all engaged in the Königsberg operations in May 1915. (FAAM)

conventional warships ever designed, while on the drawing board, to accommodate aircraft as a standard feature.

Roberts operated a Short 166 (No.164), transferred from *Ark Royal* in September 1915. It spotted for the guns of *Roberts* while she bombarded Turkish batteries on the Asiatic coast.

Meanwhile, some 3,500 miles to the south in German East Africa, seaplanes and later aeroplanes of the RNAS were about to play an indispensable part in the destruction of the cruiser SMS *Königsberg* in the Rufiji Delta.

Königsberg had arrived at Dar-es-Salaam on 6th June 1914 and, in the event of war breaking out between Britain and Germany, the disruption that she could cause to shipping in the Indian Ocean was apparent to the Admiralty.

As a preventative measure the Cape of Good Hope Squadron under Rear Admiral H.G. King-Hall was ordered to sail from Port Louis, Mauritius, on 27 July in order to find *Königsberg* and shadow her movements. The Cape Squadron consisted of HM Ships *Hyacinth*,

Astraea and *Pegasus*, all 2nd or 3rd class cruisers completed at the end of the previous century and at least five knots slower than the modern *Königsberg*, whose guns could easily outrange those of the British cruisers.

Königsberg sailed from Dar-es-Salaam at 1600 on 31 July and she was sighted in the gathering darkness that evening by *Hyacinth*, but easily outran *Hyacinth*. War had not been declared, and for the next $7^{1}/_{2}$ weeks *Königsberg* disappeared - in fact to the entrance to the Red Sea from the Indian Ocean where she was engaged as a commerce raider.

Königsberg reappeared at 0530 on 20 September off Zanzibar where *Pegasus* was boiler cleaning. *Königsberg* opened fire at 1100 yards, closing to 7000 yards, and hit *Pegasus* repeatedly. After a brief gun action *Königsberg* reversed course and once more disappeared. *Pegasus* sank at 1400 that day.

A chance encounter by the cruiser *Chatham* with one of *Königsberg*'s supply ships SS *President* on 19 October finally revealed *Königsberg*'s whereabouts. Papers recovered from SS *President* showed that she had shipped coal in lighters to *Königsberg* from Lindi to

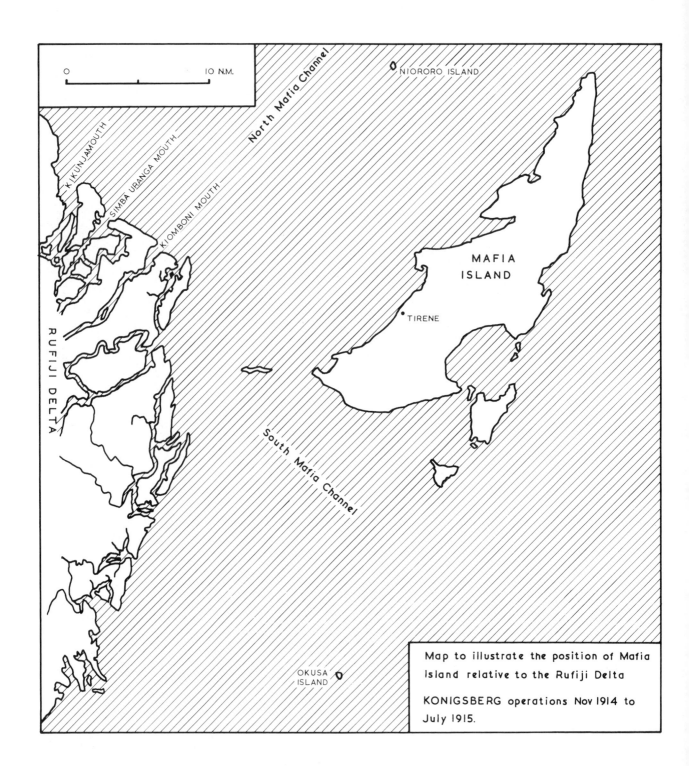

O   IO N.M.

K IKUNJAMOUTH

SIMBA URANGA MOUTH

KIOMBONI MOUTH

North Mafia Channel

NIORORO ISLAND

RUFIJI DELTA

MAFIA
ISLAND

· TIRENE

South Mafia Channel

OKUSA
ISLAND

Map to illustrate the position of Mafia
Island relative to the Rufiji Delta

KONIGSBERG operations Nov 1914 to
July 1915.

Sarari, 6 miles up the Rufiji.

On 30 October *Chatham* arrived off the Rufiji Delta and saw *Königsberg*'s topmasts above the trees. The channel was not navigable by *Chatham* as she drew two feet more than the German cruiser. Both banks of the river were fortified by the Germans, so the only course open was for *Chatham* to wait outside and blockade the ship. *Chatham* was soon joined by the cruisers *Dartmouth* and *Weymouth*.

To ensure that *Königsberg* should not attempt to escape, the collier SS *Newbridge* was sunk as a blockship in the main exit from the Simba Uranga channel under heavy fire from the German shore positions on 10th November, and the decision was taken to pin-point *Königsberg*'s position in the river by aerial reconnaissance.

At Durban were two 90 hp single engined Curtiss Model F flying boats owned by Mr Gerard Hudson, which had been demonstrated there in July by their pilot H.D. Cutler. Since there were no RNAS aircraft in the area Admiral King-Hall sailed for Durban in *Hyacinth* to negotiate the hire of a Curtiss F at £150 per month,

with a clause to cover loss of the flying boat of up to £2,000.

Cutler was awarded a commission as a Flt Sub Lt RNAS, and the AMC *Kinfauns Castle* was dispatched to Simonstown to embark Cutler and the Curtiss flying boat. *Kinfauns Castle* left Simonstown on 6 November, but during the passage the flying boat's ailerons were damaged by heavy seas. In answer to a radio message the second Curtiss's ailerons were removed and sent to Durban for collection by *Kinfauns Castle* en route to Niororo Island. These ailerons were fitted to the Curtiss by Cutler and Midshipman S.N. Gallehawk RNR, and *Kinfauns Castle* was met off Mafia Island on 15 November by *Chatham*. The plan was to use Niororo as a base for the flying boat since that island provided a good lee from the open sea for the take off. Niororo Island lay just north of Mafia Island and eighteen miles NE of the Rufiji Delta. Gallehawk had now been appointed as observer to fly with Cutler, and both men spent the next three days endeavouring to get the Curtiss into an airworthy condition. Its hull was built up of laminated wood veneer strips applied to the wooden hull

A Short 827 being towed by HMS Severn, probably off the coast of German East Africa during 1916. Although her quarterdeck afforded enough space for the stowage of a seaplane there is no evidence that HMS Severn was fitted with a derrick for handling seaplanes. (IWM SP959)

This group on Kinfauns Castle in February 1915 includes, left to right:
Back row: -?-, E.Quarman (Air Mech), W.H.Shaw (Air Mech), C.E.Tubbs (Air Mech), G.Toll (Air Mech), Brazier (Air Mech), Grant, T.Williams (Air Mech), N.M.Bois (Air Mech).
Middle row: C.V.Lacey (CPO), Mobsby (PO), H.Norrington (ERA), Flt Lt J.T.Cull, Flt Lt H.E.M.Watkins, Midshipman S.N.Gallehawk RNR, Sprot (CPO), G.W.Sutcliffe (Ldg Mech).
Front row: E.H.A.Boggis (Ldg Mech Obs), T.R.Law (Air Mech), A.H.Gregory (Air Mech), W.H.Cornelius (Ldg Mech), W.Bennett (Ldg Mech Obs). (FAAM)

frame and leaked badly, as did the radiator of the 90 hp Curtiss OX engine. Endurance was limited to about 50 minutes flying time, and it soon became evident that the Curtiss would not get off the water carrying an observer.

By 19 November all was ready for the first reconnaissance flight. *Chatham* had anchored off the mouth of the Simba Uranga to give Cutler a mark over which to fly. Although he was observed flying inland at 0715 he disappeared into thick cloud at 4000 feet and, without a compass, lost his bearings. With fuel running low he was forced to land at what he took to be Niororo Island, but was in fact Okusa Island 34 miles to the south of Niororo Island. Both Cutler and the flying boat were fortunately found some 6 hours after take off and were returned to Niororo Island, where it was discovered that the hull had been damaged on landing and that the radiator was beyond repair.

The radiator was replaced by one taken from a Ford car at Mombasa and brought down to Niororo by HMS

Fox in time for Cutler to fly a second reconnaissance on 22 November. This time *Königsberg* was at last located in the position to which she had now moved, some distance from the river mouth. Upon the flying boat's return to Niororo the hull was found to be beyond repair, so *Kinfauns Castle* was dispatched to Durban on 23 November to fetch a replacement hull from the other Curtiss, which had already been robbed of its ailerons.

Kinfauns Castle returned to Niororo Island at 0800 on 3rd December, the new hull was quickly fitted, and the intrepid Cutler took off on his third reconnaissance flight later that day, taking with him as observer Captain D.B. Crampton RN, *Kinfauns Castle*'s commanding officer, to confirm Cutler's sighting report, which had initially been disbelieved.

Königsberg was again sighted, but had moved further up river during the past ten days, putting her beyond the range of a cruiser lying off the river mouth. Further reconnaissances were flown on 4th, 7th, 8th and

9th December, but that on 10 December ended in disaster. After flying inland the Curtis developed engine problems and was seen to come down at the mouth of the Kikunja River. Cutler tried and failed to take off again under accurate rifle fire from the Germans on the bank, who eventually waded out to him and made him prisoner.

The armed tug *Helmuth* had been lying off the river mouth under Gallehawk's command. He immediately took the tug up river to the scene of the forced landing and, finding no sign of Cutler, succeeded in securing a line to the flying boat while under heavy fire from the shore and towed it back to *Kinfauns Castle*. The Curtiss was so badly damaged that it was eventually returned to South Africa.

HMS Severn c.1916. (A.K.Vicary)

Without aerial reconnaissance the blockading squadron was blind, and powerless to destroy or immobilise their adversary. Captain Loof took advantage of the stalemate on 14 December to move *Königsberg* down the Simba Uranga, across one branch of the Kikunja channel.

Admiral King-Hall now requested the Admiralty to despatch shallow draught monitors to the Rufiji and a flight of seaplanes to spot the fall of shot from the monitors on *Königsberg*.

Two monitors were selected for the operation, *Severn* and *Mersey*, each armed with two 6-inch and two 4.7-inch guns, and each previously earmarked for operations on the Danube should the Galipolli landings succeed.

On 7 January 1915 Flt Lt J.T. Cull was posted to command RNAS Expeditionary Force No 4 with Flt Lt H.E.M. Watkins as his second in command. Eighteen

ratings, including three specialists from Sopwith and the Lang propeller works were selected to complete the RNAS contingent. They were H. Norrington ERA, W.H. Cornelius Ldg Mech, A.H. Gregory Air Mech, W.H. Shaw Air Mech, G.W. Sutcliffe Ldg Mech, C.E. Tubbs Air Mech, G. Toll Air Mech, E.H.A. Boggis Ldg Mech (Obs), C.V. Lacey CPO, Brazier Air Mech, T. Williams Air Mech, N.M. Bois Air Mech, E. Quarman Air Mech, T.R. Law Air Mech and W. Bennett Ldg Mech (Obs). The three specialists, granted temporary rank, were PO Mobsby from Sopwiths, and the two from Langs - CPO Sprot and PO Burgess.

It had been hoped to equip the squadron with Short Folders, but as none were available two Sopwith 807's, 920 and 921, were substituted. Brand new machines powered with 100 hp Gnôme Monosoupape engines, they were tested at Calshot before being dismantled and crated for delivery to Tilbury. There they were loaded on board SS *Persia* which sailed with the RNAS detachment on 16 January, arriving at Bombay on 8th February. The cover story was that the men and machines were to establish a flying school at Bombay, but the intention was more warlike. The seaplanes were erected and test flown at Bombay on 11 February, to the consternation of the natives who assumed they were German, and then embarked with wings folded in *Kinfauns Castle* on 13 February for transport to Niororo Island.

Kinfauns Castle reached Niororo Island on 21 February where it was the intention to use both seaplanes to bomb *Königsberg*. Trials optimistically began to get the Sopwiths airborne loaded with four 16-lb and two 50-lb bombs, a full petrol tank, plus pilot and observer. The best that could be achieved however was a take off with just pilot and petrol. Plainly neither aircraft was suitable for their intended task, but various modifications were undertaken to increase their performance. The Gnôme engines had a hollow propeller shaft for sucking air into the engine, and a funnel was fitted onto the nose piece to achieve forced induction and a supercharging effect. The valve timings were altered to close later to induce more air into the engine. The ignition timing was retarded but the engine only ran hotter and rougher. Finally the engine cowlings were removed to improve cooling - all to no avail.

Upon arrival at Niororo Island on 21 February, 921s operational career was brief. On that day Cull with CPO Lacey in the observer's cockpit attempted to take off in a cross wind. A wing tip caught in the water and the propeller was damaged. After repairs to 921, Watkins was airborne on the 24th but the seaplane suffered engine failure, force landed and was wrecked. 920 had suffered damage to the port wingtip while being test flown at Bombay by Watkins and Gallehawk, but this had been repaired en route to Niororo Island, and the seaplane was test flown there on 21 February when Cull flew 920 to the scene of 921s crash on the 24th.

920 was crewed by Cull and Cornelius on 28 February, but suffered engine failure and force landed on the sea. *Kinfauns Castle* was on hand however to salve the seaplane, and with new float struts and starboard lower mainplane it was flying again on 4 March. However, on 9 March, flown by Cull, it started to sink after landing owing to the bottom of the starboard float peeling off. *Kinfauns Castle* again hoisted both Cull and the unfortunate seaplane on board.

It was found on investigation that the floats became weakened by a build up of pressure within them while on the ship's deck in the hot sun, causing the bottoms to peel off on landing. The floats were therefore fitted with exhaust vents, the bottoms were reinforced with sheet metal beaten to shape from empty petrol tins, and the floats were kept filled with water until the seaplanes were hoisted out. These measures solved the problem.

Requests to Egypt for engine spares were ignored, so the local works department in Zanzibar made them. These included piston rings for the rotary engines, usually made from nickel silver but now made from ordinary silver. Various expedients to try and increase performance, including reducing the diameter of the propeller to increase engine revs, produced no improvement. 920's best performance was just 30 minutes flying, carrying only a pilot, and on 14 March the C-in-C Cape wired the Admiralty to say that any further aerial operations were impossible until other aircraft were made available. The response was surprisingly swift, and upon receipt of a signal that replacement aircraft were on their way, the RNAS unit embarked in *Kinfauns Castle*, taking with them the useless Sopwith, 920, and reached Mombasa on 28th March. After moving up to Zanzibar they took passage

HMS Laurentic was a former White Star liner hired as A.M.C. in 1914. She transported two Henry Farmans and two Caudron G.III's to Mafia Island in June 1915 for Rufiji Delta operations, but never operated aircraft. (NMM P19482)

One of the two Caudron G.IIIs transported in HMS Laurentic being uncrated at Mafia Island in June 1915. (FAAM)

in SS *Chakdara* for Durban to collect their replacement aircraft.

In early April these were unloaded in their cases from the AMC *Laconia* at Durban. To the Squadron's dismay their new equipment turned out to be three Short Folders, 119, 121 and 122, all of which had seen considerable service in seaplane carriers since the previous summer.

In Cull's words, "These machines were getting very old when we left England. During the war they had spent all winter on a seaplane ship. They had been refused by Grain and Calshot as useless, but were considered good enough to send to Africa where we had no chance of refusing them." Two of them, 119 and 122, had been in fact embarked in *Engadine* for the Cuxhaven raid of 25 December 1914. The only consolation was their 160 hp Gnôme engines, which it was hoped would be an improvement on the 100 hp engines of the Sopwiths.

The Shorts were taken from their packing cases and erected on the dockside at Durban. They were then loaded back on board *Laconia* which sailed on 18 April, reaching Niororo Island on the 22nd. Mafia Island had been taken from the small German garrison by a landing on 10 January, and it was to Tirene Bay on the west coast of the island that *Laconia* sailed next day to unload the three Shorts. Mafia Island was much nearer to the Rufiji Delta than Niororo Island, and its longer length of 27 miles provided a useful lee from the open sea for seaplane operations.

Meanwhile the two monitors *Severn* and *Mersey* had left Devonport under tow on 15 March, arriving in Malta on 29 March. Still under tow they left Malta on 28 April for the long passage, reaching Aden on 15 May and finally Mafia Island on 3 June. Flight trials with the Short Folders began as soon as they were disembarked from *Laconia*. Though not in a very serviceable condition they were an improvement on the Sopwiths, being able to get airborne with an adequate load of fuel and a two man crew.

Cull flew the first reconnaissance with the Shorts on 25 April in 122, taking off at 0930 with Ldg Mech E.H.A. Boggis in the observer's seat. Flying at 800 feet up the Mssala Channel, the Short came under heavy fire from the banks. *Königsberg* was not sighted in the southern channel where she had been reported, but was finally located at Kikale in approximately the position she was reported to be in on 6 December.

Cull's report stated,

"She looked as though she had been newly painted, her sidescreens and moorings were spread, smoke was issuing from her funnels and in general she was looking very spick and span. No sign was observed of any attempt to camouflage the ship by means of branches of trees as reported in the English press. The machine had now arrived within range of *Königsberg* and on her present course would have passed about ³/₄ mile on her beam, travelling from stern to bow. As the machine,

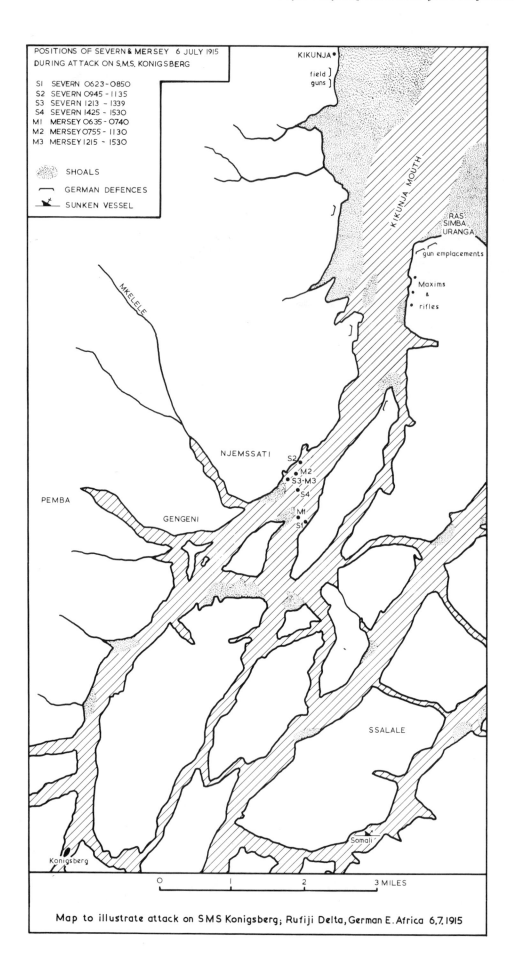

POSITIONS OF SEVERN & MERSEY 6 JULY 1915
DURING ATTACK ON S.M.S. KONIGSBERG

S1   SEVERN 0623–0850
S2   SEVERN 0945–1135
S3   SEVERN 1213–1339
S4   SEVERN 1425–1530
M1   MERSEY 0635–0740
M2   MERSEY 0755–1130
M3   MERSEY 1215–1530

SHOALS

GERMAN DEFENCES

SUNKEN VESSEL

KIKUNJA

field
guns

KIKUNJA MOUTH

RAS
SIMBA
URANGA

gun emplacements

Maxims
&
rifles

MKELELE

NJEMSSATI

S2
M2
S3·M3
S4

M1
S1

PEMBA

GENGENI

SSALALE

Somali

Konigsberg

0   1   2   3 MILES

Map to illustrate attack on SMS Konigsberg; Rufiji Delta, German E. Africa 6.7.1915

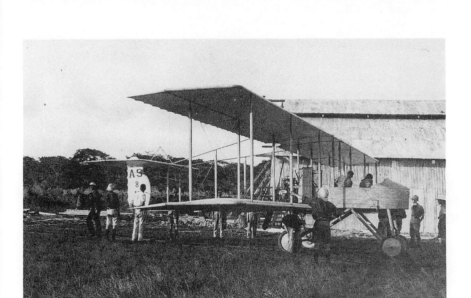

Two views of Henry Farman F.27 ''AS/8/HF'' being readied for take-off c.June 1915 on Mafia Island. Flown by Flt Lt J.T.Cull this aircraft crashed and was written off before it could be used to spot for the monitors during the operation against Königsberg in July. (FAAM)

Henry Farman F.27 ''SA/9/HF'' on Mafia Island showing the corrugated iron hangar erected on the aerodrome. This aircraft was shot down and crashed on 11th July while spotting the fire of Severn on Königsberg.

however, was not flying very well, and everything of interest had been noted, the machine was turned just before coming abreast of *Königsberg* and headed out to sea again. As it turned, *Königsberg* opened fire, and for a first attempt made some very pretty shooting, shells bursting just astern of the machine. The machine left by the same entrance as it had entered, and was speeded on her way with a considerably reinforced volley of rifle fire, German officers and Askari's being easily distinguished from the height of 600 feet, firing all for all they were worth and in no way disconcerted by pistol and Very pistol fire from the machine.

From now onwards the engine started failing gradually, and packed up altogether within some 6 or 7 miles of the anchorage where the ships were lying. On landing it was found that a rifle bullet of about $1/2$-inch bore had entered between the observer and the engine at a very flat trajectory, tearing away the air intakes and succeeding in practically closing the main oil pipe. This latter was naturally the cause of the engine failing, and several blued cylinders resulted".

The Short was soon towed back to Mafia Island where the photographs of *Königsberg* taken by Boggis with Cull's own Goetz Anschutz camera were developed. For this flight Cull was awarded the D.S.C. and Boggis the D.S.M.

Königsberg's attempts to ward off the reconnaissance flights were hampered by her lack of shrapnel ammunition - there were only 30 rounds on board. Capt Loof however gave orders for the tops of

Two views of Caudron G.IIIs at Maktau Camp, East Africa, probably after the operations against Königsberg in July 1915. However the photograph's are representative of the Caudron G.IIIs used in the operation. (FAAM)

her 4.1-inch gun shields to be removed to increase the guns' elevation for A.A.defence.

Other successful reconnaissances were flown by the Shorts, often with the Flag Commander, Cdr The Hon.R.Bridgeman, going up as observer.

Flt Lt H.E.M.Watkins was piloting 119 on one of these reconnaissances on 5 May when the seaplane was hit at low altitude by fire from the eastern Kiombini battery. The rudder was shot away, and Watkins had to put the Short down rather hurriedly across both wind and sea about half a mile of the coast. The seaplane capsized and Watkins and his Air Mechanic observer clung to the wreckage until almost nightfall, when Cull in another Short spotted them. He landed and taxied over to them and they clambered on to the floats. Cull transferred them to a whaler before flying back to *Laconia*. An attempt was made by the cruiser *Chatham* next day to salve 119's engine, but it had sunk so far in the mud that it had to be left.

By the middle of May, Cull was informed that further aerial reinforcements were on the way. These consisted of four aeroplanes shipped out in the AMC *Laurentic* - two Caudron G.IIIs and two Henry Farman F.27s to spot the monitors' fall of shot.

The RNAS detachment accompanying these aircraft was under the command of Sqdn Cdr R. Gordon RMLI who had become only the tenth naval officer to learn to fly in 1911. With him were two more pilots, Flt Lt V.G. Blackburn and Flt Sub Lt H.J. Arnold plus thirteen PO's and ratings.

To accommodate the four new aircraft, an aerodrome had to be cleared on Mafia Island, $1^1/_2$ miles inland from Tirene Bay. Trees and scrub were cut down and a landing strip some 200 yards long was levelled, and a large corrugated iron hangar was erected on the site. *Laurentic* arrived off Mafia Island on 18th June and the four aircraft in packing cases were brought ashore on pairs of *Laurentic*'s lifeboats. The cases were unpacked on the beach and the aircraft parts were carried by native labour to the hangar for erection.

Following the two monitors *Severn*'s and *Mersey*'s arrival on 3rd June, work was put in hand to fit them for the coming assault on *Königsberg*. Steel plates $^1/_2$-inch thick were laid on their decks, sandbags were placed round exposed positions and 900 empty petrol tins were stowed below decks to increase the ships' buoyancy, should they suffer any hits below the waterline. The upperworks of each ship were also painted with disruptive camouflage.

While all these preparations for the final attack continued, the Shorts kept up their reconnaissance flights. All four of the newly arrived aeroplanes had a greatly superior performance to the ancient Shorts, although the East African climate did nothing to prolong the life of either their airframes or engines.

One of the Caudrons was lost on a trial flight soon after arrival, and a Farman suffered the same fate when its engine failed. It was found that the wooden propellers had warped in transit, and on the Farman grooves had to be cut in the blades so that they might clear the HT terminal on the magneto. This unorthodox modification proved satisfactory on ground runs, but when Cull took the Farman, marked AS/8/HF, on a test flight, the weakened propeller struck the ignition terminal causing instant engine failure. The Farman crashed and was a complete write off, so that by 30 June there were only two serviceable aeroplanes left - one Henry Farman SA/9/HF, and one Caudron G.III. Tests were conducted during the last week of June to establish W/T communications between the aircraft and monitors for spotting purposes. These were unsuccessful, and it was decided that the aircraft should signal corrections to the monitors by flares and lamps if it was necessary.

The stage was set for what was hoped would be the final act in the Rufiji Delta operation. It was however preceded on 2 July by a high level bombing attack, delivered by one of the two available aeroplanes, on *Königsberg*. All bombs missed their target, and fortunately the aeroplane escaped damage from AA fire. It seems extraordinary that the machine should have been imperilled in this way on the eve of the main operation but it returned safely to Mafia Island.

Orders were given for the attack on *Königsberg* to take place on 6 July, this date being chosen to coincide with a high tide which would enable *Severn* and *Mersey* to reach their firing positions up the Kikunja river. In order to create a diversion, *Laurentic* and three transports were dispatched to Dar-es-Salaam on 5 July to fake a landing. *Severn* and *Mersey* weighed at 0400 on 6 July, and skirting the bank off Ras Simba Uranga crossed the bar at the river mouth at 0520. A field gun to the north of the entrance fired three apparently blank charges to alert the Delta Force defences, followed by live rounds. Rifles and machine guns then opened fire from the banks, but were silenced by return fire from the monitors.

At 0523 Watkins took off from Mafia Island in the remaining Caudron with a load of six bombs. These he dropped over *Königsberg* from 6,000ft, and although none hit their target the object was to create a diversion as the monitors entered the river. Cull with Flt Sub Lt Arnold as observer took off at 0535 in Henry Farman SA/9/HF, and on arrival at 0600 sighted the two monitors proceeding up river and firing on enemy positions along the banks. *Königsberg* opened fire on them while the monitors were still manoeuvring for anchoring positions at 0700 near Gengeni Island, firing salvos of two guns for ranging purposes. The first shots were 1500 yards short, but when her salvos increased to

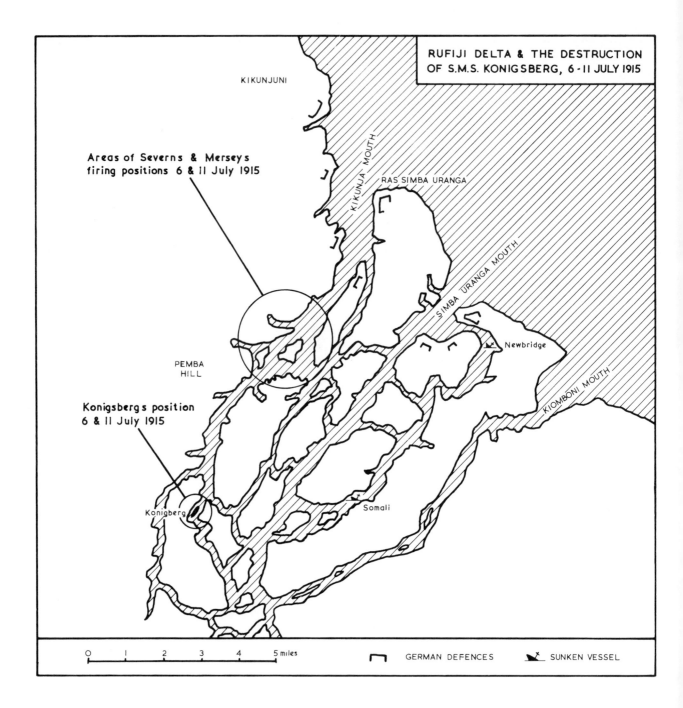

RUFIJI DELTA & THE DESTRUCTION
OF S.M.S. KONIGSBERG, 6 - 11 JULY 1915

KIKUNJUNI

KIKUNJA MOUTH

RAS SIMBA URANGA

SIMBA URANGA MOUTH

Areas of Severns & Merseys
firing positions 6 & 11 July 1915

Newbridge

KIOMBONI MOUTH

PEMBA
HILL

Konigsbergs position
6 & 11 July 1915

Somali

Konigberg

O   1   2   3   4   5 miles

GERMAN DEFENCES   SUNKEN VESSEL

five guns Cull could see shells falling all round the monitors.

Severn and *Mersey* were both seen by Cull to be anchored bow and stern, though *Severn* had experienced some problem in anchoring when the flood tide swung her round. Both monitors opened fire at 0725 approximately 11,000 yards from *Königsberg*. Their fire was very wild and Arnold had great difficulty in observing the fall of shot because so many shells fell on land. By 0740 *Mersey* had been hit twice, knocking out her forward 6-inch gun, killing four men and severely wounding three others. *Mersey* signalled that she was holed below the waterline and retired out of range while *Severn* continued firing. From the Farman it was seen that just as *Mersey* began to move a salvo of five shots fell just astern of her and in the exact spot where she had lain. *Severn* was hit at 0731, but at 0751 Arnold was able to signal that *Mersey* in turn had hit *Königsberg* with the first of several hits. The Caudron should have taken over spotting duties from the Farman at 0810, so as it had still not appeared by 0840 Cull was forced to return to Mafia Island with fuel running low.

Mersey returned to the fray at 0810, and in the absence of any spotting aircraft, both monitors closed

the range and opened fire again, *Königsberg*'s topmasts being visible over the trees. The accuracy of the monitors' fire fell off and became wild, however, in contrast to their adversary's accurate fire. The reason for this was a German spotting position up a tree which was observed from *Severn*. This was brought down by *Severn*'s gunfire. Meanwhile the Caudron, crewed by Flt Lt Blackburn and Assistant Paymaster Badger, arrived overhead to carry on spotting, but results were disappointing as confusion arose in distinguishing between the fall of shot of the two ships.

Severn now closed the range to 11,300 yards and anchored again one cable N and E of *Mersey* at 0945. Blackburn's Caudron was relieved by the Farman now piloted by Sqdn Cdr Gordon with Flt Lt Arnold as his observer. A constant shuttle of the two spotting aircraft between Mafia Island and the monitors was maintained until 1545 when *Severn* and *Mersey* ceased fire and proceeded back to the river mouth after expending 635 shells. Not many hits were obtained on *Königsberg*, but this was due to only 78 corrections being sent, owing to defective W/T and confusion about which monitor was being signalled. A total of 15 hours 19 minutes flying time by four pilots and two observers in the two available aeroplanes on 6 July over hostile and inhospitable territory is the feat achieved this day by the aircrew of the RNAS.

Aerial reconnaissance on 7 July confirmed that *Königsberg* had been damaged, but that a further attack would be necessary to finish the job. Further operations were postponed for four days so that repairs might be carried out to the two monitors.

Severn and *Mersey* left Tirene Bay under tow at 0800 on 11 July. The tow was cast off at 1045 and the Kikunja entrance was passed at 1145 where the *Mersey* was hit by two shells, causing some casualties.

Cull and Arnold took off from Mafia Island in Farman SA/9/HF at 1150 and crossed the coast at 3200 feet in very bumpy conditions. The monitors were observed getting into position, firing heavily at German positions on the river banks. *Mersey* was under way and firing at *Königsberg* while *Severn* approached her anchorage.

Königsberg opened accurate fire on the monitors at 1212 and by 1217 she was firing rapid salvos of four guns, one salvo dropping 50 yards ahead of *Severn*. *Severn* then anchored bow and stern, and at 1231 she opened fire on *Königsberg*. Her first five salvos were unobserved from the Farman. Arnold sent corrections to *Severn* for the sixth and seventh salvos, but the eighth salvo was on target and eight or nine shells burst on the forward part of *Königsberg* at 1245.

The Farman was now in trouble, and Cull's report states:

"For the last 8 or 10 minutes the machine had been

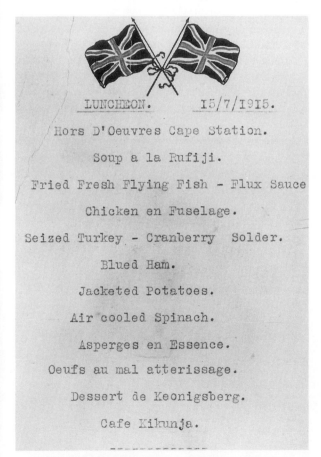

LUNCHEON.   15/7/1915.

Hors D'Oeuvres Cape Station.

Soup a la Rufiji.

Fried Fresh Flying Fish - Flux Sauce

Chicken en Fuselage.

Seized Turkey - Cranberry Solder.

Blued Ham.

Jacketed Potatoes.

Air cooled Spinach.

Asperges en Essence.

Oeufs au mal atterisage.

Dessert de Keonigsberg.

Cafe Kikunja.

The menu of celebration lunch on Mafia Island, 15th July 1915. (FAAM)

losing height rapidly though I was flying her at a speed and angle she should climb very rapidly at - something was obviously wrong with the engine and I put it down to a small injury from rifle fire. We also observed puffs of smoke in the air beneath us.''

"When at 2,400 feet about 1245 a shell must have burst just beneath us as I experienced the most violent bump I have ever felt and the machine was out of control for several seconds - this was on our journey towards *Königsberg* and I turned shortly afterwards as the engine could now be heard running very badly and the machine was losing height more rapidly.''

"A few minutes afterwards the engine stopped dead, and I started to glide towards the *Mersey*, as though the *Severn* was nearest I did not want to interfere with her fire. By prolonging the glide as much as possible we managed to reach within about 150 yards of the *Mersey*.''

"On our way down my observer, with great coolness, gave a correction to the *Severn* by W/T, bringing hits from forward on the *Königsberg* to amidships. He also informed the monitors we were hit and descending and asked for a boat, after which he wound in his aerial.'' [In a most seaman-like manner - author]

"On the way down we noticed a 1-inch hole through a cylinder, though probably there was other damage to account for so sudden a stoppage.''

"Our landing on the water was very slow but the machine on touching at once turned a somersault. My observer was shot over my head well clear - I however had foolishly forgotten to unstrap my belt and I went

down with the machine - my feet also were entangled and I had the greatest difficulty in freeing myself, tearing off my boots and legs of my trousers in so doing. When I came to the surface my observer was hunting in the wreckage for me and we both then started swimming for the *Mersey* whose motor boat picked us up after a short time and took us on board.''

At 1340 Capt Fullerton, commanding *Severn*, signalled *Mersey* to close the range to 7,000 yards and take over the bombardment from her sister ship. By the time *Mersey* opened fire, the Caudron, crewed by Watkins and Lt A.G. Bishop RMLI, had arrived to spot the fall of shot and reported a hit with the third salvo. *Mersey* got off 28 salvos before Fullerton, who had ascended *Severn*'s topmast head, could see that *Königsberg* was on fire fore and aft, her centre funnel lay across the deck and a stream of smoke was coming out of the top of her mainmast. At 1420 therefore he decided that further expenditure of ammunition would be pointless and determined to proceed up river to assess the damage to *Königsberg* since her guns were now silent. He was thwarted in this however at 1430 on receipt of a signal for the monitors to retire.

Severn and *Mersey* fired at both banks on the way down river and came under fire from field guns as they passed the entrance at 1545, though the exchange of fire inflicted no casualties to either side.

Watkins made a bad landing in the Caudron on returning to Mafia Island and overturned the machine. Watkins was thrown clear, but in the excitement of relating the destruction of *Königsberg* quite forgot his observer who, left hanging head down, was struggling to

HMS Laconia, with HMS Severn alongside, for operations against Königsberg in the Rufiji Delta c. Jun/July 1915. (FAAM)

release his belt. Bishop was eventually released unharmed!

After the successful completion of operations the RNAS unit at Mafia Island transferred its stores and personnel to *Laconia*, after burning on 13 July the two surviving Short Folders, 121 and 122. Before leaving Mafia a grand celebration luncheon was held on 15 July, attended by amongst others the RNAS aircrew and commanding officers of the two monitors.

Laconia then proceeded to Mombasa where arrangements were made to land the RNAS unit for reconnaissance duties with two Caudron G.IIIs which had recently arrived. Since it had been impossible to carry out a reconnaissance of the wrecked *Königsberg* immediately after the battle as all the aircraft had been lost or were unserviceable, a small party under Cull with one Caudron G.III returned to Mafia Island at the end of July to assess the damage to the enemy cruiser. Bad weather delayed the reconnaissance until 5 August when the Caudron took off at 1524 piloted by Flt Lt V.G. Blackburn with Cull in the observer's seat. The coast was crossed at 1545 and Blackburn brought the Caudron down from 6,000ft to 4,000ft. After proceeding over the Kikunja channel and reconnoitering the Dar-es-Salaam road the Caudron headed for the *Königsberg*.

Cull's report stated

"The *Königsberg* had a 150 degree list to starboard and her starboard battery was under water, the only visible part being the boat's davits. Her AD was a bright red colour and I take this to be rust from being submerged at high tide. We circled round her three times, coming down to 3,000ft. A large lighter one third of her length was lying alongside the port side of her forecastle with a small dhow outside."

"I could see no guns in her port battery nor any port forecastle guns, but her starboard forecastle gun was in position. Her top masts were gone and the stumps were bare of paint and rusty, while the remains of a fighting top could be seen. Her OD was lying across the ship in a heap. I could see no one working on the ship or lighter, though I observed a small group of huts on the water's edge and a sharply defined road across the sand. The supply ship and two dhows were anchored close to the west shore about 500 yards astern of *Königsberg*. We arrived home at 1710."

After the reconnaissance Cull's party left Mafia Island for Mombasa, and on 12 August Sqdn Cdr Gordon and his flight with three Short 827s left Mombasa in *Laconia* for duty in Mesopotamia. On 8 September Cull, now promoted to Flt Cdr, with Flt Lt Watkins, Flt Sub Lt Gallehawk, W/O C.V. Lacey and eleven CPO's, PO's and ratings left Mombasa by train for Maktau - some 20 to 30 miles from the border of British East Africa - where they were to operate Caudron G.IIIs.

Although *Königsberg*'s threat to shipping had been eliminated, many of her 4.1-inch guns were removed from the ship and were mounted for use in the land campaign in East Africa, echoing the final words of Capt Loof's report - "SMS *Königsberg* is destroyed but not conquered." The part played by the men and machines of the RNAS had been vital in the destruction of *Königsberg*. Without them the monitors could have achieved little. The whole operation was a vindication of naval airpower and a fine example of the courage of the aircrews of the Royal Naval Air Service and of the ships' companies of *Severn* and *Mersey*.

Short Folder 122 astern of HMS Laconia during the Rufiji Delta operation to attack SMS Königsberg in 1915. (FAAM)

Group photograph on Mafia Island 15th July 1915 taken after lunch to celebrate destruction of Königsberg.

*Left to right: Sqdn Cdr R.Gordon, Flt Sub Lt H.J.Arnold, Cdr Cullinan (flag Sec), Flt Lt H.E.M.Watkins,
Surg Lt Jones, Flt Lt V.G.Blackburn, Major –, Capt E.J.A.Fullerton (commanding HMS Severn),
Lieut A.G.Bishop RMLI, Cdr R.A.Wilson (commanding HMS Mersey), Lt Col Mackay (Military Governor),
Flt Lt J.T.Cull (seated), Lt Money (Flag Lieutenant), Col Smith. (FAAM)*

Sopwith 807 922 is here shown being hoisted on
board HMS Ark Royal in early 1915, but this
seaplane was later operated by HM Ships Doris
and Minerva. (G.S.Leslie/J.M.Bruce collection)

Schneider 1437, operated by HMS Doris
in the Gulf of Smyrna c.March 1915.
(G.S.Leslie/J.M.Bruce collection)

Two views of Schneider 1438, here seen operating from HMS Ark Royal in the
Gulf of Xeros in April 1915, but later transferred to HMS Minerva. (G.S.Leslie/
J.M.Bruce collection)

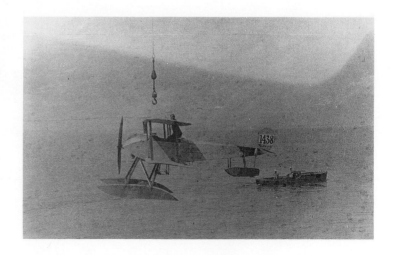

Sopwith 807, 921, after erection on the dockside at Bombay in early February 1915. Alongside is HMS Kinfauns Castle which transported two Sopwith 807's, 920 and 921, to Niororo Island for the Rufiji Delta operations. (FAAM)

The propeller shop on board HMS Kinfauns Castle c.February 1915. (FAAM)

Sopwith 807, 920, on board HMS Kinfauns Castle en route to Niororo Island February 1915. (FAAM)

Sopwith 807, 921, stowed on board HMS Kinfauns Castle February 1915. (FAAM)

Sopwith 807, 920, undergoing maintenance on Niororo Island February 1915. (G.S.Leslie/J.M.Bruce collection)

Sopwith 807, 920, with Flt Lt H.E.M.Watkins in the cockpit, being launched for take-off at Niororo Island February 1915. (G.S.Leslie/J.M.Bruce collection)

Sopwith 807, 920, alongside Kinfauns Castle, Niororo Island 1915. (FAAM)

Sopwith 807s, 920 and 921, at Niororo Island February 1915. (FAAM)

Sopwith 807, 920, beached at Niororo Island February 1915. (FAAM)

Sopwith 807 on board Kinfauns Castle en route from Bombay to Niororo Island, February 1915. Left to right: Temp PO Mobsby, Flt Lt J.T.Cull and possibly Air Mech T.R.Law. (FAAM)

Two views of Sopwith 807, 920, probably on 9 March 1915, alongside Kinfauns Castle. Piloted by Lt Cull, the seaplane damaged the starboard float on landing and started to sink, but was salved by the ship. (G.S.Leslie/J.M.Bruce collection)

Another view of a Sopwith 807 on board Kinfauns Castle. Flt Lt H.E.M.Watkins is on the left of the group and 5th from the left is probably Capt D.B.Crampton RN commanding HMS Kinfauns Castle. (FAAM)

On board Kinfauns Castle in February 1915 in the front row are left to right: C.V.Lacey (CPO), Flt Lt H.E.M.Watkins, Flt Lt J.T.Cull, Midshipman S.N.Gallehawk RNR, H.Norrington (ERA)

The P & O liner SS Persia, in which the two Sopwith 807's, 920 and 921, were shipped in packing cases from Tilbury on 16th January 1915 to Bombay for the Rufiji Delta operations. Persia was torpedoed by U38 south of Crete and sank with heavy loss of life on 30th December 1915. (FAAM)

Two views of Short Folder 122 used for reconnaissance duties over the Rufiji Delta in May 1915 (G.S.Leslie/J.M.Bruce collection and FAAM)

*Two views of Short
Folder 121 after erection
on the dockside at
Durban in April 1915.
(FAAM)*

*Short Folder 121 on the
dockside at Durban early
April 1915. 119's
packing case is in the
foreground. (G.S.Leslie/
J.M.Bruce collection)*

CHAPTER VI

Anti-Zeppelin operations by seaplanes in Home Waters 1915-1916

In Home Waters, during 1915, great efforts were made to counter the Germans' use of Zeppelins to raid this country and to report back to their bases the movements of the Harwich Force and Grand Fleet in the North Sea. Zeppelins raiding this country aimed to cross the coast at dusk to avoid detection of their approach across the North Sea. There was, therefore, little chance that defending aircraft based at Yarmouth Naval Air Station, and its associated night landing grounds, could climb to the Zeppelin's altitude for an interception before darkness hid her.

The answer to the problem seemed to be to fly standing patrols well out to sea at dusk and dawn. To this end four trawlers were taken in hand in early 1915 and fitted with a platform aft, on which a Schneider or Baby could be carried. From May 1915 these four

trawlers - *Cantatrice, Jerico, Kingfisher* and *Sir John French* - operated their seaplanes on anti-Zeppelin patrols some 50 miles off the East Coast. The routine was for the seaplane to be launched an hour before dusk, and then to patrol until dark within 10 to 15 miles of its parent trawler, before being hoisted inboard for the night. If a night raid had been made, the routine was repeated at dawn to try to intercept any raiding Zeppelins returning in daylight to their base. Lieut. Curzon RNR, commanding *Kingfisher,* even took his vessel as far as the Haaks light vessel on occasions, in the hope that his seaplane would catch a Zeppelin off its guard.

By May 1916 a fifth trawler, *Christopher*, had been added to the four carrying out anti-Zeppelin patrols. From the Daily Reports of RNAS Yarmouth it is apparent that these trawlers embarked Schneiders until October 1915, when they were generally replaced by Babies. The length of service of these trawlers as seaplane carriers varied considerably. *Kingfisher* operated a seaplane for at least twelve months between June 1915 and May 1916, but records indicate that the other four trawlers only operated a seaplane for very brief periods between these dates. *Cantatrice* was sunk

HMT Welbeck, as a minelayer in 1919, was probably a sister vessel to HMT Cantatrice for which no photograph can be traced. HMT Cantatrice operated a Schneider or Baby on anti-Zeppelin patrols in the North Sea during 1915. The platform on HMT Welbeck's stern had nothing to do with laying mines - these were laid from rails projecting through her bulwarks. It is thought that the platform was built to accommodate a Schneider - the usual position in which the anti-Zeppelin trawlers carried their seaplanes. (NMM FFL 1)

off Yarmouth on 5 November 1916 after striking a mine, but trawler patrols were continued until the middle of May 1916 at least. Pilots for the trawlers' Schneiders and Babies were provided by the Air Station at Yarmouth and included Flt Cdr W.P.de Courcy Ireland, Flt Lt F.D.G.Hards and Flt Sub Lts V.Nicholl, H.B.Smith, G.H.Bittles, F.N.Halstead, E.Cadbury, T.G.C.Wood and S.C.Beare.

Damage to the seaplanes from heavy seas encountered by the trawlers in the North Sea may have led to the two torpedo gunboats, *Halcyon* and *Dryad*, with higher freeboard, being fitted to each carry a Baby on the quarterdeck between December 1916 and July 1917 for anti-Zeppelin patrols. Flt Sub Lts Smith, Bittles and Brenton were the pilots for the seaplanes carried by these ships.

The patrols were augmented in 1916 when two former Humber paddle ferries were fitted to carry seaplanes by the addition of a pair of derricks forward to handle the seaplanes, and two 6-pdr guns. *Brocklesby* and *Killingholme*, were sister ships and both were commissioned on 27 March 1916. Brocklesby operated one Schneider and one Baby initially and thereafter two Babies between April 1916 and March 1917. *Killingholme* carried two Babies between April and October 1916, although a Schneider was substituted for one Baby in September 1916. There has been a suggestion that the smaller Humber paddle ferry *Cleethorpes* was also fitted to carry one seaplane during 1916, but confirmation of this is lacking.

They were very shallow draught vessels, with a low freeboard and were double-ended, having both bow and stern rudders operated by two wheels. *Killingholme*'s compass was defective, however, the north point

Baby 8140 was operated by HMT Cantatrice on anti-Zeppelin patrols in February 1916, but force landed off the Dutch coast on 27th April 1916. The seaplane is here depicted after being brought ashore in Holland where it was interned.
(G.S.Leslie/J.M.Bruce collection)

being always directed at the funnel! So a binnacle was borrowed from the old cruiser *Forth* at Immingham. Reserve feed water for the boiler was carried in two gallon cans, and by early April *Killingholme* was ready for her first operation. Her passage down the Humber was unseamanlike in the extreme until the tricky steering gear was mastered, but by Spurn Head she was on a fairly steady course. Her performance at sea was unusual, for each time she rolled the overhang of the deck hit the water with a bang, which shook the ship and made the funnel wobble. *Killingholme* carried on

The drifter Adele was formerly HMT Kingfisher operating a Schneider or Baby on anti-Zeppelin patrols in the North Sea during 1915. (Port of Lowestoft Research Society)

Seaplane pilots at Great Yarmouth in 1916. Left to right are: Flt Sub Lts F.W.Walker, G.H.Bittles, E.Cadbury, N.W.Leslie, H.B.Smith and G.H.Simpson. Smith flew Schneiders and Babies from HMTs Sir John French, Jerico and Kingfisher. Bittles flew Babies from HMT Kingfisher, HMS Brocklesby and HMS Halcyon. Cadbury flew Babies from HMT Kingfisher. (FAAM)

through the night, got a latitude sight at noon next day, and that afternoon picked up soundings with the hand lead on the Doggerbank. *Killingholme* patrolled back and forth that afternoon and night watching for Zeppelins, but none appeared.

The following morning it came on to blow hard from the north-west, and as conditions were quite unfit for launching the Schneiders, it was decided to return to the Humber. After an hour, crashes and bangs in the port paddle box forced the ship to stop. The cover of a manhole in the side of the paddle box was removed, and it was found that several wooden floats attached to the steel spokes of the wheel had come adrift. After great difficulty the damaged floats were cut away and the ship proceeded slowly back to the Humber with both wheels manned to keep her on course. *Killingholme* anchored in the lee of Spurn Head next morning, and had to be towed up river, since the Humber was not wide enough for her erratic steering.

Killingholme's paddles had new floats fitted and on 27 April she sailed again with one Schneider and one Baby embarked for her next sortie. While on patrol off the Doggerbank on the night of 28 April she struck a

mine. Extensive damage was caused to the port paddle and paddle box, to the bridge wing and to the saloon. A refit costing £7000 and lasting four months was considered necessary. She paid off on 17 May for a refit and this may have been completed in only three months, for the Daily Report of 1 August for the Air Station at Killingholme states that two Babies, 8141 and 8148 were allocated for HMS *Killingholme*. This indicates that she was probably returned to service as a seaplane carrier after her refit.

Under consideration also, in March 1916, was the proposal to fit all 24 paddle minesweepers of the *Ascot* class to operate two Babies from each ship on anti-Zeppelin patrols. All 24 ships of this class were completed between January and September 1916, but only two, *Eridge* and *Melton*, ever had derricks installed for handling seaplanes. Both seaplanes were to be stowed forward of the second funnel where the paddle boxes gave an overall beam of 58 feet. Apart from trials in *Eridge* and *Melton* it seems unlikely that their seaplanes were ever used operationally, although their derricks were retained throughout the war years.

A typical series of operations by *Brocklesby*,

commanded by Lt L.V. Marsh RNR, covered a four-day period. On 31 July 1916 *Brocklesby* commenced bunkering at 1330, and when this was completed at 1820, proceeded down river from Yarmouth with two seaplanes embarked, in company with the trawler HMT *Kingfisher*. By 1935 Cross Sand buoy was abeam, and by 2020 Cross Sand Light Vessel was abeam, with the weather dull and overcast. Seven Zeppelins crossed the East Coast this night, one of which, steering WSW, was sighted briefly overhead by *Brocklesby* at 0147 on 1 August. At 0345, as dawn was breaking, *Brocklesby* was to the West of Pillar buoy and the port seaplane was hoisted over the side for take-off. After a fruitless search for any Zeppelins the seaplane crashed on landing, but was picked up by *Kingfisher*.

Brocklesby returned to Yarmouth Roads at 1055 and anchored off the Air Station. At 1540 she made fast at the coaling berth, and at 1855 made fast at the Aviation Quay to take aboard, at 1930, a replacement for her crashed seaplane. Her air complement now consisted of Schneider 3736 and Baby 8149, and with these two seaplanes secured on deck she proceeded to sea.

1000 on 2 August saw *Brocklesby* cruising round Pillar buoy at dead slow speed. At 1254 Short 827, 3321, passed on patrol heading NE. As early as 1830 - with several daylight hours ahead - a Zeppelin was sighted from *Brocklesby* ten miles to the north west and flying slowly at 3,000 feet heading in a NW direction.

Both seaplanes were immediately hoisted out, and F/S/L G.H. Bittles was first away in the Baby at 1840. Bittles steered a course west by north which brought him about five miles due south of the Zeppelin at an altitude of 3,500 feet. Judging that he had a height advantage of some 200 feet Bittles began overhauling the Zeppelin on its port quarter until, when within two miles of it, the Zeppelin climbed steeply and disappeared into a cloud. Bittles then took the Baby to 6,500 feet above the cloud, but failed to sight his target and flew back to Yarmouth, landing there at 1940.

F/S/L H.B. Smith, meanwhile, had taken off in the Schneider at 1900, but once airborne his engine started missing. Steering a course to westward of the Zeppelin to intercept it before it crossed the coast, Smith coaxed his machine to 2,500 feet and, unable to climb any higher, turned in towards it. As Smith flew beneath the Zeppelin it started to rise, and before he could open fire with his Lewis gun it had got out of range. Smith then circled round two or three times and was able to make out the number on the Zeppelin's bows which he took to be L33. In fact L33 had not then been launched so it may possibly have been L13. Smith returned to Yarmouth and landed there at 2020.

Brocklesby meanwhile had increased to full speed, steering north-west, and at 1930 opened fire with her two 12-pounder AA guns at the Zeppelin, expending 51 rounds until 1935, when the Zeppelin turned east and

HMS Brocklesby in the North Sea 1916 on anti-Zeppelin patrol, with two Sopwith Babies stowed on deck. Virtually the only conversions made to the former Humber ferry were the installation of a pair of derricks forward for seaplane handling and two 12-pdr guns for defensive purposes. (FAAM)

drew out of range. All this gunfire cannot have aided the two seaplane pilots to make a successful interception.

2 August 1916 is noteworthy too for the fact that HMS *Vindex* from Harwich was also at sea this evening, and Flt Lt C.T. Freeman took off from *Vindex*'s forward flying-off deck in Bristol Scout D, 8953, at 1950. He made three attacks from above on L17 with Ranken Darts, but to no effect. He had to ditch near the North Hinder Light Vessel, but mercifully was picked up in darkness by the merchant ship *Anvers*.

By 0645 on 3 August *Brocklesby* was anchored off Yarmouth Air Station, and at 0800 made fast at the coaling berth. At 1200 she made fast at the Aviation Quay and took aboard ammunition and her two seaplanes. At 1445 she cleared the piers with the patrol boat P.32 as escort and proceeded to sea. A defect developed in the port paddle at 2030 and at 2240 the ship was stopped, one of the paddle's floats being found to be damaged. She proceeded again at 2340 at half speed, but by now the wind was freshening and the sea was causing the ship to roll and strain badly in a beam sea. Conditions were clearly unsuitable for seaplane operations, so course was set for Yarmouth, and *Brocklesby*

Schneider 1557 stowed on HMS Aurora's port side abaft the 3rd funnel, 1915.
(IWM SP1198)

anchored off the Air Station at 0715 on 4 August.

This far-sighted use of naval aviation deserved success, but the southern North Sea is a large and inhospitable area and Zeppelin sightings were infrequent.

To try to prevent Zeppelin reconnaissance of the Grand Fleet's movements in the North Sea, four light cruisers of the Harwich Force were fitted with fixed forecastle ramps to enable aeroplanes with wheeled under carriages to be launched at sea in May 1915. A Deperdussin Monoplane, 1378, was embarked in *Aurora* and a successful take off by Flt Lt R.J.J. Hope-Vere achieved, but the aircraft's frailty and poor performance led to the abandonment of this project. By the end of May *Aurora* carried a Schneider seaplane as did the other three cruisers, and the ramps were removed.

To assess the effectiveness of the Schneiders operated by the Harwich Force cruisers, Sqdn Cdr Seddon paid a visit to *Arethusa* on 10 June 1915. In discussion with her officers he was told that a Zeppelin had recently been sighted at 3,000 feet and six miles distant. The Schneider was hoisted out, and in spite of damaging its floats, got airborne, but only circled the cruisers and then returned further damaging its floats on landing. *Arethusa*'s officers blamed ''the utter incapacity of the pilot alone for failing to pick off one of the VC's which were simply hanging on to this Zeppelin''.

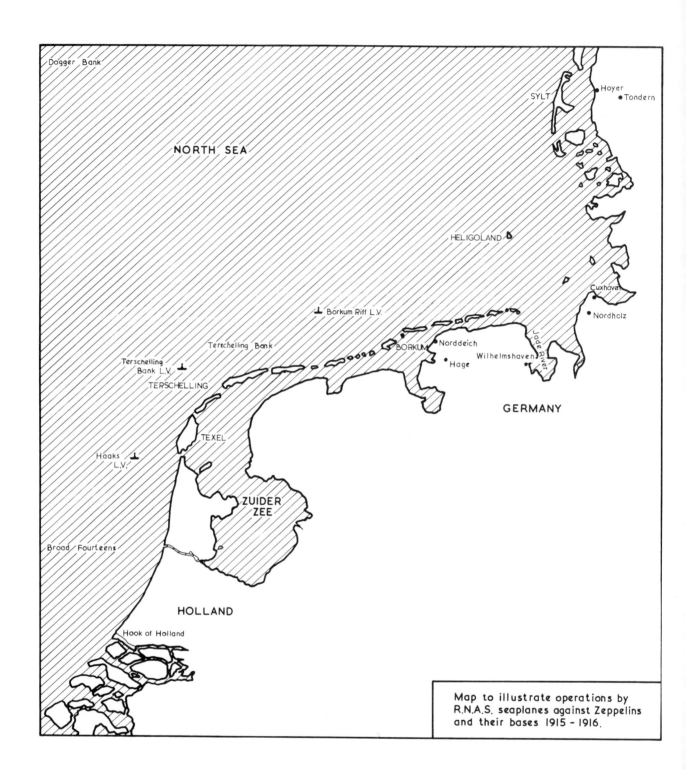

Map to illustrate operations by R.N.A.S. seaplanes against Zeppelins and their bases 1915 - 1916.

Later that day Seddon went to Felixstowe Air Station to meet Sqdn Cdr J.T. Babington who expressed surprise at the views held by *Arethusa*'s officers, and blamed the seaplane and not the pilot.

Babington maintained that the Schneider's float bottoms were too weak and that Schneiders could not work in a seaway equal to that in which a bigger seaplane could work. Babington also said that Commodore T (i.e. Commodore R. Tyrwhitt) held that Zeppelins constituted a serious menace to operations of the fleet, and that the performance of the Schneiders carried in his cruisers had been disappointing.

Babington's proposed solution to the problem of successfully intercepting the Zeppelins, and which Commodore T was willing to test, was to hoist out seaplanes in the dark, so that this operation was not observed by the enemy. The cruisers were then to retire 20 or 30 miles from the seaplanes, and by wirelessing to draw the Zeppelins over the seaplanes. As this plan would entail the seaplanes being left on the water or airborne for several hours, Babington wanted Short 184s to replace the Schneiders.

In his report to the Director of the Air Department, Seddon stated

"I feel it is not my place to discuss whether this strategy is more likely to achieve success than the Schneider strategy, but I do feel entitled to point out that when *Arethusa* encountered the Zeppelin the commencement of the operation pointed to every possibility of a successful conclusion being reached, and therefore justified this strategy."

D.A.D.'s conclusions on receiving this report were as follows:-

"I have noted Sqdn Cdr Seddon's remarks with which I fully concur. It is most unfortunate that the officer selected for working with the light cruisers has condemned the Schneider before he has ever flown one.

There are several arguments against the employment of large seaplanes in light cruisers, amongst them being the difficulty of stowage, inability to hoist in and out quickly, waste of time in starting up, and lastly the improbability of their ever making a successful attack on a Zeppelin. In the event of an enemy's squadron being met these large and valuable seaplanes would probably be destroyed and thrown overboard, owing to the danger of their presence during an action.

With the light and cheap Schneider, even if found necessary, this would not be a matter of great consideration.

The question is one of extreme difficulty to deal with to the Board, and if you decide to put it forward I propose to point out the difficulties, but adding that if required, large seaplanes can be provided when these become available in order to try the experiment.

I think a better plan would be to send a carefully worded minute to Commodore T., embodying Sqdn. Cdr. Seddon's arguments in favour of the Schneider, but if these machines are to be successfully used from the light cruisers it is absolutely essential that the pilots should believe in them.

I would go so far as to send Sqdn. Cdr. Babington back to No 1 Sqdn., and replace him by Sqdn. Cdr. Bigsworth or a younger seaplane pilot.

I think that the chances of catching a Zeppelin at sea would be far greater if Schneiders were used from armed trawlers well out to sea, such as has already been carried out by Flt. Cdr. Ireland at Yarmouth."

Unsubstantiated information does make reference to the *Arethusa* and *Aurora* operating Short 184s, but it is a fair assumption that their size presented insuperable problems with their stowage and handling on the cruisers' limited deck space, and that the experiment was not put to operational use.

And so in Home Waters, the Harwich Force cruisers each with one Schneider embarked, continued at sea during 1915 and 1916 in efforts to counter the threat posed to naval operations by the Zeppelins. Throughout the war, constant sorties were made by the Royal Navy to lay minefields in the Heligoland Bight, to hinder the exit of U-boats from their bases and to disrupt German minesweeping operations there. Zeppelins had these operations under constant surveillance, and also the movements of the Grand Fleet in the North Sea.

Lack of performance in the Schneider, or any other seaplanes of the RNAS, meant that they were no match for the Zeppelins in the air. But in their sheds at their home bases the Zeppelins were vulnerable to attacks by seaborne airpower.

No-one realised this better than Commodore R. Tyrwhitt, commanding the Harwich Force. Although the

HMS Undaunted's Schneider, 1557, is hoisted out. The seaplane was possibly camouflaged before taking part in the raid on Hoyer during March 1915. (IWM SP1141)

Cuxhaven raid of 25 December 1914 had failed to destroy any Zeppelins at their bases, the potential of air attacks from ships of the Royal Navy on such targets was quickly realised by Tyrwhitt. During March 1915 he proposed an attack by the Harwich Force on the Wireless station at Norddeich - important as a D/F station used by Zeppelins navigating over the North Sea. No seaplane carriers were available initially, so two Schneiders each were to be carried by the light cruisers *Arethusa, Penelope* and *Undaunted*. The Force was to sail on 19 March, but departure was delayed by snowstorms.

The seaplane carrier *Empress* was now available and was in company with the Force, escorted by twelve destroyers, when it left Harwich on 20 March. The take off point was reached undetected at dawn on the 21st, but a rising wind and rough seas caused the cancellation of the attack at 0500. A further attempt on the same target on 22 March was abandoned because of fog.

Another effort to attack Norddeich and the Zeppelin base under construction at Hage was made on 3 May by the Harwich Force cruisers escorting the three seaplane carriers *Engadine, Riviera* and *Ben-my-Chree*, but again high winds made the operation impracticable. A fifth attempt on 6 May was frustrated by fog.

On 11 May weather conditions were perfect, but at 1600 the force was sighted by a Zeppelin and the essential element of surprise was lost. Three seaplanes were launched in pursuit of the Zeppelin but one crashed, killing the pilot, and the other two failed to gain sufficient altitude before the Zeppelin disappeared.

Harwich Force cruisers, each with one Schneider embarked, spent much of June 1915 on anti-Zeppelin patrols in the North Sea. On 2 June Zeppelin L5 was sighted from *Arethusa* and *Undaunted*. *Arethusa* launched her Schneider but it only just managed to get off the water before being forced to return with engine failure. *Arethusa* opened fire on L5 which then made off. *Arethusa* was then attacked by a German seaplane but all three of its bombs missed her. The Force was at sea again on 19 June, but no Zeppelins were sighted during a 24 hour patrol.

By June 1915 the three seaplane carriers had been dispersed for other duties, and the Harwich Force was without a carrier until the arrival of *Vindex* in October 1915 made further strikes against the Zeppelin bases possible. Operations against Hage and another base thought to be at Hoyer were mounted on 4 December, and on 18 and 19 January 1916. Bad weather conditions caused all three attempts to be abandoned.

On 24 March 1916 *Vindex*, with five seaplanes embarked, sailed from Harwich in company with Tyrwhitt's cruisers and destroyers to attack the supposed Zeppelin base at Hoyer on the Schleswig-Holstein coast. *Undaunted's* Schneider was launched with the seaplanes from *Vindex* at dawn on 25 March in deteriorating weather conditions. By 0830 only two seaplanes had returned to their parent ships. One pilot reported attacking a factory at Hoyer, but the second pilot had made the important discovery that the Zeppelin base was in fact at Tondern. His attempt to attack it failed however when his bomb release mechanism jammed. Three seaplanes of the attacking force suffered engine failure overland and were forced down.

Like so many of the previous and subsequent attacks by naval aircraft launched from seaplane carriers and cruisers on the enemy's Zeppelin bases, this operation was a failure.

Inadequate performances of both ships and aircraft tended to strengthen the belief of many senior officers that this use of naval airpower was a waste of resources. It took the raid by seven 2F.1 Camels from the flight deck of the new aircraft carrier *Furious* on the sheds at Tondern in July 1918, during which L54 and L60 were destroyed in their sheds, to dispel these doubts at the eleventh hour.

HMS Ben-my-Chree c. March 1915, still with a temporary canvas hangar, and in the rig in which she took part in the abortive raid on Norddeich on 3rd May 1915. (FAAM)

HMT Sir John French (H262) beached at Gorleston post war. During 1915 she operated one Schneider in the North Sea on anti-Zeppelin patrols. HMT Sir John French was a sister vessel to HMT Jerico (H310) which also operated a Schneider or Baby in 1915. (K.Kent)

Flt Sub Lt H.B.Smith in the cockpit of a Schneider at Great Yarmouth in 1915. Smith was one of the pilots operating Schneiders from the trawlers Sir John French and Jerico on anti-Zeppelin patrols in 1915 and this Schneider or Baby may well be one of these embarked in these two trawlers. (FAAM)

Schneider 1568 ready for delivery to the RNAS. 1568 was briefly embarked in HMT Sir John French for anti-Zeppelin patrols during September 1915.   (G.S.Leslie/ J.M.Bruce collection)

HMS Halcyon, which operated a Baby on patrols in the North Sea during 1917. (FAAM)

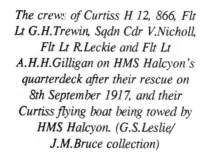

The crews of Curtiss H 12, 866, Flt Lt G.H.Trewin, Sqdn Cdr V.Nicholl, Flt Lt R.Leckie and Flt Lt A.H.H.Gilligan on HMS Halcyon's quarterdeck after their rescue on 8th September 1917, and their Curtiss flying boat being towed by HMS Halcyon. (G.S.Leslie/ J.M.Bruce collection)

HMS Halcyon's Baby with its pilot, Flt Sub Lt H.B.Smith. (FAAM)

Probably a pre-1914 photograph of HMS Halcyon wearing a light coloured paint scheme, and possibly taken at Yarmouth from where she embarked a Baby seaplane in 1917. (A.K.Vicary)

The torpedo gunboat Dryad, a sister ship to Halcyon, also carried a Baby abaft her after 4.7-inch gun during June and July 1917. (A.K.Vicary)

Lt L.V.Marsh RNR, commanding HMS Brocklesby, and Flt Lt E.L.Pulling RNAS standing on deck in front of the ship's Schneider 3736, during 1916. (FAAM)

Schneider 3736 comes alongside HMS Brocklesby for hoisting in 1916. (FAAM)

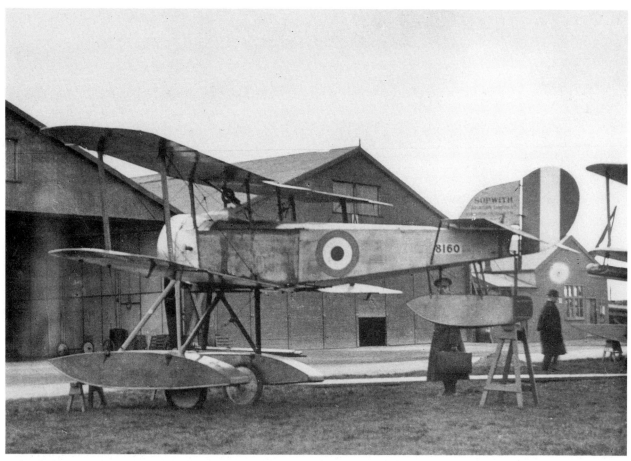

Baby, 8160, was operated by HMS Brocklesby on anti-Zeppelin patrol in the North Sea during late 1916. The mounting of a Lewis gun on a centre section strut is noteworthy. (G.S.Leslie/J.M.Bruce collection)

HMS Killingholme's port side in April 1916 with one Schneider and one Baby on deck, shortly after commissioning. Her seaplane handling derricks and armament are apparent. (FAAM)

Flt Lt G.H.Bittles in the cockpit of his Schneider at Great Yarmouth in 1916. Bittles flew many anti-Zeppelin patrols in Babies and Schneiders operated by paddle-steamers and trawlers during 1915 and 1916. (FAAM)

Damage to HMS Killingholme's port paddle box sustained on the night of 28th April 1916 after striking a mine while on anti-Zeppelin patrol off the Dogger bank. A Baby is seen stowed on her wrecked upper deck. (IWM SP3043)

Princess Victoria postwar as a passenger ferry in the livery of the Portpatrick and Wigtownshire Railways. As HMS Princess Victoria she was employed as a Seaplane tender by the RNAS in 1915. (NMM P21002)

HMS Cleethorpes photographed in 1918 after conversion to a paddle minesweeper. A former Humber ferry, she may have operated one Schneider on anti-Zeppelin patrols in the North Sea during 1916. (IWM SP2087)

HMS Eridge as a paddle minesweeper in 1916. It was the intention to embark two Schneiders in each of the twenty-four ships of this class for anti-Zeppelin patrols. Only two ships, HMS Eridge and HMS Melton, were fitted with seaplane-handling derricks, and it is unlikely that their seaplanes were ever used operationally. (NMM G5377)

Three views of Short S.74 818 stowed to port of HMS Aurora's aft searchlight platform March 1915. The difficulty of handling such a large seaplane with only a makeshift derrick rigged to a boat davit is apparent.
(NMM N22826 - 22828)

CHAPTER VII

Early operations by *Anne*'s and *Raven II* s seaplanes, East Mediterranean January-April 1915

At Port Said, in August 1914, two German merchant vessels had been seized as prizes - SS *Aenne Rickmers* and SS *Rabenfels*. Their story as seaplane carriers however begins with a soldier, Capt L.B. Weldon of the Dublin Fusiliers.

After 14 years service in the Survey Department of the Egyptian Government, Weldon had just returned to England when war broke out. His stay was brief because in September 1914 he received a cable recalling him to Egypt. General Sir John Maxwell, then GOC in Egypt had applied for someone to act as Map Officer, and Weldon had been recommended for the post. Granted the temporary rank of Captain, he was attached to General Staff Intelligence for the last three months of 1914. But towards the end of December he was informed that he was to undertake the job of Intelligence Officer, Liaison Officer and Officer Commanding a ship which had just been taken over by General Maxwell, and in which it was proposed to place two French seaplanes.

On arrival at Port Said on 16 January, Weldon was told by Col Elgood, the Base Commandant, that in addition to the duties mentioned above, he was required to land Agents from the sea behind the Turkish lines in the Eastern Mediterranean. For this purpose he was to be lent a small steam launch, five naval ratings and six Royal Marines. But to land the agents, a surf boat and native crew to man it was needed, and Weldon spent the rest of the 16th recruiting four Syrian-Christian boatmen - at a price.

Weldon joined SS *Aenne Rickmers* on 17 January. Her complement consisted of the skipper Gaskell, Bishop the chief engineer, and the naval ratings and marines who were all English. The pilots and mechanics were French - from L'Aviation Maritime Française, commanded by Capt de Lescaille in the seaplane carrier *Foudre*. The mates and crew were Greek, one of the engineers was Maltese and Weldon himself was Irish. Fortunately, Gaskell, who had formerly been skipper of the SS *Milo* engaged on the Syrian coastal trade, was able to speak Greek.

Aenne Rickmers flew the Red Ensign, and the original cargo of baulks of timber and antimony ore, worth £250,000, was still on board as ballast. To complete the story of the British genius for improvisation in time of war, the ship was run by the Ports and Lights Administration of the Egyptian Government, although still the responsibility of General Maxwell, who had guaranteed the safety of the cargo!

The two seaplanes embarked were Nieuport VIs of L'Aviation Maritime Française. The unit had left France on 2 September 1914 aboard the merchantman *Louis Fraissinet* bound for Bizerta. One flight was used over Montenegro during October and November 1914 as ''Détachment d'Aviation Maritime du Monténégro''. These machines were put at the disposal of the Admiralty in December by Admiral Boué de Lapeyrère and ferried to Port Said in the French seaplane carrier *Foudre*. Known as Escadrille Nieuport, Suez, its strength was five seaplanes augmented in January 1915 by a further three machines. On board *Aenne Rickmers* the two seaplanes were stowed on the hatch covers on the after well deck, and were protected from the elements by canvas ''hangars''.

Capt L.B.Weldon, Dublin Fusiliers, Intelligence Officer and Commanding Officer of HMFA Aenne Rickmers 1915. (via RCC)

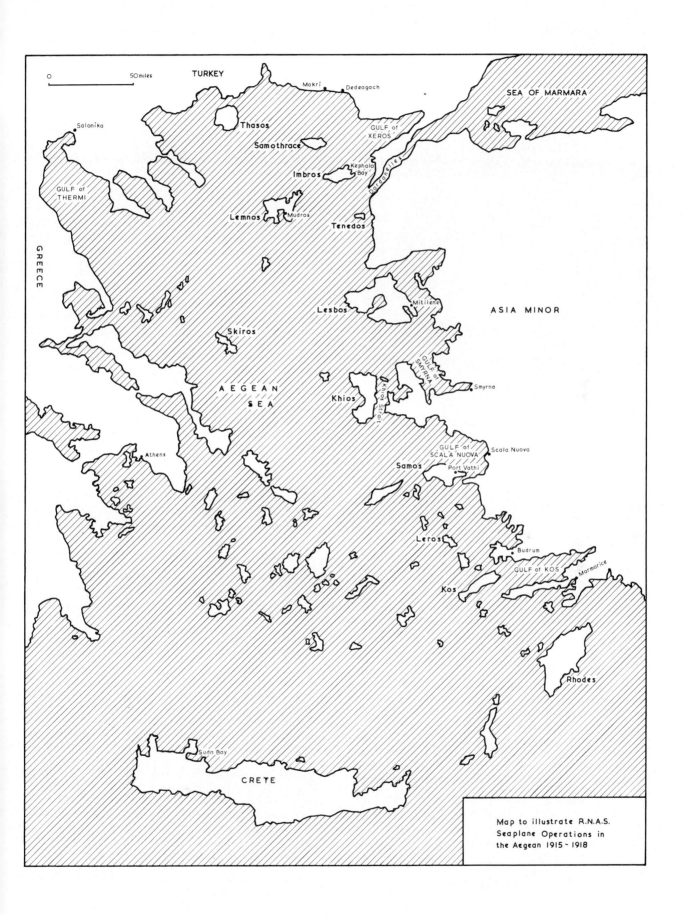

Map to illustrate R.N.A.S.
Seaplane Operations in
the Aegean 1915~1918

The portrait of Aenne Rickmers, daughter of the owner of the German shipping company Rickmers, which hung in the saloon of HMFA Aenne Rickmers throughout her service as a seaplane carrier. (via RCC)

SS *Rabenfels* was equipped and crewed in similar fashion shortly after *Aenne Rickmers*, but with Capt R.E. Todd RAMC chosen to discharge the same duties accepted by Capt. Weldon.

Both ships were then accorded the prefix SS at the commencement of their service, *Aenne Rickmers* from 18 January 1915 to 8 February 1915 and *Rabenfels* for approximately the same period. Thereafter they were designated HMFA until June 1915 when they were respectively re-named HMS *Anne* and HMS *Raven II* wearing the White Ensign. At this time too Lt J. Kerr RNR took command of *Anne*, and Lt J. Jenkins RNR commanded *Raven II*, retaining their commands until both ships were decommissioned. For the purpose of the narrative they will be referred to throughout as HM Ships *Anne* and *Raven II*.

All the Nieuport VI seaplanes embarked bore French markings and French serial numbers, ranging from N11 to N23 and latterly NB.1 and NB.2. Since no British serials were ever allocated to these machines, the French serials will be used when referring to particular machines.

Anne's second cruise commenced at 0100 on 18 January when she sailed from Port Said under the command of Capt. Weldon, with Gaskell responsible for handling the ship. Arriving off El Arish at 1200 on the 18th, Nieuport VI N16 crewed by Lt de Saizieu and Capt J.R. Herbert was hoisted out for a reconnaissance of Kosseima. Petty Officer Grall and Capt R.E. Todd RAMC in N11 then carried out a reconnaissance of El Arish, Rafa, Kahn Yunis and Gaza. After both seaplanes returned and had been hoisted on board, *Anne* stood out to sea for the night, and off Gaza on the 19th launched a seaplane. On their return the crew reported considerable movement of enemy troops along the Beersheba to Hebron road. About midnight on 19/20 January *Anne* stood in to about three miles from the shore for the purpose of landing an Agent. Here the steam launch to tow the surf boat was hoisted out, and Weldon, two of his Syrians and the Agent embarked in the surf boat. When close to the beach the tow was slipped and the Agent was successfully landed.

Both seaplanes were launched off Gaza on the 20th for further reconnaissances of El Arish and Lifan, and at 2300 *Anne* closed the coast again to recover the Agent. The prearranged light signal from the Agent was seen from *Anne* and Weldon was landed on the beach. But the man had disappeared - in fact he had been captured by Turkish coastguards - and after Weldon had returned on board *Anne* she stood out to sea again.

From a position eight miles from the coast at El Arish, N16 with de Saizieu and Herbert on board took off at 1431, overflying the town at 4,500 feet and landing close to *Anne* at 1615. The estimated number of Turkish troops at El Arish, about 1,000, appeared not to have altered since *Anne*'s first reconnaissance sortie of 1 January.

Anne returned to Port Said on 23 January, but sailed from there again at 2200 on the 25th with seaplanes N11 and N15 embarked, arriving off El Arish on the morning of the 26th. Heavy seas and low cloud prevented any flying on the 26th, as did thick fog on the forenoon of the 27th. However this eventually lifted and at 1400 N15 was hoisted out for a reconnaissance of El Arish, but failed to get off the water. N11 then managed to take off but, unable to gain sufficient altitude, had to return to the ship.

A signal from *Swiftsure* on the 28th reported that a seaplane despatched from Port Said on the 27th for a reconnaissance of Bir El Abd was now overdue, and *Anne* was requested to search for it. Weldon gave orders for the ship to cruise westwards keeping close inshore. The seaplane N14 was found near El Gralls at noon with engine "broken" and one float damaged, but abandoned and riding well on a rough sea. *Anne* launched a boat, towed the seaplane alongside and hoisted it on board. The pilot's helmet and the observer's map and notes were still there. From the latter it was learned that after flying to Kantara and running into fog they had decided to return to Port Said, but owing to engine trouble a landing on Lake Bardawil was necessary. Taking off again from here the seaplane had obviously forced landed in the sea and the crew, consisting of Lt Partridge of the Ceylon Rifles and a French naval rating, had waded ashore to try to reach Port Said on foot. They had almost reached their goal when they ran into one of our own posts, manned by Indian troops, and were fired at and both killed.

In the early days *Anne*'s time at sea was not without such risks either. When challenged by another ship one dark night, Weldon at first thought it inadvisable to reply with his ship's name as they were close inshore and about to land an Agent. Fortunately he changed his mind, for the other ship was the cruiser *Philomel* which was about to open fire.

Anne next sailed from Port Said at 0600 on 1 February 1915 with two seaplanes embarked. Off Gaza at 2300 she sent her launch ashore to land an Agent, and at 0400 on the 2nd left for El Arish. At 1100 a seaplane crewed by Petty Officer Trouillet and Lt Sir R. Paul was launched for a reconnaissance of El Auja. Unable to climb above 1,950 feet, the seaplane had to return to the ship. The second seaplane, crewed by Petty Officer Grall and Lieut Hillas, armed with bombs and pamphlets

for a flight over El Arish was now launched, but the 100 hp Gnôme engine caught fire and one wing was slightly damaged. The first seaplane then took off again and crewed by Trouillet and Hillas climbed to 4000 feet, but owing to a strong easterly wind could make little headway and was forced to return to the ship. The Nieuport's maximum speed in ideal conditions was only 68 mph.

Unfavourable weather prevented any flying, or the recovery of the Agent, from the 3rd to the 5th, but Trouillet and Paul were airborne at 0910 on the 6th for a flight to El Auja, returning short of fuel at 1208. Grall and Hillas took up the other seaplane for a reconnaissance of El Arish, but heavy rain and mist caused an early return, and at 1500 *Anne* proceeded to Gaza to pick up the Agent.

Grall and Paul flew a reconnaissance to Beersheba and Hebron on 7 February. Six hundred tents and approximately 20,000 troops were seen at Beersheba, and working parties were observed laying a tarmacadam road between Beersheba and Hebron.

Anne closed the coast to within one-and-a-half miles at 2300 and waited until 0130 on 8 February for a pre-arranged signal from the Agent, but no signal was received. An attempt at a reconnaissance of El Auja by Trouillet and Paul in the forenoon of the 8th had to be abandoned, heavy swell damaging a float on take off. *Raven II* was met off Gaza on 8 February, maps and intelligence reports were transferred to her, and *Anne*

Nieuport VI seaplane, N14, found abandoned off El Gralls on 28th January 1915 by HMFA Aenne Rickmers. Hoisted on board and subsequently operated by the ship until lost on 10th October 1915. (via RCC)

*Lt Gaskell MN, skipper of HMFA Aenne Rickmers
January 1915 to June 1915. (via RCC)*

sailed for Port Said at 1300.

   Anne sailed from Port Said again at 2215 on 24
February, on what was to be her last sortie for several
months, with two Nieuports, N15 and N17, their pilots
Destrem and Grall and three observers Capt R.E. Todd
and Lts Sir R. Paul and K.L. Williams.

   Anne met *Raven II* off El Arish on the 25th and
anchored off the Wadi Gaza for the night. Destrem and
Paul took off for a reconnaissance of Beersheba and
Hebron next morning but after climbing to 2,400 feet
were obliged to return to the ship after 37 minutes
because of thick cloud cover overland. Bad weather
prevented any flying until the afternoon of 28 February
when Grall and Todd attempted a reconnaissance of
Jaffa. The Nieuport failed to struggle above 500 feet
however and returned to the ship five minutes before a
gale sprang up. *Raven II* signalled she was returning to
Port Said. *Anne* remained at anchor off Gaza on 1
March, but was forced to weigh anchor on the 2nd and
put out to sea, as the gale increased in violence. A signal
from SNO Port Said on 3 March enquired of *Anne*'s
coal stock, to which she replied 460 tons. A second

signal from SNO Port Said then ordered *Anne* to
proceed to a rendezvous in the Gulf of Smyrna,
provided both her seaplanes were on board and in order.

   Weldon replied that one seaplane had a broken float
stay, but at very least he had one operational seaplane,
and that to save time he was proceeding immediately to
the rendezvous.

   The Greek crew became nervous about where they
were sailing to, and as the captain thought they might
damage the seaplanes, in the hopes of forcing the ship to
return to Port Said armed sentries were placed over the
seaplanes. *Anne* attained her maximum speed of 10
knots in spite of head winds on 4 March, but heavy
weather next day reduced her to 7 knots.

   Anne arrived off the Gulf of Smyrna at 1000 on 6
March and received an order from *Swiftsure* to steam in
towards Smyrna harbour where she closed with
Euryalus, Triumph and *Swiftsure* at 1230 while they
were bombarding the forts.

   The object of these operations was to prevent the
use of Smyrna by the enemy as a submarine base to
attack the Allied fleet at the Dardanelles.

   After the bombardment ceased in the evening of 6
March Capt. Weldon took his aircrew across to *Euryalus*
so that Admiral Sir R. Peirse could explain to them what
tasks he wanted the seaplanes to perform. These were to
report on the damage done to the forts by the two
previous days' bombardment, and to find out the
position of two ships sunk across the harbour entrance
and whether they blocked the entrance.

   Anne's aircrew again went aboard *Euryalus* while
she bombarded the forts next morning, so that they
could see the position of the forts, and returned by
trawler to *Anne* at noon. Destrem and Paul made a flight
that afternoon, but were unable to gain sufficient altitude
for a reconnaissance owing to strong gusts of wind
blowing down the valley between the mountains. Bad
weather prevented any flying on the 8th, but the
bombardment continued and was augmented by fire
from the Russian cruiser *Askold*'s guns. *Triumph*
bombarded the enemy's searchlights that night to
prevent them playing on the minefield, which four of
our trawlers were sweeping under cover of darkness.

   Destrem and Paul succeeded in taking off at 1415 on
9 March, and although the Nieuport refused to climb
above 2,500 feet they flew over the sunken ships in the
harbour mouth and reported two clear channels, suitable
only for small vessels, between the two ships and
between one ship and the shore. They also saw that
three guns in one of the forts had been put out of action.
Upon their return to *Anne*, Capt Weldon and Lt Paul
proceeded in *Anne*'s launch, to report the results of the
reconnaissance, on board *Euryalus*. On the way they
intercepted a shore boat flying a white flag and
containing the American Consul-General and the envoy

of the Vali of Smyrna. These two were taken aboard the flagship where a general truce was arranged until 1000 on 11 March, to give the enemy time to accede to our demands to block the port, and deny its use as a submarine base.

Meanwhile, during the night of 8 March the Turkish TBD *Demir Hissar*, commanded by the German Lt Cdr von Freigs, had left the Dardanelles for an attack on shipping at Tenedos, but encountering a destroyer patrol, had run into the Gulf of Smyrna. Here on the night of the 9th she fired two torpedoes at two ships - probably *Euryalus* and *Swiftsure* - which both missed. She then ran out of the Gulf and hid in Khios Strait during daylight hours of 10 March.

There were no flights by *Anne*'s seaplanes on 10 March while the truce was in force. All ships were normally darkened at night, but this was relaxed until the expiry of the truce.

Anne lay with the rest of Admiral Peirse's squadron, the outermost ship, under the lee of Chustan Island during the night of 10-11 March. Weldon turned in at 2300 only to be rudely awoken at 0205 by a terrific explosion which pitched him from his bunk, flinging him first to the deckhead and then to the deck. Getting into trousers and coat, for the weather was bitterly cold, he found the bridge deserted. But down on the bridge deck was the 23-stone Gaskell, clad only in a short nightshirt and shouting "We're sinking, we're sinking. Get the boats out." *Anne*'s Royal Marines had had previous orders in such an eventuality to stand by the boats with their arms. They obeyed orders as quickly as possible, but the gallant Greek crew - headed by their Greek officers - had beaten everyone to the boats.

Gaskell hailed the boat in which was the First Officer and told him to stand by the ship, but he pulled towards the warships although the boat, which could have held forty, contained only himself and three other Greeks. In their hasty exit the crew had also taken nearly all the available lifebelts. It was pitch dark and the ship was badly down by the head. All the crew had bolted with the exception of the Maltese engineer - he was caught

by Bishop and put back forcibly into the engine room to get steam on the winch. This was needed to lower five wounded men from the bombarding squadron who had been transferred to *Anne* in the charge of Surgeon Lt Patterson on 6 March. The legs were cut from their cots, and they were lowered into the first available boat to come alongside, and were taken on board *Euryalus*.

Bishop and Paul meanwhile sounded the No 1 hold and found 16 feet of water in it. On returning to the bridge Weldon ordered boy signaller Sloman to signal by lamp to the warships that *Anne* had been mined or torpedoed and required assistance. *Euryalus* replied "Are you in danger of sinking?" To Weldon it looked very like it so he signalled "Probably".

Euryalus soon sent across a cutter to take off all of *Anne*'s remaining ship's company with the exception of seven men to be left to stand by the ship. Lt Destrem was one of those to be taken off, but he refused to leave his seaplanes. In Weldon's words

"We all stood about on deck with our ankles in water, wondering when the final plunge was coming, till I suggested it would be drier if we adjourned to the saloon. Naturally we were rather excited and all complained of exceedingly dry mouths. Someone suggested that a drink would not be amiss, but the steward had bolted with the keys. Luckily I remembered that I had one bottle of Irish whiskey in my cabin and had been keeping it

A group photograph taken on board HMFA Aenne Rickmers (later HMS Anne) c. January 1915. Standing are 2nd left Lt Gaskell MN the ship's master, 3rd left probably Petty Officer Grall a French seaplane pilot, 5th left Capt J.R.Herbert and 7th left Capt R.E.Todd who both flew as observers in the Nieuport Seaplanes, and 6th left Lt de Saizieu the other French pilot. Others in the group include British and French naval ratings, Royal Marines, French air mechanics, Syrian boatmen and Greek engine room staff. (via RCC)

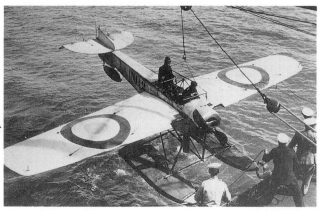

Sequence of four photographs showing HMS Anne's Nieuport VI, NB2, taxying alongside and being hoisted inboard c. February / March 1916. The difficulties of handling non-folding seaplanes on HMS Anne's after deck are well illustrated in the final photograph.
(G.S.Leslie/J.M.Bruce collection)

for St Patrick's Day. Whilst we were drinking I happened to glance at the door and saw a marine standing outside. It was my Corporal Shrimpton. I asked him why he had not obeyed my order and gone away in the last boat. Thereupon he merely saluted and said "The Marines never desert their Officers, Sir", so although annoyed I promptly forgave him and brought him out a whiskey".

The ship although down by the head was not settling any deeper. The damage had been caused on the starboard side in No 1 hold which contained baulks of timber. No 2 hold contained antimony ore which served to buttress the bulkhead between Nos 1 and 2 holds, and if the bulkhead held there was a good chance that *Anne* would remain afloat.

The other warships of the squadron had meanwhile slipped their cables and proceeded to sea, *Euryalus* leaving her cutter with a Sub Lt in charge to stand by *Anne* through the night. The Sub was invited on board for a drink before the bottle was emptied.

The squadron returned to Chustan Island at 0630 on the 11th. *Swiftsure*'s launch attempted to recover *Anne*'s

boats, cast adrift by the panicky Greek crew, which had drifted onshore. Rifle fire from the shore, however, wounded the Sub Lt in charge and two seamen, and the attempt had to be abandoned. It transpired that the fleeing Greeks had rowed alongside *Euryalus* imploring to be saved. When Cdr. Marriott asked them where the five wounded ratings were, and received the reply that they were still in *Anne*, he promptly knocked the First Officer down.

Euryalus sent a working party on board *Anne* and rigged a collision mat over the hole in her bows. The hole in *Anne*'s No 1 hold had been caused by a torpedo fired from *Demir Hissar*. Unaware of the truce in force at Smyrna, she had got up her reserve torpedo while hidden in Khios Strait, and ran into the anchorage at Chustan Island, where she fired her torpedo at the outermost ship of Admiral Peirse's squadron, which hit *Anne* on her starboard side forward.

Capt Weldon's report on *Anne*'s damage concluded by saying

"I do not think it is within my province to mention the behaviour of anybody on board, but if I am allowed I would like to mention that all the Frenchmen and all the Englishmen

HMFA Aenne Rickmers (later commissioned into RN as HMS Anne) beached at Mudros in March 1915 after being torpedoed by the Turkish TBD Demir Hissar in the Gulf of Smyrna during the night of 9th March 1915. The hole in the starboard side of No.1 hold is visible above the stern of the whaler alongside the ship. (A.K.Vicary)

Close-up of the damage inflicted by a torpedo fired by the Turkish TBD Demir Hissar at HMFA Aenne Rickmers (later HMS Anne) on the night of 11th March 1915. (FAAM)

behaved as one would expect. I would like to mention the conduct of the Chief Engineer, Mr Bishop, who prevented one of his engineers from deserting, shut him in, and made him get steam on the winches, thereby making it possible to lower the wounded. I would especially like to mention the signalman (lent from *Euryalus*) Sloman - a boy of 17 years - who stayed on the bridge and sent and received signals while the crew was in a state of panic''.

After the working party had left *Anne* she received orders to proceed to Lemnos, escorted by *Swiftsure*. The Greek crew were sent back on board, but were not allowed to take a watch or to have anything to do with the navigation of the ship. *Anne* butted into a head wind and heavy sea through the bitterly cold night of 11-12 March, steering very badly, and at 1300 on the 12th anchored close to *Swiftsure* in Mudros harbour. After all the dangers she had

overcome, *Anne*'s only welcome was a signal ordering her to lower the Blue Ensign she was inexplicably wearing and to hoist the Red Ensign in its place!

Mudros harbour at this time was the assembly point for the Dardanelles landings. The harbour was full of shipping, and here for the next two months *Anne* lay awaiting temporary repairs to enable her to proceed to Alexandria for dry docking.

During a gale in late March Gaskell thought it advisable to drop another anchor. On hearing the cable rattling through the hawse pipe the gallant Greek crew tumbled out on deck, thinking the ship had again been torpedoed. Mercifully they were all paid off a few days later.

A salvage ship from Malta was now expected to effect temporary repairs to *Anne*, but her arrival coincided with the mining of the battle cruiser *Inflexible* on 19 March, necessitating *Anne*'s repairs being delayed.

At this time *Raven II* arrived at Mudros with orders to embark *Anne*'s two seaplanes. Unfortunately Gaskell and Bishop had gone ashore in *Anne*'s launch and so the only means of transferring the seaplanes was via a line between the two ships - a lengthy process with a strong wind blowing. Wanting to sail in a hurry, de Lescaille who was in charge of the transfer to *Raven II* was enraged when Gaskell returned in *Anne*'s launch just as the job was finished. As he was being rowed back to

Lt Sir R.Paul standing in the hole made by a torpedo from the Turkish TBD Demir Hissar in the starboard side of Aenne Rickmers No.1 hold, March 1915. (via RCC)

Raven II he stood up in the boat and kept calling out in very broken English to Gaskell "You are a very bad captain"!

On the morning of 6 April while Weldon was just turning out of his bunk the ship gave a couple of shivers. A gale was blowing and both *Anne*'s cables had parted. A signal "Not Under Control" was hoisted, and after drifting among the vessels cramming the harbour, *Anne* eventually ran aground in a little bay where she remained fast. Immediately afterwards *Anne* received a signal from the flagship to say that the ship was to remain where she was. Since the only men on board *Anne* were Weldon, Gaskell, Bishop, the cook and the steward the order was easy to obey. With the best will in the world five men could hardly have pushed *Anne* from the shore!

From 19 April to 4 May Weldon embarked in the cruiser *Euryalus* and witnessed the carnage of the Gallipoli landings, while *Anne* still lay at Mudros. On 4 May he was instructed to return to Egypt with *Anne*, and took passage in SS *Dago* sailing that day for Mudros, arriving at dawn on 5 May.

Anne was at last patched up by a working party from the repair ship *Reliance* and Weldon was informed that the captain and crew of the *River Clyde*, which had landed 2,000 men on V beach at Gallipoli, were to be transferred to *Anne*.

Lt J. Kerr RNR took command of *Anne* on 10 May. A Scot from the Isle of Arran, he could speak Gaelic, and when excited always spoke with an appalling American accent. He had been at sea since the age of 13 and been skipper of square-rigged ships, salvage vessels and tramp steamers. In addition he had served for a short time in the American cavalry! The new crew came on board at 0830 on 12 May - mostly Scandinavians but also an Irishman and an Australian. The officers and engineers were Scots.

At 1030 that morning a tug towed *Anne* off the beach, and at 1100 on 14 May she sailed for Alexandria in company with a hospital ship proceeding to Malta. A big swell was running on the 15th and *Anne* soon began to take in water through her patch. Two tugs came out to tow her into Alexandria next morning as she had some 600 tons of water in No 1 hold. Here for the next month *Anne* was repaired in dry dock.

A view, looking forward, of Aenne Rickmer's after welldeck showing the canvas coverings over her two Nieuport seapolanes. Off the port bow lies the Russian cruiser Askold, known to the Royal Navy as "the packet of Woodbines" from her five funnels. It is likely that this photograph was taken early March 1915 in the Gulf of Smyrna shortly before Aenne Rickmers was torpedoed. (Collection J-P. Dubois)

CHAPTER VIII

Operations by *Raven II*'s seaplanes April-July 1915

For the next month *Raven II* was the only seaplane carrier operating in the Eastern Mediterranean, *Ben-my-Chree* being fully occupied in the Aegean between June 1915 until January 1916.

Raven II sailed from Port Said at midnight on 7 April 1915 for a reconnaissance of El Arish. Weather conditions were unsuitable for flying on the 8th and 9th. A Cingalese fireman was treated for gastritis on the 9th "which was probably alcoholic in origin"! Lt Cintré and Lt Paul flew a reconnaissance to El Sirr in the forenoon of the 10th, and Cintré and Capt. Todd flew to El Arish and Gaza that afternoon.

Raven II was off Gaza on 11 April and at 0630 her Nieuport VI, N15, was hoisted out, crewed by Lt Cintré and Lt Paul for a reconnaissance of Beersheba. When 15 miles from the coast on the return flight the engine revs fell to 1000 and their altitude to only 650 feet. As they crossed the coast at 250 feet they came under small arms fire but landed safely and were hoisted inboard.

The French battleship *St.Louis* arrived off Gaza at 0930 on the 11th and Cintré and Todd took off to spot the fall of shot from the battleship's 12-inch and 5.5-inch guns on Turkish positions, but engine trouble entailed curtailment of the flight. Twelve bottles, each containing six propaganda leaflets, were then thrown overboard from the ship in the hope of their reaching the enemy. The bottles had doubtless previously contained something more exciting than pamphlets. Cintré and Todd were airborne twice on 12 April to spot for the fire of *St.Louis* on camps at Gaza, but apparently "no harm was done to the camps". *Raven II* then proceeded back to Port Said.

Raven II next sailed from Port Said during the night of 15-16 April and rendezvoused with *St.Louis* off El Arish at 0700 on the 16th. Petty Officer Grall and Lt Paul in Nieuport N11 took off at 0928 to spot the fall of shot from *St.Louis* onto the tented camp and town of El Arish. *St.Louis* opened fire at 0954 and during the day put some 200 rounds of 5.5-inch and 3.9-inch shells into these two targets and four batteries of field guns. These batteries opened heavily on both *St.Louis* and the Nieuport but caused no casualties. N11 now undertook a detailed reconnaissance. Most of the tents at Gaza had been removed since the last flight. The Wadi El Hesi was seen to be crossed by a three-arch masonry bridge

HMS Raven II with steam up c.1915/16. Visible are her canvas hangars for seaplane stowage on both foredeck and after welldeck. Astern of her lies probably the French armoured cruiser Jeanne d'Arc. (Collection J-P. Dubois)

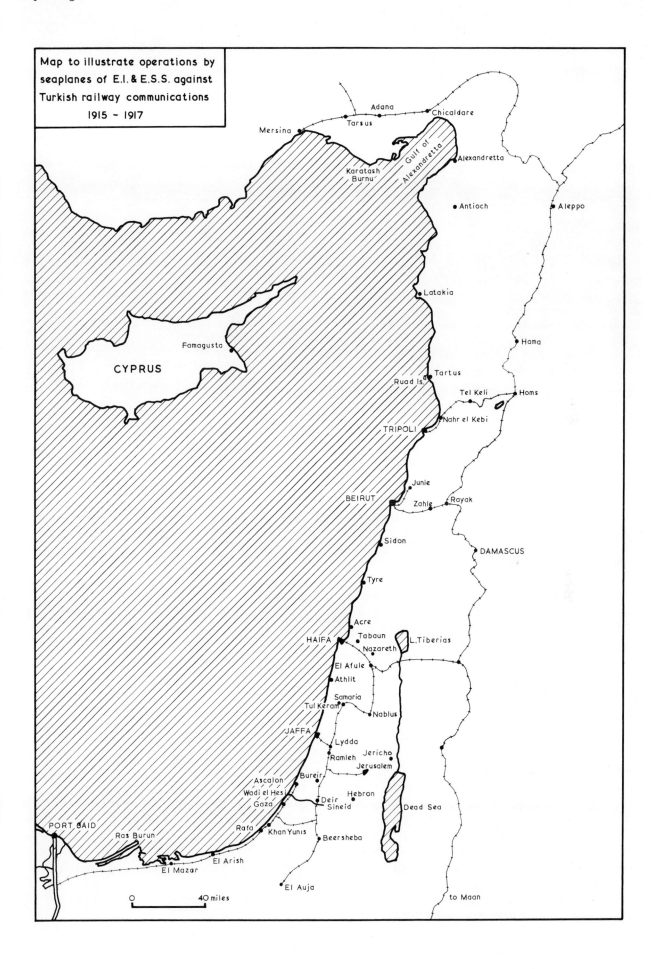

Map to illustrate operations by
seaplanes of E.I. & E.S.S. against
Turkish railway communications
1915 - 1917

N16, Nieuport VI seaplane being salved. The original caption states "Off Gaza 13 February 1915". However at 0800 on 21 May 1915 N16 was hoisted out from Raven II of Gaza and "seaplane after rising a few metres from the water appeared to lose speed and the pilot lost control. The seaplane fell in the water and damaged right wing". Possibly this is the incident depicted. Certainly N16 was returned to service and was operated by both RIMS Hardinge in the Red Sea during June 1915 and HMS Anne in the Eastern Mediterranean during August 1915. (Collection J-P. Dubois)

on the Gaza to Jaffa road, but no railway bridge was seen here. The Nahr Sukereir was similarly crossed on the same road, but again there was no railway bridge. Two large camps were found three miles SW of Ramleh, where the seaplane was fired on. No engines or tracks were seen on the line between Ramleh and Ludd. To the north of Ludd a new line branched off the existing track going due north and running parallel to the coast about eight miles inland. Bridges were necessary at two points but their construction had not started.

As petrol was now running short Grall turned towards the coast and flew over Jaffa where a large dump of square stone blocks - possibly for the construction of railway bridges - was visible. Propaganda leaflets were dropped here as they had been also at Ramleh and Ludd. N11 landed close to *Raven II* at 1115 and was hoisted on board.

Raven II was off Gaza at 0630 on 17 April, but a heavy swell prevented any flying in the forenoon. Nieuport N11 crewed by Grall and Todd took off at 1435 to direct the fire of *St.Louis* onto the Gaza camps. None of the Nieuports was equipped with W/T so that communication with the bombarding ships had to be by visual means. On this occasion "smoke balls" were

dropped by the seaplanes to mark the fall of shot. A second flight later that day had to be called off because of rough seas.

One spotting flight of two hours was possible on the 18th, by which time the camps had been pretty well ploughed up by shell fire. Grall and Paul flew a reconnaissance over Gaza, Jaffa, Ludd and Ramleh on 19 April, and after recovering her seaplane *Raven II* returned to Port Said.

Raven II's stay at Port Said was brief - sufficient only to coal ship and to embark two fresh Nieuports, N18 and N20. She sailed at 1900 on the 20th having onboard Lt Cintré and four French mechanics, Todd and Paul as observers, Mr Jackson of the Sudan Civil Service as passenger and interpreter, and the Agent Ibrahim Sayid. Cyprus was passed at 1730 on the 21st, and at 0530 on the 22nd *Raven II* met the French cruisers *D'Estrèes* and *D'Entrecasteaux* off Mersina. Rough seas, heavy clouds on the mountain sides and a steadily falling barometer made flying impossible on 22 and 23 April.

A flight over Mersina, Tarsus and Adana by Cintré and Todd was made on the 24th. After recovering her seaplane *Raven II* proceeded to Alexandretta where the

Agent, with £5 sterling, was put aboard *D'Estrées* for Ruad Island.

On the 25th Cintré and Paul flew a reconnaissance in N18 over Topra Kalle, Osmaniah and Port Ayas under anti-aircraft fire. The railway as far as Hamidri was impossible to reconnoitre owing to the difficulty of air currents among the mountains. Cintré and Todd attempted a reconnaissance of the Alexandretta coastline later on the 25th, but engine failure forced an early return to the ship. Cintré and Paul flew over Hamidri, Chicaldere and Missis on the 26th, and on landing the Nieuport came under rifle fire from the shore. After recovering her seaplane *Raven II* sailed for Alexandretta, arriving 1500. A second reconnaissance of Alexandretta was contemplated but cancelled because of worsening weather. A signal from GOC Egypt received in *Raven II* on the 27th ordered a further reconnaissance between Mersina and Adana. Flying was impossible however so *D'Entrecasteaux*'s wardroom entertained *Raven II*'s officers to dinner that evening. "A very cheery evening was spent" according to Capt. Todd, *Raven II*'s Intelligence Officer.

Cintré and Paul made a coastal reconnaissance between Alexandretta and Durtyol on 28 April, having to make a hurried descent after the petrol feed pipe sheared. Fortunately *D'Entrecasteaux* had followed the seaplane up the coast, because it was drifting on shore and was under small arms fire. The cruiser's launch soon had it in tow back to *Raven II* however, and it was safely hoisted aboard. *Raven II* sailed for Mersina at 2000 followed later by *D'Entrecasteaux* and both arrived off Mersina at 0600 on 29 April, where Cintré and Todd flew over Tarsus and Adana. Both ships then steamed for Alexandretta, arriving 1700. At midnight *D'Entrecasteaux* received a signal recalling her to Port Said. Since this would leave *Raven II* without escort off a hostile coast she too proceeded to Port Said on the 30th.

Raven II next sailed from Port Said at 2200 on 19 May with Nieuports N16 and N18 embarked, and an Agent to be landed near Haifa. A reconnaissance of El Arish was flown between 0722 and 0832 on the 20th and leaflets were dropped over the town by N18. Nieuport N16 took off at 0800 on the 21st but shortly after getting airborne suffered engine failure and went in, damaging the starboard wing. Neither pilot nor observer were hurt and the seaplane was recovered. At 1700 a two-masted Syrian schooner was intercepted and searched south of Gaza. Apart from sums of money, she carried no cargo, so she was released to proceed to Jaffa after propaganda leaflets had been concealed in her hold.

A reconnaissance of Beersheba and Gaza by N18 was accomplished in good weather conditions on 22 May. Three schooners carrying timber to Gaza were intercepted and searched in the forenoon of the 22nd but

were released. A reconnaissance and bomb dropping mission was flown over Jaffa, Ludd and Ramleh in the forenoon of the 23rd by N18 - N16 being unserviceable since the 21st. Receiving no instructions from *D'Estrées*, which was about to proceed to Port Said, *Raven II* sailed north for Tyre. Ten sailing vessels were sighted heading for Jaffa but were too close inshore to be intercepted.

A heavy swell cropped up towards sunset on 24 May rendering it impossible to land the Agent that night. Landing plans were discussed with the Agent next day, who, on being informed that he was only to receive £5 as expenses, refused to be put on shore and mentioned that he was a Russian subject. *Raven II* then wirelessed to Port Said for instructions and at 1700 was ordered to proceed thence, where she arrived at 2330 on 26 May.

Although the main Turkish threat to the Suez Canal from southern Palestine was kept under constant surveillance, troop movements along the Gulf of Akaba and on the railway from Maan to Medina and on the eastern shore of the Red Sea were closely watched during 1915. During 9-27 May 1915 the French cruiser *Montcalm* operated a Nieuport VI seaplane, with a French pilot and Lt F.O. Baxter as observer, in the Gulf of Akaba.

Montcalm sailed from Suez at 1145 on 8 May, arriving off Akaba at 1830 next evening. Between 11 and 14 May *Montcalm*'s Nieuport VI seaplane made four attempts to fly a reconnaissance up the Wadi Yetham. Owing to the rarified atmosphere and the intense dry heat, carburation of the 100 hp Gnôme engine was adversely affected, and strong gusts of wind and down draughts made it impossible to climb above 1600 feet. The seaplane took off at 0610 on the 11th and after climbing to 650 feet was forced to return at 0650. No flying was possible on the 12th, and on the 13th the Nieuport was unable to take off due to lack of wind in the early morning. A further attempt was made at 1550 on the 13th, but the seaplane failed to climb above 1,140 feet and had to return at 1610. At 0500 on the 14th a successful take off was made and the Nieuport climbed to 1600 feet, but engine failure forced an early return and *Montcalm* weighed anchor at 0915, proceeding south to Yembo via Wej.

Off Yembo on the 16th the seaplane took off at 0900 and flew over the town at 1,600 feet, but no troops or guns were observed. After being airborne for 50 minutes the seaplane was hoisted inboard and *Montcalm* left for Jeddah via Port Sudan. *Montcalm* sailed from Jeddah at 0930 on 20 May bound for Akaba once again, which was reached on the 23rd. A short flight was made here at 0455 before the ship reached her anchorage station, and from a height of 650 feet three mines were observed. A reconnaissance of Akaba was attempted at 0500 on the 24th but insufficient altitude was attained and the seaplane returned to the ship at 0622. A second attempt in the cool of the evening was successful, and Akaba and the surrounding neighbourhood were thoroughly reconnoitred from a height of 2,300 feet, the flight lasting one and three quarter hours.

Montcalm sailed at 2000 on the 24th, and proceeding up the Gulf of Suez, a reconnaissance was flown over Abu Zeminea between 0700 and 0835 on the 26th. From there on the morning of the 27th an attempt was made to fly the seaplane back to Suez, but after spending an hour trying to get airborne, the Nieuport was hoisted back on board, and *Montcalm* finally reached Suez at 1430 that day.

Along the Red Sea coast during June RIMS *Hardinge*, with Nieuport VI's from EI and ESS embarked, was active in the reconnaissance rôle. *Hardinge* sailed from Suez at 0730 on 9 June, arriving off Dibbah at 0430 on the 10th with Nieuport VI's N16 and N18 embarked. N16 took off for a reconnaissance, but was forced to return to the ship with a burnt out cylinder. The wing fabric of N16 was also in need of repair. N18 made several attempts to take off, nearly caught fire because of a petrol leak and was hoisted back onboard for repairs at 0930.

A dhow was captured by *Hardinge* on the 10th

whose crew stated that the proclamations dropped over Muwailah by *Hardinge*'s Nieuport VI, crewed by Lt Cintré and Major H.P. Fletcher, on 6 June had been found and read.

On the 11th it was found that N18 "had defective inlet valve, ball race and expanding ring to cylinder". Capt. Linberry decided to sail for Jeddah while repairs were carried out. The engine was tested at 1800 but the timing was out. *Hardinge* stopped 15 miles off Jeddah on 13 June and N18 was hoisted out for a reconnaissance of the town. After several attempts to take off however the flight was abandoned for fear of damage to the floats in a rising sea. Wind and sea had increased so much on the 14th that flying was impossible, and it was decided to return to Suez for boiler cleaning, condenser repairs, and to coal ship. *Hardinge* reached Suez at 0700 on 16 June and both Nieuports were put ashore for an overhaul.

Hardinge was at sea again before the end of the month with four Nieuports, N16 and N18, back onboard again, and N17 and N19. Off Ras Mahrash, SSE of Muwailah, N16 with Capt Cintré and Lt Hillas was hoisted out at 0545 on 27 June and flew down the coast as far as Namaan Island where they turned inland onto a

Nieuport VI, N15, on the dockside at Port Said Seaplane Base. N15 was operated from both HMS Anne and HMS Raven II during 1915. The ship at the extreme right of the picture is probably the armoured cruiser HMS Euryalus. (Collection J-P. Dubois)

R.I.M.S. Hardinge operated Nieuport VI seaplanes in the reconnaissance role in the Red Sea during June 1915.
(A.K.Vicary)

NNW heading. Leaflets were dropped near Dibbah and the flight in bumpy conditions continued up the coast again until 0652, when a heavy landing broke the petrol gauge. N16 was hoisted inboard at 0707.

Raven II was back on patrol on 29 June, when she sailed at 0430 from Port Said with Nieuport VIs N17 and N19 embarked, arriving off El Arish at 1400 that day. Lt de Saizieu with Lt H.M.C. Ledger, Indian Army Reserve, as observer took off in N17 at 1631. Climbing to 4,400 feet they made a thorough reconnaissance of the town and camps nearby but reported only about 500 troops there. Bombs were dropped on a fort and the seaplane landed at 1818. A signal to Port Said enquiring if further bombing of El Arish was required was answered in the negative, and at 2000 *Raven II* proceeded north towards Gaza in company with *D'Entrecasteaux*. Two of *Raven II*'s steam pinnace crew were now suffering from sunstroke, and a third member of the pinnace crew cut his arm badly and had to be transferred to *D'Entrecasteaux* for attention off Gaza at 0630 on the 30th.

Raven II hoisted out N17 crewed by de Saizieu and Ledger at 0941 and they flew towards Ramleh and the railhead. They suffered engine failure over Akir, only just having enough height to reach the sea, where they landed at 1043. No troops were seen, but in every village the inhabitants were busily engaged in threshing

their crops - probably using the same methods employed for thousands of years. Three schooners were seen during the forenoon anchored close inshore between Nebi Yunis and Askalon. *D'Entrecasteaux* was informed and she sank two by gunfire. N19 was hoisted out during the afternoon for a reconnaissance of the railhead, but the sea was too rough for take off and *Raven II* anchored for the night off Nebi Yunis. No flying was possible on 1 July with a high NW swell running. At 1130 a schooner was sighted to westward and *Raven II* gave chase and captured her at 1230. She was the *Twakalet Al'Allah* out of Jaffa with a cargo of beans, four crew members and a passenger. *Raven II* took off the passenger and three of the crew, and putting three members of her Syrian prize crew aboard the schooner despatched her to Port Said at 1415.

Raven II arrived off Gaza at 2000 and anchored for the night six miles offshore. Here the ship became infested with a large swarm of crickets which made an incessant noise. Hoses were turned on them and large numbers were extirpated. A heavy swell precluded all flying on 2 July, and *Raven II* lay off Gaza all day awaiting the arrival of the French motor schooner *Belle Alliance*, commanded by Capt Woolley RFA, from Port Said. *Belle Alliance* was a cloak and dagger vessel, armed with a bow gun and engaged in landing Agents and in cutting-out operations in the shallow waters off the coasts of Palestine and Syria. Two of *Raven II*'s engine room crew were now laid up with sunstroke, in spite of Lt Jenkins's warning that heads must be covered on the upper deck during daylight hours, and that men sleeping on deck at night must cover their stomachs. The same warnings were issued in HM Ships 30 years later, and were not always heeded! *Belle Alliance* was sighted at 1100 on the 3rd approaching from the south under motor and with sail furled. She came alongside *Raven II* at 1150 and Capt Woolley and the Agent Mr Dabrouge came aboard, the latter suffering from seasickness.

Raven II weighed anchor at 1445, and with *Belle Alliance* in tow proceeded north at five knots until 1945, when she anchored five miles off Nebi Yunis for the night, the schooner being tied up astern. Sea conditions on 4 July being again unsuitable for flying, *Raven II*, with the schooner in tow, weighed at 0900 and steamed north for Beirut, continuing through the night until at 0700 on the 5th when seven miles north-north-west of Beirut, the schooner was cast off to land the Agent. Weather conditions on the 5th were again unsuitable for flying or for landing the Agent, so *Raven II* and the schooner cruised off the coast until dawn of the next day.

The weather had improved by the morning of 6 July, and at 0700 de Saizieu and Ledger in N19 were hoisted out for a reconnaissance and leaflet dropping sortie over Beirut. However "after flying in the air for a little while the seaplane was found not to be acting well, so that they came down without accomplishing their object" at 0745. *Raven II* proceeded north at 0800 to look for *Belle Alliance* and met her at 1340 six miles south-west of Ramkine Island. At 1900 as weather and sea looked good for the night, *Raven II* put three of her Syrians on board the schooner to assist in landing the Agent and cast off the schooner.

Raven II met *Belle Alliance* at 0230 on the 7th and took her in tow, proceeding slowly towards Beirut. The Agent had been successfully landed at 2330 the previous night - probably thankful to be ashore and no longer afflicted with seasickness! Several schooners were sighted at 0600, and the wind being light, *Raven II* gave chase. However they escaped close inshore, and the surf was too heavy to send in the steam pinnace after them. At 0802 de Saizieu and Ledger got off in N17, and climbing to 4200 feet flew over Beirut where leaflets were dropped. Nothing of importance was seen and the seaplane was hoisted back onboard at 0935. *Belle Alliance* came alongside at 1015 with a captured sailing vessel and the crew of three, being of military age, were taken on board as POW's and *Raven II*, with the schooner in tow, made for Jaffa at seven knots, keeping well out to sea so that those ashore might assume the ship was bound for Port Said, and closed in again after

R.I.M.S. Hardinge in Red Sea June 1915. (Collection J-P.Dubois)

dark. About 15 miles off Cape Carmel at 2330 a vessel showing many lights and steering north was seen. Although challenged she did not reply, and was probably the cruiser USS *Chester* which was known to be in the area.

At 0330 on 8 July three miles north-north-west of Arsuf the schooner was cast off to proceed southward along the coast. At 0700 off Nebi Yunas *Raven II* hoisted out N17, and de Saizieu and Ledger flew over Ramleh, Abu Hareira and Gaza at 2700 feet. The railhead was found to be extended two miles south of Gaza with about 5000 troops engaged in extending the line. The seaplane was fired on from four camps and returned to the ship at 1010. *Belle Alliance* was sighted approaching from the northwards and at 0930 when close inshore off Nebi Yunas she was fired on by some field guns and shrapnel burst in her sail, wounding one French sailor. A signal was sent to *D'Entrecasteaux* and at 1800 she shelled the scene of the morning's action, proceeding with the wounded man aboard back to Port Said at 1930. *Raven II* and *Belle Alliance* remained anchored overnight off Nebi Yunas.

N17 with de Saizieu and Ledger was hoisted out at 0825 on 9 July and flew over Jaffa and Ramleh at 4,000 feet, dropping leaflets at Jaffa. Three new camps were seen at Ramleh and after hoisting the seaplane back on board at 1104, *Raven II* proceeded to Port Said with *Belle Alliance* in tow, arriving there at 0515 on 10 July.

Raven II left Port Said again, at 1815 on 14 July with Nieuports N15 and N20 aboard, and arrived off El Arish at 0600 on the 15th. Destrem and Hillas were hoisted out in N20 in conditions of a calm sea with no wind at 0857 and spent 20 minutes trying to take off. From 3,500 feet several camps and store buildings were observed and the seaplane returned to the ship at 1050, which then proceeded northwards at 5 knots three miles offshore. Many groups of camels were seen moving in both directions between El Arish and Gaza. Askalon was passed at 2100 and at 0615 on the 16th *Raven II* arrived off a Wadi from which a proposed flight to Samaria was to be made. Weather conditions were good, but in view of the heavy load of fuel to be carried for such a long flight Lt Destrem decided to wait for perfect conditions.

Lt Jenkins noted however "that similar reconnaissances have been made from this ship under more difficult circumstances and successfully accomplished".

Raven II remained at anchor during the night of 16-17 July. *D'Entrecasteaux* arrived from the south on the 17th and sent across a boat with leaflets to be dropped by Raven II's seaplanes.

The sea was too rough for any flights on the 18th, and at 0630 *D'Entrecasteaux* returned with a prize schooner in tow. She had been damaged up aloft and *Raven II*, after putting four of her Syrian prize crew on board the schooner and putting her former crew of six under guard in No.3 hold, weighed at 1118 and proceeded at seven knots toward Port Said with the schooner in tow.

Raven II arrived off Port Said at 0700 on 19 July and handed over the prize and six POW's to a tug which towed the schooner in. Orders were now received for *Raven II* to proceed to Aboukir Bay for a reconnaissance by the seaplanes to search for submarines.

Raven II stopped at 0538 on 20 July four miles south-west of Rosetta lighthouse and hoisted out N20 crewed by Destrem and Major H.P. Fletcher. Flying at 900 feet about $3^1/_2$ miles off the coast they traversed a line from Rosetta to Bourg and back, and then back over the coastline to Nelson Island. Nothing was seen and the seaplane returned to the ship at 0803, which then proceeded at full speed toward the Syrian coast. A signal from *D'Entrecasteaux* ordered *Raven II* to meet her 11 miles SW of Caesarea at 0700 on the 21st, but on account of the wretched quality of her coal *Raven II* could make no better than 9 knots and did not meet *D'Entrecasteaux* until 1140 that day. The aircrew went on board the French cruiser to receive their instructions, and at 1515 *Raven II* weighed anchor and stood further out to sea.

Destrem and Fletcher took off in N15 at 1619 and flew over Samaria at 3600 feet. New buildings south of the town were bombed, also a camp at Tulkeram causing panic among the troops there. The railway at Samaria running north-west and south-east, and at Tulkeram running parallel to the coast, was reconnoitred and the seaplane was hoisted in at 1834. *Raven II* proceeded slowly up the coast at 2200 reaching a position off Haifa at 0700 on the 22nd, where Grall and Hillas took off at 0830 to drop leaflets over Haifa and Acre. Engine trouble however forced an early return at 0920, and at 1000 the ship set course for Beirut. A schooner was sighted off Ras en Nakoura and fire was opened with the Maxim, but the swell was too great to launch the steam pinnace to prevent her escape inshore.

The scene at Port Said on 18th August 1915 as Lieutenants de Vaisseau de L'Escaille and Cintré are decorated with the D.S.C. by Admiral Sir R. Peirse RN.

D'Entrecasteaux was met off Beirut at 0600 on 23 July, and Destrem and Fletcher in N20 failed to take off for a reconnaissance of the town. It had been reported that there was to be a review of Turkish troops in the town, so at 0755 Grall and Hillas took off in N15, armed with darts, but no troops were seen and they landed at 0921. N20 made a further attempt to take off but again failed, and at 1053 in company with *D'Entrecasteaux* the ship proceeded at $7^1/_2$ knots toward Tripoli. Just north of the town some 500 camels and a large stores encampment were seen. *Raven II* closed the coast to within 2500 yards then opened rifle fire, and sent her steam picket boat in even closer. The camels and men rapidly dispersed leaving stores littered over the ground. At 1900 *Raven II* anchored for the night five miles off shore. *D'Entrecasteaux* joined *Raven II* at 0730 off Nahr El Kebir. Destrem and Fletcher in N20 flew up the river at 1300 feet, sighting two small tugs, and reported that yesterday's stores encampment was almost deserted. Destrem and Fletcher attempted to take off again in N20 without success, but were airborne in N15 for a second reconnaissance of the same area.

Parting company with *D'Entrecasteaux* at 1400, *Raven II* headed for Latakia. A Turkish schooner out of Mersina was captured at 1940 on the 24th, and a second schooner at 0600 on the 25th, both loaded with wheat,

rye and barley mixed. Prize crews were put on board both schooners and they were left while *Raven II* proceeded closer to Latakia. N15 with Grall and Hillas was hoisted out at 0727 to search for a suspected submarine base at Latakia but nothing was found and the seaplane was hoisted in again at 0816. *Raven II* then rejoined her prizes, and with "everyone in the ship working with the greatest zeal" managed to unload 39 tons of cereals by 1500. One can't help admiring their "zeal" - a relatively small ship's company working in probably very high temperatures.

With the two schooners in tow, *Raven II* proceeded to Famagusta at 1540, and at 0900 on 26 July she took her prizes into the inner harbour where Customs took charge of them. *Raven II* weighed anchor at 1330 and set course for the Bay of Acre to do a reconnaissance of the district north-west of Nazareth.

Unfortunately there was too much swell to operate the seaplanes on the morning of the 27th off Haifa. Destrem and Fletcher in N20 made an attempt to take off at 1613 but failed, and were hoisted inboard again at 1638. A shortage of fresh water now compelled a return to Port Said. *Raven II* arrived off Port Said at 1030 on 28 July, transferred her aircrew and seaplanes on board a tug, and proceeded with a prize schooner to Alexandria.

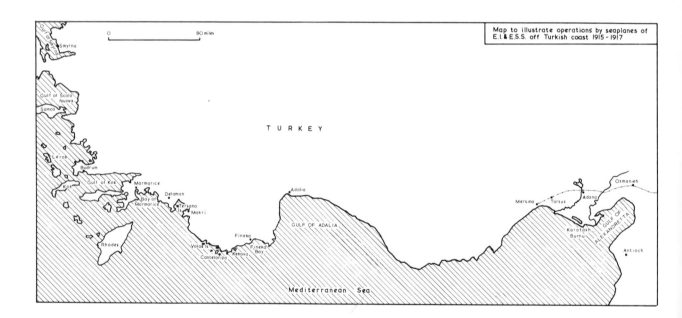

CHAPTER IX

Anne, returns to service, June-December 1915

While *Anne* was still in dry dock at Alexandria, her seaplane crews including de Saizieu, Herbert and Hillas rejoined the ship on 28 May from Tenedos. On the 29th Weldon was informed that *Anne* was to be commissioned into the Royal Navy wearing the White Ensign, and that the captain and officers, including Bishop the chief engineer, were to be given RNR commissions. Junior engineers were to be given warrant rank. The previous lash-up arrangement whereby the ship had been run by the Ports and Lights Administration under orders from GOC Egypt had proved unworkable.

Anne came out of dry dock on 18 June, and anchoring in the Arsenal basin discharged her valuable cargo. *Anne* sailed for Port Said on 30 June, arriving there on 1 July after an uncomfortable voyage without ballast.

The passage to Port Said had been made with a scratch crew who had then returned to their own ships. One signaller and five ratings were drafted by the Navy to *Anne*, but Weldon was told to raise his own crew to work the ship. The sweepings of Port Said were engaged, only one of whom had ever been to sea before. He was appointed bo'sun, but having spent the previous four years as head waiter at the Eastern Exchange Hotel, was a bit out of practice!

With two seaplanes embarked, *Anne* sailed from Port Said at 2000 on 7 July on her first sortie for four months to search for a reported submarine off Borollos. Nothing was seen, and after hoisting in her seaplanes *Anne* set course for Aboukir Bay for a further search. However the sea was too rough to launch a seaplane here, so Weldon decided to launch one in Alexandria harbour for a flight to Aboukir. No sooner had the Nieuport returned than a very excited Staff Officer arrived on board *Anne* demanding an explanation for an "unauthorised" flight. The seaplane had flown over Ras El Tin and the Ramleh shore where everyone was bathing. Mistaken for a German aircraft, it had created considerable panic on the beach!

On 18 July Weldon received a despatch from the American Consul at Cairo for delivery to the US cruiser *Des Moines* then lying at Beirut. Before sailing at midnight on 18/19 however, he wrote to Col. Elgood setting out in writing the conditions under which he was sailing. *Anne*'s crew consisted chiefly of fellahin, she had no steam launch, hardly a man capable of pulling a boat, no-one except the ship's officers able to take the wheel, and no armament except for a few revolvers. Weldon requested a crew of naval ratings, a steam launch and armament of a maxim and one 12 pounder as defence against German submarines, now appearing in the waters in which *Anne* had to operate.

At Beirut *Anne* signalled to *Des Moines* that she bore despatches from the Consul, but received no reply. After wirelessing to the American cruiser the only reply received was a repeated "Impossible to communicate with you"!

Her captain undoubtedly had orders not to break his country's strict neutrality. *Jeanne D'Arc* signalled to *Anne* on 21 July to rendezvous with her at Pegodia Bay, Isle of Scarpanto, so that the seaplanes might search along the Asia Minor coast for submarine bases. Off Delaman Chai *Anne* sent away one of her Nieuports for a one and a half hour reconnaissance but nothing was seen. Later that day Petty Officer Trouillet and Capt. Herbert were airborne off Makri and bombed some Turkish barracks.

Lt J.Kerr RNR, commanding HMS Anne from June 1915.(via RCC)

*One of the agents put ashore on the Syrian coast from
HMS Anne. (via RCC)*

Repairing on board *Jeanne D'Arc* to report the
results of these flights, it was suggested to Weldon by
Admiral Dartige du Fournet that, if one of the two ships
was torpedoed, the other ship was to steam away at full
speed and not to stop to pick up survivors. However,
after consultation, Weldon and Kerr agreed to reject this
rather unsporting suggestion should the eventuality arise!
Anne and *Jeanne D'Arc* then sailed for Rhodes, arriving
there on 22 July. Both ships sailed for the Bay of
Marmarice that day at 1500 to search again for
submarine bases, but results were negative. *Jeanne
D'Arc* left for Port Said on the 23rd, leaving *Anne* to
return unescorted at her best speed of nine knots.

Anne reached Port Said on 24 July, where the old
ship was in Luck's way. A 12 pounder gun was fitted
and on 5 August she was ordered to haul down the Red
Ensign and hoist the White Ensign. *Aenne Rickmers* had
now become His Britannic Majesty's Ship *Anne*. At
about this time *Rabenfels* also became HMS *Raven II*
entitled to wear the White Ensign, and both ships'
motley crews were paid off and replaced by naval

ratings.

August saw the first operation, timed for the 18th in
the Gulf of Alexandretta, involving the use of the two
seaplane carriers, each with two Nieuport VIs
embarked. *Anne* sailed first from Port Said at 1930 on
12 August with two pilots (Destrem and Grall), two
observers (Fletcher and Herbert) and seaplanes N11 and
N20.

Anne met the French cruiser *Jeanne D'Arc* off El
Arish at 0600 on the 13th, and Destrem and Fletcher in
N20 located four guns in a fort, and a building which
might be an ammunition store on the north bank of the
Wadi El Arish. The French admiral however ''did not
think expenditure of ammunition advisable''.

Anne sailed for Haifa at 1100, arriving in the Bay of
Acre off Haifa at sunrise on the 14th. Grall and Herbert
flew in N11 over the Bay to see if any mines had been
laid, but none were found. At 1130 the French flagship
of the Syrian Division, the battleship *Jauréguiberry* fired
two rounds of 12-inch shell on the railway junction east
of Haifa. The second round demolished the station.
Sailing at 1330, to pick up fresh provisions at
Famagusta en route to Alexandretta, a schooner was
spotted inshore south of Ruad Island at 0700 on the 15th
and *Anne* gave chase. At 0830 when within 1,000 yards
of her the schooner ran into shoal water. *Anne* had no
launch to follow her in, so a shot was put across her
bows. She then lowered her sails, got out sweeps and
rowed towards *Anne*. The 12-pounder shell meanwhile
had ricocheted and burst ashore just north of the Nahr El
Kebir amongst a troop of 50 cavalrymen. The schooner
had been bound from Beirut, to ship a cargo of onions at
Ruad, with a crew of three. From them it was learned
that there were 2,000 troops at Beirut, that the harbour
was not mined, that no German submarines used it as a
base and that food there was scarce. Famagusta was
reached on the 16th, with the captured schooner on
board, where *Anne* took in fresh provisions.

Raven II meanwhile sailed from Port Said at 1000
on 16 August with Nieuports N14 and N17 and their
aircrews of pilots Lt de Saizieu and PO Trouillet, and
observers Lts Paul and Ledger to join *Anne* and *Jeanne
D'Arc* in the Gulf of Alexandretta on the 18th.

Anne sailed from Famagusta at 1200 on the 17th and
all three ships met at the top of the Gulf of Alexandretta
at 0600 on the 18th. It was intended that all four
Nieuports should take off to bomb the railway bridge at
Chicaldere, but the weather prevented any flying in the
forenoon. All three ships sheltered from a thunderstorm
and high seas in the Bay of Ayas during the afternoon,
and no flying was possible on that day. *Anne* and *Raven
II* were ordered to rendezvous with *Jeanne D'Arc* at
dawn on the 19th in the Bay of Tarsus for a bombing
attack on Tarsus and Adana.

At 0700 on 19 August both ships commenced

hoisting out their seaplanes with the intention of bombing Adana and Tarsus. *Raven II*'s two seaplanes N17 (de Saizieu and Ledger) and No 14 (Trouillet and Paul) both found a thick mist inland and very soon returned to the ship. *Anne*'s N11 crewed by Grall and Fletcher reached Adana and dropped a bomb on or near the station, and then flew on to Tarsus where another bomb was dropped near the station. Meanwhile Destrem and Herbert in N20 failed to get off the water with their bomb load, and soon had to return to *Anne*. N20, without bombs, took off later and took photographs of the town and station at Adana.

Raven II's two seaplanes made another attempt to reach Adana in the afternoon. However N17 broke a float stay in taking off and had to return to the ship. And N14 also broke a float stay resulting in the propeller striking the floats and damaging both. More seriously the engine bearers were strained, rendering No 14 unserviceable for the rest of the cruise. N17 was repaired, but not in time for any flight that day. At the conclusion of the day's operations the French admiral sent a well earned signal of commendation on Grall's and Fletcher's sortie to Adana and Tarsus, and ordered the two carriers to rendezvous with him at the top of the Gulf of Alexandretta next morning. The rendezvous was kept at 0700 on 20 August, and *Anne*'s N20 with Destrem and Herbert was hoisted out at 0830 to fly a reconnaissance of Osmanieh and the railway tunnel at Bageh, with the object of making a bombing attack with the three serviceable seaplanes on locomotives supposed to be on the line between Osmanieh and Bageh. However, with no wind, No 20 was unable to take off, and since low cloud was accumulating on the hills over Osmanieh the operation was cancelled.

The squadron then proceeded to the shelter of Ayas Bay to launch a bombing attack on the railway bridge at Chicaldere near Missis. The three seaplanes were hoisted out at 1500. *Anne*'s N11 bombed the bridge without result and returned with two bullet holes in the fabric, but N20 had to return with engine failure after being airborne for 20 minutes. *Raven II*'s N17 took off at 1512, bombed the bridge with unknown results, and returned at 1700. All three ships left Ayas Bay at 1800 on the 20th proceeding south, *Raven II* bound for Jaffa and *Anne* bound for St George's Bay at Beirut.

On 21 August *Raven II* met *Jauréguiberry* proceeding north at 1230, and at 1330 passed *Jeanne D'Arc, D'Entrecasteaux* and *Anne* lying off St George's Bay. At the same time *D'Estrées* was sighted ahead proceeding south and USS *Chester* lay at anchor off Beirut. *Raven II* stopped off Sidon at 1700 and swung ship for deviation of the compass. Jaffa was reached at 0530 on 22 August and although a considerable swell was now running, de Saizieu thought a flight was quite feasible. As the wind was at right angles to the swell the ship could be manoeuvred so as to give a minimum of

Syrian boatmen, whose task was to land agents on the enemy coast. The photograph was taken on board HMY Managem, but the men are typical of those employed by HMS Anne for the same purpose. (via RCC)

roll, and at the same time to give a lee to the seaplane. Ship handling and seamanship practised by both the captains of the seaplane carriers had reached such a fine art by 1915 that a seaplane could be hoisted out in one and a half minutes and recovered in two minutes. Both operations were now under the orders of the ships' RNR skippers, and it speaks volumes for the abilities of these professional seamen that they could so adapt to the needs of a new aerial dimension.

Trouillet and Paul in N17 made a perfect take off at 0653 and at 3,200 feet overflew Jaffa and returned to *Raven II* at 0756 to report only a new hospital to the south of the town. As soon as the seaplane was hoisted in, *Raven II* proceeded at full speed to Port Said.

Anne, meanwhile, in St George's Bay, hoisted out Destrem and Fletcher in N20 on the morning of 21 August for a flight along the Beirut-Damascus railway as far as Aliya, where three machine guns opened on them from a camp on the hill. Fletcher had a narrow escape, "a bullet piercing the car just alongside of him''. *Anne* proceeded to sea for the night of 21/22 August and returned to St George's Bay at 0900 on the 22nd, where Capt Weldon repaired on board *Jeanne D'Arc* to report the result of the previous day's flight. The admiral told Weldon that both Fletcher and Herbert would be ''mettre à l'ordre du jour'' in recognition of the excellent work they had done.

Major Fletcher reported that Lt Destrem, when they were under machine gun fire, was most cool and collected and manoeuvred his machine in such a way as to give as difficult a target as possible to the enemy.

Anne received orders at 1030 on the 21st to return to Port Said, and that the ship and her seaplanes would not be required by the admiral for at least ten days. Shortly after 1100 when south of Beirut *Anne* sighted and chased a schooner. When she attempted to run inshore a shot was put across her bows to make her heave to. When close in however, her crew deserted her and swam ashore. *Anne* then opened fire on her, and she was left dismasted and aground, and *Anne* proceeded to Port Said at 1130.

Anne's ten day rest from operations did not run its course, for at 2300 on 30 August she again sailed from Port Said with Nieuports N16 and N17 embarked. The aircrew consisted of de Saizieu, Trouillet, Fletcher and Hillas and five French mechanics to service the seaplanes. Also on board were the Agent Mr Knesovich, 23 Prisoners (including another Agent) with their escort of one sergeant and 10 men of the Glasgow Yeomanry, and three additional Agents shipped as ''crew'' for a captured native boat carried aboard.

Anne was off El Arish by 0700 on the 31st, where Trouillet and Fletcher took off in N16 at 0845 to discover if any Turkish reinforcements had arrived in the area since the reconnaissance of 13 August by N20. No further reinforcements were seen and at 1000 *Anne* sailed for Ruad to land the prisoners who were being repatriated. The north end of the island was reached at 1320 on 1 September where *Jeanne D'Arc* and *Jauréguiberry* lay at anchor. The French flag was flying from the lighthouse and from the fort at the harbour, the island having been occupied by the French at the inhabitants' request as they were starving. One of *Jauréguiberry*'s officers, Lt Trabaud, had been appointed Governor, and to him were handed over the 23 prisoners which were landed from *Anne*. The Agent among them was pointed out to the Governor, who was requested to aid him in every way possible.

Anne left Ruad at 1700 for Haifa, and at 2200, when 15 miles north of Beirut and 10 miles off shore, the captured native boat was lowered with the three Agents to land on the coast. On completion of their mission they were ordered to return to Ruad and report to the Governor there.

Anne arrived off Haifa at 0800 on 2 September and

at 0900 de Saizieu and Fletcher in N17 flew via Shafa'Amr to Nazareth, returning over Hartiya and Haifa. No camps were seen, and over Haifa leaflets and letters from POW's were dropped. Shortly after N17's take off, Trouillet and Hillas searched Acre Bay for mines in N16, but none were observed. As soon as both seaplanes were back onboard at 1115, course was set for the region of Jaffa, where at 0945 on 3 September de Saizieu and Hillas in N17 flew over Ramleh, Kheimel, Wadi Burshein and to the mouth of Nahr Sukereir. The bridge over Wadi Burshein was still in course of construction and the guns previously reported near the mouth of Nahr Sukereir were not observed. Leaflets were dropped over Ramleh and *Anne* returned to Port Said on 4 September.

After sailing from Port Said at 2200 on 19 September, *Anne* hoisted out N20 crewed by Destrem and Ledger at 0730 on the 20th for a flight lasting an hour and twenty minutes over and around El Arish. No change in the situation was observed since the last reconnaissance. Grall and Paul took up N11 in the afternoon and found no changes at the railhead, and nothing was seen at Khan Yunis.

Anne arrived off the coast south of Jaffa on the morning of the 21st where Destrem and Paul flew N20 to Ludd and Ramleh, returning via Jaffa. The only thing of note seen were two camps at Ramleh. A signal from the admiral in *Jauréguiberry* ordered *Anne* to rendezvous with him at Ruad at 1400 on the 23rd. Ruad was reached at 1330 on the 22nd where *Anne*'s Intelligence Officer, Capt. Weldon, went ashore to see the Governor, whose latest intelligence suggested that an offensive against the island from the mainland might be contemplated. The Governor wanted an immediate aerial reconnaissance of gun emplacements opposite the islands, but Capt. Weldon advised caution until the arrival of *Jauréguiberry* next day. After the French battleship reached Ruad *Anne*'s seaplanes, N11 and N20, made flights over the coastline opposite the island on the 23th and 24th. The conclusion drawn was that the emplacements were purely defensive to resist a landing on the mainland - a task beyond the capability of the island's small French garrison - and no further action was taken.

Anne sailed at 1200 on the 24th, cruising towards Cape Andreas en route to Famagusta, where N20 was fitted with a new propeller on the 25th. Destrem made a short flight in N20 next day to test the new propeller, and at 1100 *Anne* sailed for Port Said. The Belgian steamer *Fanny* was boarded en route. She was empty and was bound for Famagusta to ship 500 head of cattle for Mudros. Her papers being in order she was allowed to proceed, and *Anne* arrived at Port Said at 1630 on 27 September. *Anne*'s next sortie was marred by the loss of one of her long serving aircrews. She left Port said at

Nieuport VI seaplane, 21, of l'Aviation Maritime Française operated by HMS Anne - seen close inshore with her escort of two French destroyers. (P.H.T.Green)

1530 on 9 October, and was off Wadi Gaza at 0800 on the 10th. N14 crewed by Trouillet and Paul was hoisted out at 1010 for a flight to Beersheba with enough fuel for a three hour reconnaissance. At 1400 when N14 had not returned N17 crewed by de Saizieu and Ledger was sent out to search for the missing seaplane, but without success. N17 flew to within three miles of Beersheba and made a reconnaissance of the railway from Tel El Sharia to the Gaza to Beersheba road. Many store dumps were observed and an elaborate trench system between Gaza and Wadi Esh Sharia. About 100 cavalry were seen in bivouac at Sheikh Nebhan just south of Wadi Gaza, but there was no sign of the missing seaplane.

When Trouillet's and Paul's N14 had taken off, the crew had been issued with two red flares for use if they were brought down over land. One red flare would indicate that they wished to be taken off by *Anne*'s boat, and the second flare was to be used when the boat was close inshore. All crews were also instructed to burn their aircraft if forced down. *Anne* cruised a mile off-shore all night but no signal was seen.

N14 had actually been forced down with engine trouble near Beersheba and had made a perfect landing. Both floats were smashed but neither of the crew were injured at all. They were at once surrounded by Arabs who stripped them of all their personal possessions and some of their clothing. Fortunately some Turkish officers rode up, returned Trouillet's and Paul's belongings, mounted them on camels and took them to Beersheba.

About two months later Weldon had a censored letter from Paul, written from a POW camp. Paul stated that after their capture his camel had shied at some railway trucks on entering Beersheba and had thrown him. But knowing what a good man Paul was on either a horse or a camel, Weldon concluded that he was letting him know that the railway had reached Beersheba - the very information that he had been sent on the flight to obtain. He also mentioned that the Turkish officers, including some aviators, had treated him well. This also was a way of informing Weldon that the enemy now had aeroplanes on this front.

Anne was off Nebi Yunis on the morning of the 11th intending to fly a reconnaissance down the railway to Tel Esh Sharia, but clouds were too low to make the attempt. N17 was hoisted out in the afternoon but after two unsuccessful attempts to take off in rough seas the flight was abandoned, and *Anne* returned to the vicinity of Wadi Gaza in the vain hope of getting a signal from her missing aircrew. The seas off Nebi Yunis on the 12th were again too rough for flying, and after sending a signal to Port Said for a spare propeller for N17, *Anne* returned to Wadi Gaza and cruised all night off the coast.

The sea was still running high off Nebi Yunis on the morning of the 13th, and after seeking permission from Port Said, *Anne* proceeded to Ruad where she arrived at sunrise on 14 October. The Governor asked for a reconnaissance of the mainland opposite the island,

and of Tartus, which N17 accomplished that afternoon, but no new developments were seen since the last flight on 24 September.

Capt. Weldon learned that, since the French occupation of Ruad, 500 people had left the island in small boats - 300 of whom were women. His report concluded "They are very fanatical on Ruad, and I think they are nervous concerning their womenfolk!"

Anne sailed from Ruad at 1730 on the 14th to rendezvous with the French cruiser *Dupleix* off Wadi Rubin south of Jaffa on the 15th. A flight by N17 off the Wadi had to be abandoned when the propeller was damaged while attempting to take off. However *Dupleix* arrived and handed over the spare propeller sent from Port Said, and *Anne* stood out to sea for the night.

At 0845 on 16 October N17 was hoisted out four miles from the mouth of Wadi Rubin for a reconnaissance of Ramleh and the railway to Wadi Esh Sharia. Although the sea was not heavy, the bolts sheared on one of the float struts and the seaplane was hoisted in again. Since one float was already cracked, it was decided at 1045 to return to Port Said to pick up two new seaplanes. Port Said was reached at 2400 on 16 October.

Anne only had 72 hours in Port Said, sailing at 2400 on 19 October with Nieuports N19 and N20 embarked. Their aircrews consisted of Lt Destrem and Petty Officer Bourgeois (pilots) with Fletcher and Ledger as observers. Low cloud on the morning of the 20th off El Arish prevented flying, but Bourgeois and Fletcher flew a reconnaissance over the town in N19 in the afternoon. The seaplane was fired at from a fort, but nothing of importance was seen.

Off Askalon on the afternoon of the 21st Destrem and Ledger attempted a flight over the railway from Kheima southwards. N20 took 40 minutes to attain sufficient altitude to cross the coast with safety, but as they were flying inland the engine started missing and they had to return to the ship. It now being too late to hoist out the other seaplane, *Anne* stood out to sea for the night.

Anne came close inshore off Nebi Yunis at dawn on the 22nd. Bourgeois and Fletcher in N19 flew to Kheima and thence north over the railway to Ramleh, where a train of four coaches was seen in the station. N20 attempted the same flight as planned on the previous day, and with exactly the same engine trouble. Destrem and Ledger changed to N19 and were hoisted out at 0842 on the 23rd, five miles off the mouth of Wadi Esh Sukereir, for a third attempt at the southward reconnaissance of the railway. The line was followed to within six miles of Beersheba and Destrem only turned back then because of some difficulty with the oil pump. After a two hour flight the seaplane landed alongside *Anne* which had steamed down to meet it between

Lt Destrem of l'Aviation Maritime Française, pilot of French Nieuport VI seaplanes operated by HMFA Aenne Rickers/Anne during 1915/16, and of Nieuport seaplanes operated by HMS Raven II and Campinas during 1915/16. (via RCC)

Askalon and Gaza. Since N20 was now unserviceable, the planned reconnaissance of the railway north of Ramleh was abandoned and *Anne* set course for Port Said at 1000 on 24 October, arriving there at 1745 that evening.

Anne's next sortie was on 5 November, primarily to land an Agent named Frienberg at Athlit. Early on the 6th she was off Wadi Gaza where at 0920 N11 with Grall and Fletcher was hoisted out. Crossing the coast over the Wadi at 1000 at 2500 feet a course was set for a point ten miles south of Beersheba. At a height of 4000 feet they did a thorough reconnaissance of the camp between 1020 and 1040. What was thought to be a hangar, measuring approximately 100 feet x 40 feet, was seen just outside the camp, and some 50 men were observed working on a three mile stretch of Decauville railway laid on the Beersheba to El Auja road. Various activity on the railway was seen en route to Gaza including a bridge under construction at Tel El Sharieh. Gaza was reached at an altitude of 5200 feet at 1125, and at 1145 the seaplane was hoisted back on board. N22 was hoisted out in the afternoon with the intention of bombing the camp and railway at Beersheba, but after taking off, and a 40-minute flight over the sea, de Saizieu had to bring the seaplane down again with engine trouble.

Anne moved north to a position off the mouth of Wadi Rubin by dawn of the 7th, where de Saizieu and Fletcher were hoisted out in N22 for a flight northwards along the railway from Ramleh to Tul Keram, and details of all the bridges on the line were noted. N22, with petrol running low, had to be landed some three miles from the ship. There was a heavy swell running, and being unable to take advantage of the lee of the ship, a float and wing were quite badly damaged before the seaplane could be hoisted inboard.

Anne steamed close inshore off Athlit at 1300 on the 8th to select a spot for landing the Agent. The Agent pointed out his house to Capt. Weldon and a code of signals was arranged. The Agent also asked to be sent a small wireless set with a range of 10 miles and a good telescope. *Anne* then proceeded slowly north as far as Acre until darkness, when "darken ship" was piped and she turned back to the south, arriving off Athlit at 2230. A Syrian took the Agent ashore and *Anne* immediately proceeded south, arriving off Wadi Gaza at 0930 on the 9th. It was intended to launch N11 armed with one bomb for an attack on Beersheba, but on both the 9th and 10th the sea was too rough. Conditions were ideal for flying on the 11th, but after being airborne for 40 minutes Grall and Ledger in N11 had to return with two burnt cylinders. The spare engine was fitted and a further attempt made in the afternoon, but again a cylinder burnt out. That cylinder was replaced, and N11 was hoisted out on the 12th for a bombing attack on Gaza, but another cylinder went. There was no alternative but to return to Port Said, which was reached on 13 November.

Reconnaissance of the railway system on the southern Turkish shore continued again during December, where on 10 December both of *Anne*'s seaplanes, N19 and N23, made a detailed observation of the line from Mersina to Adana. Bourgeois and Fletcher in N19 dropped a bomb on a factory west of Mersina causing a loud explosion and clouds of smoke. Both seaplanes came under fire, but returned safely to the ship south-east of the mouth of Seihan Irmak.

Anne sailed from Port Said at 2200 on 20 December for further reconnaissance around Beersheba. The ship was off Wadi Gaza by 0900 on the 21st, but heavy seas and a strong wind ruled out any possibility of flying. A fog came up at noon and *Anne* stood out to sea for the night.

By the morning of the 22nd the weather had improved, and coming in to the mouth of Wadi Gaza, *Anne* hoisted out N17 at 0858 crewed by de Saizieu and Ledger. They took off at 0907 and spent the next 40 minutes gaining altitude before heading in over the coast. They carried petrol for a three-hour flight, but by 1230 had not returned. An immediate flight by the second seaplane to search for them was not attempted because there was now a thick fog overland and rolling up from the south-west. However at 1430, as the fog had not advanced much, the ship was taken in to within three miles of the beach at Khan Yunis. Grall and Williams in N22 took off with instructions to search for the lost seaplane in the region of Khan Yunis and Rafa, but returned after one and a half hours without having sighted it. *Anne* cruised all night close inshore and 12 watch fires were observed along the shore line, indicating that the shore was being closely patrolled. At 0837 on the 23rd N22 was hoisted out again for a

Lieut H.M.C.Ledger, Indian Army Reserve, who flew as an Observer in Nieuport VI seaplanes operated by HM Ships Anne, Raven II and RIMS Hardinge between June and December 1915. He was killed on 22 December 1915. (E.Ledger)

HMS Anne's Nieuport VI seaplane alongside and about to be hoisted in. (G.S.Leslie/J.M.Bruce collection)

reconnaissance of Beersheba. The seaplane came under fire at Beersheba, and on their return after a two-hour flight Grall and Williams reported extensive change in the camp layout at Beersheba, but that the Decauville railway from there to El Auja had not been extended. No trace was found of de Saizieu and Ledger, or of their seaplane.

A signal was sent to Port Said suggesting that it was useless to continue patrolling off this fairly thickly populated coast in the hope of taking off the lost aviators. At 2000 *Anne* was recalled to Port Said, arriving there at 0915 on 24 December.

Shortly after Christmas *Anne* picked up an enemy wireless message stating that N17 had force landed with engine trouble on the 22nd and that de Saizieu was a POW. Unfortunately Ledger had been shot when he fired at the Turks as they approached.

H.M.S. RAVEN II.

CHAPTER X

Operations by *Anne* and *Raven II* January-May 1916, and *Ben-my-Chree* February 1916

*R*aven II now took over duties from *Anne,* sailing from Port Said at 2200 on 28 December with Nieuports N20 and N23 on board. Arriving off the eastern end of Lake Bardawil at 0700 on the 29th, weather conditions were unsuitable for any flying that day, and *Raven II* stood out to sea for the night.

At 0700 on the 30th she was 10 miles north of Ras Burun, and although it was possible to launch seaplanes, the confused condition of the sea was considered likely to damage their floats, and course was set for Haifa.

Arriving off Athlit at 0630 on the 31st, *Raven II* waited for a signal from the Agent's house, but none was made and she proceeded towards Haifa.

The ship's engines had to be stopped for minor adjustments during the forenoon, and it was thought inadvisable to launch a seaplane while the engines were out of action. Destrem and Fletcher in N20 took off at 1213 however for a reconnaissance over Nazareth, returning to the ship at 1405. After hoisting the seaplane inboard *Raven II* closed the coast at Athlit again, and at 1630 received a signal from the Agent's house requesting the ship to return again in three day's time.

Raven II proceeded seaward for the night and arrived off Nebi Rubin at 0700 on 1 January 1916, where weather and sea conditions were excellent. Destrem and Fletcher in N23 were hoisted out for a reconnaissance and bombing of Ramleh, Ludd and Jaffa, returning to the ship at 1100. After hoisting N23 on board *Raven II* cruised south as far as Askalon and then stood out to sea for the night. Adverse weather conditions off Arsuf on the morning of the 2nd prevented any flights that day and *Raven II* cruised along the coast between Nebi Yunis and Athlit. The wind freshened from the south during the night, and cruising off the coast between Arsuf and Askalon on the 3rd, *Raven II* was forced to reduce speed to avoid damage to the seaplane hangar. At 1330 on the 4th when 10 miles off Cape Carmel, with no sign of the weather abating, Lt Jenkins reversed course and proceeded at slow speed towards Port Said. During the night of 4/5 January the seaplane hangar suffered considerably from the effects of wind and rain.

At daylight on the 5th the French cruiser *D'Entrecasteaux* was met approaching from the south-east, and at 0900 Jenkins had to put his ship about and

run before the gale for two hours to avoid further damage to the canvas hangar and seaplanes on the after welldeck. At 1100 course was again set for Port Said in the teeth of a south-west gale and driving rain, and *Raven II* finally reached Port Said at 1900 on 6 January.

From October 1915, when the Allies landed forces at Salonika, the military situation in the East Mediterranean underwent considerable change. With the evacuation of the Gallipoli Peninsula in January 1916 the Navy's role in the Aegean changed to one of supporting the Salonika landings, watching the Dardanelles to prevent a sortie by the German battle-cruiser *Goeben* and denying the use of the Aegean Islands as bases for U-boats. It was also apparent from the many reconnaissance flights by the Nieuport seaplanes along the East Mediterranean

Capt de L'Escaille of l'Aviation Maritime Française (left) who commanded the French Seaplane Squadron at Port Said 1915 - 1916, and Capt. E.L.Chute of the Duke of Wellington's Regiment who flew as observer in Nieuport seaplanes operated by HMS Anne in 1916.
(via RCC)

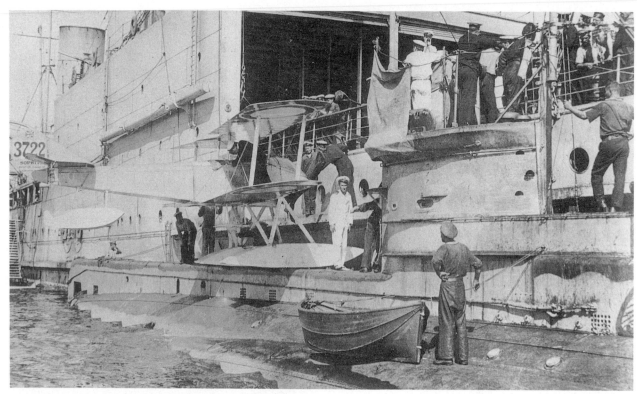

Schneider 3722 is here seen on the casing of HM Submarine E7, lying alongside HMS Ben-my-Chree in Kephalo Bay on 3rd September 1915. 3722 embarked in HMS Raven II and, flown by Flt Lt Bankes-Price, took part in a series of bombing attacks on Turkish camps round Aden between 31st March and 2nd April 1916. (G.S.Leslie/J.M.Bruce collection)

coastline that a substantial build up of Turkish forces was taking place for another attack on the Suez Canal. Their railhead had now been extended south as far as El Auja. Simultaneously Arab resistance to the Turks along the Red Sea coast needed backing with Naval support and aerial reconnaissance. The East Indies Squadron's two seaplane carriers were insufficient for all these tasks, and accordingly, in early January 1916, the much larger and faster seaplane carrier *Ben-my-Chree* was transferred from the Aegean to Port Said to join the East Indies and Egypt Seaplane Squadron then being formally constituted under the command of Cdr. C. L'Estrange Malone. A base for the Squadron was established on one of the islands in the harbour at Port Said for accommodating the crews when ashore, and for servicing the seaplanes.

Meanwhile, before *Ben-my-Chree* began operations with the Squadron, *Anne* sailed at 1530 on 10 January with N22 and N19 embarked, arriving off Athlit at 1300 on the 11th to make contact with the Agent there. However, his house appeared to be deserted, and course was set for Beirut.

Anne was 25 miles west of Beirut by the morning of the 12th, and at 0933 N19 was hoisted out, out of sight of land, with Grall as pilot and Capt. E. L. Chute as observer. A submarine had previously been reported in Haifa harbour, but no sign of her was seen. Two

mines were located however, and N19 returned to the ship at 1108. *Anne* stopped 25 miles off El Mina at 1400 to hoist out N19 again, this time crewed by Bourgeois and Williams, to search for submarines or mines in El Mina roads and harbour. Nothing was sighted, but when the Nieuport was over the town "people assembled and waved handkerchiefs to it!" N19 was hoisted inboard again at 1525, and *Anne* proceeded to Athlit to see if any signals were being made by the Agent. No signals were seen from the Agent's house on the 13th. On the 14th it was the intention to sail for Ruad, but a south-west gale sprang up and *Anne* ran for shelter at Famagusta as the seaplanes were being strained by the rolling and pitching of the ship. Famagusta was reached on the 15th after a very rough passage, and here *Anne* lay in the harbour until the 19th when the storm had blown itself out.

Anne arrived off Jaffa on the 20th in the hopes of flying a reconnaissance between Ramleh and Tul Keram, but heavy seas, low cloud and rain frustrated those hopes. Later that day the weather again prevented a flight over El Arish. It still blew hard on the 21st. *Anne* steamed to Jaffa on the 22nd but the seas were too heavy to hoist out a seaplane. Returning to El Arish at 1500 she found the seas had moderated, and here Grall and Chute were hoisted out in N22. After take off, 6 photographs were taken of the camp and Wadi. On the

Two views of HMS Anne's Nieuport VI seaplane being hoisted out and on the water, crewed by Lt Destrem and Lt E.Williams (E.Yorks.Regt.) in February 1916. Noteworthy are the three - step floats, and the tube protruding vertically between the float struts down which bombs were dropped. (FAAM)

23rd *Anne* returned to Jaffa where Bourgeois and Chute in N22 made a 2 hour flight over the railway from Ramleh to Tul Keram. Much traffic was observed on the railway, and on recovering her seaplane *Anne* sailed for Port Said.

Ben-my-Chree's debut with the East Indies and Egypt Seaplane Squadron was untypical of her performance over the next year. She sailed from Port Said on 10 February, and at Alexandria picked up her escort of an Italian destroyer. Early on the 11th Short 184, 849, was hoisted out in the Gulf of Sollum for a photographic reconnaissance of Sidi Barrani and Sollum, preparatory to an advance against the Senussi by the Western Frontier Force from Mersa Matruh. 849 suffered engine failure after take off and was forced to ditch. Fortunately the aircrew were picked up by HM Trawler *Charlsin* and returned to the ship, and *Ben-my-Chree* then sailed for Port Said.

At the beginning of February 1916 *Anne* put into Ruad, and at the request of the Governor flew a seaplane over the mainland opposite to see what the enemy was doing there. Nothing of importance was seen, and the sea now being too rough for further flights, *Anne* ran for shelter at Famagusta. The Governor was instructed to wireless to Famagusta when the weather had moderated enough for further flying at Ruad. *Anne*'s departure was well timed, for two hours after she sailed a German submarine cruised round the island evidently looking for her.

Anne was at sea again on 11 February off Rafa, where at 0940 N22 crewed by Grall and Chute took off for a reconnaissance of the railway between Beersheba and El Auja. At 1012 the coast was crossed at a height of 3,250 feet at Tel El Ajjul until the railway was met, and from here the flight was continued northward to Beersheba. Considerable traffic was observed on the line south of Beersheba, and although a camera was carried, Capt Chute's entire time was taken up in making notes of all that was seen, and no photographs were taken. N22 was hoisted back on board at 1159.

On returning to Port Said in late February Weldon went on board *Ben-my-Chree* and had a long talk with the Squadron Commander, L'Estrange Malone. With the advent of *Ben-my-Chree* the Squadron's war-weary Nieuports began to be replaced by Short 184s and Schneiders, but Weldon and Malone agreed that for the time being *Anne* would continue to operate Nieuports, and that Weldon should consider himself as Intelligence Officer attached to L'Aviation Maritime Française under the orders of de Lescaille. Malone now took over an island at Port Said and rigged hangars and quarters for his staff on it.

By the end of February things in the Squadron were not running smoothly. Weldon and Malone did not see eye to eye, and the appointment of Lt R. Erskine Childers as Intelligence Officer on board *Ben-my-Chree* was a classic example of a square peg in a round hole. Childer's knowledge of the North Sea and German coastal waters was unrivalled, but the Admiralty sent him to a ship working off the coasts of Sinai, Syria and Asia Minor!

One of *Anne*'s final sorties with Nieuport seaplanes embarked took place during March, when on the 7th a reconnaissance was made of the Turkish positions in the El Arish area. Both seaplanes were new machines and most of their aircrews were operating from *Anne* for the first time. NB2 crewed by Ldg Seaman Roussillon and 2nd Lt A.D. Finney was airborne at 1420, crossing the coast at 2500 feet over the mouth of Wadi El Arish 25 minutes later. Climbing to 4000 feet over El Arish and

H.M.S. ANNE.

HMFA Aenne Rickmers anchored in Castelorizo harbour. (via RCC)

El Murra very little of any importance was seen, and at 1618 NB2 landed and was hoisted on board. Meanwhile NB1 with Lt Jean Blanc and Capt E.L. Chute aboard had been hoisted out, and took off at 1438 to report on any troop concentrations at El Auja. After spending a long time gaining height NB1 crossed the coast at El Arish. Various camps were observed en route to El Auja where it was estimated about two battalions were encamped. A reconnaissance of Rafa had been intended, but petrol was running low, and a direct return flight to the ship had to be made, landing alongside at 1731 with only sufficient fuel left for another 10 minutes flying.

Anne next sailed from Port Said on 15 April with the French torpedo boat No.250 as anti-submarine escort, and took Malone as passenger to see how things were done. One of her seaplanes, N22, was launched off Wadi Gaza on the 16th, but while attempting to take off in a heavy swell it was hit by a big wave, capsized and sank, though the crew were saved. The other Nieuport, NB2, flew a reconnaissance to Shellal in the afternoon. It had just been hoisted on board on its return when there was a loud explosion in the sea between *Anne* and her escort, followed by two more. Two German aeroplanes had bombed the ships from 2,000 feet and fortunately missed their target. As they flew off, *Anne*'s 12-pounder was elevated to its maximum and one round fired to speed their departure. The only damage inflicted was to *Anne*'s wireless aerial which her 12-pounder had shot away. After flying a reconnaissance over El Arish

with her remaining seaplane on 17 April, *Anne* returned to Port Said.

Next day Malone sent for Weldon and informed him that on returning from *Anne*'s next patrol the French Seaplane Squadron would be leaving Port Said and that he (Weldon) was required to go and work with the British Squadron at the EI and ESS Squadron's base on the island. This did not suit Weldon's book. It should perhaps be mentioned that, at 24 years of age, Malone was probably too young to be given command of the Squadron.

Anne coaled at Port Said on 18 April, and after embarking 2 Short 184's, 8004 and 8054, sailed on the 19th and arrived at Castelorizo on the 21st. Weldon went ashore to see the French Governor of the island, who outlined the flights he required to be flown by *Anne*'s seaplanes. The plan was to keep the ship concealed in the harbour while a flight was made from there to Makri and Tersana, and thence to Marmarice where it was suspected there was a German submarine base.

Some of *Anne*'s air mechanics, with a supply of petrol for refuelling the seaplane, were embarked in the French trawler *Nord Caper* which landed them safely under cover of darkness at Tersana on the 21st.

8054 crewed by Flt Lt M.E.A. Wright and Lt A.K. Smith HLI was hoisted out at 0632 on the 22nd and carrying three bombs was airborne at 0638. Between 0700 and 0735 a reconnaissance was carried out in the area of Makri from an altitude of 2,000 to 4,000 feet, but no worthwhile targets for the bombs were seen, and at 0812 the seaplane was waterborne at Tersana. 8054 was refuelled during the forenoon of the 23rd and Wright and Smith took off at 1642 for a reconnaissance of Makri and Levisi in bad flying conditions. The crew reported a blue oily film on the water at Makri which might have indicated the presence of a submarine. The only other sighting of note was at Kis il Ada where men were seen lying down with a white flag! The seaplane returned to Tersana at 1714, was again refuelled and at 1309 on the 24th Wright again took 8054 up with Lt T.V. Hughes as observer to search for submarine bases at Ikinjik Liman and Marmarice and to look for French mines in the passage to Marmarice. Flying at 4,000 feet one bomb was dropped at Karagach and two more at Marmarice, and since there were no signs of either submarine bases or mines the seaplane was waterborne again at Tersana by 1512.

After flying back to Castelorizo on the 25th, the seaplane was hoisted back on board *Anne* and the ship sailed for Port Said that evening with 45 Turkish prisoners on board.

After *Anne*'s return to Port Said on 26 April a tragedy occurred on board. Lt Kerr's bull terrier "Major" fell overboard in harbour and hit his head on the last step of the gangway. He managed to walk all the way back up to the bridge, licked Weldon's hand, and died. There was not a man on board who was not upset at losing him.

In spite of all the intelligence reports of suspected enemy submarine bases and submarine activity in the East Mediterranean, there were few enemy submarines operational in this area. There were more tempting targets for their torpedoes farther west. A month before *Anne*'s trip to Castelorizo the French seaplane carrier *Campinas* with two Nieuport VI seaplanes, N19 and N23, had been despatched there to search for

The French seaplane carrier Campinas with one of her Nieuport VI seaplanes alongside, possibly at Malta during 1915 or 1916. Campinas operated as a unit of the East Indies and Egypt Seaplane Squadron during March 1916. (R.D.Layman)

HMS Ben-my-Chree rigged as she sailed with the East Indies and Egypt Seaplane Squadron based on Port Said during 1916. (G.S.Leslie/J.M.Bruce collection)

submarines and mines.

On 24 March *Campinas* hoisted out N19 crewed by Lt Destrem and Lt J.H.B. Wedderspoon RFA in Castelorizo harbour at 0650. Armed with a magazine carbine with two magazines of 20 rounds each and a 105 mm melenite bomb the seaplane was airborne at 0705 to examine the coast between Andifilo and Volos for mines and submarines to try to destroy them with bombs.

A camera was also carried to photograph Kalamaki and Andifilo, but since the seaplane was unable to climb above 1,600 feet no photographs were taken. No mines or submarines were seen and with the engine missing at 0742, Destrem turned back for Castelorizo and was hoisted aboard again at 0755.

Destrem and Wedderspoon took up N23 at 1520 that afternoon for a second attempt at the same reconnaissance flight as that attempted in the forenoon. Again nothing of note was observed, but an altitude of 3,250 feet was attained. Returning to the harbour at 1,600 feet, Destrem circled twice and put the seaplane down on the water at 1635.

Destrem and 2nd Lt J.M. Burd RFA in N23 were hoisted out at 1443 for a reconnaissance of the coast between Andifilo and Yali Bay and to bomb the castle on Kekova Island. The 105 mm melenite bomb was duly dropped from 3,000 feet at 1525 scoring a direct hit, and returning to Castelorizo the seaplane landed at 1610.

One last flight from Castelorizo was made by Destrem and Wedderspoon in N23 at 1410 on the 26th

to reconnoitre the neighbourhood of Fineka for defence works. None were found, and although Wedderspoon had prepared the 105 mm melenite bomb and placed it in the tube before reaching Fineka, the place seemed of no military value. The bomb was dropped at the castle on Kekova Island on the return flight but fell into the sea, and N23 was waterborne and hoisted back on board *Campinas* at 1606. By 29 March *Campinas* had shifted to Ruad Island from where two flights were made to examine fortifications between Tel Busire and El Mina. Petty Officer Gramant and Burd took up N19 in the forenoon, but engine trouble forced an early return to Ruad. Destrem and Burd in N23 flew a reconnaissance between 1428 and 1530 and although trenches and blockhouses were observed none of them appeared to be manned.

At 0756 on 31 March *Campinas* stopped 20 miles West of Beirut to hoist out N23 crewed by Destrem and Wedderspoon. Airborne at 0805, the seaplane reached the harbour at 1,400 feet beneath the low cloud base. Besides numerous small vessels and several sunken ships, nothing more noteworthy than a large oily stain in the harbour was seen, and this was thought to be the discharge from a drain! N23 landed close to *Campinas* at 0922 but in doing so struck the water and damaged the floats. However, it was safely hoisted inboard and *Campinas* set course for a return to Malta via Port Said, where her two seaplanes were landed.

The last few days of April were occupied with loading all the French Nieuport VI's - dismantled and in packing cases - on board *Anne*. Before sailing for Malta,

Weldon and Destrem attended a farewell dinner given by the British aircrew of the EI and ESS. One of the young RNAS pilots asked Destrem "Why are all you French pilots such old men?" Looking up and down the table at all the British boys Destrem replied "Ah, we do not rob the nurseries". In spite of his beard and stoutness Destrem was only 33, but our men were only boys.

By the time operations by the Nieuports with the Squadron came to an end the seaplanes had flown 1,072 sorties including 500 hours flown over enemy held land territory. The unit was mentioned in dispatches by General Maxwell, the wording of which was:

"L'Escadrille française d'hydravions, basée sur Port Said, sous le commandement du Lieutenant de Vaisseau de L'Escaille, placée sous mes ordres pour le service d'informations, a été employée d'une manière continue pour des reconnaissances sur les côtes de Syrie et d'Anatolie, avec les bâtiments *Anne* et *Raven*. Je ne pourrais apprécier trop hautement l'oevre de l'Escadrille d'hydravions. Les vols prolongés sur la terre, avec des hydravions, sont extrêmement dangereux, mais rien n'arrêta les vaillants aviateurs français dans leur enterprises"

Late in the evening of 3 May, when all the personnel of the French Squadron had come on board and Malone had said farewell, *Anne* set sail for Malta. *Anne* arrived off Valetta harbour at 0900 on 9 May where she was escorted in through the minefield by the torpedo gunboat *Hazard*. At Malta all the Frenchmen and their seaplanes were transferred to the French seaplane carrier *Campinas* which was under orders to sail for Cephalonia. *Campinas* sailed on 12 May, and as she passed *Anne* the latter's ship's company lined the upper deck to give their gallant French commrades three cheers.

Anne underwent a quick refit at Malta, and the mounting of her 12-pounder was modified to enable it to be used against enemy aircraft.

Ben-my-Chree meanwhile had been out of action temporarily. She had suffered quite severe damage to her bows while at anchor in Port Said on 19 February, when SS *Uganda* had collided with her. Dry docking at Suez was considered necessary, but as this was not available for three weeks, temporary repairs were made. On 7 March off Gaza two of *Ben-my-Chree*'s Short 184s, 846 and 850, reconnoitred the area before the ship returned to Port Said. Here she remained until 13 March, when she entered dry dock at Suez until 24 April.

H.M.S. BEN-MY-CHREE.

CHAPTER XI
Operations by the three seaplane carriers of East Indies and Egypt Seaplane Squadron April-August 1916

*A*nne returned from Malta, arriving at Port Said on the evening of 21 May to find that Cdr C.R. Samson had arrived there on 14 May to take over command of the EI and ESS from Malone. Weldon went on board *Ben-my-Chree* next day to ask Samson if he was now to return to soldiering. Samson's reply was that he understood *Anne* could not do without him, and that he was to carry on exactly as before. Weldon was delighted. With a new and aggressive commander and new seaplanes with a higher performance than the faithful Nieuports, a new era was to dawn for the

Squadron.

With the increase of German aerial and submarine activity in the East Mediterranean, Samson took immediate steps to increase his ships' AA armament, and to reduce the time taken to launch and recover their seaplanes. Gone were the days of 1915 when *Anne* and *Raven II* could lie stopped off an enemy coast while their Nieuport seaplanes operated overland.

Ben-my-Chree sailed from Port Said on the evening of 17 May escorted by the French destroyer *Voltigeur*, and at dawn on the 18th met the sloop HMS *Espiègle* and the two monitors *M 15* and *M 23* at a rendezvous off El Arish. *Ben-my-Chree* hoisted out Short 184, 8054, fitted with W/T to spot for the first 6 rounds of the monitors' 9.2-inch guns. 8054 was forced to return with an overheating engine after 50 minutes, and its place was taken by the ship's two Babies 8188 and 8189. *Ben-my-Chree* then closed the land, and with her 12-pounder fired 27 rounds at the trenches in front of the town and at a fort to the north-east. Before returning to the ship *Ben-my-Chree*'s two Babies reported several 9.2-inch hits on the fort and a hangar at El Arish. After the bombardment *Ben-my-Chree* proceeded north with

Short 184, 846, alongside HMS Ben-my-Chree probably during 1915. This Short was still on board when the ship joined the E. Indies and Egypt Seaplane Squadron in 1916 although it was lost on 3rd April 1916. The long padded poles at the top of the picture were used to fend off the seaplane from the ship's side. (FAAM)

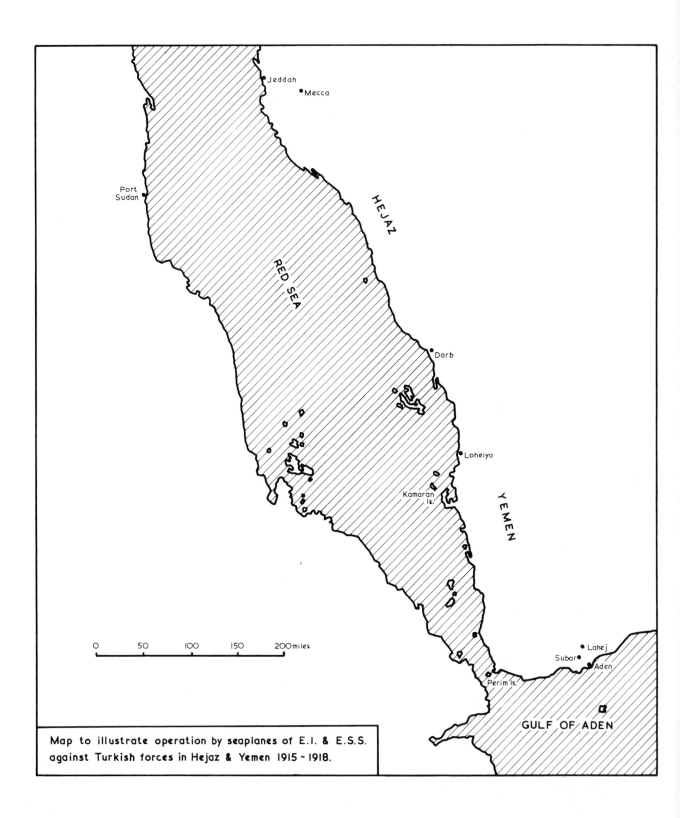

Map to illustrate operation by seaplanes of E.I. & E.S.S. against Turkish forces in Hejaz & Yemen 1915 - 1918.

Voltigeur, and that afternoon 8189 was launched again for an attack on the camp at Kahn Yunis, where four 20-lb bombs and propaganda leaflets were dropped. Rough seas off Jaffa on 23 May made conditions difficult for hoisting out seaplanes but Samson, with Lt J. Wedgwood-Benn of the Middlesex Yeomanry as observer, attempted to take off for a reconnaissance in 8087. However, a float was smashed by a wave and the Short 184 sank, though the crew were picked up.

By 27 May the weather had abated and *Ben-my-Chree,* from a position 10 miles south-west of Jaffa, hoisted out Schneider 3790 piloted by Flt Lt T.H. England at 0439 to reconnoitre and bomb the camp at Ramleh. A fair sea was running and the seaplane, carrying two 16-lb bombs and six petrol bombs, was unable to get airborne. After jettisoning three bombs England attempted to take off again. But after attaining a speed of 35 knots the seaplane hit a wave and broke the port top aileron pulley. England taxied back to the ship and was hoisted back on board at 0447.

At 0641 *Ben-my-Chree* was off Gaza where Short 184, 850, crewed by Flt Lt M.E.A. Wright and 2nd Lt A.K. Smith and Schneider 3774 piloted by Flt Lt Bankes-Price were hoisted out.

A military post south of Jaffa was attacked by both seaplanes with machine gun fire and the Short dropped two 65-lb bombs. Bankes-Price flew on to Ramleh where he dropped five 20-lb bombs on a camp. After recovering her seaplanes the ship turned south, and later that day 850 was again hoisted out off Gaza, where Flt Cdr England dropped two 65-lb bombs and one incendiary on a camp, and a further incendiary on Kahn Yunis on his way back to the ship. Still proceeding south *Ben-my-Chree* again hoisted out 850 for the final operation of the day off El Arish. In addition to pilot and observer the Short carried camera, Lewis gun, and ten bombs (two 65-lb, one 16-lb, six petrol and one Thermite). The HE bombs were dropped on a fort and on the south-west corner of the town, and the incendiaries on gun emplacements with varying success. It was observed that two hangars at El Arish aerodrome had been damaged by the bombardment on the 18th.

While the Short was away *Ben-my-Chree* was bombed from 5000 feet by a German aeroplane whose four bombs straddled the ship. An inconclusive exchange of fire then took place between ship and aircraft, and after recovering her seaplane *Ben-my-Chree* proceeded to Port Said, entering harbour at 1530 that day, 27 May.

While these operations had been in progress concern had been felt for the security of the British and Indian troops garrisoning Aden. A Turkish force had advanced from the Yemen in July 1915 and had occupied Lahej, 20 miles north of Aden. The Aden garrison was strong enough to resist the Turks, provided

A Short 184 is hoisted on board HMS Ben-my-Chree 1916. The extension to the after derrick post is a mast supporting the wireless aerial. The hangar measured approx. 70 ft by 30 ft and A.A. armament is visible on the hangar roof. (G.S.Leslie/J.M.Bruce collection)

the latter were not supported by the local tribes.

While *Ben-my-Chree* had been in dry dock at Suez a show of strength in support of the Aden garrison had been decided upon. Six Schneiders and one Short 184 were transferred from *Ben-my-Chree* to *Raven II* which left for Aden towards the end of March 1916.

In order to mount a surprise air attack on the following day, *Raven II* stopped off Perim Island at 1330 on 30 March, being well out of sight of land and of all shipping, to hoist up seaplanes from the hold and erect them and stow them on deck. Under cover of darkness *Raven II* entered Aden harbour that night with five Schneiders (3721, 3722, 3727, 3774, 3790) and Short 184 (850) on deck, derricks plumbed, and bombs in place ready for hoisting out next morning. The spare Schneider was kept below in the hold.

Raven II anchored in the outer harbour and Flt Cdr C.H.K. Edmonds went on board *Euryalus*, which was flying the flag of the C in C, in obedience to a signal received. After consultation with the C in C and the GOC Aden who was on board *Euryalus*, it was decided to make a reconnaissance to locate enemy camps early next morning, and to follow this up as quickly as possible with a bombing attack. It was also provisionally agreed to bomb the enemy again in the afternoon. Edmonds suggested to the GOC that after the bombing was finished propaganda leaflets might be dropped on the camps and villages, in which he concurred and promised to see about the printing. Edmonds also arranged for a Staff Officer with a good knowledge of the country to be sent aboard *Raven II*. 850, crewed by Edmonds and Lt V. Millard of the Essex Regiment, was hoisted out at 0615 on 31 March. Airborne at 0625, Edmonds climbed to cross the coast east of Wadi Kabir at 2,000 feet. Low cloud hampered observation, but the enemy's main camp near Subar was located at 0703, where at 3,300 feet the seaplane was received with considerable fire from the ground. Edmonds landed back in the harbour at 0750 and after briefing the other pilots an immediate attack was decided upon on the camp near Subar.

All the five Schneiders were hoisted out, the first one getting airborne at 0837 followed at short intervals by the others carrying 16-lb and 20-lb bombs. Flt Cdr Edmonds in 3721, 3722 flown by Flt Lt Bankes-Price, and F/S/L Clifford's 3774 with the sun and wind behind them bombed the camp at heights varying from 100 feet to 600 feet in the face of considerable rifle and machine gun fire from the ground, but all three returned safely to Aden harbour. Flt Lt England in 3727 suffered engine trouble and dropped his bombs on Waht. Flt Lt Wright

flying 3790 dropped two bombs on Sharaj and two into some mule lines south-east of Waht. The last of the seaplanes returned at 0940.

The five Schneiders were then refuelled and re-armed for an attack on two villages near Subar where activity had been noticed during the early morning reconnaissance flight. Each pilot flew the same machine as in the morning's attack and the first seaplane was airborne at 1503. Three of the Schneiders reached their objectives and two of them bombed successfully, but Bankes-Price was unable to release his bombs over the target owing to a defect in the bomb dropping mechanism. Despite engine trouble, England bombed a camp east of Waht, although his Schneider was unable to get airborne with more than two bombs. These he dropped on Waht, and the last seaplane returned safely at 1544 in spite of very bumpy conditions at heights between 1,500 feet and 2,500 feet.

On 1 April a second attack was mounted on the camp near Subar by four of *Raven II*'s Schneiders, Edmonds's 3721 being unserviceable. The first seaplane took off at 0615, and attacking from 800 to 1500 feet a total of 15 bombs fell in the camp. There was very little ground fire on this occasion and the last seaplane

HMS Ben-my-Chree's Short is hoisted in at Thud Island, Suez Canal 1916. The observer, Capt J.Wedgwood Benn stands on the float and the pilot is Flt Cdr W.G.Sitwell. Although 8085 is stencilled on the port float, this may not be the Short's serial number. Floats were interchangeable between seaplanes. (FAAM)

returned at 0709. At 0845 Edmonds, taking Capt C.P. Paige, GSO Aden, as observer, took off in the Short to reconnoitre the enemy positions at Waht, Lahej and Subar during which twelve 20-lb bombs were dropped on trenches and gun emplacements. The seaplane returned to the ship at 0709, but further operations planned for that evening had to be cancelled owing to a strong wind and low cloud.

The weather was still threatening at dawn on 2 April, but had cleared sufficiently for the first of the four still-serviceable Schneiders to take off at 0638 for a low level attack on Fiyush. Clifford in 3774 failed to find the target and bombed Waht, but an advanced army outpost reported that twelve of the bombs from the other three Schneiders fell in the village of Fiyush. All the Schneiders had landed by 0700, and at 0747 Wright and Millard took off in 850 to fly a reconnaissance over the targets attacked since 31 March and to drop propaganda leaflets urging the Arabs to desert the Turkish cause. In spite of a failing engine several photographs of enemy positions were taken, and at 0838 the ageing Short was put down safely on the waters of Aden harbour. Edmonds, while at Aden, had tried to persuade old 850 to stagger into the air with a 500-lb bomb but the attempt had failed. In fact examination of the engine in the forenoon of 2 April proved the trouble to be extensive. No further flights by *Raven II*'s seaplanes were required; all the Schneiders were struck down below on the afternoon of the 2nd, and the ship sailed for Suez in the early hours of 3 April.

Flying conditions during the three days of operations had been difficult. Early mornings were calm but the cloud base was down to about 1,500 feet. Later in the day the heat caused turbulence problems and adversely affected the water cooled engine on the Short, and in the evenings there was usually a strong wind. Bomb aiming on the Schneiders was via an aperture in the cockpit floor. Alongside the sighting aperture three angles were marked on the footboard, viz. from the pilot's eye in his normal sitting position to the front, the middle and the rear of the aperture respectively, all measured from the vertical. A total of 91 bombs was dropped during the three days, and a high proportion found their targets. While physical damage was not great the effect on the Turks' Arab allies was considerable.

Following her return from Aden, *Raven II* was off El Arish on the morning of 25 April where F/S/L Clifford took off at 0625 in Schneider 3774 to observe enemy troop movements between El Arish and Bir Mazar. When over Lake Bardawil Clifford noticed an enemy aeroplane astern at 5,000 feet and about six miles away. Since Clifford's only weapon was a Webley pistol he altered course to seaward and put down the Schneider's nose attaining a speed of 80 knots. The

HMS Ben-my-Chree's Short 184,8087, crewed by Cdr Samson and Capt Wedgwood Benn sinking on 23rd May 1916 after the floats smashed attempting to take-off. (via RCS)

enemy aircraft gave chase for 15 miles out to sea, firing with his machine gun mounted in the rear cockpit. Clifford jettisoned his four 20-lb bombs at 200 feet and swung towards the ship, when the enemy sheered off. Clifford put 3774 down safely at 0710 with one bullet in a strut and two more in the fuselage fabric.

It was now *Ben-my-Chree*'s turn to continue operations off Aden, and after embarking three Short 184's (850, 8054 and 8082), two Schneiders (3789 and 3790) and a Baby (8189) she sailed from Port Said at 0600 on 2 June.

Before arriving in Aden harbour, Short 184, 8054 was hoisted out at dawn on 7 June and flying east attempted a reconnaissance of enemy camps in the Lahej Delta. The intense heat caused the coolant of the Short's engine to boil, so the flight had to be restricted to the camps south-east of Waht.

On the ship entering Aden harbour the GSO supplied the latest intelligence on the disposition of enemy forces, and plans were made for operations on the next day. At dawn on 8 June two Schneiders and one Short 184 were hoisted out and took off. The Short headed north and reached the camps on the farther side of Lahej. The seaplane was under heavy fire from two guns at Waht. A 16-lb bomb was dropped on a camel camp at Malhalla on the way to Lahej. It had been intended to bomb the ammunition store at the north-west corner of Lahej, but as the seaplane could not reach a greater height than 700 feet above sea level (only 300 feet above the town) it was impossible to drop the

Two views of a Short 184 and a Baby at Port Said Seaplane Base, both of which types were operated by HMS Anne during 1916/17. In each photograph HMS Anne lies at anchor in the background. (G.S.Leslie/J.M.Bruce collection)

112-lb bomb without damaging the machine. The bomb together with two 16-lb bombs was accordingly dropped on a gun emplacement north of Lahej in the face of intense AA fire from four 10-pounder guns.

The Waht guns also fired at the Schneider which immediately followed the Short. Flechettes were dropped on the gun crews and a bomb was dropped in the town. The second Schneider, under heavy AA fire, dropped eight bombs on Waht. Two Short 184s and the Baby were hoisted out on the morning of 9 June. One Short reconnoitred Darb and Waht, where preparations to repel a British night attack were observed. The other Short flew a reconnaissance over Darb, Subar and Fiyush and was hit by AA fire.

After the Baby had climbed to 1,000 feet the engine suddenly cut, so the pilot jettisoned his bombs and turned to glide back within our lines. However the engine picked up again and the pilot was able to regain Aden harbour, landing unharmed in about two feet of water.

On the afternoon of the 9th a Schneider attacked the camp at Darb, as did a Short 184 with a 65-lb bomb and 112-lb bomb respectively. A second Short 184 dropped

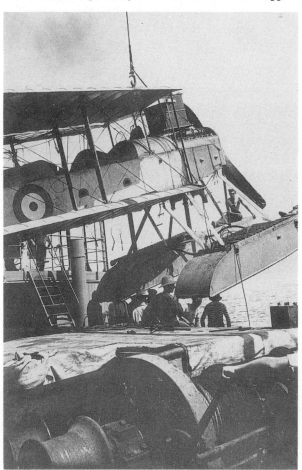

One of Ben-my Chree's Short 184's being hoisted out, possibly in the Red Sea if the wearing of sun helmets is any indication. (G.S.Leslie/J.M.Bruce collection)

a 112-lb bomb on Waht and all three seaplanes dropped propaganda leaflets dealing with the German hostility towards Islam.

No flying was undertaken on the 10th to give the impression that the raids had ceased, but two Short 184's and a Schneider were hoisted out on the morning of 11 June. One Short with engine trouble failed to get airborne but the other bombed the camp with four 20-lb bombs and two incendiaries. The Schneider attacked the Subar camp with a 65-lb bomb which fell 50 yards short of the tents. The final sortie was flown on the morning of 12 June when the Baby started a good fire in the camp at Subar with two 20-lb and six incendiary bombs. During five days' operations *Ben-my-Chree*'s seaplanes had dropped HE bombs totalling 845 lbs plus incendiaries and flechettes. Again the material damage was not great, but that to the will of the Arabs to assist the Turkish forces certainly was.

Ben-my-Chree left Aden harbour on the evening of 12 June and arrived off Perim Island at 0400 on the 13th where Short 184 850, fitted with W/T, was hoisted out to spot the fall of shot for *Ben-my-Chree*'s guns. 850's engine however gave trouble; it was hoisted in again at 0525, and its place taken by a Schneider. *Ben-my-Chree* took up a position north of the camps at Jebel Malu and Jebel Akrabi and 2000 yards from the shore which permitted of enfilade fire. The Schneider dropped two incendiary bombs to give the line of the camps to the ship's guns and then five HE bombs into the camps themselves. At a range of 4,600 yards the port forward 12-pounder opened fire and the seaplane observed four shells fall into the camp. A gun which had been firing on both the ship and the seaplane then ceased firing.

Ben-my-Chree moved farther offshore in order to launch a Short 184 out of range of the guns, but then came under fire from two guns on the western slopes of Jebel Akrabi to which she replied - one round bursting close to them. Their return fire straddled the ship and one round passed through the forward funnel. After silencing one of the two guns *Ben-my-Chree* moved out of range and launched a W/T equipped Short 184, which directed the ship's resumed gunfire on Jebel Akrabi. The Short returned after an hour's spotting for refuelling and re-arming, and was hoisted out again at 0803 and attacked a camp at Khor Ghorera with a 112-lb and two 20-lb bombs.

At 0848 the Short was again sent out and bombed a camp at Akrabi. After a flight of 47 minutes the seaplane was hoisted in and at 1000 on 13 June, since coal stocks were now running low, *Ben-my-Chree* set course for Port Sudan to replenish. During the gun action the ship had expended 39 rounds of shrapnel, lyddite and common shell.

Before *Ben-my-Chree* could reach Port Sudan, however, orders were received to proceed at once to

Jeddah, where the Turkish garrison was being besieged by the Arabs. Here the cruisers *Fox* and *Perth* with the AMCs *Hardinge* and *Dufferin* had been bombarding the town with little success, having no seaplanes to spot the fall of shot.

Ben-my-Chree arrived at Jeddah on the morning of 15 June, and in accordance with the requirements of the SNO Red Sea, Capt. Boyle, Samson arranged for bombing and reconnaissance flights that evening, after the bombardment had ceased. Samson and 2nd Lt Wedgwood-Benn at 1708 took off in a Short 184 and flew over the town. Photographs were taken of the enemy guns and trenches north and south of the town, and after the seaplane had bombed and missed a gun battery, Samson came down to low level to enable Wedgwood-Benn to fire his Lewis gun at men in the trenches.

Return fire hit the Short repeatedly. The propeller was pierced and other shots hit the fuselage, one by the pilot's foot and another behind the observer nearly severing the elevator control wire. Bankes-Price in a Schneider bombed the trenches south of the town and then fired his Lewis gun into them from 100 feet. Flt Lt England unsuccessfully attempted, in another Schneider, to breach the east wall of the town with a 65-lb bomb, the gate itself being too close to a Mosque to be attacked. Preparations for further attacks were halted by the surrender of the town on 16 June and *Ben-my-Chree* proceeded, via Port Sudan for coaling, to Port Said where she arrived on 21 June.

May 1916 was an inactive period for *Raven II*, but she was at sea again off El Arish on 7 June when at 0518 Flt Lt J.C. Brooke and Lt N.W. Stewart took off in Short 184, 8090, for a 2-hour photo reconnaissance and bombing flight in the vicinity of El Arish. Similar flights in the same area were made by *Raven II*'s seaplanes on 22 and 26 June.

On 29 June *Raven II* commenced coaling and taking on board bombs, ammunition and stores for a nine-day cruise. Four seaplanes were embarked next day - two Short 184s 8090 and 8091, a Schneider 3786 and a Baby 8189. Her aircrew consisting of four pilots and three observers under the command of Flt Lt G.B. Dacre reported onboard by 2200, and *Raven II* sailed from Port Said at 0630 in company with the armed tug *Laborieux* as escort. A position 15 miles north-north-east of El Arish was reached at 1600, where between 1635 and 1645 the Schneider and a Short 184 were hoisted out. The Short, 8091, had its wings spread and the engine started in a heavy swell. By 1700 the seaplane had climbed to 1,000 feet when the cooling water boiled and the oil pressure dropped. Unable to gain further altitude Dacre reversed course and landed close to the ship at 1715. The wings were folded and the machine hoisted aboard at 1720.

Flt Lt Brooke's Schneider 3786, which had been meant to escort 8091 to El Arish, was airborne at 1655 getting off from a considerable swell. Brooke carried out a reconnaissance of El Arish under heavy and accurate AA fire. Two 16-lb bombs were dropped from 3,000 feet and one was seen to hit the outhouse of the ammunition store east of the town. AA fire followed Brooke to the coast which he crossed at 4,000 feet and by 1745 the seaplane was safely hoisted onboard, 10 miles north of El Arish.

Raven II soon got under way and by 0615 on 2 July was in position eight miles north-west of Haifa. Dacre with Lt Ravenscroft RFA as his observer in 8091 were hoisted out in a considerable swell at 0645, as was F/S/L Man in Schneider 3786, and both seaplanes were airborne by 0700. Flying at 3,000 feet the Short bombed the railway bridge and Custom House at Haifa but no direct hits were observed and the seaplane landed close to the ship at 0820.

At 0715 Man's Schneider developed engine trouble when one-and-a-half miles east of Haifa and he was forced to land half-a -mile west of Haifa. Man found that a tappet rod had broken and that it had carried away others as it whirled round. By 0830 it was realised on board *Raven II* that the Schneider was overdue, so Dacre ordered 8091 to be hoisted out, and taking Lt Brown as observer, set off to search for the missing seaplane. The Schneider was seen floating half-a-mile off Acre town, drifting towards the shore in a sinking condition, and with Man standing on the upper mainplane clear of the water. A crowd had now appeared on the beach but no attempt was made by them to open fire or board the machine. At 0905 Dacre put the Short down close to the Schneider and Man swam across to the Short. Brown emptied a full hopper from his Lewis gun into the Schneider which then sank, after which the Short flew back to the ship with Man in the rear cockpit and Brown astride the top petrol tank. This position, the only possible one to keep a balance of the machine, was extremely uncomfortable during the 12-minute flight. The heat from the radiator and the bumps in a cramped position had to be endured by Lt Brown.

Leaving Acre at 0945, *Raven II* shaped a course for Famagusta which was reached at 0500 on 3 July. That day and most of the 4th were spent unloading coal onto the jetty, the Air Mechanics also being used to accelerate the work. *Raven II* sailed from Famagusta at 1830 on 4 July and reached Castelorizo at 0430 on the 6th. Here Dacre went ashore and saw the Governor, Lt de Vaisseau de Saint Salvy and the Intelligence Officer. From them he got their requirements, the most important work being in the area of Makri. The coast near Castelorizo could be reconnoitred from *Raven II*, but the Makri district, as far as reconnaissances were required, entailed a flight of three hours working from Castelorizo. This could not be done by the Sunbeam-engined Short 184's in their present state of unreliability. It was decided therefore, with the Governor's approval to form an advanced base at Tersana Island in Makri Bay. It was inadvisable to take *Raven II* into this potentially dangerous area, so it was planned that *Laborieux* should carry personnel and petrol to Tersana Island to establish a base.

Raven II's seaplanes made two reconnaissance flights from Castelorizo harbour as far west as Volos Island. Brooke and 2nd Lt King KOSB in 8090 were hoisted out

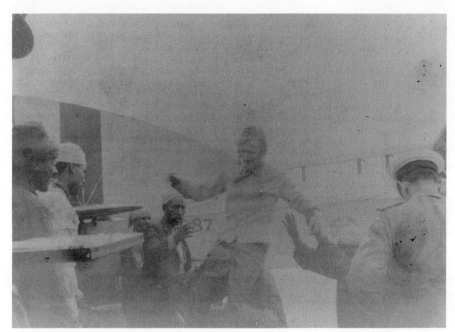

Flt Lt G.B.Dacre with his observer Capt J.Wedgwood Benn on his shoulders. HMS Ben-my-Chree's Short 184, 8087 is in the background. (FAAM)

first at 1615. Soon after getting airborne at 1640 the Short's radiator boiled, and unable to gain sufficient altitude for a bombing run, the 112-lb bomb was dropped unfused into the sea. Photographs were taken from 1,500 feet of Kalmaki and Port Vathi, and after landing at 1747 the Short was hoisted in at 1810. Dacre in Baby 8189 was airborne at 1710, flying eastwards as far as Cape Pyrgo. At Fakdir Dacre dropped four 16-lb bombs on a hill outpost which set fire to the scrub. The fire spread rapidly and was still burning two days later. At 1750 Dacre landed back in the harbour and was hoisted in. At 2330 that night *Laborieux* left for Tersana Island, taking with her seven Air Mechanics, 150 gallons of petrol, 20 gallons of oil, two spare propellers, twenty 16-lb bombs, spare Lewis gun hoppers and various spares.

Brooke and King with 8090 remained at Castelorizo until at 0500 on the 7th Dacre and Lt Ravenscroft RFA in 8091 and Man in the Baby 8189 took off to fly to Tersana Island. The other observer, Brown, had gone

ahead on board *Laborieux*.

Man had orders to fly directly to Tersana Island, but the Short made a reconnaissance along the coast towards Makri Bay before heading for Tersana. At 0540 however the Short's radiator boiled badly, engine revs began to drop and at only 400 feet three 16-lb bombs had to be dropped into the sea. The Short reached Tersana Island at 0645 and taxied into the small harbour to await the arrival of *Laborieux*. The right hand float touched the bottom before reaching the shore, and because the beach was rocky the seaplane had to be moored out with the tail on the beach.

The Baby had landed at the next island, but on discovering his mistake Man took off again and reached Tersana Island at 0700. *Laborieux* arrived at 0745. In the afternoon the Short's starboard float had shipped a lot of water and two hours were spent pumping it out. When this was completed, Man and Brown attempted to take off in the Short at 1710 for a reconnaissance of Makri and Levisi. First the radiator boiled and then the starboard float took in so much water that the wingtip float became submerged. After taxying back into the harbour 8091 was beached tail first at 1735. Dacre then took off in the Baby at 1718, and after dropping three 16-lb bombs at Makri harbour returned to Tersana at 1740. Because it was impossible to beach the Short properly, and in the absence of an efficient pump, an attempt was made to hoist the submerged float with *Laborieux*'s davits and syphon out the water, but this was unsuccessful. At daylight on the 8th therefore the starboard mainplanes were removed from 8091. They were then floated off and hauled across *Laborieux*'s gunwale. The floats were removed after strengthening up the forward davit and hoisting up the Short to the limit of the block. The floats were hauled aboard by the after davits, while the fuselage with port mainplanes attached was strung up to the side of *Laborieux* by two davits. In this way the Short was brought back to *Raven II* at Castelorizo, the only damage being a bent elevator and one wingtip float carried away by heavy seas.

Man in the Baby left Tersana at 0500 on the 8th and after dropping bombs at Levisi landed at Castelorizo at 0555. While taxying over the boom at the harbour entrance the tail float was damaged. *Laborieux* reached Castelorizo at 1245, and after transferring the Short to *Raven II*, both ships sailed for Port Said at 1700 on 8

July, arriving there on 9 July.

Anne lay at Port Said for three weeks following her return from Malta. Weldon's time was occupied by running the office of the Military Intelligence Officer, Capt. Woolley - he of the schooner *Belle Alliance* - while he was in Cyprus. But on 15 June *Anne* received orders to steam through the Canal to Suez, and there to ship ammunition for the Hejaz. Suez Roads were reached on the 16th and on the 19th *Anne* moved into the inner harbour to take on board tons of coffee, rice and barley. Also coming aboard was Sayad Bey Ali of the Egyptian Artillery, who was to command two Egyptian mountain batteries. These were to be embarked at Port Sudan and shipped to Jeddah, where they were to join the King of the Hejaz's army. Port Sudan was reached on 26 June, where the batteries and 150 mules were loaded. £30,000 in gold was also shipped. *Anne* sailed for Jeddah on 27 June with all the mules on her foredeck. They had a pretty warm time, standing on iron decks with no awnings over them, and with a shade temperature of 120 degrees fahrenheit.

Anne arrived off Jeddah on the 28th, the town having fallen to the Arabs on 16 June, and next day proceeded to unload the batteries and mules - the latter being hoisted over the side in slings and lowered into dhows. After half this task was completed, an order was received to keep one battery on board and proceed with it to Rabegh, which was reached on 30 June. On entering harbour *Anne* was surrounded by dhows crewed by a wild looking lot of Arabs. They refused to unload *Anne* saying all they wanted was food and ammunition. Capt Linberry of RIMS *Hardinge* went off in a boat to see what he could do, but the Arabs threatened to shoot him if he stepped ashore. *Anne* wirelessed to Jeddah for instructions and was told to await the arrival of the transport *Surada* with a local Sheikh Nassir on board who would sort things out. *Surada* arrived at Rabegh on 1 July, having on board the other mountain battery *Anne* had landed at Jeddah! Sheikh Nassir failed to persuade the Arabs, and so *Anne* returned to Jeddah, where on 3 July the artillery and mules, who had been on board for six days, were unloaded and the ship was given a thorough washing down. *Anne* lay at Jeddah for the next three days unloading the rest of her cargo. Sailing on the 7th she arrived at Suez on 11 July where she was to be dry docked, not returning to Port Said and her proper rôle as a seaplane carrier until early August.

While *Anne* was at Suez, Weldon and Kerr found at Alexandria an ex-Austrian Lloyd vessel of 8,000 tons and with a speed of 18 knots which would have converted to an ideal seaplane carrier. However, the Prize Court at Port Said refused to part with her, and *Anne* was reprieved for a further year! *Anne* made a brief sortie from Port Said in the early hours of 6 August, when at 0558 F/S/L Man and Sub Lt Kerry

RNVR took off in Short 184, 8090, to reconnoitre the roads between El Mardan and to within 7 miles of El Arish. A camp was observed at El Mardan, but no movement on the roads, and after the Short was hoisted in at 0702 *Anne* proceeded back to Port Said.

Ben-my-Chree meanwhile had sailed on 6 July, to relieve *Raven II* off the Syrian coast, escorted by the French destroyer *Dard*. Off El Arish a Schneider was launched to bomb a Turkish trench system, and flying farther inland towards the aerodrome was headed off by two German aeroplanes and had to return to the ship. Off Beirut on the 7th a Short was launched for a reconnaissance of the harbour, where some schooners were unsuccessfully bombed. Proceeding north, a Short was launched off the mouth of Nahr El Kebir for a flight to the railway station at Tel Keli, but engine trouble forced an early return. Two tugs were observed in the river mouth. *Ben-my-Chree* sailed for coaling at Famagusta, and by the 10th was back off Nahr El Kebir, where two of her Schneiders unsuccessfully bombed the tugs. After recovering her two Schneiders, a Short 184 was despatched to spot for her 12-pounder gun which scored several hits on the tugs. Further flights were made over Beirut and Haifa before the ship returned to Port Said on 11 July.

Ben-my-Chree was at sea again on 24 July for a reconnaissance of the El Maadam to El Arish roads, and to search for mines off El Arish. Short 184, 8054, crewed by Flt Lt Maskell and Lt Stewart, Royal Scots was hoisted out at 0920. Bombs were dropped on a camp at Ujret El Zol, and shortly after the seaplane had been hoisted in at 1020, *Ben-my-Chree* and the escorting French destroyer *Arbalette* were near-missed by three bombs dropped from high altitude by a German aeroplane.

By dawn on 26 July *Ben-my-Chree* was in position off Haifa to launch a series of reconnaissance and bombing missions by her Short 184s and a Schneider. Samson and Wedgwood-Benn in 8372 were hoisted out at 0451, and getting airborne within 5 minutes, crossed the coast over Haifa at 1,000 feet. The railway was followed south-east to the junction at El Afule where a train and 1,500 troops were seen. Despite heavy AA fire they scored a hit with a 16-lb bomb on the train, setting it on fire. Samson landed the seaplane at 0615 and it was hoisted in ready for another sortie. Flt Lt England and 2nd Lt Smith were airborne in 8372 again at 1012, but flying conditions were so bad that after ascertaining that there were no troop movements on the road leading south from Nablus, it was decided to return to the ship after a 40-minute flight. Two more reconnaissance flights by Schneider 3771 and Short 184 8054 were made over Jaffa, Ludd, Ramleh and El Falugeh. Bankes-Price in the Schneider bombed the railway station at Ludd, Maskell and Stewart in the Short

Four photographs taken over Palestine in 1916 by one of HMS Anne's Short 184s. (FAAM)

A bomb bursting in a Turkish camp north of the railway at Shemmune from 1,800 feet.

Rolling stock on the railway at El Afule (top right) and two bomb explosions near some tents.

Trenches (top right) facing the sea south east of Haifa from 2,500 feet.

Two Turkish camps at Warakani from 1,800 feet.

bombed the station at Arak El Mensbiyeh, but neither seaplane saw any troop movements. A second attempt to reach Nablus and Samaria was successful when England and Smith took up 8372 at 1650 in better flying conditions. Camps were seen at Tulkeram and Nablus but no signs of military activity. As soon as the Short had been hoisted in at 1812, *Ben-my-Chree* set course for Port Said arriving there early on 27 July, where she was taken in hand for boiler cleaning.

While *Ben-my-Chree* was in dockyard hands, *Raven II* was despatched to the Gulf of Akaba for her Short 184s to make photographic reconnaissance flights with a view to selecting suitable landing places for an expedition to cut the railway at Ma'an. The British naval blockade of the Hejaz coast had effectively cut off supplies to the Turkish garrisons along the east coast of the Red Sea from Port Sudan, but supplies were still getting through to them via the Hejaz railway running south from Ma'an to Medina.

On 30 July *Raven II*'s seaplanes made two flights over Akaba to photograph the town vertically from 2,500 feet, and also the country round the head of the Gulf. 8091 with F/S/L G.D. Smith and Lt V. Millard of the Essex Regiment was hoisted out at 0645. After getting airborne at 0653 the camera slide shutter broke and 8091 had to land again at 0715 to obtain another camera. Taking off again after seven minutes the flight was successfully concluded, and at 0807 the seaplane was hoisted inboard. 8075 crewed by Flt Lt A.W. Clemson and 2nd Lt K.L. Williams completed a similar photographic reconnaissance of the town between 0655 and 0745. Smith and Millard in 8091 flew another photographic sortie over Akaba and trenches between Wadi Ithm and Akaba on 1 August, taking off at 0642 and landing alongside the ship at 0725.

By 4 August *Raven II* had moved south to Muweilah where at 0600 Clemson and Williams were hoisted out in 8075. Armed with one 65-lb and two 16-lb bombs they crossed the coast at 2,300 feet 7 miles north of Muweilah. Turning south they were over the town at 2,700 feet by 0635, where the fort was bombed. All bombs missed their target, and after examining the channels into Sherm Yahar and Sherm Jubba, 8075 returned to the ship at 0713.

Moving farther down the coast *Raven II* hoisted out 8091 crewed by Smith and Millard off Wej at 0723 on the 5th. Carrying one 65-lb and two 16-lb bombs the seaplane spent 17 minutes trying to get airborne. After jettisoning the 65-lb bomb they got off at the third attempt. At 1,000 feet they were fired at from Wej, but after climbing to 3,000 feet they photographed the town, and dropped the two remaining bombs on a Bedouin camp. Both bombs missed, and returning to the ship the seaplane was hoisted in at 0835. *Raven II* returned to Port Said on 7 August.

Following an unsuccessful Turkish attack on Romani, *Raven II* sailed from Port Said at 1900 on 9 August with two Short 184s, 8075 and 8091, embarked to spot for the monitor *M 21* in a bombardment of the retreating Turks at Bir El Mazar. *M 21* was met at 0415 on 10 August 12 miles north-north-west of Bir El Mazar, and *Raven II*'s aircrew went on board the monitor to make arrangements for spotting *M 21* which then proceeded to her firing position.

Clemson and Williams in 8075 were hoisted out at 0555 and 30 minutes later had climbed to 3,500 feet over the Turkish camp north-east of Bir El Mazar, where four 16-lb bombs were dropped to mark the target for the monitor, which then fired one round. The Short stayed over the target for an hour constantly wirelessing the monitor, but apparently they were not received by *M 21* and at 0740 the Short landed and was hoisted in.

Meanwhile 8091, crewed by Brooke and Smith, had taken off to continue the operation. The camp was reached at 0745 and three 16-lb marker bombs were dropped from 3000 feet. The signal to *M21* to open fire had just been made when a burst of machine gun fire

Flt Lt D.G.Smith RNAS, who between July 1916 and March 1918 flew seaplanes from all five seaplane carriers of the East Indies and Egypt Seaplane Squadron. (FAAM)

from below hit the seaplane and ruptured the petrol tanks. The Short had been attacked by a German aeroplane and a running fight ensued as Smith replied with his Lewis gun. The Short was hit in the radiator as Brooke dived seawards, and when close to *M 21* the enemy aircraft sheered off, and Brooke put the seaplane down close to the monitor at 0805. *M 21* wirelessed to *Raven II* for assistance, and at 0930 *Raven II* closed the monitor and hoisted in the Short, which by then was in a sinking condition. At 1015, while still stopped, *Raven II* was near missed by one of five bombs dropped by a hostile aircraft flying at about 6,000 feet. *Raven II* immediately got under way, zig-zagging seaward and set

Capt V.Millard, Essex Regiment (attached RFC) flew as an observer in seaplanes of the East Indies and Egypt Seaplane Squadron between March 1916 and March 1918 (FAAM)

course for Port Said.

Following her boiler clean, *Ben-my-Chree* sailed from Port Said on 14 August with three Short 184s and a Schneider for a series of reconnaissance flights along the Haifa Valley to El Afule. By dawn on 15 August the ship lay two miles north of Haifa. The Schneider was hoisted out first piloted by Bankes-Price, but failed to take off, and 8372 crewed by Samson and Wedgwood-Benn was hoisted out at 0455. At El Afule six

locomotives, 30 passenger coaches and 40 goods wagons were seen. Four bombs were dropped on the junction, one of which hit the track, and the Short returned at 0606.

Flt Cdr England and 2nd Lt King KOSB in Short 184, 8080, were hoisted out at 0512 to reconnoitre the Carmel Range for troops and trenches, and then to bomb the camp at Tabaun. The latter could not be found so the Short bombed a group of buildings at Jeida before returning to the ship at 0627.

F/S/L Dover and Lt Woodland RNVR in Short 184, 8054, however located the camp at Tabaun, and under heavy fire from six guns dropped four 16-lb and two petrol bombs into the camp, returning to *Ben-my-Chree* at 0555 after a flight of only 34 minutes. After 8054 had been re-armed and re-fuelled, Bankes-Price and Woodland were airborne in the Short at 1035 for a reconnaissance of Ludd and Ramleh. Over the camp at Ludd their 112-lb bomb failed to release, but four incendiaries were dropped there before alighting close to the ship at 1124, by which time Dover and King were airborne in 8080 to reconnoitre the roads between Nahr Sukereir and Falugeh for troop movements. The 112-lb bomb carried was not dropped as no suitable targets were seen, and the seaplane was hoisted in at 1225.

Flt Lt Maskell and Sub Lt Kerry RNVR made the last reconnaissance of the day in 8054 at 1300. A large camp was observed at Bureir, and because their use by the Turks to carry supplies made them a legitimate target, Kerry emptied a hopper from his Lewis gun into many camels on the road near Shellal.

8054 was hoisted in at 1435 and *Ben-my-Chree* set course for Port Said, her seaplanes having reconnoitred 165 miles of coastline to a depth of 20 miles. As a result of these flights a series of air attacks by the seaplanes of all three carriers of the Squadron was planned for the end of August.

Following her brief sortie of 6 August, *Anne* next left Port Said on the evening of 8 August with a Schneider, 3777, and a Short 184, 8090, embarked and escorted by the French destroyer *Voltigeur*. By 0330 on 10 August both ships had reached a pre-arranged rendezvous five miles south of Mersina. At 0415 the French bombarding squadron, consisting of the armoured cruiser *Pothuau*, three TBD's, five trawlers and the armed tug *Laborieux*, was sighted and closed. A channel having been swept by *Laborieux*, *Pothuau* followed by *Anne* steamed down it and anchored two miles off Mersina town at 0558. Both seaplanes were then hoisted out, the Short to spot *Pothuau*'s fall of shot and the Schneider to fly anti-submarine patrols round the ship.

The Short crewed by Flt Lt Dacre and F/S/L Man was airborne between 0621 and 0740 and from 2,000 feet spotted for *Pothuau*'s fire on a factory north-east of the town. Dacre with Lt Stewart as observer took off again in 8090 at 0948, this flight being delayed by 40 minutes through the engine failing to attain sufficient revs. *Pothuau*'s fire was now directed onto a factory north-west of the town, and by the time the Short returned to *Anne* at 1048 this target was practically demolished.

At 1035, while the Short was still airborne, a hostile biplane with Turkish markings appeared from the south-west at about 8,500 feet and dropped four small bombs, none of which fell closer to *Anne* than 400 yards. *Anne* fired two rounds at the aircraft which then made off to the south-west.

Both Dacre and Man took turns in flying the Schneider, armed with two 16-lb bombs, on anti-submarine patrols while the bombardment took place. A signal from the French admiral thanking the ship and her aviators for their co-operation was received and at 1115 *Anne* proceeded back to Port Said escorted by *Voltigeur*, arriving there on 12 August.

HMS Raven II moored in the harbour at Castelorizo. From here on 7 July 1916 she despatched two seaplanes to Tersana Island for an attack on Makri. (FAAM)

Three groups photographed at Port Said, headquarters of the East Indies and Egypt Seaplane Squadron. Uniforms of RNAS, Army and RFC can be seen. (FAAM & G.S.Leslie/J.M.Bruce collection)

{ Very few aircrew members' names serving with the East Indies and Egypt Seaplane Squadron have been applied to those in the above photographs. Any help with identification from readers would be invaluable.}

CHAPTER XII

Further operations by the three carriers of East Indies and Egypt Seaplane Squadron August 1916- January 1917

T he stage was now set for operations by all three seaplane carriers of the EI and ESS, the objectives being to deliver a rapid series of attacks on enemy communications with their army in Sinai, and to reconnoitre the whole of the lines of approach from Adana.

Although the railway ran parallel to the coast, most of its length was behind a range of mountains, and for this reason the Turks considered it immune from aerial attack. Enemy sea transport had been virtually eliminated by the patrols of the French Navy, so that the Turkish army still menacing the Suez Canal was dependent on being supplied by the railway from the north.

The most attractive means of disrupting the railway supply line was to attack the junction at El Afule. The junction could be approached through a narrow valley between the Nazareth and Carmel ranges without the necessity for heavily-laden seaplanes to climb over the mountain ranges. This route had been thoroughly reconnoitred by *Ben-my-Chree*'s seaplanes on 15 August.

The plan adopted was for the three ships of the Squadron to rendezvous off Haifa just before dawn on the morning of 25 August. For this purpose the two slower ships sailed from Port Said early on the 24th, *Raven II* escorted by the trawler *Paris II* and *Anne* by the French destroyer *Hache*. *Ben-my-Chree* in company with the French destroyer *Arbalette* sailed at 1640 on the afternoon of the 24th, and all three carriers rendezvoused off Haifa at first light on the 25th.

The operation orders called for the ten seaplanes - *Ben-my-Chree*'s three Short 184s and two Schneiders, *Raven II*'s two Short 184s and a Schneider, *Anne*'s one Short 184 and one Schneider - then to be hoisted out, and as soon as Samson's Short had taken off and circled the ships once, the other seaplanes were to get airborne. They were then to formate on Samson's Short,

Short 184, probably 8372, in which Cdr Samson flew to lead the attack on El Afule railway junction, 25th August 1916. This photograph was taken in 1915 while the Short was in HMS Engadine. (FAAM)

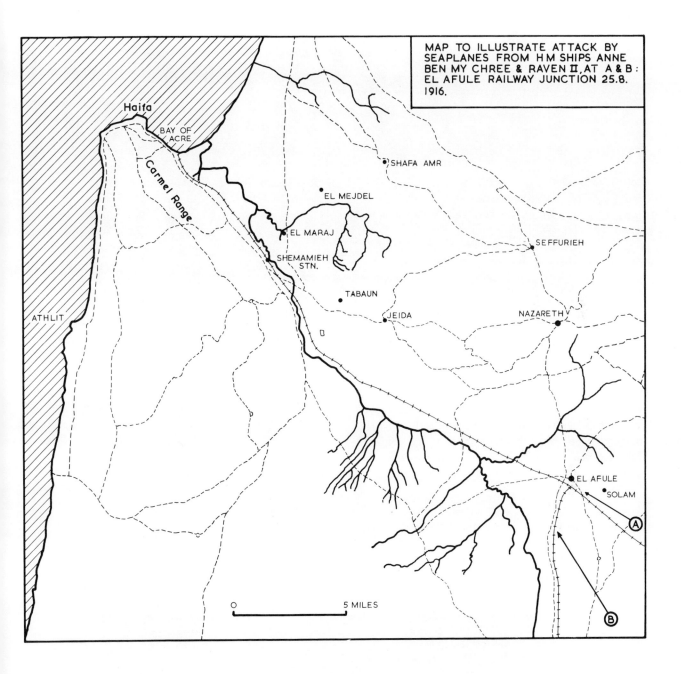

MAP TO ILLUSTRATE ATTACK BY
SEAPLANES FROM H M SHIPS ANNE
BEN MY CHREE & RAVEN II, AT A & B:
EL AFULE RAILWAY JUNCTION 25.8.
1916.

65-lb bomb from Cdr Samson's Short 184 bursting between two trains at El Afule junction on 25th August 1916.
(via RCC)

distinguished by a red fin, in quarter line to starboard with *Ben-my-Chree*'s five seaplanes leading and over to port, *Anne*'s two seaplanes in the centre and *Raven II*'s bringing up the rear on the starboard side. The staggered formation was necessary because of the narrow valley up which they must fly to reach their targets.

Samson's own summary of this operation, and all published accounts of the raid state that this is exactly what happened. However from the pilots' and observers' Report of Flight forms it is evident that the composition of the raiding force consisted of only nine seaplanes made up as follows:-

BEN-my-CHREE	Short 184,	probably 8372	Cdr C.R. Samson and Capt J. Wedgwood Benn
	Short 184,	8080	F/S/L M.G. Dover and Lt P. Woodland
	Short 184,	8035	Flt Lt J.T. Bankes-Price (no observer)
	Schneider (probably, but no serial quoted)		Probably Flt Cdr T.H. England
ANNE	Short 184,	8091	Flt Lt J.C. Brooke and 2nd Lt K.L. Williams
	Schneider,	3777	Flt Lt W. Man
RAVEN II	Short 184,	8045	F/S/L G.D. Smith and Lt V. Millard
	Short 184,	8075	Flt Lt A.W. Clemson and Sqdn Cdr C.J.L'E.Malone
	Baby,	8189	F/S/L L.P. Paine

From the foregoing it would appear that one of *Ben-my-Chree*'s two Schneiders failed to take part in the raid for some reason, and the identity of her Schneider, and its pilot who did take part have not been confirmed. The duty of the Schneiders and the Baby was to act as escort to the Shorts after each machine had bombed.

The ships began hoisting out their seaplanes at 0450, and by the time all the seaplanes had been hoisted out at 0540 Samson's Short had been airborne for ten minutes. All seaplanes then crossed the coast north of Haifa between 0540 and 0545 with the exception of Dover and Woodland in 8080 which was not airborne until 0539. However Dover's Short crossed the coast at 0555 and must soon have caught up with the formation, for all the seaplanes attacking the junction bombed the target within 15 minutes of each other.

The formation flew up the valley at altitudes varying between 1,200 and 1,900 feet and were subjected to heavy rifle and machine gun fire from hilltop positions on both sides of the valley during the 20-minute flight. Plunging fire from the camp north-west of Tabaun was directed at the three seaplanes from *Raven II* on the starboard side of the formation, but each machine emerged safely at the head of the valley into the Plain of Esdraelon - Armageddon, scene of the final battle between the kings of the earth at the end of the world, described in Revelations XVI.16.

At El Afule, just short of the junction, *Raven II*'s flight swung south to attack the line south of the junction, while the flights from *Ben-my-Chree* and *Anne* pressed on to the main target. Their approach precipitated the hurried departure southward of a train standing in the station, which did not go unnoticed by *Raven II*'s seaplanes. Paine in Baby 8189 dropped his first 16-lb bomb from 1,000 feet and damaged the embankment. Descending to 700 feet he dropped his remaining three bombs, scoring a hit on the line and on the rear coach of the train which caught fire. The two Shorts, 8045 and 8075, then made their bombing runs at 0608 and 0615 respectively. From only 300 feet 8045 dropped two 16-lb bombs one of which was a direct hit and took the roof off a carriage, while one of the two 65-lb bombs fell on the line five yards behind the train. Clemson and Malone in 8075 bombed from 500 feet and scored one direct hit on the line and machine gunned the train. All three seaplanes of the *Raven* flight encountered small arms fire on their return flight. The Baby's floats, wing and main spar all had bullet holes in them, 8075 was hit in several places, but all three seaplanes landed safely between 0637 and 0700 and were hoisted in.

The main force meanwhile had commenced their attack on the junction at 0600. *Anne*'s flight opened the proceedings, when Man's Schneider approached the station from the south-east and dropped a line of three 16-lb bombs on the station buildings. Brooke and Williams in 8091 flying at 1700 feet also bombed these buildings three minutes later, dropping one 112-lb bomb, two 16-lb and three incendiaries. Both seaplanes then climbed to 4,000 feet and returned to the ship at 0623 and 0645 respectively. The objective of the *Ben-my-Chree* flight was the locomotives and rolling stock in the station, and all four seaplanes began their attack from 1,500 feet at 0606 as those from *Anne* flew off. In the face of heavy AA fire from two guns at the station, Samson's Short dropped two 65-lb bombs, one of which fell between two trains in a siding. The other two seaplanes caused extensive damage to the track and buildings with HE and incendiary bombs, and two fires were burning as they left to return to the ship. Approximately 1,500 lb of bombs had been dropped on the two targets within the space of 15 minutes.

The last of the seaplanes was hoisted in at 0715, and while *Anne* and *Raven II* proceeded

Flt Lt J.T.Bankes-Price is hoisted inboard in Schneider 1437 or 1438 by the derrick of HMS Ben-my-Chree during operations in the Eastern Mediterranean in 1915. Bankes-Price later flew seaplanes from Ben-my-Chree with the EI & ESS until he was killed in action on 17th September 1916. (FAAM)

southward to a rendezvous off Askalon, *Ben-my-Chree* hoisted out Short 184, 8054, crewed by Flt Cdr Dacre and Wedgwood Benn at 0825. Airborne at 0842 and carrying a 112-lb bomb and two 16-lb bombs, the objective was the rolling stock at El Afule. Flying east along the Haifa railway the Short was unable to climb above 800 feet, so before returning to the ship at 0919 the bombs were dropped on the track. *Ben-my-Chree* then steamed south to meet the other two carriers for the purpose of attacking the camp at Bureir, making a general reconnaissance and bombing the railway bridge crossing the Wadi El Hesi. *Raven II* hoisted out Short 184, 8045 at 1520 on 25 August and reached Bureir half an hour later. Only one 16-lb bomb had been dropped from 2,000 feet on the camp when accurate AA fire holed the radiator. The remaining bomb load was dropped to lighten the machine and it returned to the ship at 1625. Paine in Baby 8189 bombed the camp with four 16-lb bombs and was hoisted back on board *Raven II* at 1700.

While *Ben-my-Chree*'s seaplanes were reconnoitering the area, *Anne* hoisted out Schneider, 3777, and Short 184, 8091, at 1555. Man in the Schneider dropped four 16-lb bombs in a line along the embankment 50 yards north of the bridge at Wadi El Hesi from 1,000 feet at 1630. He was followed two minutes later by Brooke and Williams in the Short whose 112-lb bomb dropped from 2,800 feet damaged the railway line, and *Anne* hoisted in both seaplanes by 0538. The operation was marred by the loss of Dacre whose Short 184, 8054, flying from *Ben-my-Chree*, suffered engine failure on a flight to Bureir. Dacre was taken prisoner and spent many months in captivity. *Anne* remained off the coast for some time in the hope of finding Dacre and then proceeded south. Meanwhile *Ben-my-Chree* and *Raven II* both steamed north to Tripoli and Adalia respectively.

By the morning of 26 August *Anne* lay five miles west of Nahr Iskanderuneh where at 0948 Short 184, 8091, was hoisted out for a flight to Nablus returning via Tul Keram. In perfect flying conditions and with the Sunbeam engine delivering full revs for once, Nablus was photographed from 4,000 feet, and Tul Keram bombed from 5,200 feet before the Short returned to the ship at 1118. Continuing southward *Anne* stopped six miles off Nahr Rubin at 1614 to again hoist out 8091, for the second time that day crewed by Brooke and Williams. A 20-minute flight took them to the camp at Ramleh which they bombed with one 112-lb and four 16- bombs, and as soon as the seaplane was hoisted back on board, *Anne* proceeded to Port Said which she reached on 27 August.

Raven II after steaming north through the night of 26 August stopped in the Gulf of Adalia at dawn on the 27th and at 0520 Clemson and Millard were hoisted out

in Short 184, 8075, to reconnoitre for a suspected submarine base at Adalia and to bomb a factory north-east of there. All bombs missed the factory although one fell within 20 yards, and the Short returned at 0810. Clemson and Kerry took off at 1310, again in 8075, to search Fineka Bay and Jeronda Bay for mines or submarine bases, but nothing was seen. *Raven II* sailed for Port Said as soon as her seaplane was hoisted in at 1402, arriving there on 28 August.

Ben-my-Chree steamed north during the night of the 25th, arriving off the mouth of Nahr El Kebir where two Short 184s were hoisted out on the morning of the 26th for a reconnaissance of the railway between Homs and Tripoli. The first Short flown by Samson failed to climb above 1,000 feet and only flew a coastal reconnaissance, but the other Short crewed by England and King reached Homs, 45 miles inland, in conditions of low cloud and a head wind. A Schneider was sent out to bomb a camp at Tel Keli, and after *Ben-my-Chree* had recovered her seaplanes she sailed for Famagusta to coal.

Ben-my-Chree left Famagusta early on the 29th, and off the headland of Karatash Burnu two Shorts were launched. One failed to gain height, but the second flown by Samson reached Adana and bombed a troop train in the station and a railway bridge over the river. A Schneider was later launched and bombed some lighters on a salt lake to the west of Karatash.

With the increased risk of submarine attack while launching and recovering seaplanes, Samson had cut down the time spent on these operations in *Ben-my-Chree*. The seaplanes had previously been run out of the hangar on trolleys, hoisted off the quarterdeck by derricks powered by a steam winch, lowered, and the derrick purchase unhooked. A motor boat was then employed to tow the seaplane away from the ship, or back to the ship after landing. By using a slip toggle, worked either from the ship or from the seaplane, the seaplane was dropped 6-12 inches above the water, while the ship was still under way. On returning the seaplane alighted to leeward, taxied to the ship which was kept stationary at 45 degrees to the seaplane's course, creating a patch of calm water for hoisting in. Alongside, the pilot stopped his engine and the observer caught a heaving line which was attached to the hook of the derrick purchase. Men along the ship's side fended off the seaplane with bearing-out spars, and once the seaplane was hoisted clear of the water the ship went ahead. Samson's claim of launching one seaplane and recovering another within 45 seconds must be taken with a pinch of salt! But a combination of ship handling and a precise routine undoubtedly reduced the danger of the carrier being torpedoed.

Knowing the vital part an observer had to play in seaplane operations, Samson took a great interest in the

Schneider 3789 flown by Cdr Samson on 14th September 1916. The upper longerons were rotten, and as the seaplane landed the engine fell out of its mountings. Here the imperturbable Samson waits to be hoisted in. (IWM Q99388)

training of the East Indies and Egypt Seaplane Squadron's observers.

Besides mastering air gunnery and bombs and bomb dropping, the observer had to operate his W/T transmitting and receiving sets. By 1916 the transmitter used in Short 184s was either a Type 52 Sterling 8-volt accumulator set or a Type 52B Marconi set, each with a 300 feet trailing aerial. The receiving set was either the Sullivan TB or Paul TD.

But most importantly the observer had to be trained to use his eyes (and his camera) to record what was happening below him, whether on sea or on land.

To help in this training, and guided by his own experience as a pilot, Samson wrote many useful notes for observers, some of which are quoted below:

"The observer should be able to help quite a lot by knowledge of how to dope the engine, shift sparking plug, etc."

"When returning to the seaplane carrier, he should get on the float when the seaplane is taxying back to the ship and look out for a heaving line. As soon as you have caught a heaving line remember first of all catch a turn with it."

"In HMS *Ben-my-Chree* the practice is for the seaplane to taxi towards the ship with wings spread at right angles to the ship fore and aft, and, when close alongside, the pilot stops his engine; a heaving line is then thrown to the pilot who hooks on. The observer should be ready to catch the second heaving line if the first misses and also to bear the seaplane off from the ship's side. Always remember to keep well clear of the propeller until it finally stops; also never touch the propeller unless you have first asked the pilot if the switch is to OFF.'

"Before going on a flight make certain that your W/T, camera and gun are in working order, and that you have:

1. Plates for the camera

2. Ammunition for the gun

3. Observer's board with plenty of pencils

4. Maps and charts

5. Binoculars

6. Codes (to be destroyed if there is any chance of them falling into the hands of the enemy)

7. Special instructions, ready reference tables, etc

8. Adequate clothing, life belt, etc

9. Even in hot climates, always have a uniform tunic or coat with you in case of capture, as if you appear well dressed it impresses your captors and makes them realise that the RNAS is a well organised and efficient force. Remember every little helps.''

"If you have a forced landing in enemy's territory carry out the following routine:

1. Smash the W/T on the way down. The best way is a blow with your pistol and then chuck it overboard from not less than 2,000 feet

2. Destroy all codes, maps, etc. all on the way down, as you may get damaged when alighting on land in a seaplane.

3. Damage your gun and throw it and your ammunition overboard if you have time. Even if they do not get damaged they might hurt somebody falling from a good altitude.

4. Never carry private letters or orders in your pocket as you might forget to destroy them

5. After alighting assist the pilot to destroy the machine by fire. The quickest way is to break the petrol gauge, and then ignite the petrol that streams out of it onto the ground.

"Get into the habit of continuously estimating the size of ships, general appearance of men-of-war, etc.

On every flight you make, keep a dead reckoning going and check it continuously with observations when possible.

In tropical countries remember that the wind generally rises and falls with the sun. The more you train yourself in observing the little details of life, the better observer you will be and the more you will see on a flight and will be able readily to answer questions and give

information that you have not noted down, but have subconsciously engraved on your memory.

Above all, do not forget the possible presence of hostile aircraft, and always keep your weather eye lifting.

Don't worry the pilot on a bumpy day or if he is having trouble with his engine.

Always be ready to point out your approximate position to the pilot.

Never forget your way home.

Always wind in the aerial before alighting. Nothing looks more unseamanlike than to alight with your aerial dragging in the water.''

Possibly Samson's last comment was aimed at the Army officers, unused to the ways of the Senior Service, who comprised most of the Squadron's observers. But he was a great leader of men.

Preparatory to a sortie into the Red Sea for operations off the Hejaz coast, *Raven II* was lying at Port Said on 31 August when she was put out of action. *Anne* lay 30 yards from *Raven II,* with hatches off for loading bombs, when three German aeroplanes flew over the harbour and dropped 12 bombs.

Weldon was on *Anne*'s bridge with Bishop, watching the enemy aircraft and the effects of the AA fire, when a bomb hit the water and burst just 20 feet off *Anne*'s counter. A second bomb then burst on *Raven II*'s foredeck, blowing a large hole in her deck, badly damaging her seaplanes and killing twelve of her native crew who were sitting there. A third bomb fell in a coal dump on the far side of the canal, sending up a dense black cloud.

Raven II was now out of action and in her place *Anne* was ordered to sail for the Red Sea where she remained until relieved by *Raven II* on 26 October. *Anne* sailed on the evening of 31 August, taking with her Sqdn. Cdr. Malone who had returned to Port Said and been put in charge of the seaplane base on the Island. Abu Zenima was reached on 2 September, but as wind and sea were too strong for flying Malone went ashore and accompanied a camel patrol 10 miles up country to inspect the nature of the surrounding area.

On 3 September *Anne* hoisted out Short 184, 8004, at 0455 to reconnoitre the road from Abu Zenima towards Nekhl to see if the Turks were advancing to

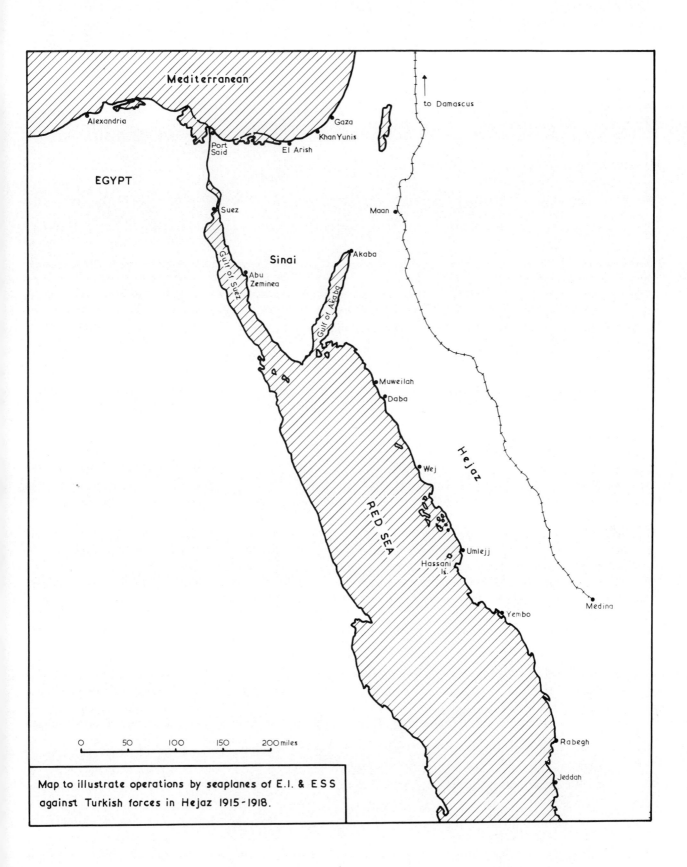

Map to illustrate operations by seaplanes of E.I. & E S S
against Turkish forces in Hejaz 1915-1918.

attack Abu Zenima. Clemson and Malone were airborne in the Short at 0535, but flying at 4,000 feet in very bumpy conditions no enemy troops were seen and the seaplane returned to the ship at 0719.

On receipt of orders from the SNO in the cruiser *Fox*, *Anne* then proceeded to Ras Malak which was reached on the evening of the 6th. Clemson and Malone were airborne in 8004 next morning at 0535 to impress a camp of 8,000 Arab recruits, and to carry out a W/T spotting exercise with *Fox*. A repeat of this flight was made in 8075, crewed by Smith and Millard, early on

HMS Ben-my-Chree's Short 184, 8090, taking off. This seaplane had been modified to Samson's design to increase its performance during October 1916, the lower mainplane being reduced by one bay and the fin area reduced. After service in HMS Ben-my-Chree the Short was transferred to HMS Raven II and was lost on 28th March 1917.
(G.S.Leslie/J.M.Bruce collection)

the 8th. It was hoped that, with British arms, the Arab recruits would make themselves unpleasant to the Turkish garrisons along the Red Sea coast. Perhaps inevitably the Arabs shipped many of these arms, provided by a benevolent British Government, to the Egyptian side of the Red Sea and sold them to the Bedouin. Thereafter "friendly" dhows were boarded and searched!

Anne sailed on 8 September bound for Sherm Rabegh, anchoring there that evening. At 0509 next morning F/S/L Smith and 2nd Lt Williams took 8075 on a photo reconnaissance flight over villages adjacent to Sherm Rabegh and conducted a W/T practice with *Anne*.

Orders were then received to proceed to Sherm

Yembo. The charts of this coast were very inaccurate, and as *Anne* felt her way into the little harbour at dawn on the 10th she ran onto a coral reef. No damage was done however, and at high water *Anne* went astern and slid off easily. Here Smith and Millard in 8075 made a photo reconnaissance flight over Yembo between 0502 and 0545 before *Anne* received orders to proceed to Hassani Island where at dawn on 11 September she met *Fox* and *Hardinge*. Weldon and Malone went ashore to survey the island for possible use as an aerodrome, and found it suitable from which to operate aeroplanes for coastal patrols.

The Turks had evacuated Umlejj, leaving only the Arab population, but news was received that 200 Turks with four guns were advancing southward from Wej in four dhows to recapture Umlejj. Accordingly Smith and Millard in 8075 took off at 0619 on the 12th to search for the Turkish raiding force. The Short flew north as far as Agra without sighting anything, and at 0915 with petrol running low course was reversed, and the seaplane was hoisted back on board *Anne* at 0951. The ship sailed for Marduna Island that evening

R.I.M.S.Northbrook operated one Short 184, transferred from HMS Anne, during September 1916 in the Red Sea. (Via RCC)

R.I.M.S Dufferin operated one Short 184, transferred from HMS Anne, in the Red Sea during September 1916.
(NMM D3569)

and proceeding to the lee of the island, hoisted out Short 184, 8075, next morning at 0533. Smith and Williams took off in the Short and for the next 2 hours spotted for the bombardment of Wej by *Fox* and *Hardinge*. Clemson and Millard in 8004 performed a similar task between 0833 and 1017. The last flight of the day was made by Clemson and Millard in 8004. They were airborne at 1742 to reconnoitre Sherm Munnaiburra, where 200 Turkish troops were reported, but no sign of them was seen. Clemson landed the Short at 1820, by which time it was almost dark. Clemson and Millard took off in 8004 again next morning at 0744 and found that the town of Wej was deserted, but nevertheless *Fox* kept up the bombardment all morning. Further reconnaissance flights by *Anne*'s Short 184s on the 15th and early on 16 September showed that the Turkish force had been withdrawn from the town.

On the 16th *Anne* received orders to proceed to Hassani Island to await *Northbrook*. On arrival *Anne* anchored off the island, and to pass the time her crew fished - the bag was 200 lbs of fish of all sorts. Short 8075, and some air mechanics were transferred to *Northbrook* on 17 September, and after coaling and re-provisioning *Anne* headed south again to Yembo where on the 21st one of her Shorts (8004) was

transferred to the AMC *Dufferin*.

Dufferin hoisted out 8004 at 0525 on 23 September off Sherm Rabegh and, crewed by Clemson and Millard, the Short took off at 0546 to reconnoitre Sh-Al-Khahrar and vicinity to find a suitable aerodrome site, and to fly over Rabegh camp to impress the Arabs. The Short was waterborne at 0710. *Anne* arrived at Sherm Rabegh on the 26th, where next day Short 184, 8075, was transferred from *Northbrook* back on board *Anne*.

By 0500 on 30 September *Anne* lay off Ras Duleidela, where at 0514 Smith and Williams took off in 8075 to locate the road between Medina and Mecca and to ascertain if it was within range of the ships' guns. Many separate camel tracks were observed and it was apparent that the road was much used. The Short returned at 0628 and was hoisted back on board *Anne* at 0639. The C-in-C visited Sherm Rabegh in *Hardinge* on the 30th, and a military mission, including a representative of the RFC from Egypt, accompanied him. *Anne* was sent with the RFC officer to show him the proposed landing grounds selected by her aircrews and of these Bureika was considered the most suitable between Rabegh and Medina.

Anne lay at Rabegh for the next two weeks in company with *Dufferin* and the sloop *Espiègle*. Warlike activities were mainly confined to the Arab troops ashore who continually fired their rifles. *Anne* was hit by bullets several times, fortunately causing no casualties on board. Clemson and Millard in 8004 made a reconnaissance flight over Rabegh between 0625 and 0725 on 10 October to find out what defence works had been constructed by the "friendly" Arabs, and photographs were taken of these trenches.

On 12 October the military mission left Sherm Rabegh and Malone was informed by the SNO Red Sea that they had reported that landplanes should not be sent unless accompanied by a guard of at least 4,000 men! Malone's concern was that his seaplanes were required to work upwards of 100 miles inland in support of land operations - a task better suited to landplanes. It was apparent that the stipulation that a guard of 4,000 men was necessary was merely a way of saying that no landplanes were going to be sent! Malone accordingly prepared a design for converting his Short 184s to aeroplanes with wheeled undercarriages. Construction of as many parts as possible was made on board and Port Said was requested to send those parts which could not be made, but apparently this novel idea came to nothing.

Anne sailed for Port Sudan on 14 October to complete with provisions, and to bring back 29 Egyptian gunners to Yembo. From there she was ordered back to Rabegh in case the Turks advanced along the road through Rabegh to Mecca. *Raven II* had now had her bomb damage repaired and she arrived at Rabegh on 26

October, but without any seaplanes, to allow *Anne* to return to Port Said. Before sailing *Anne* transferred both her Short 184s, 8004 and 8075, to *Raven II*. *Raven II* returned briefly to Port Said during November, but left there again on 30 November to return to the Red Sea. On her way down the Gulf of Suez orders were received from SNO Red Sea Patrol for the ship to proceed to Sherm Yembo, where she remained until 16 December in a good anchorage with smooth water for seaplane operations.

HMS *Suva*, formerly a vessel belonging to the Australasian United Steam Navigation Company, but now armed with three 4.7-inch guns, arrived at Yembo harbour on 5 December to discharge rifles and ammunition. Flt Lt Burling then flew over to Yembo harbour to arrange operations with the SNO on board *Suva*.

Both Shorts, 8004 and 8075, were airborne on 7 December and discovered a Turkish force of 300 to 400 men entrenched 24 miles inland north-east of Yembo. Both seaplanes attacked and dropped 20 bombs on the trenches in the face of heavy fire from the enemy. Burling and Lt Stewart flew 8004 over to Yembo harbour on the morning of the 8th and went on board *Suva* for instructions. The Short took off for a reconnaissance at 0715 and returned to *Suva* at 0810 for further instructions, after which the seaplane flew back to *Raven II* and was hoisted in at 0845.

F/S/L Worrall and 2nd Lt Williams in 8075

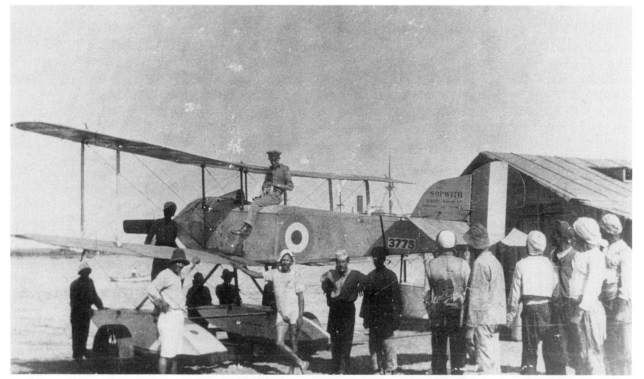

Schneider 3778 at Port Said. This seaplane was flown from HMS Ben-my Chree by Flt Lt Clemson during the attack on Chicaldere Bridge on 27th December 1916. (G.S.Leslie/J.M.Bruce collection)

Baby 8188 flown by Flt Lt Brooke also took part in the attack on Chicaldere Bridge on 27th December 1916.
(G.S.Leslie/J.M.Bruce collection)

repeated this routine on 9 December, but while taking off from Yembo harbour the compression tap blew out and the seaplane returned to *Raven II* for a replacement.

F/S/L Man and Stewart flew a reconnaissance on the 10th in 8004 on instructions from *Suva* and bombed a camp in the foothills near Yembo and received several hits from ground fire.

Burling and Williams in 8075 attacked the same target again with 16-lb bombs as soon as the first Short had returned to the ship. Both Shorts continued bombing and reconnaissance flights between 11 and 16 December on likely targets at Yembo and Mubarak. Agents had reported a force of 10,000 Turkish troops at Mubarak but this was discounted. All these flights were opposed by AA fire and on the 11th 8075 had a large hole smashed in the port float by shrapnel. Too badly damaged for repair, it was replaced by the last of *Raven II*'s stock of spare floats. The monitor *M 31* arrived at Sherm Yembo on 15 December and both *Raven II*'s Shorts spotted for gun practice with the monitor on the 15th and 16th.

Orders were now received for *Raven II* to return to Port Said, but she stopped at dawn on the 19th off Wej and Burling and Williams in 8075 took off at 0634 and bombed the inland fort at Wej from 3,000 feet. A total of six sorties by both seaplanes were flown between 0634 and 1055 and nine 65-lb and fifty 16-lb bombs

were dropped on the fort and an entrenched camp one mile north of Wej. All attacks were carried out from 1,000 to 3,000 feet, and both Shorts were frequently hit by ground fire. After both seaplanes had been hoisted in *Raven II* proceeded to Suez and then on to Port Said to prepare for an attack on the railway bridge at Chicaldere on 27 December.

Following her hectic week of operations in late August, *Ben-my-Chree* returned to Port Said on 30 August where she remained for the next two weeks. With growing German air activity from the aerodromes at El Arish and Ramleh towards the end of 1916, *Ben-my-Chree*'s Short 184s were, whenever possible escorted by two Schneiders on sorties inland. On short range operations at least this involved embarking up to four Schneiders and two Short 184s for each sortie.

Ben-my-Chree sailed from Port Said on 13 September for a reconnaissance of Gaza, Beersheba and Shellal. Arriving off Gaza early on the 14th *Ben-my-Chree* hoisted out a Short 184, a Baby and two Schneiders between 0524 and 0532. The Short was airborne first shortly followed by Samson in Schneider 3789 and Bankes-Price in Baby 8135 as escorts. Heavy AA fire at Beersheba was encountered by all three seaplanes, the Short having one of its floats damaged. Flt Lt Leigh in Schneider 3779 had engine trouble and was not airborne until 0600, and finding it impossible to

Two views of a bomb from Cdr Samson's Schneider 3770, bursting on the Chicaldere railway bridge on 27th December 1916. (via RCC)

overtake the Short returned to the ship and flew an anti-aircraft patrol at 8,000 feet until 0702 by which time the other three seaplanes had returned. As Samson in Schneider 3789 returned across the coast the engine was vibrating badly, and after landing it fell out of its mountings. The upper longerons were found to be rotten, a result of old age and extreme climate. *Ben-my-Chree* returned to Port Said that day, but was ordered to sea again for her seaplanes to spot for a bombardment off El Arish on two separate targets. Samson's request to concentrate on one target and so provide better protection for the Shorts was overruled, and his force had to be divided.

On 17 September between 0522 and 0526 *Ben-my-Chree* hoisted out Short 184, 8080, crewed by Flt Lt Maskell and Sub Lt Kerry RNVR, a Baby 8135 flown by Flt Lt Bankes-Price, and Schneider 3778 flown by F/S/L Nightingale to spot for the monitors *M 15* and *M 31* at El Arish.

Ten minutes later *Ben-my-Chree* hoisted out three more seaplanes - Short 184, 8372, crewed by Flt Cdr England and 2nd Lt King KOSB, and two Schneiders 3777 and 3770 flown by F/S/L Man and Cdr Samson respectively. They were to spot for *Espiègle* firing on positions eight miles south of El Arish. King in the Short called up *Espiègle* repeatedly on W/T but could get no reply, so England flew back to *Espiègle* but could see no signal from her lamp. Since there appeared to be no worthwhile targets Samson's three seaplanes turned to reinforce those spotting for the monitors. England took the Short back to the ship and landed at 0620. Man's Schneider was flying over El Arish at 3,000 feet when the engine revs dropped to 975, height was lost rapidly and as it passed over the coast at 1,000 feet was hit by machine gun fire in the wings and petrol tank. Man saw a damaged Schneider on the water as he came in to a forced landing six miles north-east of El Arish at 0637, and as soon as his floats touched the water the undercarriage collapsed. The machine turned over and sank but Man was picked up by HM Trawler *Rononia*. Samson meanwhile saw that the monitors had ceased firing and flew inland to search for Maskell's flight. Failing to find them he returned to the ship at 0643.

Soon after Maskell's flight began climbing, W/T signals were sent to both M 15 and M 31 but neither monitor acknowledged. At 0556 the Short was flying at 5,000 feet to the east of El Arish when an enemy aeroplane was seen taking off from the aerodrome. The signal for M 15 to open fire was given but the fall of shot was not seen. The enemy machine climbed very rapidly and endeavoured to attack the Short from underneath, but Maskell put the seaplane's nose down and Kerry opened fire on the attacker from the rear cockpit with his Lewis gun. Both escorting seaplanes then attempted to engage the enemy, but Bankes-Price's

Baby, for no apparent reason, burst into flames and fell into the water and the pilot was killed. Nightingale's Schneider was attacked from the rear by the enemy aircraft, whose fire shattered the Schneider's petrol tank, so Nightingale turned out to sea and landed close to M 15. The monitor took him on board and towed the seaplane back to *Ben-my-Chree* where it was hoisted inboard. Maskell meanwhile managed to get his Short into position below the German aircraft, where Kerry fired a long and accurate burst into the enemy which then turned for home.

While all this action had been going on three more German aeroplanes bombed *Ben-my-Chree* but all three bombs fell wide, and after Maskell's Short was hoisted in at 0635 *Ben-my-Chree* returned to Port Said to lick her wounds. For the next six weeks, until her losses in seaplanes had been made good, *Ben-my-Chree* remained at Port Said while her remaining seaplanes flew anti-submarine patrols, but on the morning of 2 November she left Port Said and proceeded to an agreed rendezvous off Adalia, arriving at 1100 on 3 November. Here were assembled Admiral de Spitz's yacht, the French destroyer *Dard* and three trawlers. *Ben-my-Chree* was to provide seaplanes to spot for the bombardment of enemy batteries which had recently fired on *Dard*. Two flights were immediately made by *Ben-my-Chree*'s seaplanes to locate the enemy's guns, their positions being found north of Lara. At 1320 England and Wedgwood-Benn took off in Short 184, 8080, and directed by W/T the fire of *Ben-my-Chree* and the French trawler *Canada* onto the gun emplacements which were hit repeatedly. After the Short was hoisted in at 1505 the ships moved further along the coast. When they were south-east of Adalia a battery of guns opened fire on the squadron and *Ben-my-Chree* hoisted out 8080 again crewed by England and Lt Woodland. The Short located and bombed the guns, whose fire straddled *Ben-my-Chree* while she was stopped. She immediately got under way and engaged the battery with her own guns. Thirty-six rounds of 12-pounder and six rounds of 3-pounder were fired from the ship at ranges between 4500 and 8300 yards. As soon as *Ben-my-Chree* had hoisted in the Short at 1654 she steamed to Castelorizo, arriving there early on the morning of 4 November.

Two flights were made that morning to find guns believed to be on the hills facing Castelorizo and probably able to fire into the harbour. However, it was impossible to locate them with certainty so *Ben-my-Chree* sailed for Port Said.

Ben-my-Chree left harbour on the evening of 1 December escorted by the French destroyer *Dard*. Off Haifa on the 2nd, Short 184 8080, crewed by England and Wedgwood-Benn made a reconnaissance flight to El Afule where much railway traffic was seen. The

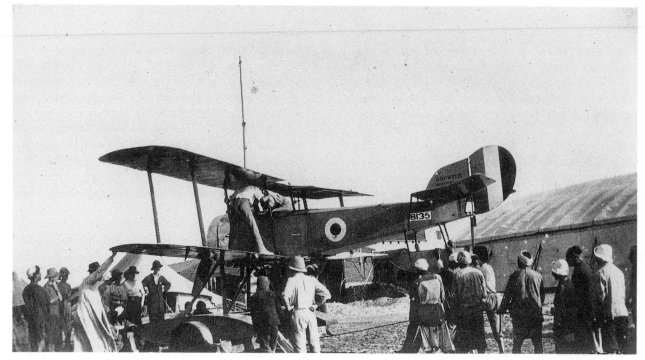

Baby 8135, seen here at the seaplane base for the East Indies and Egypt Seaplane Squadron at Port Said, was lost off El Arish on 17th September 1916 while operating fron HMS Ben-my-Chree. (G.S.Leslie/J.M.Bruce collection)

seaplane came under heavy fire from the ground and a float was holed, but the seaplane landed safely on its return and was quickly hoisted in before it could sink. A Schneider was also launched to reconnoitre the road between Tul Keram and Samaria before *Ben-my-Chree* moved south. Off Jaffa Short 184, 8372, with F/S/L Nightingale and Lt P.M. Woodland took off to fly over Ramleh to Bureir, but while over Ramleh the seaplane came under heavy AA fire and received a direct hit. From the ship it was seen to go down out of control behind the hills. *Ben-my-Chree* was immediately stopped, and after hoisting out 8080, England and Wedgwood-Benn took off to search for the crashed seaplane. Nothing was seen of it, but a German wireless message intercepted later in the day said that the missing crew were safe but prisoners of war. Two further flights were made on 2 December, a Short flying to Falugeh and a Schneider making a reconnaissance of the area between Bureir and Gaza before *Ben-my-Chree* returned to Port Said early on 3 December.

During *Ben-my-Chree*'s enforced period of inactivity during October, mechanics at the Base in Port Said were employed in modifying a Short 184, 8090 to Samson's design. This involved shortening the lower mainplanes to a position just outboard of the second pair of interplane struts, reducing the fin area and fitting more aerodynamically shaped wingtip floats.

The first flight of the modified Short was made on 23 November, and it was found that its rate of climb and top speed were far superior to the unaltered Shorts. Four further flights made by the modified Short between

3 and 16 December proved equally satisfactory.

Ben-my-Chree left Port Said at 1630 on 21 December, and by 0705 next morning hoisted out two Shorts to reconnoitre the camps between Gaza and Falugeh. This was the first operational use of the modified Short. After recovering her seaplanes the ship was proceeding north when she was attacked by an enemy aeroplane. Six bombs were dropped and missed, the ship's AA fire keeping the enemy above 7,000 feet. A reconnaissance was flown over Jaffa at 1050 and, still steaming north to a position off Haifa, a reconnaissance of the Haifa Valley was made. 8080 was hoisted out at 1505, and crewed by F/S/L Henderson and Air Mechanic Lloyd, took off to follow the railway inland and bomb the camp at Tabaun. Five 16-lb bombs were dropped on the camp and three more on the railway bridge at Jelamah. On conclusion of these operations *Ben-my-Chree* returned to Port Said at dawn on 23 December.

Seaplane carriers and their seaplanes of the RNAS were no strangers to action during the season of "goodwill toward all men". And the Turks were made no exception. The advanced Turkish forces threatening the Suez Canal in 1916 were supplied and reinforced by the railway running southward from Aleppo. But to reach Aleppo they had first to travel from east to west along the railway between Tarsus and Alexandretta. On either side of the headland of Karatash Burnu the rivers Jeihan and Seihan flow into the sea, and across these two rivers, on iron girder bridges, ran the railway from Tarsus to Alexandretta.

An attack during December 1916 by *Ben-my-Chree* and *Raven II* on the Chicaldere bridge spanning the Jeihan river was planned, and on Christmas Day 1916 *Raven II* sailed from Port Said, followed by *Ben-my-Chree* on the 26th for a rendezvous on the 27th in Ayas Bay. It had been decided that the seaplanes from both carriers should make the first attack together, but owing to mines in the channel, *Raven II* was delayed and arrived late at the rendezvous.

Pending *Raven II*'s arrival *Ben-my-Chree* hoisted out four seaplanes - Short 184, 8080, crewed by F/S/L G.D. Smith and Capt J. Wedgwood-Benn, two Schneiders 3770 and 3778 piloted by Cdr C.R. Samson and Flt Lt A.W. Clemson respectively, and a Baby, 8188, flown by Flt Lt J.C. Brooke.

All four seaplanes were airborne by 1100 and headed for the bridge, where Smith's Short dropped one 65-lb bomb at the bridge and two 16-lb bombs at a train, but all the bombs failed to explode. Smith then turned his attention to the defences at the south side of the bridge, to divert any fire away from the other three seaplanes, and having dropped his remaining 16-lb bombs, which exploded on the water and damaged the bridge, he machine gunned the bridge's guard who promptly fled.

The Schneiders and the Baby now attacked at heights ranging from 400 to 700 feet. Samson scored one hit on the bridge and both Brooke and Clemson caused damage with their bombs. By 1200 *Raven II* had got both her Short 184s airborne, 8075 with Flt Lt E.J. Burling and Lt K.L. Williams of the 2nd Rajputs, and 8004 with F/S/L E.M. King and Lt N.W. Stewart of the 7th Royal Scots. Each armed with one 65-lb and two 16-lb bombs, they scored one hit on the bridge. The third phase of the attack took place at 1330 when *Ben-my-Chree* sent away Short 184, 8080, crewed by Flt Lt A.S. Maskell and Lt W.L. Samson RNVR, carrying two 65-lb bombs. Both these bombs missed the bridge, but the ship's two Schneiders following up the Short's attack had more success with their 16-lb bombs. F/S/L Henderson flying 3770 hit the bridge with both his 16-lb bombs. Although the bridge was now temporarily unusable, Samson realised that another attack next day was needed to put it out of action for any appreciable length of time. This was not to be however, and as the carriers left the Gulf of Alexandretta to stand out to sea during the night a signal was received from the C in C ordering them to return at once to Port Said.

Ben-my-Chree returned briefly to the Gulf of Alexandretta between 2 and 5 January 1917 but bad weather prevented any flying. On 8 January she sailed for Castelorizo to operate her seaplanes under French orders, arriving there on the 9th. At 1410 while lying in the harbour with her bows facing seawards there was a loud explosion close to the ship's port side. Initially it was thought the ship was under air attack, but in fact she was being shelled from the mainland. The third round started a petrol fire in the hangar which was soon out of control, and at 1445 the order to abandon ship was given. *Ben-my-Chree* burned until the next morning and was a total loss.

French aircrew and mechanics pose for the camera with Raven II's ship's company in front of two folded Short 184s on the aft welldeck. The date is probably May 1916, just before the French contingent of EI and ESS transferred to Campinas. It is certain that no members of L'AMF ever flew or serviced British seaplanes, however. (FAAM)

9th January 1917, and the end of HMS Ben-my-Chree in Castelorizo harbour. Repeatedly hit by shellfire from Turkish batteries on the mainland, she caught fire and had to be abandoned. (G.S.Leslie/J.M.Bruce collection)

HMS Ben-my-Chree with Short 184, 841, on deck in 1915 before joining EI & ESS. (IWM SP916)

Two views of an investiture at the Seaplane Base, Port Said c.1917, with aircrew in the front rank and air mechanics behind receiving their medals from a French admiral - possibly Admiral de Spitz. Both the variety of uniforms and the style of RNAS architecture (formerly seaplane packing cases) is interesting (FAAM and G.S.Leslie/J.M.Bruce collection)

CHAPTER XIII
Operations by *Anne* and *Raven II* Red Sea and Indian Ocean January-June 1917

*R*aven II's sortie into the Gulf of Akaba and along the Red Sea coast in August, to select landing sites for a force to cut the Hejaz railway, had shown that the coast was too well defended for a landing attempt to be made. But over the next four months the strength of the Arab revolt grew. With naval bombardment to assist them Akaba, Muweilah, Yembo and Rabegh had all fallen to the Arabs, and only Wej was still held by the Turks.

After returning from the Red Sea in October, *Anne* spent most of the remainder of 1916 lying at Port Said, relieved (if that be the correct term) only by a voyage to Cyprus in November with her holds crammed with coal. At Famagusta the "coalies" doing the unloading were a mixture of Greek men and girls, and while watching them it was not difficult to see which were the best workers! Christmas 1916 found *Anne* still at Port Said.

Weldon and Kerr went the rounds of the messdecks and at each mess they were presented with a tumbler half full of whisky. The ship's company was lent the piano from the wardroom, and the day closed without any regrettable incidents!

At the beginning of January 1917 *Anne* put to sea once more, but ran into such bad weather that she had to return to Port Said to land one of her seaplanes, damaged by the heavy seas.

Orders were received on 11 January for *Anne* to embark her seaplanes and proceed to the Red Sea. Sailing that evening she reached Suez on the 12th, where she remained for three days awaiting orders. At last on the 15th *Anne* received instructions to proceed to Sherm Hanab south of Wej. Here *Anne* rendezvoused on the 17th with *Espiègle* and proceeded to Daba, where her two Short 184s flew along the coast to try to locate Turkish troops. After recovering her seaplanes *Anne* steamed to Hassani Island where she found *Hardinge*. The Turks were present in some force at Wej and the plan was that *Fox, Espiègle* and *Hardinge* should bombard the town, with *Anne*'s seaplanes spotting the fall of shot, while an army of Arabs under Lawrence and the Emir Feisal should attack and drive out the enemy.

At 0920 on 21 January Flt Lt Burling and 2nd Lt

HMS Raven II, showing her rudimentary canvas hangars abaft the funnel for seaplane stowage. The significance of the Japanese ensign flown from her mainmast is not known, but by 1917 Japanese destroyers were serving in the Mediterranean with the Allies. (A.K.Vicary)

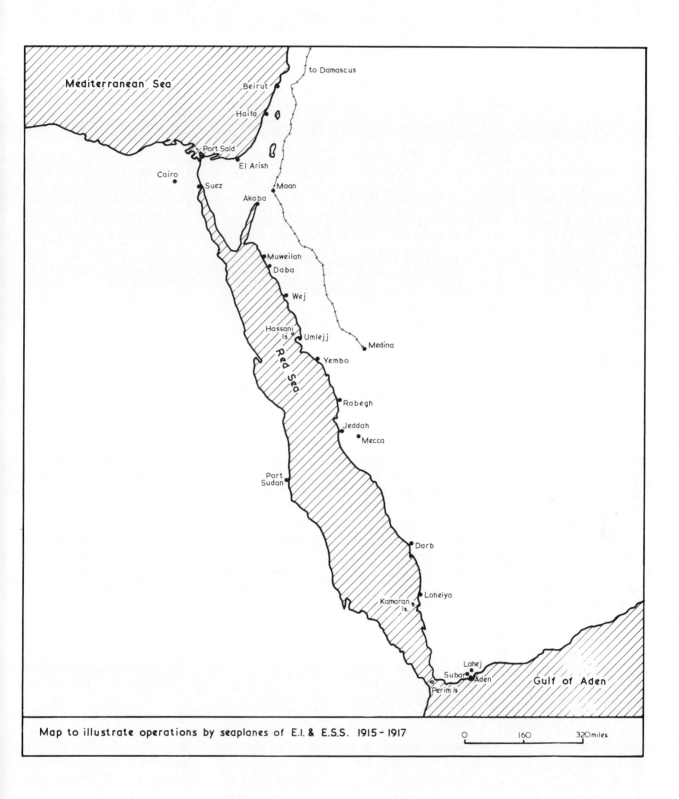

Map to illustrate operations by seaplanes of E.I. & E.S.S. 1915-1917

Short 184, 8075, with wings folded and canvas cover on propeller, being prepared for hoisting out from HMS Raven II's after welldeck 1917. (G.S.Leslie/J.M.Bruce collection)

Williams took off under the lee of Hassani Island in Short 184, 8075, to spot for *Hardinge* and *Espiègle* bombarding Wej. The first smoke bomb to mark the target was dropped at 0930, but the fall of shot from *Espiègle* was hard to see as she was firing with a high angle gun and the explosion of the shell was very small. *Hardinge* did not open fire, so after *Espiègle* had ceased firing a W/T exercise with *Fox* and *Hardinge* was conducted until 1032. Ranging on smoke bombs was carried out, and the difference between the range on the smoke bombs and the range obtained from a spotting station on shore was only 25 yards.

On the 22nd a practice landing of marines and naval ratings was carried out on Hassani Island, and at 0825 Burling took up Short 184, 8004, with Capt Boyle (SNO Red Sea) in the rear cockpit to make a reconnaissance of Wej prior to making an attack on the town, and to locate the Arab army. No sign of them was seen, so the ships decided to do the job themselves.

Anne moved to Marduna Island from where on 23rd at 0817 F/S/L King and Lt Stewart 7th RS took off in 8004 to bomb enemy trenches if manned and afterwards to spot for *Fox*. All trenches had been evacuated but enemy refuges were bombed with six 16-lb bombs. After spotting for *Fox* the Short came under rifle fire from Wej, and when the seaplane was hoisted back on board at 1015 it was found that Stewart had been hit by a stray bullet and had been killed. That evening the chaplain from *Fox* came on board and Stewart was buried over the side.

A landing party of 450 ratings and marines and 400 Arabs had meanwhile been assembled that morning, and having been landed they stormed the town. *Anne* shifted to a position off Sherm Dumrigh during the forenoon, and at 1247 launched 8075, crewed by King and Williams, to try to locate a Turkish force proceeding north from Wej. Nothing was seen however, and at 1349 when north of Noman Island the Short reversed course and returned to the ship at 1426. By the time the 6,000 strong Arab army arrived at Wej on the evening of the 23rd, they were too late to do any fighting, but in plenty of time for looting, which they did most enthusiastically.

Anne sailed for Port Said on 26 January, and on arrival there Weldon went ashore for the last time from the ship which had been his home for the past two years.

During February *Anne*'s seaplanes flew reconnaissances over Haifa and Beirut and then returned to Port Said before her next sortie.

Escorted by the French trawler *Nord Caper, Anne* left Port Said at 0700 on 26 February with Short 184s embarked, 8021 and 8022. Arriving off Haifa at 0530 on the 27th, 15 miles from the coast, both seaplanes were hoisted out between 0640 and 0650 for a reconnaissance of the Carmel range and Haifa valley. 8022 crewed by F/S/L G.D. Smith and Sub Lt Kerry RNVR was first away at 0647, carrying a Lewis gun and six hoppers, W/T set and two cameras.

The coast was crossed at 3,000 feet over Haifa, and on the approach to the coast smoke signals appeared on the Carmel range, which were immediately answered down the valley. The flight followed the road and railway to El Afule, where from 4,000 feet two locomotives were seen east of the town proceeding eastwards.

At 0750 over El Afule the seaplane turned north and flew over Nazareth and Shafa Amr, where the condition of the roads was noted. At Shafa Amr course was set west for a return to the ship, which had now closed the coast to within five miles, and the seaplane was hoisted in at 0830.

Meanwhile Flt Lt H. deV. Leigh and 2nd Lt G.H. Pakenham-Walsh of the Cheshire Regiment in 8021 had taken off at 0710, 20 minutes after being hoisted out, carrying a Lewis gun and 12 hoppers (the latter were circular Lewis-type magazines). Crossing the coast at 4,500 feet, smoke signals were seen on the hills south of Haifa. The coast road was followed to Athlit and thence to Zimmarin, where at 6,200 feet, the seaplane turned inland to cross the hills to Jelameh. From here course was set north-west to Haifa and a return to the ship. 8021 was hoisted back on board *Anne* at 0835, with a detailed report on the condition of the roads and railways in the area covered, and the ship then proceeded towards Beirut.

At 0530 on the 28th *Anne* approached Beirut. When 20 miles off the coast she hoisted out 8022 at 0645, crewed by Flt Cdr A.W. Clemson and Sub Lt Kerry RNVR, for what was to prove to be an epic flight. 8022 was loaded with two Lewis guns and nine hoppers, W/T set and a camera plus sufficient fuel for a three hour flight. 8022 was airborne at 0703 and crossed the coast three miles south of Beirut at 0730, flying at 5,000 feet. A course was now set due east to follow the railway to Zahle situated on the eastern slopes of the Saddle of Lebanon. To cross this range the seaplane climbed to 7,600 feet and reached Zahle at 0755. Proceeding on to

Rayak at 7,000 feet they turned north-east for half-a-mile up the railway, to photograph and reconnoitre the railway workshops at Baalbik, which was reached at 0802. The workshops consisted of 25 large sheds, and the sidings contained much rolling stock. From Baalbik the seaplane turned south, following the road from Zahle to Damascus. A battalion of troops on the march was seen at Dumar, two miles north-west of Damascus, and fire was opened on the seaplane from five or six guns which were brought into action. Damascus was reached at 0845 and as nothing of importance was observed, the return flight, following the road leading north-west to Beirut, was commenced. Another battalion of troops was seen marching towards Damascus, and at 0930 the seaplane crossed the coast two miles south of Beirut at 6,000 feet. *Anne* was sighted eight miles to the south-west, and 8022 was waterborne again at 0948 and hoisted in at 1000 after a flight of 150 miles, most of it over land.

Anne's swan-song took place between 21 and 23 March 1917. She left Port Said at 1030 on 21 March escorted by the French destroyer *Arbalette*, and at 0705 on the 22nd when 20 miles west of Haifa hoisted out Short 184, 8020. Flt Lt Leigh and Lt Millard were airborne in the Short at 0715 and crossing the coast at 4,800 feet reconnoitred the camp at Tabaun. Climbing to 7,800 feet over Jenin the Short headed north, reached Nazareth at 0836, and then headed west to return to the ship and was hoisted in at 0920. Flt Cdr. Brooke had taken off in Baby, N1016, at 0715, and flying as escort to the Short had flown to a position east of El Afule when the engine gave trouble. Brooke fortunately had

Short 184, 8090, which while operating from HMS Raven II on 28th March 1917 in the Indian Ocean crashed and was wrecked. This photo was taken after modifications undertaken by air mechanics in HMS Ben-my-Chree in October 1916 to reduce the lower mainplanes by one bay and to reduce the fin area. This considerably increased the Short's performance. (G.S.Leslie/J.M.Bruce collection)

Short 184, 8018 (visible on torn fabric forward of tailplane) at Male Island c. May 1917. The Short had flown a reconnaissance of Ari Atoll on 21st April and after being blown off course was unable to return to the ship. The photo shows 8018 about to be recovered by HMS Raven II on her way back from Colombo to Port Said. (FAAM)

sufficient altitude to reach the sea less than one mile off Haifa at 0830. After taxying on the water for three miles the engine failed completely. The Baby was taken in tow by *Arbalette* and was hoisted in by *Anne* at 0910. The ship then returned to Port Said, reaching there at 1100 on 23 March. So ended her last operational sortie.

Anne finally paid off and her White Ensign was hauled down for the last time in August 1917, and as RFA *Anne* she served as a collier from January 1918 until the Armistice. Her proud record from the first day of 1915 was not surpassed by many of HM Ships. With the loss of *Ben- my-Chree* and *Anne*, and with the departure of Samson in the not too distant future, the operational rôle and composition of the EI and ESS changed. But Samson had one more task with the Squadron before leaving for England.

The German raider *Wolf*, armed with two 5.9-inch and two 4.1-inch guns and carrying a Friedrichshafen FF33E seaplane had sailed from Germany on 30 November 1916 to seek and destroy Allied merchant shipping.

However, her presence in the Indian Ocean was not

known for certain until 5 March 1917. As one of the measures taken to hunt her down Samson sailed in *Raven II* from Port Said on 10 March with four Short 184s (8018, 8019, 8021, 8090) and one Baby (N1014) embarked. Samson realised that a lot of flying would have to be undertaken, and to this end the aircrew was increased to six pilots and five observers.

Several reconnaissance flights were made over the Hejaz coast as *Raven II* proceeded to Aden, which was reached on 16 March. While waiting there to be joined by the French cruiser *Potuhau*, further bombing and reconnaissance flights were made by *Raven II*'s seaplanes. Both ships then sailed for a search of the Laccadive Islands, but no sign was seen of *Wolf*. Proceeding next to the Maldive Islands, 8090 was launched for a reconnaissance on 28 March crewed by F/S/L T.G.M. Stephens and Capt R.E.C. Knight-Bruce. When 15 miles north of Kalpeni the Short crashed and was severely damaged. The wreckage was hoisted on board *Raven II* and both pilot and observer were picked up uninjured. 8090 was the Short which had been modified by *Ben-my- Chree*'s air mechanics to increase its performance the previous October.

Further reconnaissances of the Maldive Islands were made between 29 and 31 March in 8019 and 8021, but *Wolf* was not sighted and *Raven II* proceeded to Colombo for coaling. Before entering harbour on 2 April, 8019 crewed by Samson and PO Mech E. Groucott was hoisted out at 0853 to search for mines in the swept channel. None were seen, and the Short landed in the harbour at 0915 to await the ship's arrival.

Another intensive search of the Laccadive and Maldive Islands took place between 16 to 23 April, a total of 21 reconnaissance sorties being flown by the three Shorts during this eight day period. Most flights were made in early morning or late evening when flying conditions were best in an area close to the Equator.

One of these flights took place on 21 April when at 1608 F/S/L G.D. Smith with Lt W.C.A. Meade RNVR as his observer were hoisted out for a reconnaissance of Ari Atoll in 8018. The Short was airborne at 1614 and was last seen 15 miles from the ship on its correct course. However, the seaplane had not returned before darkness fell. Two flights were made next day to search for the missing seaplane but without success. The Short had been blown off course by high winds, and an emergency landing was made near an island, and the

machine was beached for the night. To cut a long story short (!) Smith and Meade flew the Short to Male Island next morning, where the seaplane was protected by a native-built "hangar" and after many adventures the aircrew were safely returned to *Raven II* at Colombo on 6 May. The Short was eventually recovered by *Raven II* from Male Island during mid May.

Between 9 and 11 May *Raven II*'s Baby, N1014, was transferred to HMAS *Brisbane*, and flown by Flt Cdr A.W. Clemson, made six flights to search for *Wolf*. But *Wolf* had by now moved to the Pacific, eventually returning safely to Kiel on 24 February 1918.

Raven II then proceeded to Bombay, where she and *Brisbane* sailed in company with the battleship *Exmouth* to escort a convoy on the 21st bound for the Red Sea. At Aden on 1 June *Raven II* hoisted out 8019 crewed by Flt Lt Burling and Sub Lt Kerry RNVR, and during an hour's flight the camps at Waht and Subar were bombed from 5,000 feet. Next morning F/S/L Smith flew a reconnaissance over the Lahej Delta, carrying Major Paige (on the staff of GOC Aden) as observer in 8019. Further reconnaissances were flown as *Raven II* proceeded up the Red Sea, and she returned to Port Said on 12 June.

HMS Raven II coaling ship, probably at Colombo, during her search for the German commerce raider SMS Wolf in the Indian Ocean 1917. (FAAM)

Flt Lt A.W.Clemson is hoisted out in HMAS Brisbane's Baby, N1014, Indian Ocean May 1917. (FAAM)

HMAS Brisbane, which during 1917 embarked a Baby, transferred from HMS Raven II, to search for the German commerce raider 'SMS Wolf' in the Indian Ocean. (Maritime Photo Library)

CHAPTER XIV
Operations by *Empress*, East Mediterranean May-October 1917

To replace the loss of *Ben-my-Chree* the seaplane carrier *Empress* was withdrawn from the East Mediterranean Squadron in the Aegean, and after refitting at Genoa, sailed to join the EI and ESS at Port Said in late February 1917.

For her first operation with the squadron, *Empress* sailed from Port Said late on 6 March and at 0905 on the 7th Short 184, 8088, crewed by Flt Cdr Sitwell and Lt Williams, East Yorkshire Regiment, was hoisted out ten miles west of Tubeh for a reconnaissance of Tul Keram and Nablus. No troop concentrations were observed and at 1034 the Short returned to *Empress*. The ship turned south after recovering her seaplane and at 1155 hoisted out Short 184, 8381, when nine miles west of Jaffa to reconnoitre Ludd, Ramleh and Falugeh. Flt Lt Field and Lt Bourne RFA were airborne in the Short at 1200 and after a flight of nearly two hours landed four miles west of Askalon. *Empress* after hoisting in 8381 then returned to Port Said.

For her next operation with the squadron *Empress* left Port Said at 1145 on 12 May, and escorted by the French destroyers *Coutelas* and *Pierrier,* arrived off Beirut at 0400 on the 13th. As the ship's position was uncertain, Short 184, 8004, crewed by F/S/L E. King and 2nd Lt A.D. Ferguson, was hoisted out at 0430 some 15 miles off the coast. 8004 carried two 65-lb bombs with 25-second delayed action tail fuses, a camera with 12 plates, a Very pistol with six white and six red flares, and a Lewis gun with four hoppers. From 2,000 feet at 0435, when seven miles off the coast, Beirut was located in the distance and 8004 returned to circle round *Empress* while she hoisted out two more Short 184's between 0505 and 0520. 8020 was armed with one 500-lb bomb and was flown by Flt Cdr J.C. Brooke, and understandably no observer. Airborne at 0510 Brooke circled the ship until 8075, crewed by Flt Lt H.de V. Leigh and Lt V. Millard, was airborne at 0525. 8075 carried two 65-lb bombs with 25-second delayed action fuses, a Lewis gun with four hoppers and a camera.

At 0530 all three seaplanes headed east for Beirut, 8004 at 3,000 feet, 8020 at 2,300 feet and 8075 at 1,600 feet. 8020 reached Beirut at 0550, and after observing that there were no submarines in the harbour, Brooke dropped his 500-lb bomb from 4,000 feet, which fell on open ground just west of the Customs House. It made a

HMS Empress at Port Said after joining the East Indies and Egypt Seaplane Squadron in February 1917. (FAAM)

Reconnaissance photograph of trenches covering the crossroads immediately north of Tul Keram, taken by a Short from HMS Empress 1917. (FAAM)

large hole and doubtless was the source of endless "bomb stories" among the natives! Ferguson photographed the explosion of this bomb at 0555 from 3,500 feet. Climbing to 4,500 feet, 8004 now dropped two 65-lb bombs at 0600 and 0610, which both exploded in the harbour entrance and were duly photographed by Ferguson.

8075 dropped two 65-lb bombs from 6,000 feet at 0617 and 0625, which fell in and just outside the harbour entrance, both being photographed by Millard. 8004 remained over the harbour between 0610 and 0620 photographing bridges over Nahr Beirut and trenches west of the town. All three seaplanes then set course back to *Empress*, 8020 landing at 0638, 8075 at 0645 and 8004 at 0646.

Intelligence reports had indicated that Beirut was being used as a supply base for German submarines, but no submarines were seen, and although the attack was well planned the results were disappointing. But *Empress* was new to operations off the Syrian coast, and her seaplanes were soon to redeem this failure.

Her next operation commenced at 1720 on 22 June, when *Empress,* escorted by the French destroyer *Hache*, sailed from Port Said for an attack on the railway junction at Tul Keram.

Cdr Samson had now relinquished command of the

EI and ESS to return to England, where in November he assumed command of Yarmouth Naval Air Station. He was succeeded in command of the Squadron by Wg Cdr C.E. Risk RMLI. Intelligence reports indicated that there were seven German aeroplanes based at Ramleh, and to prevent their interference with *Empress*'s seaplanes a combined operation with No 14 Squadron RFC was arranged. W/T communication was arranged for between No 14 Squadron's base at Deir El Belah and the carrier. The plan was that No 14 Squadron should take off at 0400 on the 23rd, signalling their departure by W/T to *Empress,* arriving over the German aerodrome at Ramleh at 0500. They were then to drop bombs at intervals until 0530 and return to Deir El Belah.

Shortly before reaching her launching position at 0415 on the 23rd, seven miles off Nahr Iskanderuneh, *Empress* received the pre-arranged W/T signal from the RFC, and at intervals between 0423 and 0444 hoisted out four Short 184s. All were armed with two 65-lb and between four and eight 16-lb bombs, twin Lewis guns and a camera apiece. 8020 crewed by F/S/L Bronson and Lt V. Millard took 31 minutes spent taxying before getting airborne. 8019 with F/S/L E. King and 2nd Lt G.H. Pakenham-Walsh was airborne 21 minutes after hoisting out. Flt Lt Barr and 2nd Lt A.D. Ferguson in

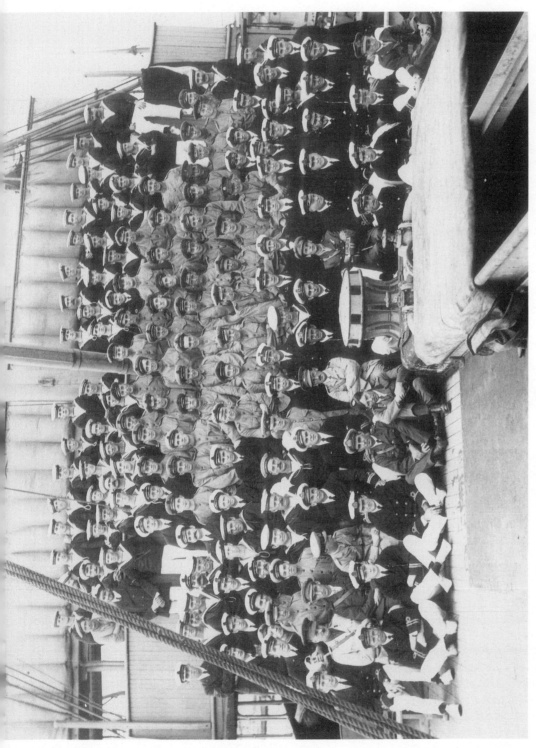

The Ship's Company of HMS Empress 1917, commanded by Cdr E.D.Drury, RNR. On his right is Sqdn Cdr C.E.Risk, RMLI, commanding El&ESS. Flt Lt Worrall is fourth from the left in the front row, and Flt Lt H. de V. Leigh is also known to be in the group. The officer on Worrall's left is probably 2nd Lt A.D.Finney (observer) of the Highland Light Infantry. (FAAM)

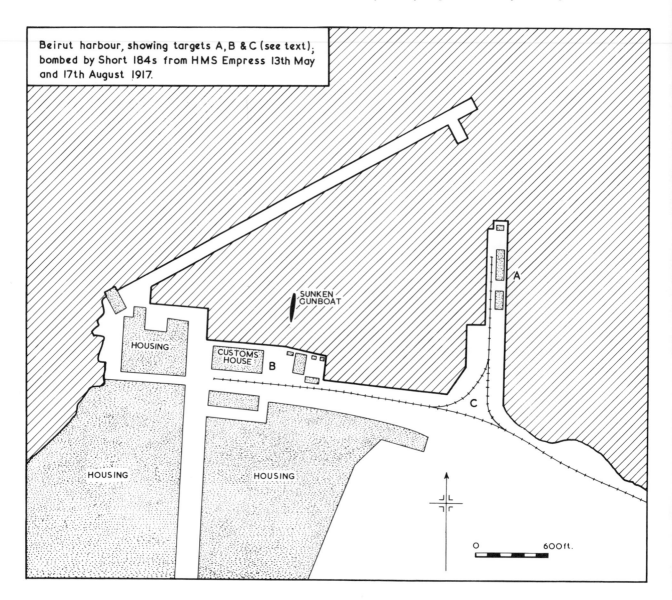

Beirut harbour, showing targets A, B & C (see text), bombed by Short 184s from HMS Empress 13th May and 17th August 1917.

8076 failed to take off and were hoisted in again at 0510. Finally hoisted out at 0444, Flt Lt Worrall and Wg Cdr Risk in 8004 were airborne at 0450. The three Shorts then formed up in single line ahead, at an interval of 800 yards from each other, and headed for the coast.

8004 was first across the coast at 0500 flying at 3,000 feet, and at 0520 Tul Keram was bombed from 2,000 feet with two 65-lb and four 16-lb bombs. 8004 was waterborne again at 0549 and was hoisted in at 0554. 8019 crossed the coast at 0507 at 2,000 feet, and climbing to 3,500 feet bombed the station with two 65-lb and eight 16-lb bombs. Only four 16-pounders hit the target, all the rest falling short to the east of the station. 300 Turkish troops were scattered by fire from the seaplane's Lewis gun on the return flight. 8019 was waterborne at 0608 and was hoisted in at 0617.

Last over the coast at 0510, by which time conditions were becoming very misty, was 8020 flying at 1,800 feet. Climbing to 2,500 feet over the target, two 65-lb and four 16-lb bombs were dropped on the station.

The first 65-pounder failed to explode, but the second burst among the station buildings. Of the 16-pounders one failed to explode, two fell wide and one scored a direct hit on the station. 8020 recrossed the coast at 3,700 feet, landed at 0556 and was hoisted in at 0604. The three Shorts had all carried out their attacks on Tul Keram ten minutes before No 14 Squadron left their target at Ramleh, but owing to the long period needed for the RNAS seaplanes to get airborne, the timing of the joint operation nearly did not succeed. As soon as all three seaplanes were hoisted in, *Empress* proceeded back to Port Said, arriving at 1715 on 23 June.

The next task assigned to *Empress* was for her seaplanes to bomb two cotton factories north-west of Adana and to destroy crops in the district with petrol bombs.

Empress, with four Short 184s embarked and escorted by the French destroyer *Voltigeur*, sailed from Port Said at 0500 on 14 July. At 1855 that evening *Voltigeur* signalled that her boilers were damaged, and

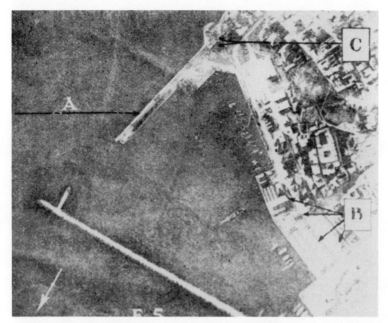

*Reconnaissance photograph of Beirut harbour taken on 13th May 1917
from a Short 184 from HMS Empress. A, B and C on the photograph
indicate the aiming points for a bombing attack carried out on 17th August
1917 by Short 184's from HMS Empress. These points are referred to in
the text and sketch map on page 248. (via RCC)*

M.C. Wood with 2nd Lt G.H. Pakenham-Walsh as observer, airborne at 0503, and seeing the fire at the factory attacked the target with two 65-lb bombs from 1,200 feet at 0558. Next to attack was 8019, armed with two 65-lb and eight 16-lb bombs and crewed by Flt Lt E.J. Burling and Sub Lt Kerry RNVR. Although subjected to vigorous infantry fire, Burling took his seaplane down to 400 feet, after bombing the factory, to enable Kerry to retaliate with his Lewis gun.

Flt Lt H. de V. Leigh and Capt V. Millard of the Essex Regiment in 8020 were last away from *Empress* at 0514 and bombed the factory with two 65-lb and two 16-lb bombs from 2,000 feet at 0600. Both 8004 and 8020 each dropped six petrol bombs on the return flight in an endeavour to burn any standing cereal crops.

Most crops had by then been harvested, and results were not very effective. Propaganda leaflets were also dropped from all four seaplanes, which returned safely, and were hoisted in between 0630 and 0650. *Empress* proceeded to Port Said at 0655 on the 15th, and when ten miles north of there at 0423 on the 16th stopped to hoist out 8020, crewed by Flt Lt H. V. Worrall and 2nd Lt G.H. Pakenham-Walsh to fly an anti-submarine patrol. 8020 circled round *Empress* at 500 feet until she entered the breakwater at 0605 on 16 July.

that she was obliged to proceed to Famagusta for repairs. Like so many French light craft in the Mediterranean her machinery was worn out after three years of wartime escort duties.

Empress sailed on alone and arrived off Karatash Burnu at 0400 on 15 July. Proceeding to a point five miles south of Merkez salt depot, she began hoisting out her seaplanes at 0500. Crewed by Flt Lt G.D. Smith and Capt W.R. Kempson 8018 was airborne at 0502 and crossed the coast heading north at 1,000 feet. Climbing for the next 30 miles, Adana was reached at 0542 and from 4,000 feet two 16-lb bombs were dropped on a camp of 150 bell tents. Smith immediately took 8018 down to 2,000 feet to attack the factory where two 65-lb and six 16-lb bombs were dropped and two hits obtained, starting a fire.

8004, piloted by Flt Lt

*8076, a Short 184 which was embarked in HMS Empress on 23rd June 1917 for a raid on
Tul Keram. Here pictured in "factory fresh" condition and with four 65-lb bombs on
carriers beneath lower mainplanes. (G.S.Leslie/J.M.Bruce collection)*

Beirut harbour under attack on 17th August 1917, taken from the East by one of HMS Empress's Short 184s. (See sketch map page 248 (FAAM)

A second attack on Beirut by *Empress*'s seaplanes was planned for August, using reconnaissance photographs taken during the raid of 13 May to identify the targets to be bombed. *Empress* sailed from Port Said at noon on 16 August with four Short 184s embarked, and was in position 20 miles off Beirut by dawn on the 17th. 8022 crewed by Worrall and Risk, and 8004 with Bronson and Walsh took off first at 0430, with instructions to bomb any submarines in the harbour, or if no submarines were seen, to wait to bomb the port installations until the two following seaplanes - 8019 piloted by Burling and 8018 piloted by King, both flying without observers - had both made their bombing runs. The latter two Shorts' objective was the store sheds on the eastern arm of the harbour (marked A on map and photographs) which they bombed from 500 feet. Their bombs fell through the roof of one shed starting a fire, and rolling stock on the railway line outside the sheds was hit.

After taking photographs of the damage, 8022 and 8004 then bombed the railway offices and store sheds on the harbour foreshore (marked B on map and photographs), scoring several hits from low level. All four seaplanes returned safely, and when the last one was hoisted in at 0650, *Empress* proceeded back to Port

Said, arriving at 0815 on 18 August. Beirut was not left in peace for long however, since intelligence reports indicated that the harbour was still being used as a submarine supply base. Accordingly *Empress* left Port Said at 1249 on 26 September, arriving at a rendezvous with the cruiser *Grafton* at 0504 on the 27th some 25 miles west of Beirut. *Grafton* was to bombard the sheds (at A on map and photograph) at the eastern end of the harbour from a position east of Beirut, so that any shot falling beyond the target would cause no damage in the town.

Empress hoisted out 8018 piloted by F/S/L E.M. King and 8019 piloted by Flt Lt Burling at 0520 for a bombing attack and reconnaissance of the harbour, but 8019 was unable to take off due to a bent distributor disc. 8018 returned to the ship at 0704, and a signal was then made to *Grafton* giving details of the reconnaissance of her bombardment target.

Grafton replied at 0745 that she would be in position to commence firing at 1000. Accordingly Flt Lt Worrall and 2nd Lt Pakenham-Walsh in N1090 was hoisted out at 0930 to spot for *Grafton*, followed shortly afterward by 8021 crewed by Flt Lt Bronson and Capt Millard to fly anti-submarine patrol round *Grafton*. With her armament of 9.2-inch and 6-inch guns *Grafton* scored numerous hits on the sheds on the eastern mole and a fire was started.

The majority of the projectiles however pierced the side of the building and burst in the water beyond. Numerous shell holes were observed, and the mole itself was damaged, but no damage was done to the residential quarter either by bombing or by shell fire. The objective at B bombed by 8018 at the start of the attack received direct hits from one 65-lb and sixteen 16-lb bombs, and a fire was started inside the building.

All the Shorts were hoisted back on board by 1146 and *Empress* set course for Port Said at 1257, arriving there at 0755 on 28 September.

Empress had not long returned to harbour before Wg Cdr Risk had formulated a plan for her seaplanes to carry out attacks in the Gulf of Alexandretta. Their objectives were to be railway installations at Adana, and the railway bridge at Chicaldere.

Throughout 1916 and 1917 the British Army had been gradually pushing back the Turkish forces, following the failure of their offensive at Romani in August 1916. El Arish was taken in December

Bombing attack by Short 184 from HMS Empress at aiming point A, Beirut harbour 17th August 1917. (via RCC)

Bombing attack by Short 184 from HMS Empress at aiming point B, Beirut harbour 17th August 1917. (via RCC)

1916, Rafa the following month and Khan Yunis by the end of February 1917. It was therefore important to disrupt the flow of Turkish supplies and reinforcements conveyed south on their railway system.

Accordingly *Empress* left Port Said at 0500 on 8 October to attack the railway bridge at Chicaldere and locomotive sheds at Adana, arriving ten miles south of Karatash Burnu at 0600 on the 9th. *Empress* began

hoisting out her four Short 184s at 0628, but a slight swell made it difficult for the seaplanes to leave the water. Flt Lt Wood, flying in 8018 without an observer and carrying three 65-lb and sixteen 16-lb bombs, was airborne at 0640 but was seen to be unable to climb above 700 feet as he approached the coast. Wood therefore dropped some of his bombs and reversed course to return to the ship, but as he landed at 0730 the rest of his bomb load exploded, blowing the Short to pieces and killing the pilot. In consequence of this Flt Lt Leigh and 2nd Lt Newton ASC in N1091, who had been detailed to accompany Wood's Short, returned to the ship and flew an anti-submarine patrol until being hoisted in at 0830.

The other two Shorts, 8021 crewed by Flt Lt Stephens and Capt Kempson, and 8019 piloted by Flt Lt Popham, meanwhile had taken off at 0650 and proceeded in company to bomb the bridge at Chicaldere. Stephens's machine had to jettison one 65-lb bomb to get airborne but still carried one 65-lb and four 16-lb bombs. Popham's Short had difficulty in taking off with three 65-lb and sixteen 16-lb bombs. 8021 bombed the bridge first from 1,000 feet at 0741, closely followed by 8019 at 0748, when Popham took his machine down to 800 feet before releasing his bombs. Considerable and accurate rifle fire was experienced, also shrapnel fire from the village of Kurt Kulak on the return flight.

Direct hits were made on the bridge with two 65-lb and nine 16-lb bombs, but damage observed was slight. It was thought that most of the bombs fell through the bridge, which was open metal-work and open sleepers, and exploded in the water below it. The line at the south end of the bridge was damaged, and troops guarding the bridge were engaged with the seaplanes' Lewis guns.

8019 returned to the ship at 0848 and was found to have its radiator shot through. 8021 alighted at 0902 with the starboard float and lower petrol tank holed in several places, a float chassis bracing wire shot away and the metal tubing of tailplane and elevator shot through in several places.

As soon as the seaplanes were hoisted in *Empress* proceeded to Famagusta to coal and refit her machines, arriving there at 1800 that evening.

Next day a satisfactory test flight was carried out with 8021, after the tailplane and elevator had been replaced by those from 8019. The latter was found unfit for further use, several sections of radiator being wrecked.

Empress left Famagusta at 1730 on 10 October, arriving ten miles south-west of Karatash Burnu at 0600 on the 11th. Half an hour later 8021, armed with two 65-lb and four 16-lb bombs, was hoisted out for an attack on the locomotive sheds at Adana. After spending 20 minutes attempting to take off, Flt Lt A.W.Clemson and Newton finally got the Short airborne, and were last seen flying inland at 2,000 feet.

N1091, crewed by Leigh and Kempson, was hoisted out at 0638 to accompany the other Short to Adana, but

Reconnaissance photograph of the road and railway bridge over Nahr Beirut, between Beirut and Junie, taken by a Short 184 from HMS Empress on 17th August 1917. (FAAM)

Six aircrew members of the East Indies and Egypt Seaplane Squadron, probably on board HMS Empress, c.1917
(G.S.Leslie/J.M.Bruce collection)

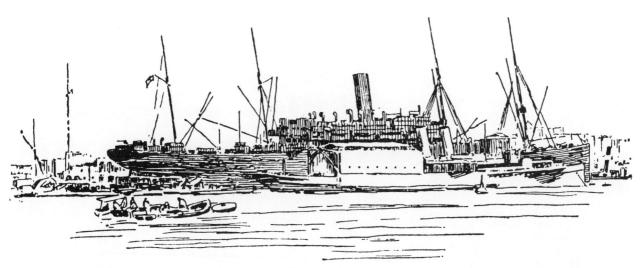

H.M.S. EMPRESS AT PORT SAID LYING ALONGSIDE THE MINNETONKA, AFTERWARDS SUNK BY SUBMARINE.

it was found impossible to start N1091's engine. A boat then put out from *Empress* with air mechanics to inspect the engine, which they managed to start at 0708. The Short was airborne soon after, but further engine problems caused a return to the ship and it was hoisted in. The engine trouble was located and repaired, and as 8021 was now overdue N1091 was hoisted out again at 0918, and crewed by Leigh and Ldg Mech A. Prince took off to search for the missing seaplane. However,

after climbing to 1,000 feet, recurring engine trouble caused an immediate return to the ship.

Empress cruised along the coast until noon, but 8021 was not sighted. The Short had crashed inland and both Clemson and Newton were killed.

Further operations being impossible, *Empress* proceeded to Port Said, arriving there at 1200 on 12 October.

HMS Empress with a Schneider in her hangar before she joined EI & ESS in February 1917. She then only operated Babies and Short 184s. (IWM SP242)

HMS Empress. (FAAM)

CHAPTER XV
Operations by seaplanes of the East Indies and Egypt Seaplane Squadron off Palestine October-November 1917

As 1917 drew towards its close the role of the EI and ESS changed from indirect support of operations on land to direct support of the Army's advance northwards in Palestine. Gaza, protecting the only practicable line of advance along the coastal plain was heavily defended by the Turks, and attacks by the Army at the First and Second Battles of Gaza in March and April had both ended in failure. For the next six months the opposing forces remained static, each side bringing up reinforcements for the forthcoming Third Battle of Gaza.

To replace *Anne* in the Squadron, the Kite Balloon Ship *City of Oxford* had been taken in hand during June 1917 for conversion to seaplane carrier. She joined *Raven II* and *Empress* at Port Said in August 1917, and by the end of October all three carriers were ready to support the attack on the Turkish right flank at Gaza.

Short 184, 8019, transferred from *City of Oxford*, was hoisted on board the monitor *Raglan* at 1000 on 28 October at Port Said. The Short's aircrew, Flt Lt E.J. Burling and Capt W.R. Kempson, together with six mechanics, embarked at 1200, and at 1800 *Raglan* proceeded to sea. *Raglan* was off Gaza at 0500 on 30 October, and then steamed nine miles northward to take up her firing position off the Wadi El Hesi. While on passage at 0630 her escorting trawlers were bombed by hostile aircraft, and were fired on by Turkish batteries sited north of Sheikh Hasan. *City of Oxford* arrived off Wadi El Hesi and closed *Raglan* at 0830.

Raglan's seaplane, 8019, was hoisted out at 1000 to spot for her 6-inch and 14-inch gunfire onto the railway station south of Deir Sineid. *Raglan* opened fire with her 6-inch gun and obtained several hits on the station. 8019's observer, Capt. Kempson, meanwhile signalled back that there was an ammunition dump near the station. Fire was switched to the dump and the eighth round exploded the stored ammunition. Explosions continued for 35 minutes destroying the station and wrecking many yards of the track.

Raglan's 6-inch now fired several rounds on the railway bridge crossing the Wadi to get the range. The 14-inch gun then opened fire on the bridge, registering a direct hit with the second round, leaving only the pillars standing. The bridge was so vital to the Turkish line of communication that within two days they had built a sand embankment across the Wadi and relaid the track upon it. At 1230 8019 landed alongside *City of Oxford* and was hoisted on board her with leaking floats.

City of Oxford hoisted out Short 184, N1262, at 1445 with the same crew of Burling and Kempson to continue spotting for *Raglan*'s guns. *Raglan* re-opened fire on the railway south of Deir Sineid and the road bridge over the Wadi, scoring several direct hits on both targets. As the seaplane was returning to *Raglan* it was attacked by a Halberstadt scout with forward firing guns. Burling took the Short down to within 800 feet of the sea, and Kempson in the rear cockpit got off two trays from his Lewis gun at close range. As they neared *Raglan*, Burling banked sharply to starboard to give *Raglan*'s anti-aircraft gunners a clear field of fire. This drove off the enemy and Burling landed N1262 close to *Raglan* at 1647. The seaplane was hit in about 36 places in the fuselage and top centre section, and one elevator control was shot away. The floats were also holed, one became waterlogged, and the seaplane turned over before it could be hoisted in. *Raglan* eventually salved N1262, but it was subsequently wrecked by the blast from her 14-inch gun while on board. The only injury sustained by the crew was a slight splinter wound in Capt Kempson's thigh.

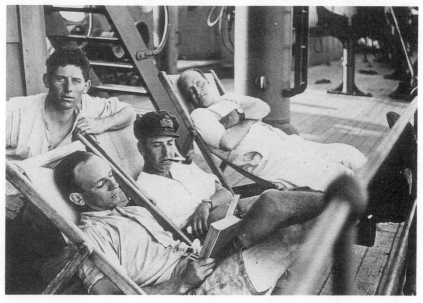

Aircrew of the East Indies and Egypt Seaplane Squadron relaxing, probably on board HMS Empress c.1917 (G.S.Leslie/J.M.Bruce collection)

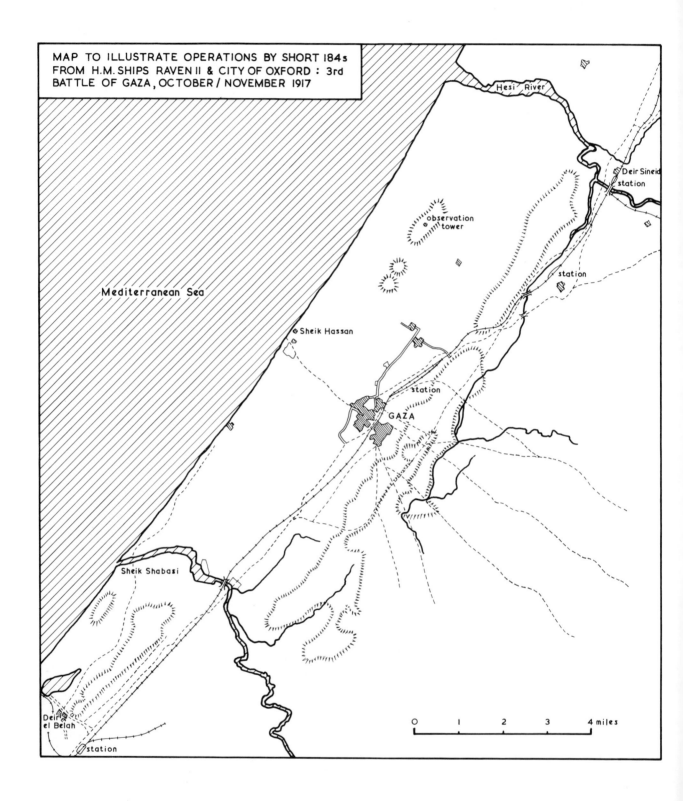

MAP TO ILLUSTRATE OPERATIONS BY SHORT 184s
FROM H.M. SHIPS RAVEN II & CITY OF OXFORD : 3rd
BATTLE OF GAZA, OCTOBER / NOVEMBER 1917

Mediterranean Sea

Hesi River

Deir Sineid
station

observation
tower

station

Sheik Hassan

station

station

GAZA

Sheik Shabasi

Deir
el Belah

station

0   1   2   3   4 miles

On land, the Third Battle of Gaza opened on 31 October. General Allenby's main objective was Beersheba, followed next day by a subsidiary attack on Gaza. At 0900 on 31 October *City of Oxford* closed with *Raglan*, and at 1020 hoisted out Short 184, N1090 crewed by Flt Lt G.D. Smith DSC and Capt W.R. Kempson.

N1090 took off to spot for *Raglan*'s 14-inch turret firing on the roads and bridge at the Wadi El Hesi once more, and returned to *City of Oxford* at 1204. *Raglan* left the Wadi El Hesi at 1400 for Deir El Belah.

HMS Raglan's Short 184 is hoisted aboard by the derrick on her port side. (G.S.Leslie/J.M.Bruce collection)

Raven II had meanwhile sailed from Port Said at 1700 on 31 October, escorted by the trawler *Veresis* and HM Yacht *Managem* and proceeded to a rendezvous off the Wadi El Hesi to meet the French battleship *Requin* (two 10.8-inch, six 3.9-inch), which she reached at 0900 on 1 November.

Requin signalled *Raven II* at 0930 to hoist out a seaplane, and Short 184, N1263, crewed by Flt Lt Bronson and 2nd Lt Pakenham-Walsh took off to spot for *Requin*. Firing commenced at 0958, concentrating on the railway north and south of the station at Deir Sineid, and continued until 1125. *Raven II* recovered the seaplane at 1130 and a signal was received from *Requin* that she would be ready to fire again at 1400. Short 184, 8022, with Flt Lt H.V. Worrall as pilot and 2nd Lt Pakenham-Walsh, was hoisted out from *Raven II* on a signal from *Requin* at 1412, but *Requin*'s wireless was not serviceable, and she signalled by searchlight to the seaplane to that effect. 8022 was recovered by *Raven II* at 1555.

At 1000 on 1 November Flt Lt Burling and Capt Kempson went ashore from *City of Oxford* to obtain information from the RFC about the area round Deir Sineid. *Raglan* left Deir El Belah at 1800 on 1 November, returning to her original firing position off the Wadi El Hesi by 0900 on the 2nd. At 1000 *Raven II* closed with *Raglan* and hoisted out Short 184, 8022, crewed by Burling and Kempson to spot for *Raglan*'s fire on the newly constructed railway embankment across the Wadi El Hesi. 8022 was forced to return at 1145 owing to poor visibility, but the weather cleared between 1445 and 1545, and 8022 took off once more.

Raglan was ranged on the embankment with her 6-inch guns, after which her 14-inch gun caused considerable damage to the embankment with several direct hits.

Raven II's Short 184, N1263, was hoisted aboard *Raglan* after dark and Burling and Kempson also transferred to the monitor. *Raven II* proceeded to Port Said at 1900. The seaplane carrier *Empress* had sailed at 1030 the previous day, 1 November, from Port Said to take part in operations designed to persuade the Turks that a landing behind their lines was imminent, in order to hasten their withdrawal. At 0600 on 2 November *Empress* rendezvoused with *City of Oxford*, some of whose pilots were transferred to *Empress*, which then proceeded to a position off El Haram by 0900. *Empress* hoisted out four of her seaplanes for an attack on the Jaljulye bridge - two Hamble Babies N1209 (Flt Lt King) and N1210 (Flt Lt Popham), and two Sopwith Babies N1129 (Flt Lt Leigh) and N1038 (Flt Lt Smith). Unfortunately Baby N1038 began to sink by the tail, turned over and became waterlogged. Efforts to salve the Baby had to be abandoned owing to the wind vanes on the seaplane's two 65-lb bombs becoming unwound by the action of the water, and the consequent danger of an explosion. *Empress* sank N1038 by gunfire. The three remaining seaplanes then took off, finding their overland flight to the target very bumpy. Six 65-lb bombs were dropped, but the wind was directly across the target and the bridge was not hit. Damage was however caused to the railway track north and south of the bridge.

After recovering her seaplanes *Empress* moved north to attack an oil refinery near Haifa, and reached her launching point at 1345 that day. Five seaplanes were hoisted out - two Hamble Babies N1209 (Flt Lt King), N1210 (Flt Lt Popham) and three Sopwith

Babies N1036 (Flt Lt Stephens), N1129 (Flt Lt Leigh) and N1028 (Flt Lt Smith).

The first seaplane to attack, Baby N1036, had orders to drop two 16-lb bombs in the vicinity of the refinery in order to give the Christian employees time to evacuate the area. The first seaplane to return to *Empress* reported that two Babies had been sighted in the water in Haifa Bay.

A signal was made to the French destroyer *Coutelas* which made full speed to Haifa. On her return at 1830 she made the signal "All saved, machine lost". Apparently Popham had suffered engine failure in Hamble Baby N1210, but had made a safe landing in the bay. This had been seen by Stephens who, after dropping his warning bombs near the refinery, had landed alongside Popham's seaplane. Popham made an unsuccessful attempt to burn his Baby, and then swam over to and boarded Stephen's Baby N1036. The combined weight of the two men almost submerged the floats during the take-off run, throwing up so much spray that it broke the propeller - a common fault of seaplanes. *Coutelas* destroyed N1036 by gunfire, after Stephens had removed the examination doors of the main floats.

Four hits by 65-lb bombs on the oil refinery were claimed, for the loss of two seaplanes and damage to Schneider N1129 after a heavy landing in a confused sea. *Empress* after finishing the recovery of her seaplanes proceeded to Port Said.

On 3 November at 0610 *Raglan*'s Short 184,

N1263, was hoisted out to spot the fall of shot from the cruiser *Grafton* onto trenches south-east of El Nezele, where fire from Turkish batteries was holding up our advance northward. On arriving over the cruiser, the seaplane was ordered by signal from *Grafton*'s searchlight to return to *Raglan* because the rising sun obscured the cruiser's point of aim.

N1263 was hoisted on board *Raglan* at 0643, but at 1000 was again hoisted out to spot for *Raglan*'s 14-inch turret onto the railway embankment and road bridge crossing the Wadi El Hesi. Several direct hits were obtained and visibility from the air was good. However, a sandstorm blew up and obscured the point of aim on shore, and Burling and Kempson had to return to *Raglan* at 1130 and the seaplane was hoisted on board.

By 4 November Beersheba had fallen and our cavalry had advanced some 10 to 12 miles further northwards. The main defences of Gaza had been overcome and Sheikh Hasan was in our hands, but the advance up the coast towards the Wadi El Hesi was being held up by Turkish batteries dug in around El Nezele.

City of Oxford, now with her pilots lent to *Empress* for the raids of 2 November returned aboard, entered the fray once more and arrived off the Wadi El Hesi at 0900 on 4 November, where she closed with *Raglan*.

Short 184, N1263, crewed by Burling and Kempson was hoisted out from *Raglan* at 1000 to spot her fire on the batteries at El Nezele. A very effective rapid fire

HMS Raglan in 1915 operated one Short 184 transferred from HMS Ark Royal. (A.K.Vicary)

was kept up by her 6-inch gun.

Two enemy aircraft attacked N1263 but both were eventually driven off by the ship's anti-aircraft fire. On landing the seaplane was hoisted on board *City of Oxford*, as she was better equipped for the task in a disturbed sea than *Raglan*. Seaplane handling by the monitors was always a tricky operation, even under ideal conditions. Four seaplanes were now on board *City of Oxford*.

Between 1145 and 1345 *City of Oxford*'s Short 184, N1091, piloted by Flt Lt E.M. King with 2nd Lt A.D. Ferguson as observer,

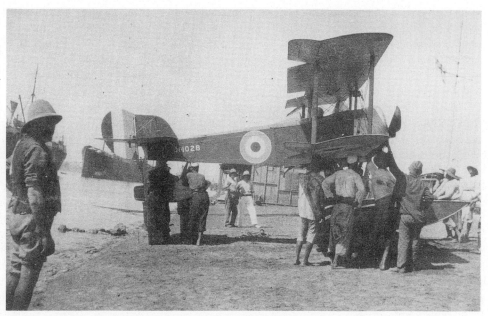

Baby N1028, which Flt Lt Smith flew from HMS Empress in the attack on the Haifa oil refinery on 2nd November 1917. (G.S.Leslie/J.M.Bruce collection)

carried on spotting for *Raglan*. Her 14-inch turret obtained three direct hits on the newly constructed railway embankment and also destroyed sections of the track north and south of the bridge over the Wadi.

At midnight on 4/5 November *Raglan* received an urgent signal from the flagship to destroy the batteries at El Nezele, and at 0300 *City of Oxford* closed with *Raglan. City of Oxford*'s Short 184, N1090, was readied for take off by 0415, but a thick fog rolled up and it rained, causing a postponement of the operation. By 0600 the fog had lifted slightly but the shore was still obscured. N1090, crewed by Flt Lt A.E. Popham and Capt W.R. Kempson, finally got away at 0800, but low cloud prevented accurate spotting and the seaplane returned to *City of Oxford* at 0900.

The weather cleared during the forenoon and at 1330 Flt Lt A.E. Popham and Capt V. Millard took off in Short 184, N1091, to spot for the monitor M 29 (two 6-inch guns) onto the trenches west of El Nezele. Turkish anti-aircraft fire kept N1091 at a distance but several hits were obtained on the target.

Between 1430 and 1530, N1091 crewed by King and Ferguson continued to spot for both *Raglan* and M 29 onto the same target, but further spotting had to be abandoned at 1530 when rain clouds came over.

Early morning spotting on 6 November again proved impossible owing to low cloud over the coast, and at 0900 *Raglan* was relieved off the Wadi El Hesi by *Requin*. Burling and Kempson with their six mechanics then transferred permanently to *City of Oxford*.

Following intelligence reports that the Turks were retreating northwards along the road leading through

Deir Sineid, and that large convoys were concentrated at Deir Sineid Junction up the Wadi El Hesi, *Requin* took up her firing position off the Wadi at 0930. Spotting flights for *Requin* were provided throughout 6 November by *City of Oxford*'s Short 184, N1091, with three crews taking their turn.

Smith and Pakenham-Walsh were airborne from 1000 till 1150, and were attacked first by two enemy aircraft and then by one single seater. Pakenham-Walsh replied with his Lewis guns from the rear cockpit, and anti-aircraft fire from the ships eventually drove off the attackers.

Popham and Ferguson took over spotting duties between 1330 and 1500, and in spite of being attacked by an enemy aircraft, succeeded in getting *Requin*'s guns onto the Wadi El Hesi railway embankment and road bridge.

The last flight of the day was undertaken by King and, for a second time, Ferguson. Hits were obtained on Deir Sineid Junction and the line to the north of it.

Gaza fell on 7 November, and as the Turks regrouped their field guns north of Deir Sineid and occupied previously prepared trenches south of Askalon, *City of Oxford*'s seaplanes were again in action in an intensive effort to dislodge the retreating enemy.

N1091 crewed by Burling and Kempson was hoisted out at 0650 on 7 November, but low cloud made spotting impossible and the seaplane returned to *City of Oxford* at 0727. 8019 with King and Millard was airborne at 0810 and spotted *Requin*'s fire onto the trenches south-east of Askalon. Visibility was still poor and the seaplane returned at 0930. Burling and Kempson went on board the flagship at 0900 to arrange spotting for the monitor *M 15*'s 9.2-inch turret onto the railway junction south-east of Askalon as large convoys were reported there; this would be the last junction within range of the ship's guns at sea. An enemy aircraft dropped four bombs close to *City of Oxford* at 0915, but these caused no damage.

From 1138 until 1421 Burling and Kempson in N1263 spotted *M 15* onto Julis Junction, but the cloud base was now down to 1200 feet and spotting had to be carried out below this height. Popham and Ferguson with N1091 took over these duties from N1263 until 1640, and observed many hits on the junction. *Raglan* had by now joined in the attack on this target with her 14-inch turret, after taking up position off Askalon.

City of Oxford was ordered north to the coast off Ramleh and Jaffa at 1430, but was ordered to return to *Raglan* at 1700 owing to operations being abandoned. N1091 flew back to *City of Oxford* and was hoisted aboard off Ramleh. Enemy aircraft were seen overhead but no bombs were dropped.

A bombardment of Ramleh was planned for next day, 8 November, and to that end Burling and Kempson were sent over to *Raglan* by trawler to arrange spotting for the bombardment. The plan was for *City of Oxford* to cruise offshore during the night and close with *Raglan* at dawn, but bad weather caused the operation to be abandoned, and *Raglan* was ordered to return to Port Said.

Burling and Kempson were transferred by trawler from *Raglan* before she sailed, and by 1030 on 8 November they were back aboard *City of Oxford* off Askalon.

The previous evening at 1700 our guns and some cavalry advanced along the coast as far north as the Wadi El Hesi, although Turkish troops still occupied positions some five miles inland up the Wadi. These positions, behind some sandhills, threatened the right flank of our advance up the coast, and all ships now took up firing positions, from the Wadi El Hesi to a few miles north of Askalon, to shift the Turks further inland.

By 1130 on 8 November all three of *City of Oxford*'s Short 184s were airborne to spot the fire of the assembled fleet onto high ground north-east of the Wadi El Hesi, trenches north-east of Askalon and onto the railway line, running east and west through Bruberah. N1091 (King and Millard) spotted for *M 15*'s 9.2-inch gun, 8019 (Popham and Ferguson) for *Requin*'s two 10.5-inch and four 3.9-inch guns, and N1263 (Smith and Pakenham-Walsh) for the monitor *M 31*'s two 6-inch guns. By 1400 our troops had advanced close to Askalon and N1263 landed alongside *Ladybird* for further orders. In attempting to take off again N1263 smashed her floats, but was taken in tow by *M31* and safely hoisted on board *City of Oxford* at 1422.

The only other casualty was float damage to 8019 caused by shrapnel. *City of Oxford* hoisted all her seaplanes aboard at 1500 and proceeded with escort to Port Said, where she arrived at 0900 on 9 November.

Short 184 N1091 which was operated from HMS City of Oxford in 1917. (G.S.Leslie/J.M.Bruce collection)

This outstanding example of inter-Service co-operation culminated with General Allenby's entry into Jerusalem in December 1917.

Soon afterwards *Raven II* paid off after nearly three years service as a seaplane carrier, during which time her seaplanes had flown over the coastlines of Asia Minor, Syria, Palestine, Egypt, the Hejaz, the Yemen and across the Indian Ocean and Arabian Sea to Colombo. Like *Anne*, she was converted to a collier and served with the RFA until the end of the war.

Short 184 N1639 which HMS City of Oxford operated in 1917/1918, here provides a backdrop to ''press-ups'' at Alexandria. The enjoyment on the faces of the participants is evident. (FAAM)

CHAPTER XVI
Operations by *City of Oxford*, Red Sea February-March 1918

After *Empress* and *City of Oxford* had returned to Port Said in November 1917, their seaplanes carried out a series of convoy escort duties to counter the increasing German submarine activity in the East Mediterranean.

But on 20 January 1918 news reached Port Said of the sortie from the Dardanelles of *Goeben* and *Breslau*. At Kephalo they had sunk the monitors *Raglan* and *M 28* on the 20th and intended bombarding the shipping at Mudros. However both ships ran into a minefield, and *Breslau* was lost. *Goeben*, though damaged, extricated herself from the minefield and ran back to make her escape through the Straits. But off Nagara Point she ran aground.

Empress was immediately despatched from Port Said, taking with her some of *City of Oxford*'s aircrew to join the aerial attack already being conducted against the stranded German battle-cruiser.

Empress arrived at Mudros at 1700 on 24 January, and orders were received for two of her Short 184s to deliver a night attack on *Goeben*. None of *Empress*'s aircrew had previously flown at night, but N1581 crewed by Flt Lt H.V. Worrall and Lt L.H. Pakenham-Walsh and N1582 crewed by Flt Lt C.G. Bronson and Lt A.D. Ferguson were each armed with two 65-lb bombs.

N1581 was hoisted out in Mudros harbour at 2220 and was airborne at 2230. By 2350 the mouth of the Dardanelles had been reached at an altitude of 3,000 feet, and proceeding north N1581 bombed *Goeben* at Nagara Point from 3,000 feet at 0015, scoring one direct hit. Worrall landed again at 0115 and was hoisted in at 0120.

Bronson and Ferguson in N1582 were hoisted out at 2300 and were airborne five minutes later, climbing to 3,000 feet off the south-east corner of Imbros. Their bombing runs were made from only 800 feet at 0025. The first bomb fell 150 feet on *Goeben*'s port beam and the second 100 feet on her port beam. N1582 was waterborne in Mudros harbour by 0130 and was hoisted in at 0135. During the 25th and 26th the weather was unsuitable for flying, but on the 27th orders were received for the seaplanes to make a further night attack. Accordingly N1582, armed with one 230-lb bomb, and crewed by Bronson and Pakenham-Walsh, was hoisted

Short 827, 8649, here seen on the quayside at Kilwa, East Africa was operated by HMS City of Oxford in June 1918.
(MAP)

HMS City of Oxford in 1918 with canvas hangars rigged on her foredeck. She embarked up to four Short 184's during 1917/18, operating in the E.Mediterranean and Red Sea. (IWM SP513)

HMS City of Oxford in 1918 without hangars rigged. Her four seaplanes, with wings folded, were stowed in pairs forward and abaft her foremast, which was fitted with derricks for handling the seaplanes. (IWM SP3041)

out at 2220 and was airborne five minutes later. N1581 was held in readiness to make an attack later, but this was cancelled owing to adverse weather reports received from seaplanes returning to *Ark Royal*.

By the early hours of the 28th nothing had been heard from N1582, so at 0845 Worrall and Capt W.R. Kempson were hoisted out in N1581 to conduct a search for the missing seaplane. A two hour flight revealed no trace of it, but showed that *Goeben* had in fact been towed off by a Turkish battleship, and although she had been hit by many bombs none were powerful enough to disable her. Flt Lt H. de V. Leigh and Capt V. Millard in N1590 made one last flight from *Empress* on 29 January to search for the missing seaplane but saw nothing. Later enemy reports indicated that N1582 had been brought down by machine gun fire at a low altitude, and that Bronson and Pakenham-Walsh had been taken prisoners unhurt. *Empress* returned to Port Said on 4 February.

On regaining her aircrew lent to *Empress, City of Oxford* sailed from Suez on 13 February to work under the orders of the SNO of the Red Sea Patrol in the cruiser *Fox*. Arriving off Loheiya on the 22nd, *City of Oxford* anchored three miles off shore. Instructions were received to make daily bombing flights against the Turkish positions on Jebel Al Milh, and the hostile Arab positions around the Jebel as far east as Zohrah.

Operations commenced at 1500 on the 24th, when Short 184, 8020, crewed by Flt Lt King and CPO Goodwin was hoisted out. Direct hits were obtained on the village at the base of Jebel Al Milh with one 65-lb and two 16-lb bombs, and four 16-lb bombs were dropped on trenches on the Jebel. Returning to the ship 8020 was re-armed with six 16-lb bombs which were dropped on the summit of the Jebel, and two hoppers of Lewis gun ammunition were fired into trenches on the Jebel. Flt Lt Smith and Capt Millard in N1263 obtained a direct hit on a tower at Beit Al Mokhay with a 16-lb bomb. Three more 16-lb bombs were dropped on villages, but their 65-lb bomb aimed at a village west of the Jebel failed to explode. 8022 was then hoisted out for an attack on the village at the foot of the Jebel with F/S/L Pennington and Lt Ferguson aboard. They obtained hits with one 65-lb and four 16-lb bombs, and considerable smoke was seen rising from the village for some time afterwards. 8022 dropped another 65-lb and two 16-lb bombs which missed the target. Flt Cdr. Leigh and Lt Kennedy took N1639 up on the last sortie of the day, dropping two 65-lb bombs on the Jebel Al Milh. One was a direct hit on trenches and a gun emplacement on the southern end of the western spur, and the other exploded on the slope of the spur. Of six 16-lb bombs dropped on the village north of the Jebel four were direct hits. Visibility had been good throughout the operations, but flying conditions were difficult overland

due to thermals. Operations were completed by 1615 on the 24th.

Poor weather on the 25th ruled out any flying, but N1263 crewed by Flt Lt King and Lt Ferguson commenced operations at 1500 on the 26th. Early morning flying was found impracticable owing to heavy ground mist, and in the heat of the day air conditions were too bumpy. No difficulty was found in taking off from Loheiya, as the anchorage was well protected from the open sea by reefs and islands. N1263 flew due east after crossing the coast north of the Jebel, penetrating up to 15 miles inland for the purpose of a photographic reconnaissance. The existing maps of the Yemen were found to be totally inaccurate, and cameras were carried on all flights, with a view to mapping the whole area.

F/S/L Pennington and Capt Millard were airborne in 8022 later on the 26th, and on a north-easterly course, flew to Zohrah, about 25 miles inland, which was the Turkish GHQ. They were fired on two miles east of Zohrah, but were not hit, and when their engine gave trouble, course was set back to the ship, dropping two 65-lb bombs on Jebel Al Milh before crossing the coast.

On 28 February continuous patrols were flown by *City of Oxford*'s Short 184s between 1100 and 1700 over Jebel Al Milh, to prevent the Turkish guns firing on the Idrissi troops who had obtained a footing on the hill. Between 1300 and 1400 the Turkish positions on the north-east and west spurs of the Jebel were attacked by the Shorts with 65-lb bombs and Lewis gun fire, and photographs were taken. A seaplane was hoisted out at 0620 on 1 March for a reconnaissance of the Jebel, but the flight had to be abandoned owing to heavy ground mist. Operations were postponed until 1600 on the 1st, when attacks on Turkish trenches and gun emplacements were continued until 1820, when bad visibility put an end to flying for the day.

From 6 March to 11 March no flying was possible owing to the heavy swell and strong winds prevailing. But operations recommenced on the 15th when Smith and Ferguson were hoisted out in 8022 at 1633. Airborne at 1644 they crossed the coast at 4,000 feet and at 1710 dropped two 65-lb bombs half way down the west side of the east spur of Jebel Al Milh. 8022 was waterborne at 1750 and hoisted in at 1756.

N1263 crewed by Flt Cdr. H.de V. Leigh and Lt R.C. Kennedy bombed two houses in Zohrah, thought to contain the Turkish GHQ, on the 16th, the sortie taking place between 1649 and 1728. Four 16-lb bombs were dropped. Flt Lt King and Lt Leish RNVR also took off that evening in 8020 for a test flight at 1623 with two 16-lb bombs. At 1,000 feet however the bombs shifted and the Short had to land again to replace them. Airborne again at 1638, both bombs were dropped from 4,800 feet over the crest of the Jebel. The pin broke in one bomb and it exploded on contact wide of the Jebel.

The engine ran satisfactorily and 8020 was hoisted in again at 1754.

City of Oxford proceeded to an anchorage off Habil on the 20th where considerable swell was encountered, there being lack of good shelter from the open sea. Here three of the Shorts made demonstration flights over Habil and Midi to impress the Arabs, and one Short was also sent to reconnoitre and bomb the Turkish positions at Jebel Abs.

On 22 March *City of Oxford* proceeded south again to Loheiya, and a seaplane was hoisted out on the way down for a reconnaissance over Jebel Al Milh and Loheiya.

Bad weather conditions on the 23rd prevented a further flight being made over the Jebel, so *City of Oxford* proceeded to Kamaran where at 1640 Leigh and Ferguson were hoisted out in 8022. The ship was now under orders to return to Suez, so only a 30-minute reconnaissance and demonstration flight over Salif was possible. *City of Oxford* left Kamaran on the 23rd, arriving at Suez on 29 March.

From 22 February to 23 March the ship's four Short 184s had made 58 flights, been airborne for a total of $51\frac{1}{2}$ hours, and had dropped sixty-three 16-lb and fifty-two 65-lb bombs on enemy positions. Of the Short 184s, N1639 was out of commission with a cracked piston. N1263, 8080 and 8022 were all still serviceable, but were not fit for overland flying until they had undergone a thorough overhaul.

So ended the last RNAS involvement of the war in the Red Sea. And within two days of *City of Oxford*'s return to Suez the Royal Naval Air Service had ceased to exist.

H.M.S. CITY OF OXFORD.

CHAPTER XVII
Seaplane operations from *Laconia, Himalaya* and *Manica,* East Africa April 1916-May 1917

T he destruction of *Königsberg* in July 1915 eliminated a threat to our trade routes in the Indian Ocean, but following that operation, many of HM Ships blockading the mouth of the Rufiji River were dispersed to other stations or were in need of refitting.

At the beginning of 1916, because of the shortage of warships, there were no plans to launch a seaborne invasion of German East Africa, over which the German forces under General von Lettow-Vorbeck still exercised control. These forces could only be supplied by sea and it was the Royal Navy's task to intercept the German supply ships.

During March 1916 Portugal declared war on Germany, which eliminated the use by the Germans of Mozambique as a port to supply their forces. And during the same month the RNAS established a seaplane base at Chukwani Bay, on the island of Zanzibar, for operations in the East African campaign.

Four Voisins and four Short 827s - 3096, 3097, 3098 and 8218 - were sent out from England in January 1916, arriving at Mombasa in March. Here they were loaded aboard SS *Clan Macpherson* for delivery to No 8 (Naval) Squadron at Zanzibar. On arrival the aircraft, in packing cases, were lightered ashore and assembled on the quayside.

Besides operating from Chukwani Bay, the Short 827's were frequently taken to sea by the two AMC's then on station - *Himalaya* and *Laconia* and by the seaplane carrier *Manica*, each of which had a temporary canvas hangar erected on deck to protect their seaplane. This considerably increased the Short's radius of action. Hoisting in and hoisting out was effected with the wings folded, and the seaplanes were handled by the ship's derricks.

Laconia arrived at Zanzibar to operate No 8 Squadron's Short 827's in April 1916, and was joined in May by *Himalaya* and *Manica*.

Manica's seaplane was first in action during the

S.S.Clan Macpherson which transported Short 827s to Zanzibar in March 1916 for use aboad the A.M.C.'s Himalaya, Laconia and Manica. (FAAM)

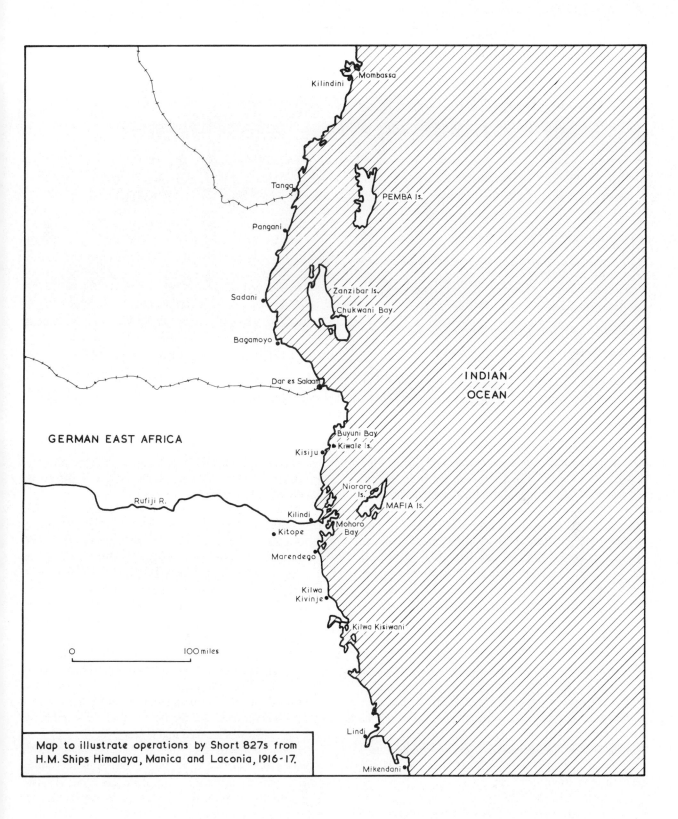

Map to illustrate operations by Short 827s from
H.M. Ships Himalaya, Manica and Laconia, 1916-17.

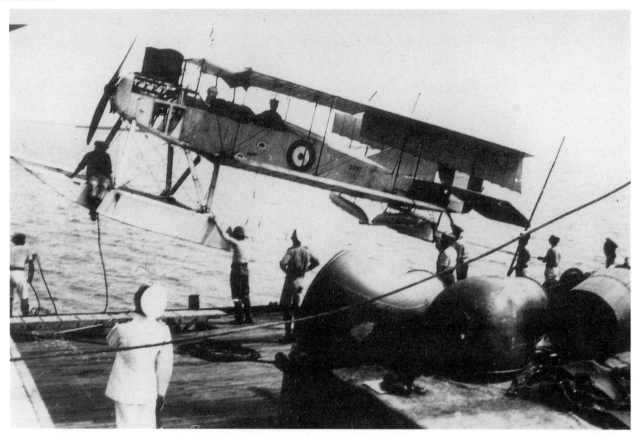

Short 827, 3097, is hoisted out from HMS Laconia off the coast of German East Africa in 1916. (FAAM)

third week in May for a reconnaissance of Kilwa. After flying a reconnaissance of Quirini on the 25th, *Manica* left for a patrol off Lindi, returning to Zanzibar on 2 June. Between 3-12 June she patrolled off Kilindi, during which time her kite balloon was used to spot for the naval bombardment of Tanga. After briefly returning to Zanzibar on the 14th, *Manica* was off Pangani from the 17th to 19 June, before proceeding south to Kilwa for seven days. *Manica* left Zanzibar on 1 July for Dar-Es-Salaam to prepare for operations off Tanga in mid-July.

Himalaya was at sea between 28 June and 4 July off Lindi. Her Short 827, crewed by Sqdn Cdr Cull and F/S/L Gallehawk, found four dhows in a creek at Gingwea on the 28th and spotted for the cruiser *Challenger* when she opened fire on them. No hits were made but the operation was repeated next day when the cruiser obtained five direct hits on the dhows. Cull and Gallehawk flew a reconnaissance over Mikendani on 3 July, and over Port Beaver and Port Nisus on the 4th, but nothing of interest was observed.

Off Tanga between 17-29 July *Manica*'s seaplane was engaged in bombing and reconnaissance flights over Tanga, Pangani Bagamoyo, and Sadani.

Flt Lt MacLean and Sub Lt Fitzherbert reconnoitered Tanga and the railway running north-east to Pongive on the 17th, where six 16-lb bombs were dropped on the village. "Damage not apparent but natives panic stricken"!

MacLean and Fitzherbert flew a reconnaissance over Sadani on the 26th where they came under machine gun fire and retaliated with bombs. MacLean took up WO Lacey as observer next day for a flight over Sadani which was bombed. MacLean and Fitzherbert were airborne again on the 28th spotting the fall of shot from the monitor *Mersey*, firing on a target at Sadani. The same aircrew flew a reconnaissance over Bagamoyo on 29 July, where incendiary and HE bombs were dropped. South of the town the Short came under machine gun fire. A bullet passed through the starboard float into the fuselage and hit the brass clip for the air bottles. The brass splintered, wounding MacLean in the leg and arm. The observer bandaged the pilot's arm, and shortly after the seaplane was recalled to the ship.

Manica returned to coal at Zanzibar on the 29th, after which she sailed to rendezvous with the cruiser *Talbot* off Bagamoyo on 1 August. Here her seaplane spotted the cruiser's fall of shot as she bombarded the German positions on 1 and 3 August.

Manica's Short 827 was employed on photo reconnaissance duties at Dar-Es-Salaam on 9 August preparatory to a landing there, and on 15 August spotted

HMS Manica off German East Africa in 1916, with canvas hangar rigged aft for her Short 827 seaplane.
(IWM SP1216)

for the fire of the battleship *Vengeance*, the cruiser *Challenger* and the two monitors *Severn* and *Mersey* on targets at Bagamoyo, before the assault on the port. Unfortunately the seaplane suffered engine failure and was forced down at the mouth of the Kingani River. It was later recovered, but meanwhile *Himalaya* was despatched to Zanzibar to fetch a replacement machine.

Manica's Short was operated over Dar-Es-Salaam during early September, spotting for *Vengeance, Hyacinth, Severn* and *Mersey*, and the town surrendered on 3 September. Her seaplane supported the landing at Lindi until 12 October, and flew a reconnaissance over the wrecked *Königsberg* in the Rufiji River on the 14th before returning in company with *Himalaya* to Zanzibar on 26 October.

Manica returned to the Rufiji Delta in early November with two Short 827s embarked - 3098 and 8641. Flt Lt MacLean with Ldg Mech E. Groucott as observer took off on the 1st in 3098 at 0530 in perfect flying weather for a reconnaissance of the delta, and reported no changes from the flight of 14 October. The seaplane returned to the ship at 0730.

The same aircrew flew a reconnaissance over the Delta and north to Kiwale Island on 3 November, leaving the ship in 8641 at 0510. Crossing the coast at Dodoni village they turned south, following the roads and dropped bombs on the supposed camp at Mangisani. Proceeding over the delta via Lokotemba Kijujani and Njemssati, they turned inland over Kikwale camp and photographed *Königsberg* before landing again at 0725.

MacLean and Groucott made another reconnaissance of the Delta in 8641 on the 8th, taking off at 0520 and crossing the coast at Kiombini Mundung. Nothing of interest was observed and the Short was waterborne again at 0720.

Manica had shifted to a position off Ras Wanga by 11 November, when MacLean and Groucott in 8641 took off at 0530 for a reconnaissance over Mtingi and district. However engine trouble, later traced to a broken valve spring, forced an early return at 0630. Next day, while the ship was off Kilwa, they took 8641 up at 0540 for a reconnaissance over Kitope Hill and district to try and locate enemy troops. Nothing was seen however, and owing to a low cloud base and very gusty conditions the seaplane returned at 0700. *Himalaya* meanwhile was operating her seaplane farther south off Lindi, where on 9 November a reconnaissance flight was made over Mto Mbanja. Flt Lt E. R. Moon and Air Mechanic Wilmshurst took off in 8642, carrying $2^{1}/_{2}$ hour's fuel, a camera and two 65-lb bombs. Airborne at 0745 they flew over Mto Mbanja at 700 feet, where no dhows were visible in the river. After proceeding up the river for two miles weather conditions deteriorated, and unable to maintain a safe altitude, Moon was forced to turn back. Crossing the coast at under 200 feet Moon flew out to sea to gain altitude and then flew over Lindi

A Short 827 is hoisted aboard HMS Himalaya by dockyard crane at Dar-es-Salaam 6th August 1916. (G.S.Leslie/J.M.Bruce collection)

harbour at 1,200 feet. When over the harbour at 0835 he saw the recall signal flashed from *Himalaya* and returned to the ship at 0845.

8642, crewed by Moon and Wilmshurst, was airborne again at 0600 on 11 November for a reconnaissance and bombing flight in the vicinity of Lindi, carrying fuel for two hours, W/T, a camera and two 65-lb bombs. The two bombs were dropped from 1,800 feet, aimed at the sisal factory at Mrweka, but both just missed the target. Photographs were taken of the bombing and also of the abandoned SS *President - Königsberg*'s former supply ship - which had been

immobilised by a demolition party from the cruiser *Chatham* in October 1914. No movement of any enemy was observed, and this information was wirelessed to the torpedo gunboat *Salamander*, which had been lying offshore ready to commence a bombardment.

Low cloud and rain now made further reconnaissance difficult, so 8642 returned to *Himalaya* at 0750. Moon and Wilmshurst in 8642 were engaged on 17 November in spotting the fall of shot on targets at Lindi from the steel screw sloop *Rinaldo*. 8642 took off at 0530 carrying $2^1/_2$ hour's fuel, two 65-lb bombs, W/T and a camera. Climbing to 1,700 feet by 0605, the

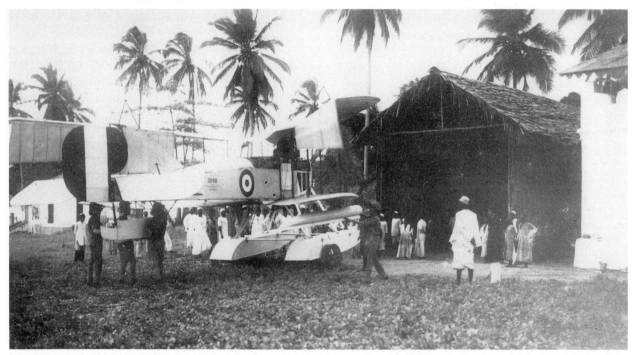

Short 827, 3098, being folded before hangaring at Kokotoni, East Africa during the Tanga campaign 1916. This seaplane was operated by both Manica and Himalaya. (FAAM)

HMS Himalaya at Simonstown 1915/16. Hired as an Armed Merchant Cruiser in 1914, she operated one Short 827 off German East Africa. (NMM P712)

seaplane commenced spotting as *Rinaldo* opened fire. All shots were observed to fall in the required area.

> "The Arab house was hit immediately and the hill was constantly hit. The trenches on the near side of the pier received special attention. Some difficulty was experienced in getting the ship to fire into the trenches just on the far side of the pier. During the bombardment troops were seen to move from the farther trenches to the presumed funk hole at either end of them. I presumed the gun position to be situated in the near trenches. If this supposition be correct, it was most probably hit".

Moon's report concluded by saying that only two shots fell off the target. The seaplane now dropped one bomb, which fell just beyond the far trenches, and after the firing had ceased flew over SS *President* and then followed the road from Mioreka 10 miles inland. Here the second bomb was dropped near an Arab house, and on the return flight the road from Kilwete to Lindi was reconnoitered, but nothing was seen, and at 0740 the seaplane returned to *Himalaya*.

Bad weather prevented any early morning flight next day, the 18th, but at 1010 Moon and Capt C. MacKenzie DSO RN (commanding *Himalaya*) acting as observer took off for a reconnaissance of Lindi harbour. A photograph of the positions shelled by *Rinaldo* on the previous day was taken from 1,800 feet and at 1110 the seaplane returned to the ship.

During November two new Short 827s had arrived for No 8 Squadron at Zanzibar, 8253 and 8254, which after being erected were test flown. The new arrivals enabled a complete overhaul to be carried out on 3096, 3097 and 3098, which had all seen a lot of service over the 8 months since arriving in Zanzibar in March. The four new Shorts 8641, 8642, 8253 and 8254 were now converted to hand starting. Air starting was taken out to save weight, and as they were taken to sea aboard ships with no air compressor, hand starting had considerable advantages. Henceforth no air bottles had to be carried in the seaplanes. Double oil tanks and enlarged radiators were also fitted to assist in cooling their 150-hp Nubian engines.

Off Kissidyu on 24 November, *Manica* launched 8254 in Buyuni Bay. Crewed by F/S/L Deans and Lt Fitzherbert it took off at 1540 with 28 gallons of petrol,

Short 827, 3096, which was operated off German East Africa by HMS Himalaya. (G.S.Leslie/J.M.Bruce collection)

Another of HMS Himalaya's Short 827s, 3098, with HMS Himalaya in the background. (FAAM)

Being detailed off for seaplane handling party had its good points. Short 827 3098 off Zanzibar c. June 1916. (G.S.Leslie/J.M.Bruce collection)

one 65-lb bomb, W/T and camera.

Turning inland at 2,200 feet the whole of Kissidyu village was seen to be on fire, and dense clouds of smoke from the village made observation of the road to Utunda difficult. However about 40 Askaris and a wagon were seen just west of Mawundja, and after making a circuit a bomb was dropped on them from 3,000 feet. The bomb missed the target by 300 yards and the seaplane then turned out to sea and landed astern of *Mersey* at 1640 to report the position of the troops. 8254 took off again at 1700 to spot for *Mersey*, and flew inland to behind the position where the troops were seen, and where some remained with the wagon. *Mersey* opened fire but did not receive the first three corrections, but afterwards got on target and scored five hits, and men were seen running away. Flying behind the target at 2,000 feet, spotting from the seaplane became difficult owing to haze and the setting sun, so the Short returned to *Mersey* at 1800 and from there flew back to *Manica*.

Dawn on 25 November saw *Manica* off Koma Island. Deans and Fitzherbert in 8254 took off from the lee of the island at 0800 carrying 30 gallons of petrol, W/T and camera. Proceeding up the coast the seaplane turned inland at 2,000 feet a mile south of Ras Funguni, and for the next 2¹/₂ hours conducted an extensive survey of roads in the area. On landing alongside *Manica* at 1050 the front strut lug on the starboard float

fitting carried away, due to defective welding. The strut then went through the top of the float and the propeller cut through the side of the float.

Repairs were carried out as soon as the seaplane was hoisted in, and 8254 was back in action again on the 28th, when Deans and Fitzherbert took off at 0707 for a reconnaissance over the north part of the Rufiji Delta. Very little of interest was observed, no photographs were taken, and the seaplane returned to *Manica* at 0835. Deans and Fitzherbert spent two hours between 0600 and 0800 on 29 November trying to get 8254, carrying two 65-lb bombs, to unstick from the water. After the bombs were taken back on board *Manica* the seaplane took off from the lee of Hatambura Island at 0938 for a reconnaissance over the Kissidyu district. After the fire on the 24th, most of Kissidyu village was seen to be destroyed. A reconnaissance of the road through Utunda was abandoned on the approach of a bad storm, which broke just after the seaplane was hoisted on board.

From the South Mafia Channel on 30 November *Manica* hoisted out 8254 again, and Deans and Fitzherbert were airborne at 1625 from the lee of Mange Reef. The Short turned down the coast to Mohoro Bay where, turning west, it headed for Marendego where the camp had been partly destroyed by fire. At 2,000 feet the wind had risen to about 35 mph and was very gusty. The sun was hidden behind heavy clouds, making the

Flt Lt E.R.Moon in October 1916. (FAAM)

*Flt Lt E.R.Moon on the day after his release as a
Prisoner of War (FAAM)*

*Flt Lt E.R.Moon and Cdr Hon R.Bridgeman about to take-off in HMS Himalaya's Short 827, 8254, from
Niororo Island 6th January 1917 for a reconnaissance of the Rufiji River. The Short was forced down
with engine failure, and Bridgeman lost his life and Moon was made Prisoner of War. (FAAM)*

light bad for observation, but two 65-lb bombs were aimed at the remaining sheds. They fell about 400 yards short and started a large bush fire. As the weather was now deteriorating Deans turned back at 1715 and landed astern of *Manica* at 1755. There was a bad sea running and the seaplane was slightly damaged while being hoisted in.

Off Niororo Island on 6 January 1917, *Himalaya* hoisted out Short 827, 8254, for a reconnaissance of the Rufiji Delta. The Short was piloted by Flt Lt E. R. Moon with the Flag Commander, Cdr The Hon R. Bridgeman, flying as his observer. 8254 was airborne at 0720 and after completing a reconnaissance of the Delta, a return flight to *Himalaya* was commenced at 0820. Shortly after the engine revolutions dropped and a forced landing had to be made in a creek. While taxying the engine was kept running with Bridgeman in the pilot's seat while Moon tried to trace the fault. It was found that the after magneto drive had failed. Pressure in the petrol tank then gave out, the engine stopped and resisted all attempts to restart it.

Bridgeman decided against trying to effect a repair because there were still Germans in the vicinity, so Moon flooded the seaplane with petrol and fired it with a Very's light. Moon and Bridgeman then set off on foot towards the mouth of the river, which they swam to cover their tracks. By high tide they had reached a point opposite to the abandoned German SS *Somali* (one of *Königsberg*'s former supply ships) where one of *Manica*'s seaplanes was seen apparently searching for them. Moon swam across the river to *Somali* but could find no water nor anything of use to them and was unable to recross the river until dawn on the 7th. Bridgeman had gone so Moon swam down river and eventually found him at some native huts. Here they found three spars and some window frames which they lashed together with sisal to make a raft, and filled two empty bottles with coconut milk. At the turn of the tide they launched the raft with Bridgeman amidships submerged to his shoulders, and Moon, armed with a paddle, submerged to his neck seated aft. By nightfall they had reached Mnasi Moja point and at dawn on 8 January beached the raft close to SS *Newbridge* which had been sunk in 1914 as a blockship to prevent the escape of *Königsberg* from the Rufiji. Here Bridgeman wrote a message on the starboard stanchion of *Newbridge*'s bridge and both men drank the last of their coconut milk. Before dawn on the 9th they launched the raft again, hoping to make the bank on the still rising tide, to wade to the river mouth and to cross it at slack

Short 827 stowed on HMS Manica's deck, Zanzibar 1917. (FAAM)

water to where they believed they might see a boat.

The raft was carried upstream and down again, and unable to make either bank, was carried through the mouth and out to sea. Outside the wind against the tide upset the raft. By midday Bridgeman's speech became unintelligible, and in Moon's own words

> "I turned to see him let go. I managed to get hold of him, I could not keep his head and my own above water. I struggled as long as I could, but finally I lost my hold and he sank immediately."

Moon got ashore late in the afternoon of the 9th where he was held by some Askaris until the Germans came next day and marched him inland. He remained as a POW until his release in November 1917.

Manica returned to Zanzibar on 8 January but was on patrol again off Rufiji between 12 and 29 January, and by 9 February was in position off Lindi. 8641, crewed by Deans and CPO W. J. Harris, was hoisted out here, armed with two 65-lb bombs and one 16-lb incendiary, to look for a gun reported stuck in the mud three miles south of Mrweka. Taking off at 0800 a search was made but no signs of the gun were observed. All the bombs were dropped near trenches west of Mrweka village. Heavy clouds and rain made observation difficult, so a return to *Manica* was made and the seaplane landed at 0925.

Manica was re-equipped with a Short 184, in place of the war-weary Short 827s, which operated off Lindi in April, bombing German positions and spotting for the steel gunboat *Thistle*.

Laconia had left the station in 1916, and *Himalaya* by early 1917. During May 1917 as the East African campaign drew to its close *Manica* also was withdrawn, finally leaving Zanzibar on 4 May.

It was the intention that *Manica* be returned to a UK dockyard for full scale conversion to a seaplane carrier, but this was never carried out. Arriving at Suez on 18 May she was dry docked there in early July and then sailed for Bombay. Here she decommissioned on 19 August, was renamed *Huntball* and served as a collier until June 1918.

Typical reconnaissance photograph of German East African coast taken from a Short 827 operating from HMS Himalaya during 1916/17. (FAAM)

CHAPTER XVIII

Seaplanes embarked briefly in ships on anti-submarine and anti-Zeppelin duties 1915-1918

Mention must also be made of the operations of seaplanes embarked in cruisers in support of land operations in the East Mediterranean during 1915-1916. There were frequent "cross-decking" of seaplanes from their parent carriers to cruisers such as *Diana, Doris, Euryalus* and *Minerva*.

One of the Royal Australian Navy's cruisers HMAS *Brisbane* also embarked a seaplane during the fruitless search in the Indian Ocean in 1917 for the German commerce raider SMS *Wolf* - which herself carried a seaplane, a Friedrichshafen FF 33E, No 841.

Brisbane, newly commissioned, was transferred from Malta to Colombo where in April 1917 she was joined by the French armoured cruiser *Potuhau* and the seaplane carrier *Raven II* from Port Said.

After coaling at Colombo *Potuhau,* and *Raven II* with two Short 184's embarked, sailed to search the Maldive Islands for *Wolf*. Before sailing *Raven II* transferred her Baby N1014 and Flt Lt A.W. Clemson to *Brisbane*. N1014 was stowed on the quarterdeck and was operated successfully for some weeks, often making two flights a day.

No sightings of *Wolf* were made however, and in fact she returned unscathed to Kiel on 24 February 1918 after an epic voyage of 64,000 miles, which had begun on 30 November 1916, and which left a trail of sunken merchant shipping across the oceans of the world.

On 21 May 1917 *Brisbane* and *Raven II* with the battleship *Exmouth* left the area to escort a convoy from Bombay to the Red Sea. In June *Brisbane* was ordered back to Australia and her Baby was returned to the East Indies and Egypt Seaplane Squadron.

The successful operation of *Brisbane*'s Baby prompted the Australian Naval Board to request that seaplanes and RNAS personnel be attached to the cruisers *Brisbane* and *Encounter*. The Admiralty refused this and another request for the loan of a seaplane carrier of the *Riviera* type. Beyond discussion, nothing was done to form a Royal Australian Naval Air Service before the Armistice in November 1918.

By 1920 however, Commander J.S.Dumaresq, by now commanding the Australian Fleet, persuaded the

The drifter Tarlair was hired between January 1915 and 1919, and was commissioned into the Royal Navy as HM Drifter Tarlair. In the Auxiliary Patrol Red List for January 1916 and throughout 1917 she is shown as based at Granton ''for Capt Ryan's hydroplane experiments.'' Records show that named pilots of the RNAS were on board 'Tarlair' between December 1917 and March 1918 at least, which suggests that she too embarked a Baby. (NMM D3571)

HMS Euryalus in 1915. She operated a Short 184 for a brief period in the E.Mediterranean during October 1915.
(NMM BBG6)

Naval Board that the battlecruiser *Australia* and the cruiser *Melbourne* could each usefully employ an Avro 504L seaplane to be transferred from the Australian Air Corps. Avro 504L H3034 was embarked in *Australia* between July and September 1920, when the ship paid off, and H3042 was briefly operated by *Melbourne* during September 1920. The handling of the seaplanes with non-folding wings was difficult, however, and their performance under tropical conditions was

unsatisfactory. Accordingly they were both landed, renumbered A3-46 and A3-47 respectively, and returned to the AAC in 1921.

For the next three years, due to indecision and political restraints, the RAN was without an air arm. The first seaplane of six Fairey IIIDs, ANA-1, for the RAN was launched in August 1921 and all the remaining five aircraft had been delivered by November, only to be taken over by the newly formed Royal

Short 184, 842, operated by HMS Euryalus in October 1915 after transfer from HMS Ben-my-Chree. This is the seaplane that on 12th August 1915 had delivered the first aerial torpedo attack in history.
(G.S.Leslie/J.M.Bruce collection)

*Two stern views of HMAS Geranium in about
June 1924 with IIID, A10-2, embarked for a
survey of the Great Barrier Reef with wings
folded and about to be hoisted out by the
derrick mounted on the port side.
(RAN Photographic Section 3795 and 977,
via J.P.Barr)*

Avro 504L H3034 is hoisted on board HMAS Australia in Sydney harbour during July - September 1920. The seaplane went to the Australian Air Corps as A3-46 in 1921.
(K.Molson via G.S.Leslie)

Australian Air Force and re-serialled A10-1 to A10-6. All the many proposals for the employment of the IIIDs in warships foundered for various reasons.

The ex-RN sloop *Geranium* had been assigned the task of surveying the Great Barrier Reef in 1921. To speed these operations the Fairey IIID was selected to join the Hydrographic Branch of the RAN, and to this end *Geranium* was taken in hand during February 1924 to adapt her to carry a seaplane. Her existing kite balloon deck was extended further aft to accommodate the seaplane and aviation fuel tanks, and a seaplane handling derrick was fitted to her mainmast. One IIID,

A10-2, joined *Geranium* in June 1924 at Sydney for trials, and the ship sailed from Townsville later that month. It was found that in the open sea the added tophamper aft adversely affected the ship's stability, so the IIID flew independently to Townsville, though within the sheltered waters of the Reef the seaplane could be safely embarked.

Over the ensuing months A10-2, flown by Flt Lt Pard Mustar proved invaluable as an adjunct to the ship's survey work. A10-2's service ended on 18 December 1925 when the seaplane crashed and was written off, and in May 1929 the Navy's remaining

HMS Orotava operated a Short 184 on convoy escort in the South Atlantic 1918. (FAAM)

Short 184, N1774 "Avatoro" being hoisted on board HMS Orotava in 1918. The observer is Obs Lt F.L.Morrison, and the pilot is probably Flt Sub Lt V.W.Lamb. (FAAM)

IIIDs were authorised for disposal. But between 1925 and February 1929 when the new seaplane carrier *Albatross* embarked her complement of Seagull III flying boats from No.101 Flight RAAF, Australia's navy was again without aircraft in her warships.

Several unlikely types of ships embarked seaplanes before the end of the war. In June 1917 approval was given by the Admiralty for the minelayer HMS *Princess Margaret* to be fitted to carry two Schneiders. On 24 September 1917 she was one of a minelaying force, with the Harwich Force and the seaplane carrier *Vindex* as escorts, despatched to lay mines north of the Terschelling Light Vessel. Eleven Zeppelins left

Germany that evening to raid England and between 1900 and 2100 no fewer than seven of these airships were sighted from *Princess Margaret* on her outward passage. Although both Schneiders were embarked, neither were launched, and AA fire was not operated because she was streaming paravanes at the time, which restricted her manouverability. Zeppelins heading back to Germany were sighted again early next morning, but again no attempt appears to have been made to launch her seaplanes.

When the convoy system was belatedly introduced in 1917, seaplanes, flying boats and aeroplanes, operating from RNAS Air Stations ashore, had an

HMS Mantua which in late 1918 operated one Short 184 in the South Atlantic. (IWM SP1065)

HMS Princess Margaret c.1917. This former Canadian Pacific liner was hired as a minelayer in 1914, and between June and September 1917 embarked two Schneiders or two Babies. (IWM SP2742)

Short 184, either N2816 or N2817, stowed on board HMS Mantua while the ship was on convoy escort duty in the South Atlantic 1918. (FAAM)

immediate effect in restricting U-boat attacks on convoys which had an air escort.

Air escort preceding a convoy forced the U-boats to submerge, which reduced their ability to manoeuvre into an attacking position, and when in company with the convoy, aircraft could pinpoint the U-boat's position by observing the torpedo tracks. Although the problem of actually sinking U-boats by aircraft was not overcome before November 1918, the tactical problem of sighting and attacking U-boats was solved, and acted as a powerful deterrent during the hours of daylight. Aircraft were "blind" at night in 1917/18, so U-boats were forced to attack on the surface at night. The value of land-based air escorts for convoys however was limited by the comparatively short range of these air escorts.

When the convoy system was extended to the South Atlantic in August 1917, Dakar was selected as the assembly port to service ships for homeward bound convoys from South America, South and West Africa, Australia and the Far East. Initially these HD convoys sailed from Dakar every four days, but eventually every eight days.

U-Boats were still operating in the Western Approaches some 200 miles off Fastnet to intercept the HD convoys - well beyond the effective patrol areas of shore based aircraft. The Armed Merchant Cruiser HMS *Orotava* embarked Short 184, N1774, in late May 1918 and sailed for Dakar to escort a homeward bound convoy. Piloted by Capt J.A. Sadler RAF with Lt F.L. Morrison RAF as observer, N1774 took off from Dakar harbour carrying one 230-lb bomb and one 100-lb bomb at 0750 on 25 June, and carried out an anti-submarine patrol of $2^1/_4$ hours without sighting a U-boat. Just prior to the HD convoy's sailing on 3 July, N1774 again took off with the same bomb load at 0805, to patrol ahead of the convoy. Again no U-boat sightings were made, and after a safe landing the Short was hoisted inboard again at 1015.

The other AMC with a seaplane for escort duties with HD convoys was HMS *Mantua*. *Mantua* took Short 184, N2817, aboard at Plymouth on 29 September 1918. No flights were possible on the outward passage because of rough weather, and *Mantua* reached Dakar on 10 October. N2817 made two test flights at Dakar on 11 and 14 October, but both were curtailed by engine trouble.

Similarly an attempt at a reconnaissance flight before the convoy sailed on 16 October proved impossible because of engine failure. Bad weather throughout the homeward passage prevented any flights

HMS Peony operated Schneiders and Babies in the Aegean during 1917/1918 on anti-submarine patrols. No wartime photograph is available, and she is shown here after being converted to passenger ferry and renamed Ardena.
(NMM P20292)

HMS Ark Royal at Mudros c. April 1918 with a Baby on her foredeck. HMS Ark Royal was then the H.Q. of Nos 62 and 63 Wings RAF comprising 220 to 223 Squadrons. From these units HMS Peony embarked Babies for anti-U-boat patrols.
(R.W.Peel via R.D.Layman)

before the convoy reached the UK on 1 November, and in fact N2817's rudder and ailerons were badly damaged by storms.

Not a story of great successes, but it shows that minds were active in trying to bridge the gap without air cover which ocean convoys had to face. There were few days when sea conditions allowed the operation of wood and canvas seaplanes in the South Atlantic, and captains of AMCs were reluctant to stop their ships to hoist seaplanes out and in for patrols, offering an inviting target for any U-boat captain. Realizing this fear the Admiralty issued special instructions exhorting AMC captains to launch their seaplanes at every available opportunity.

The Armistice came into effect on 11 November, and on 20 November the Admiralty instructed all AMCs equipped with seaplanes that they were to be disembarked and not carried in future. The RNAS having been absorbed into the RAF seven months previously, the junior service showed no enthusiasm for the continuance of this far sighted project. Another 25

years were to pass before aircraft of the Fleet Air Arm, flying from AMCs CAM ships, MAC ships and escort carriers were again belatedly able to help bridge those critical air gaps in mid-ocean. The lessons of convoy had to be relearned - at the cost yet again of thousands of sailors' lives.

Through Mediterranean convoys were started in October 1917, though here land-based air cover had adequate range to escort most convoys. There was however a fear that the Germans would establish U-boat bases among the many islands and rocky inlets of the Aegean. Accordingly the sloop HMS *Peony* was equipped with three Schneiders to search the Aegean Islands in May 1917. On 1 June *Peony* launched two Schneiders off Cape Phuka. The first seaplane flew a reconnaissance between Keramus and Budrum. The other Schneider reconnoitered the Gulf of Kos but was damaged following engine failure and a forced landing. The damaged Schneider was replaced by a Baby from the Air Station at Thermi during the middle of June.

Both seaplanes searched for SS *Newmarket* on 27

Baby N1424 piloted by Flt Sub Lt R.W.Peel flying over Mudros harbour c.early 1918. Typical of the Babies embarked in HMS Peony, N1424 while part of No.2 Wing RNAS based on HMS Ark Royal participated in the attack on S.M.S.Goeben on 20th January 1918 and was hit by A.A. fire and force landed at Imbros.
(R.W.Peel via R.D.Layman)

HMS Albion as a private yacht pre-1915. Hired in February 1915 as an Auxiliary Patrol yacht, she was commissioned into the Royal Navy as HMS Albion III and armed with 2 x 12 pdr and 1 x 6 pdr. She was based at Loch Larne, and in September 1917 was reported to be fitted to carry a Seaplane. The Red List for 2nd January 1918 confirms that she was fitted to carry a Baby. (NMM P946)

July after she had mistakenly been reported as having been torpedoed, but she was not sighted. A reconnaissance of Samos Strait was carried out on 31 July and Turkish gun positions were bombed. By now *Peony*'s seaplanes had searched the whole of the Asiatic coast and islands north from Rhodes as far as the Gulf of Scala Nuova.

Following a report that enemy motor boats were using the estuary of the Mendere River as a base, *Peony*'s seaplanes made a reconnaissance on 4 August but no motor boats were sighted. By now the seaplanes, stowed on deck, were suffering severe fabric damage from the effects of salt spray and funnel smoke.

In August 1917 *Peony* shifted her base from Leros to Port Vathi, Samos for reconnaissance and anti-U-boat patrols until a permanent RNAS Air Station opened in December 1917 on the island of Syra.

One of *Peony*'s seaplanes was wrecked on a reconnaissance flight on 7 January 1918. Anti-submarine patrols over the islands south of Samos on 8 March, and between 17-24 March over the channel between Stampalia and Kos produced no U-Boat sightings.

By 1 April 1918 *Peony* was based with HMS *Ark Royal* at Mudros, which by then became HQ of Nos 62 and 63 Wings RAF, comprising Nos 220-223 Squadrons. The last of *Peony*'s Schneiders was exchanged for Babies in April 1918, and these she continued to operate during the month from satellite bases at Port Vathi and at Port Laki on Leros. Pilots for the Babies at this period were Lts Coveney and Evans, RAF. Although *Peony*'s seaplane complement is listed as three aircraft, it is unlikely that more than two seaplanes could be stowed on deck at any one time.

The only other comparable ship to embark a seaplane was HMS *Halcyon*, an old torpedo gunboat operating out of Lowestoft on anti-submarine patrols, and in October 1917 performing air-sea rescue duties.

Halcyon embarked a Baby at 1510 on 4 October and sailed on patrol shortly after. On 6 October *Halcyon* was ordered to search for two aircraft from Yarmouth, both overdue and presumed to have landed in the sea. They were a D.H.4 and a Curtiss H.12, 8666, which had been sent out to search for the missing D.H.4 on 5 October. *Halcyon*'s Baby was hoisted out on 6 October and was airborne between 1325 and 1430 without sighting anything. The Baby was found to be unserviceable for a further search on 7 October, but at 1214 on 8 October the Curtiss flying boat was sighted on the sea five miles from *Halcyon*. 8666 had landed to rescue the DH4's crew of two on 5 October but was then unable to take off with the extra weight. *Halcyon* stopped at 1228, took both crews on board and towed 8666 back to Yarmouth, arriving about midnight on 8 October.

Information also exists, from September 1917, that four others of HM Ships were fitted to carry a seaplane. These were the Armed yachts *Albion III* based at Loch Larne and *Beryl* based at Queenstown. Also the trawler *Lordship* based at Killingholme and the minelayer *Angora*. A search of these four ships' logbooks, either side of September 1917, reveals no mention of any seaplanes embarked, and the only possible clue so far is an entry in *Lordship*'s log of 21 August 1917 at Immingham of "Flying Officer from aerodrome on board".

Details of these four ships are given in an addendum to the main listing of HM Ships operating seaplanes.

By 1918-1919 naval aviation was still in its infancy, just a few short years away from the beginning of flying. The Royal Navy's use of aircraft in naval operations was mainly confined to the defensive rôle - reconnaissance, convoy escort and defensive air combat. The offensive employment of naval aviation was largely concerned with support of the Army's operations in the Eastern Mediterranean and East Africa.

Nevertheless, by November 1918, the advocates of naval aviation could justly claim that the Royal Navy had seen the potential of airpower at sea, and had taken steps to implement it.

Parallel developments had been taking place in the navies of France, Germany and Russia during the war. But by November 1918 only the Royal Navy's air arm was in a position to lead the field in naval aviation. That lead was immediately thrown away and the lessons quickly forgotten. The reasons are not within the scope of this story. Nor is the terrible price in men and ships that Britain had to pay some 20 years later as a consequence.

"History teaches us that history teaches us nothing".

The private yacht Beryl was hired as an Auxiliary Patrol yacht between 11th January 1915 and 15th March 1919.
Commissioned into the Royal Navy as HMS Beryl, she was armed with 2 x 3'' and 1 x 12 pdr and was based at
Queenstown. In September 1917 she was reported to be fitted to carry a seaplane - presumably a Baby. (NMM D3570)

CHAPTER XIX
Seaplane operations from *Alader Youssanoff* and *Orlionoch,* Caspian Sea 1919

O ne final theatre where seaplanes were operated from small carriers, converted from merchant ships, was in South Russia during the Allied intervention against the Bolsheviks in late 1918 and early 1919 in support of General Deniken's White Russian forces.

The Bolshevik Revolution, and subsequent Treaty of Brest-Litovsk in March 1918, providing for a separate peace between Germany and Russia, opened the way for Turkish expansion into the Caucasus.

The Russian army which had been facing the Turks in the south Caucasus - and which had been in touch with the British on the Persian-Mesopotamian border - just melted away, leaving nothing to prevent a Turkish advance.

Britain realised that the capture of Tiflis would give the Turks control of the Batum railway to Baku, linking the Black Sea and Caspian, and control of the oil wells at Baku.

Accordingly a small British force, commanded by Major-General L. Dunsterville and known as Dunsterforce, was despatched in February 1918 in an attempt to stiffen the resistance of the White Russians on the Caspian. Dunsterforce arrived at Baku in August 1918.

The Caspian Sea is 630 miles long and varies in width from 125 to 300 miles, the northern end being shallow, and frozen from January to April. In 1918/19 some 240 Russian merchant vessels, mostly small tankers, were plying on the Caspian.

Dunsterforce had to abandon Baku to the Turks by 14 September. The Turkish occupation was brief however, because on 30 October the Ottoman Empire signed an armistice with the Allies on board HMS *Agamemnon* at Mudros. From now on the threat to the Caucasus and the Caspian would come solely from the Red Army, so Baku was re-occupied by 2,000 men of the British 14th Division on 17 November 1918.

With the Allied occupation of the Bosphorus ports in November 1918, access was gained to the Black Sea ports of Batum and Novorossisk, both essential to supply the anti-Bolshevik forces on the Caspian.

HMS Alader Youssanoff with two Short 184's of 266 Squadron RAF, N9079 and N9082, stowed on her foredeck, Caspian May 1919. (RAFM P1341)

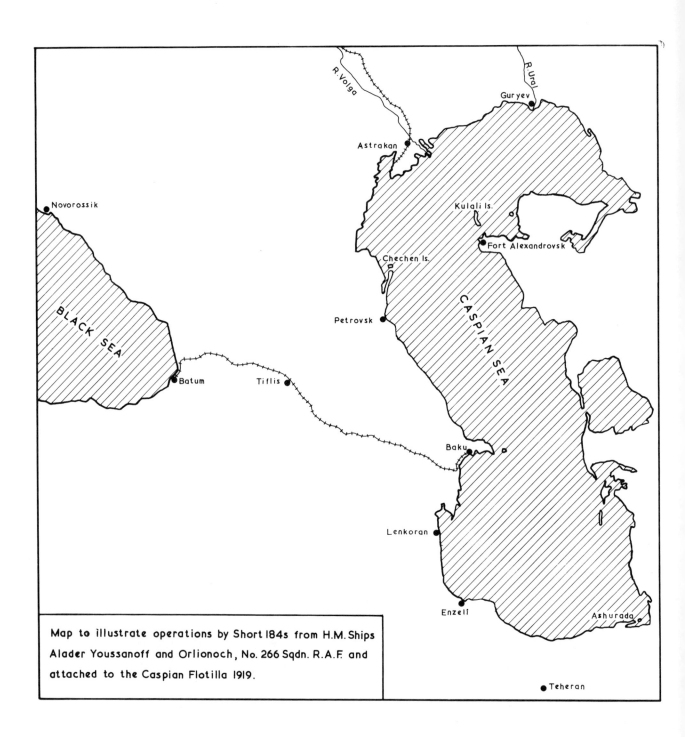

Map to illustrate operations by Short 184s from H.M.Ships Alader Youssanoff and Orlionoch, No. 266 Sqdn. R.A.F. and attached to the Caspian Flotilla 1919.

The first three of some 25 Russian merchant ships which eventually comprised the Royal Navy's Caspian Flotilla were captured in August 1918. All 25 were eventually armed during 1918/19, and two of these -*Orlionoch* and *Alader Youssanoff* - were fitted to carry two seaplanes each. All these ships initially flew the Russian Naval Ensign until 2 March 1919, when the White Ensign was hoisted for the first time.

The first naval party under Commodore D. Norris left Baghdad on 27 July 1918, arriving at Enzeli on 6 August in lorry transport, and embarked in the Caspian Flotilla flagship *President Kruger*. A second party from HM Ships *Diana* and *Juno* reached Enzeli in September 1918 by the same route.

It was decided to establish a seaplane base at Petrovsk for servicing the seaplanes which were to equip the two seaplane carriers.

The personnel selected to service and fly the seaplanes were drawn from No 437 Flight, which with No 438 Flight comprised No 266 Squadron RAF in No 63 Wing, commanded by Wg Cdr F. W. Bowhill. 437 Flight was based at the Squadron HQ at Mudros, flying Short 184s in January 1919 when they were chosen to form the Russian draft. Capt J. A. Sadler took over command of 437 Flight on 1 February and the Flight was re-designated No 266 Squadron in No 62 Wing RAF.

The advance party of 266 Squadron sailed in early February 1919 from Lemnos in the former LSWR ferry *Princess Ena* through the Black Sea to Batum, where they disembarked. From here they travelled by train via Tiflis to Baku, where the 4 CMBs they had brought with them were unloaded. The advance party proceeded to Petrovsk, arriving on 1 March, where with Russian labour they set about providing a seaplane jetty and crane, and converting existing buildings into seaplane hangars and workshops.

The main body of 266 Squadron with ten new Short 184's (Maori III engines) embarked in HMS *Engadine* on 18 February at Mudros, and sailing on the 20th finally reached Petrovsk on 12 March, by the same route taken by the advance party.

Alader Youssanoff and *Orlionoch*, both formerly small tankers, were meanwhile being fitted out and armed at Baku.

Fitting out all the ships of the Caspian Flotilla was a slow business. Continual strikes at the yards in Baku held up the work, but by 10 May *Alader Youssanoff* was finally ready for sea.

April was spent in erecting and test flying the Short 184's, and conditions on the Caspian created some unexpected problems. Being a fresh water sea the Caspian provided less buoyancy than salt water, and as a result the seaplanes' floats sank much deeper. An urgent signal had to be sent to Malta requesting finer pitch propellers to be despatched, in order to allow the Maori III engines to develop more power at lower forward speeds, to enable the seaplanes to become airborne.

The twin exhaust pipes fitted to the Maori IIIs were found to be unsatisfactory, and home-made modification was carried out to them, with bracing to prevent excessive vibration. Under more civilised conditions the engines would have been started by compressed air, but as neither of the two carriers was fitted with a compressor the Shorts had to be converted to hand starting. The extra weight penalty imposed by carrying compressed air bottles in the seaplanes was unacceptable since it reduced the weight of bombs that could be carried. It was also later found that the overhead valve Maori III's tended to burn out their valves after 30 hours.

Test flying proceeded satisfactorily, except for an accident to N9081 on 25 April. While attempting to take-off the wind suddenly increased and the seaplane crashed, wrecking both starboard mainplanes, but was safely towed in by a launch and hoisted onto the jetty by the crane.

On 12 May it was reported that the Bolsheviks had re-occupied Fort Alexandrovsk on the eastern side of the Caspian, and that their fleet had sailed into the harbour. *Alader Youssanoff* embarked two Short 184s on the morning of 12 May, N9080 and N9082, and at 1115 sailed for Chechen arriving there at 2030.

From Chechen on the 14th, N9080 crewed by Sadler and Lt F. Kingham was hoisted out for a $3^1/_2$ hour flight as far as Beryouzak, and then back along the coast to Chechen. The seaplane carried one 230-lb, one 100-lb and one 65-lb bombs but no suitable target was found for them. But the seaplane put the wind up some villages with Lewis gun fire north of Chechen.

Alader Youssanoff sailed from Chechen at 1600 on the 14th to rendezvous with *President Kruger, Asia, Emile Nobel, Venture, Edinburgh Castle, Sergie* and *Windsor Castle* off Kulaly Island at dawn next day. Enemy ships were sighted off Fort Alexandrovsk at 0530 on the 15th and they retreated into the harbour leaving two barges behind, both of which were sunk by shellfire from *Kruger* and *Emile Nobel*. Heavy swell and rain prevented any flying on the 16th. An attempt to reconnoitre Fort Alexandrovsk on the 17th was thwarted by continuing bad weather. *Alader Youssanoff* hoisted out N9080 at 0500, but with the ship rolling heavily, the starboard float and wingtip were damaged against the ship's side.

N9082 was launched successfully but was unable to take off owing to the heavy swell, and coming alongside for hoisting in was also damaged. *Alader Youssanoff*, escorted by *Emile Nobel* sailed for Petrovsk at 1100, arriving there at 0500 on the 18th. Here the damaged N9082 was put ashore and N9079 hoisted on board in its place. Repairs to N9080 were completed and these two seaplanes were aboard when *Alader Youssanoff* sailed from Petrovsk again at 1615, in company with *Emile Nobel*, for a rendezvous with the main Caspian Flotilla 20 miles south of Chechen at 1700. Here they met Commodore D. T. Norris flying his flag in *Kruger* with *Windsor Castle, Bibi Eibat, Slava, Dublin Castle, Edinburgh Castle, Venture, Asia* and *Sergie*.

The fleet steamed through the night to a position 20 miles south of Fort Alexandrovsk by dawn of the 20th. Here N9080, crewed by 2nd Lt H.G. Thompson and Lt F.R. Bicknell, was hoisted out for a raid on Fort

Youssanoff hoisted out N9080 for a bombing attack on Fort Alexandrovsk. Sadler and Kingham were airborne at 0415, but the same trouble was experienced as on the previous day, and the Short returned to the ship at 0440. The carburettors had to be stripped down and the fuel drained and filtered, which meant that the seaplane was out of action for the next 11 hours.

Meanwhile the main squadron was approaching Fort Alexandrovsk from the north-north-east and at 0740 from *Kruger* a bearing was obtained on the lighthouse on the hilltop above the harbour. The outline of the land was barely visible, while Kulaly Island, very low lying,

Short 184 N9079 of 266 Squadron. After launching from HMS Alader Youssanoff to make a reconnaissance of Fort Alexandrovsk on 20th May 1919, the floats collapsed in a heavy sea while attempting to take-off. The crew of 2nd Lt's R.G.K.Morrison and H.G.Pratt were rescued. (RAFM P1339)

Alexandrovsk. They dropped 230-lb, 100-lb and 65-lb bombs from 2,500 feet but obtained no direct hits. They came under heavy AA fire but returned safely with a comprehensive report of shipping in the harbour. 2nd Lt R.G.K. Morrison and Lt H.G. Pratt were next away in N9079, but while in a climbing turn at 200 feet the engine failed, and the seaplane went in and was lost. Both men however clung to the wreckage and were picked up. Sadler took up N9080 for a second flight on the 20th, with 2nd Lt F.L. Kingham as observer, to bomb shipping in the harbour. However water in the petrol caused carburation problems, and the seaplane had to return without carrying out the attack.

Alader Youssanoff was now detached to the south to be out of harm's way before darkness, and in company with *Edinburgh Castle* proceeded S24E at 5 knots till midnight, when she turned 16 points to starboard and proceeded to a rendezvous with the main fleet at dawn on the 21st, 40 miles from Alexandrovsk. The main fleet meanwhile took up night cruising stations to the north, turning south again at midnight.

On reaching the rendezvous at first light *Alader*

could just be seen to the east.

At 0922 course was altered to S66E, speed five knots. At about this time three enemy MLs were sighted clear of the cape on the eastern side of the harbour mouth and altering course to north-west to close the British force. One TBD and two smaller vessels were seen under the land, and next a large AMC and the icebreaker *Kaspy* appeared, apparently coming out in support. At 1100 the TBD opened fire, but her shot fell some four miles short! These five ships then turned and made for the harbour, the TBD again firing with no better result. The enemy were difficult to distinguish against the land.

Course was altered at 1106 to south to prevent the enemy escaping to the west, and again at 1148 to N40E when speed was increased to 9 knots - the squadron's maximum - to cut off the MLs now astern. At 1203 the squadron altered course to N55E, and crossing *Kruger's* bows, the MLs opened fire with 3-inch guns. *Kruger* returned the fire, and as the MLs turned away, two more ML's joined them from the direction of the harbour. *Venture* was straddled by the AMC at 1211, and all

Short 184 N9085 of 266 Sqdn on the quayside at Petrovsk c.April 1919, showing the twin exhaust pipes for the Maori engine. (RAFM P1336)

ships opened fire by signal and general action commenced. *Venture*'s shot fell short but *Emile Nobel*'s 6-inch did good work, setting the AMC on fire and put a salvo of three 6-inch shells into a large Volga barge armed with two 6-inch guns. The barge was set on fire and abandoned.

Course was altered to north-north-east at 1225 and to east at 1230 to take the squadron across the harbour mouth, and both *Emile Nobel*'s and *Venture*'s guns scored hits on the icebreaker *Kaspy*, setting her on fire aft. Unluckily *Venture* shifted target and the fire on board *Kaspy* was later got under control.

At 1242 course was altered to east by north to give a wide berth to the end of the shoal, from which the mark beacons had been removed. Two MLs now ran ashore and *Kaspy* turned away, with heavy smoke coming from aft, and retreated to shelter behind barges at the head of the harbour.

All our ships were now under heavy fire, in which the shore battery on the eastern cliffs joined. *Emile Nobel* was hit in the engine room, and still firing, was forced temporarily to haul out of line.

At 1303 Commodore Norris in *Kruger* made a general signal "We are going up to Ramoth-gilead". Since Ramoth-gilead was in the Holy Land (see 1 Kings 22) this caused some consternation in the following

ships of the squadron. However as *Kruger* altered to south by east the other ships followed round, and in line ahead sailed into the harbour mouth in the order *Kruger, Venture, Asia, Windsor Castle* and *Emile Nobel*. Only *Kruger*'s two 4-inch were able to fire ahead during the approach down harbour, both guns incidentally being controlled by the Commodore's secretary Lt H.G. Pertwee, an event probably unique in naval history. One hundred rounds of 4-inch were fired during the approach.

At 1320 course was altered to west, when all ships' 4-inch guns could range on targets ashore and afloat, the turn to starboard enabling their port broadsides to be brought into action - a total of three 6-inch and twelve 4-inch.

As the line turned to starboard the 75 mm battery on the cliffs north of the lighthouse opened fire again, hitting *Kruger* on the port side amidships and severing the engine room telegraphs. The battery was silenced by *Kruger*'s port 4-inch and by *Asia*'s broadside of four 4-inch.

With a grand total of only three RN seamen comprising the crews for *Kruger*'s five guns, a system of "general post" had to be employed during the action. Similar conditions existed in other ships of the squadron.

At 1325 course was altered to north-west and a

HMS Alader Youssanoff's aircrew, Caspian c.May 1919. (RAFM P1340)

withdrawal commenced. *Venture* reported that the Bolshevik crews were abandoning their ships and fleeing up the hillsides. The narrow V-shaped harbour was by now almost obscured by thick smoke from burning Bolshevik ships, following the expenditure of 729 rounds of 4-inch and 6-inch by HM Ships. The final shots of the action were fired by *Emile Nobel*'s aft 4.7-inch as she withdrew at 1345.

A popular toast in the wardrooms of Nelson's ships was "A willing enemy and searoom". Neither condition was met, but Nelson would have approved of the action of 21st May.

While the squadron withdrew to the westward, repairs were completed to *Alader Youssanoff*'s remaining seaplane, and at 1515 Sadler and Kingham

were hoisted out in N9080 to attack ships in the harbour of Fort Alexandrovsk. Although the Maori engine seemed to be developing full power it was throwing out a lot of oil. Climbing to 3,000 feet over *Alader Youssanoff* and *Sergie*, and setting course for the harbour, the seaplane passed over the bombarding squadron returning to the south-west. While still some distance away a series of explosions in the harbour were seen. The guard ship at the entrance was bombed but not hit. Circling the harbour the Short machine gunned shipping and the town, and took photographs of a tanker on fire. N9080 returned to *Alader Youssanoff* at 1755 and after being hoisted in, the carrier retired southward for the night, while *Kruger*'s squadron patrolled between Fort Alexandrovsk and Astrakan.

Aircrew of 266 Sqdn RAF at Petrovsk c.May 1919. Uniforms of RNAS, Army, RFC and RAF are all in evidence. (RAFM P1347)

From a position 20 miles south of Fort Alexandrovsk at dawn on the 22nd *Alader Youssanoff* hoisted out N9080 again, crewed by Morrison and Pratt, for what was to be the first of five raids on Fort Alexandrovsk that day by the seaplane. This was only possible because the carrier had on board three aircrews. Morrison and Pratt were airborne at 0530 and bombed without result.

Thompson and Bicknell took off at 0730 and claimed one hit on a "Finn" class TBD. Sadler and Kingham undertook the third raid, attempting to take off at 0930 with one 230-lb, one 100-lb, one 65-lb and two 16-lb bombs. However, the seaplane's tail would not get up, and returning to the ship the bomb load was changed to one 230-lb and four 16-lb bombs. N9080 finally got off in the wake of the ship at 1045 and dropped the 230-lb bomb between a TBD and the icebreaker *Kaspy*, which were alongside the pier. It was later reported that both ships had sunk. Coming down to 2,500 feet the Short sank several fishing boats with the 16-lb bombs, and machine gunned the shipping. After taking photos the oil pressure dropped and the Lewis gun jammed, so Sadler headed back to the ship.

Morrison and Pratt took up N9080 at 1445 for the fourth raid. Their bombs missed their targets, as did those of Thompson and Bicknell who were airborne at 1630 for the fifth raid of the day. Sadler and Kingham made an unsuccessful attempt to get off in N9080 at 1800, and shortly after returning to the ship a dense mist came down. In his report Commodore Norris drew "particular attention to the seaplane operated by *Alader Youssanoff,* which made five raids in one day on the harbour".

Sergie and *Alader Youssanoff* turned south after N9080 was hoisted in, and standing out to sea, stopped engines at 2100 and drifted.

At 0500 on 23 May Norris's squadron sighted two Bolshevik TBDs to the north-west and steering to the south. The squadron's slow speed made it impossible to head off the two TBDs, who were now heading for *Sergie* and *Alader Youssanoff.* At 0930 they received a signal to run to the south, but *Sergie*'s captain, Cdr. Robinson VC, had other ideas and "turned a blind eye" to the Commodore's signal.

At 1030 *Alader Youssanoff* hoisted out N9080, crewed by Sadler and Kingham, to search for and bomb the enemy TBDs, and before managing to take off the 65-lb bomb had to be jettisoned. The Short climbed to 4000 feet and made a search 40 miles to the north, but no ships were seen, so the seaplane turned east to Fort Alexandrovsk and bombed the Volga barge, armed with 6-inch guns, in the harbour before heading back to the

Short 184's of 266 Sqdn at Petrovsk seaplane base 1919. (RAFM P1343)

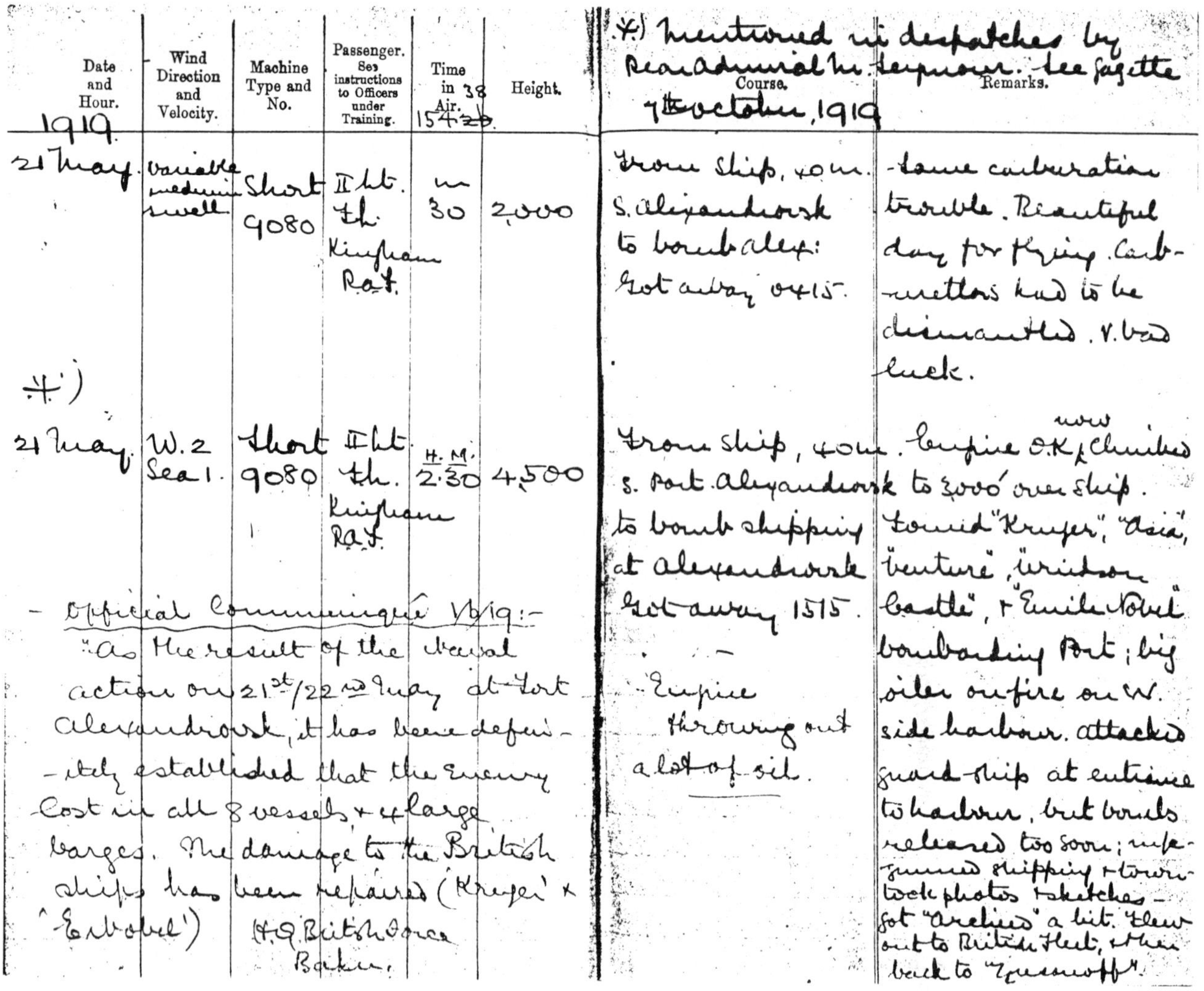
(*) Mentioned in despatches by Rear Admiral Mr Seymour. See Gazette 7th October, 1919

Date and Hour.	Wind Direction and Velocity.	Machine Type and No.	Passenger. See instructions to Officers under Training.	Time in Air.	Height.	Course.	Remarks.
1919							
21 May.	variable medium swell	Short 9080	2 Lt. Kingham RAF	1 hr 30	2,000	From ship, 40 m. S. Alexandrovsk to bomb Alex: Got away 0415.	Same carburation trouble. Beautiful day for flying. Carburettors had to be dismantled. V. bad luck.
(*)							
21 May.	W. 2 Sea 1.	Short 9080	2 Lt. Kingham RAF	H. M. 2.30	4,500	From ship, 40 m. S. Port Alexandrovsk to bomb shipping at Alexandrovsk. Got away 1515. Engine throwing out a lot of oil.	Engine now O.K. & climbed to 3000' over ship. Found "Kruger", "Asia", "Venture", "Windsor Castle", & "Emile Nobel" bombarding Port; big oiler on fire on W. side harbour. attacked guard-ship at entrance to harbour, but bombs released too soon; inspected shipping & town took photos & sketches - got "archies" a bit. Flew out to British Fleet, & then back to "Youssanoff".

- Official Communiqué 1/6/19:- "As the result of the Naval action on 21st/22nd May at Fort Alexandrovsk, it has been definitely established that the Enemy lost in all 8 vessels, & 4 large barges. The damage to the British ships has been repaired ('Kruger' & 'E. Nobel') H.Q. British Force Baku.

Flying log book entry of Capt J.A.Sadler, RAF for 21st May 1919. (via RAFM)

ship.

In the words of Capt. Sadler's flying logbook

"Mist had meanwhile come up from southward and was unable to see ships, so sent position by W/T to *Youssanoff.* Landed on outskirts of fog and taxied from 1145 till 1430, when bottom tank was emptied. Then put out drogue and waited till 1700; then tried to make land by taxying east on top tank; no land sighted by 1830. Tail float very low in water; wind got up and at 2330 tailplane, elevator and rudder were wrenched off by swell and machine sunk by the stern. An hour later machine turned upside down. Kingham and I clung to floats till 1830 on the 24th when we were picked up by HMS *Asia* (Lt Wilson) 20 miles south-west of Cape Orlok. I had given up hope and was in a pretty rotten state. *Asia* very decent, gave us hot drinks, hot bath, grub and bed. Arrived Petrovsk 1700, 24 May. Reported to Commodore".

Sergie meanwhile had hoisted out her two CMBs at 1100 on the 23rd and kept them alongside ready to attack the Bolshevik TBDs. However the weather was now worsening, and thick fog was imminent, so the CMBs were hoisted in at 1120. *Sergie* patrolled north and south at five knots for a distance of 20 miles during the 23rd with *Alader Youssanoff* to search for the missing seaplane, and at nightfall both ships proceeded back to Petrovsk.

Alader Youssanoff embarked two replacement Short 184s on 25 May, when they both flew on reconnaissance between Chechen and Petrovsk but sighted nothing. On the 27th *Alader Youssanoff* sailed for Fort Alexandrovsk with a force consisting of *Windsor Castle, Venture, Slava, Bibi Eibat* and 4 CMBs, and at dawn on the 28th launched both her seaplanes for a reconnaissance of the harbour, where they reported three undamaged barges. While *Slava* and *Bibi Eibat* patrolled to the north, *Windsor Castle, Venture* and the four CMBs proceeded up harbour where all the remaining shipping was sunk with torpedoes, and the Bolshevik garrison surrendered.

29 May saw this squadron off the mouth of the

Short 184 N9078 being hoisted from the quayside at Petrovsk onto the foredeck of HMS Orlionoch by the derrick on her foremast. (RAFM P1338)

Volga, whence the surviving Bolshevik ships of 21 May had fled. *Alader Youssanoff*'s seaplanes made four sorties, bombing and machine gunning barges and tugs in the river.

The commander of the remaining Bolshevik fleet was relieved by Sub Lt Roscalnikov, and Madame Roscalnikov was given command of the motor launches! By 31 May *Alader Youssanoff* had returned to more peaceful duties, escorting a convoy to Guryev in the north-east corner of the Caspian at the mouth of the Ural River. Her seaplanes were busy throughout June, undertaking a further reconnaissance of Fort Alexandrovsk on the 3rd, and again between the 10th and 12th prior to its occupation by the British.

Between 13 and 18 June *Alader Youssanoff* was at Petrovsk for much needed boiler cleaning, and on the 21st her seaplanes flew a reconnaissance over the Ural River. In spite of boiler cleaning her maximum speed was very low, and on 22 June a report from Commodore Norris to Rear Admiral commanding Black Sea stated "*Alader Youssanoff* not very satisfactory as carrier".

Her seaplanes bombed and machine gunned a paddle steamer, three tugs and an ML in the mouth of the Volga on the 24th, and on the 25th they bombed shipping at Lagan. On the 28th *Alader Youssanoff* returned to Chechen, from convoy escort duties, where she hoisted out N9082 crewed by Bicknell and Thompson. Unable to get airborne the 112-lb bomb was released to lighten the load. The bomb exploded blowing the seaplane in half, but mercifully the crew were not seriously injured. A Court of Inquiry was ordered to determine the cause of the destruction of one of His Britannic Majesty's seaplanes.

Alader Youssanoff returned to Petrovsk from Seal Island on 8 July on what was her last sortie as a seaplane carrier. Sadler test flew N9078 locally around Petrovsk on the 10th, giving Cdr. Watts in the rear cockpit his first experience of aerial travel.

Alader Youssanoff's top speed was now reduced to 5 knots, and on 11 July the Commodore approved of *Alader Youssanoff* taking the place of *Orlionoch* the CMB depot ship at Petrovsk, and work was at once started changing over gear to *Orlionoch*.

Orlionoch, with Short 184s N9078 and N9081 embarked, sailed from Petrovsk at 0700 on 17 July to test two newly installed 4-inch guns and one 12-pounder. Port engine trouble caused a return towards Petrovsk at 1000, but after the Engineer Commander came aboard, course was set for Chechen at 1145. Chechen was reached at 0700 on the 18th, and at 1200 *Orlionoch* left for Seal Island in company with *Edinburgh Castle* and *Emile Nobel*, arriving there at 1600.

Orlionoch hoisted out both her seaplanes at 1650 that evening, N9078 crewed by Sadler and Lt Turton-Jones and N9081 crewed by Lts McCughey and Wake for an attack on enemy shipping at Lagan. Nothing was seen at Lagan except a sunken paddle steamer, and on the return flight to the ship a strong headwind was met. Underestimating the wind strength, and having missed Seal Island, the two seaplanes tried to reach Chechen

before dark. However at 2030, as dusk fell, they landed and beached the seaplanes at Krynovka, where they all enjoyed an excellent meal in a fisherman's house. *Orlionoch* was sighted at 0400 next morning, and after calling her up by Aldis lamp both machines were taxied out to her and were hoisted inboard before she returned to Seal Island. *Orlionoch* sailed for Fort Alexandrovsk at 1700 on 20 July, and at 1400 on the 21st anchored 20 miles north-west of the harbour to hoist out both seaplanes. Taking-off loaded with 100-lb and 65-lb bombs in rough conditions, N9078 and N9081 flew to Dolgoi Island to locate reported enemy ships. None were seen so the two Shorts flew south along the Turkestan coast to Kochak Creek, and thence back to *Orlionoch* at 1640.

Sadler and Turton-Jones took off in N9078 next morning at 0700, and in company with two CMBs again reconnoitered Dolgoi Island but nothing was observed. Landing again at 0835 the seaplane's starboard float was damaged in the heavy swell then running. *Orlionoch* sailed at 2045 that evening for Seal Island where she arrived at 1900 on 23 July. Both seaplanes were hoisted out at 0530 on the 24th, each carrying one 100-lb and two 65-lb bombs, for a flight to Lagan lighthouse via the mouth of the Volga. Nothing was seen at Lagan and after coming under fire from a village near the lighthouse, Sadler and Turton-Jones in N9078 attacked an armed tug proceeding north-west. The tug returned fire with a machine gun while the seaplane was at 800 feet. One shot passed through the port lower mainplane,

HMS Orlionoch at Petrovsk c. July 1919, with two Short 184s of 266 Sqdn RAF stowed on deck. (R.D.Layman)

Short 184 N9081 after damage sustained attempting to take-off on 25th April 1919. The Short was repaired and was operated by HMS Orlionoch during July and August 1919. (RAFM P1335)

cowling, scavenger pump, main oil pipe and eventually lodged in the starboard engine bearer. Sadler immediately turned south-east belching clouds of smoke, until the engine seized up 20 minutes later, but successfully put the seaplane down on the water. Seeing what had happened, McCughey and Wake in N9081 flew back for assistance. CMB 60 and CMB 51 shortly arrived on the scene and towed the seaplane back to *Orlionoch*, which hoisted it on board at 1430. The ship sailed for Petrovsk at 2100, arriving there at 1130 on the 25th.

Orlionoch sailed at 1130 on 27 July bound for Guryev. On board were two Short 184s accompanied by Capt C.N.H. Bilney, commanding A Flight of 266 Squadron. With him were three other officers and maintenance personnel. The object was to land the two seaplanes in the mouth of the Ural River, and having instructed the White Russians in their operation, to hand them over.

Only one Russian pilot - Capt Igoroff, who demonstrated his daring by looping a war-weary flying boat - volunteered to fly the Shorts.

After some basic instruction, Igoroff announced his intention of bombing the Bolsheviks on the Western Front. With two days' sorties successfully accomplished, he took off on the third day, scorning the use of bomb racks. His observer carried the bombs on his knees, and shortly after take off the seaplane exploded into very small pieces. *Orlionoch* arrived back at Petrovsk at 0630 on 1 August.

Between 1 and 26 August she was almost continually at sea, generally with at least one seaplane embarked. On the 8th she sailed with *Bibi Eibat* to clear the Bolsheviks out of Ashurada, in the south-east corner of the Caspian, and the operation was successful. Four ships and six barges were captured, together with 200 prisoners and a quantity of arms.

The rest of the month was spent by *Orlionoch* convoying prize ships and POWs to Petrovsk, and covering the final evacuation of British forces from Baku in conjunction with other ships of the Caspian Flotilla. On 26 August *Orlionoch* was turned over to the Russian Volunteer Navy, and next day Sadler and the last few remaining members of 266 Squadron left Petrovsk at 1400. And so ended the RN and RAF contribution to the Allied intervention in south Russia.

CHAPTER XX

TABLES OF H.M. SHIPS OPERATING OR TRANSPORTING SEAPLANES 1913-1920

HMS *ANNE*

Seaplane carrier. Gross tonnage 4083. Armament 1 x 12-pounder.

Areas of Operation: East Mediterranean 1915-1917; Red Sea 1916.

Types embarked:

Nieuport VI (1915/16).	Examples:	N11, N14, N15, N16, N17, N18, N19, N20, N21, N22, N23, NB1, NB2
Schneider (1916).	Example:	3777
Baby (1916).	Example:	N1016
Short 184 (1916/17).	Examples:	8004, 8021, 8054, 8075, 8084, 8090, 8091, N1263

Notes: Ex-German SS *Aenne Rickmers* (1911) seized at Port Said 1914. Operated 2 Nieuport VI's from January 1915 as HMFA *Aenne Rickmers*. Commissioned into RN as HMS *Anne* August 1915. From early 1916 her Nieuport VI's were replaced by Short 184'S and Schneiders or Babies.

Paid off August 1917 and served as Collier (RFA) from January 1918. Sold 1922 and renamed *Ithaki* (Japanese). Still in mercantile service 1956 as *Moldava*. Scrapped 1958.

HMS *ALADER YOUSSANOFF*

Seaplane Carrier. Gross tonnage 2071. Armament 1 x 12-pounder.

Area of Operations: Caspian Sea 1919.

Type embarked:

Short 184 (1919).	Examples:	N9079, N9080, N9082

Notes: Ex-Russian tanker, commissioned as RN Seaplane Carrier at Baku January 1919. Operated 2 Short 184's of 266 Squadron RAF on Caspian against Bolsheviks between 30 April 1919 and 11 July 1919. CMB Depot Ship August 1919 until transferred to White Russians. Renamed *VOLGA* October 1919.

HMS *ARETHUSA*

Light Cruiser. Displacement 3500 tons. Armament 2 x 6'', 6 x 4''.

Area of Operations: North Sea 1915.

Types embarked:

Schneider (1915). Examples: 1439, 1441, 1556

Short 830 (1915) Examples: 819

Notes: Fitted with fixed forecastle ramp 1915 for operation of aeroplane with wheeled under-carriage, but probably never used. One Schneider embarked during May/June 1915 for anti-U-boat or anti-Zeppelin patrols. Wrecked 11 February 1916 after hitting mine off Harwich.

HMS *AURORA*

Light Cruiser. Displacement 3500 tons. Armament 2 x 6'', 6 x 4''.

Area of Operations: North Sea 1915.

Types embarked:

Short S74 (1915). Example: 183, 818

Short 830 (1915). Example: 819, 821

Schneider (1915). Examples: 1439, 1440, 1441, 1556, 1557

Notes: Fitted with fixed forecastle ramp 1915 for operation of Deperdussin Monoplane 1378. One Schneider embarked May/June 1915 for anti U-boat or anti-Zeppelin patrols. Commissioned into RCN 1 November 1920. Sold August 1927.

HMAS *BRISBANE*

Cruiser. Displacement 5400 tons. Armament 8 x 6'', 1 x 3''.

Area of Operations: East Indies 1917.

Types embarked:

Baby (1917). Example: N1014

Notes: One Baby (ex *Raven II*) embarked April 1917 to join hunt in Indian Ocean for German raider SMS *Wolf*. Sold July 1936.

HMS *BROCKLESBY*

Paddle Air Service Scout. Gross tonnage 508.

Area of Operations: North Sea 1916/17.

Types embarked:

Schneider (1916).	Example:	3736, 3776,
Baby (1916/17).	Example:	8149, 8150, 8160, 8164

Notes: Double-ended paddle steamer, built 1912 as New Holland-Hull ferry. Commissioned into RN February 27 March 1916. Operated 2 Schneiders or 2 Babies in North Sea on anti-Zeppelin patrols. Very unhandy ship. Returned to ferry service 1918. Sold 1935 for cruises in Firth of Forth as *Highland Queen* until broken up December 1936.

HMT *CANTATRICE*

Trawler. Gross tonnage 302. Armament 1 x 12-pounder.

Area of Operations: North Sea 1916.

Type embarked:

Baby (1916).	Examples:	8120, 8122, 8140, 8156, 8163

Notes: Hired 1915. One Baby carried on platform aft, and operated in North Sea 1915/16 on anti-Zeppelin patrols. Sunk by mine off Yarmouth 15 November 1916.

HMT *CHRISTOPHER*

Trawler. Gross tonnage 316.

Area of Operations: North Sea 1916.

Type embarked:

Baby (1916).	Example:	8149

Notes: Hired 1915. One Baby carried on platform aft, and operated in North Sea 1916 on anti-Zeppelin patrols. Sunk by mine off Southend 30 March 1917.

HMS *CITY OF OXFORD*

Seaplane carrier. Gross tonnage 4019.

Areas of Operations: East Mediterranean 1917-1918; Red Sea 1917-1918.

Types embarked:

Short 184 (1917/18).	Examples:	8019, 8020, 8022, N1090, N1091, N1262, N1263, N1639
Short 827 (1918)	Example:	8649
Baby (1918).	Example:	N1126
Hamble Baby (1918)	Example:	N1209

Notes: Purchased 20 October 1914 and converted to dummy battleship *St Vincent*. Kite Balloon Ship by July 1915. Converted to Seaplane Carrier July 1917, embarking up to 4 Short 184's. Sold 1920.

HMS *CLEETHORPES* (use unconfirmed)

Paddle Air Service Scout. Gross tonnage 273. Armament 1 x 6-pounder.

Area of Operations: North Sea 1916.

Type embarked:

Schneider (1916)?

Notes: Built 1903 as New Holland-Hull ferry. Hired early 1916 and possibly operated one Schneider from Yarmouth on anti-Zeppelin patrols in North Sea from March 1916. To Paddle Minesweeper April 1919.

HMS *DIANA*

Cruiser. Displacement 5600 tons. Armament 5 x 6'', 6 x 4.7'', 9 x 12-pounder.

Area of Operations: Red Sea 1914.

Type embarked:

Nieuport VI (1914).

Notes: One Nieuport VI embarked for reconnaissance of Gulf of Akaba December 1914.

HMS *DORIS*

Cruiser. Displacement 5600 tons. Armament 5 x 6'', 6 x 4.7'', 9 x 12-pounder.

Area of Operations: East Mediterranean 1914-1915.

Types embarked:

Nieuport VI (1914/15).

Sopwith 807 (1915).   Example: 922 (ex *Ark Royal*)

Schneider (1915).   Example: 1437 (ex *Ark Royal*)

Notes: Embarked in turn, one each of the 3 types above, mainly to spot for naval gunfire on Turkish shore
               positions. Sold 20 February 1919.

HMS *DRYAD*

Torpedo Gunboat. Displacement 1070 tons. Armament 2 x 4.7'', 4 x 6-pounder, 5 x TT.

Area of Operations: North Sea 1917.

Type embarked:

Baby (1917)   Example: 8150, N1066, N1108

Notes: Sister ship to *Halcyon*. Operated one Baby out of Yarmouth for patrol duties during June and July 1917.
               Renamed *Hamadryad* January 1918 for harbour duties and sold 24 September 1920.

RIMS *DUFFERIN*

Armed Merchant Cruiser. Displacement 7457 tons. Armament 8 x 4.7'', 8 x 3-pounder.

Area of Operations: Red Sea 1916.

Type embarked:

Short 184 (1916).   Example: 8004 (ex *Anne*)

Notes: Formerly Troopship of Royal Indian Marine. Operated one Short 184 (ex *Anne*) in the reconnaissance rôle
               along Red Sea coasts September 1916.

HM S/M *E22*

Submarine. Displacement 660 tons. Armament 5 x TT, 1 x 12-pounder.

Area of Operation: North Sea 1916.

Type embarked:

Schneider (1916).   Examples: 3730, 3743

Notes: Two Schneiders taken to sea 24 April 1916 stowed on a twin track platform constructed abaft conning
              tower. Both seaplanes were floated off the platform, with the submarine's stern submerged, and flew back
              to Felixstowe. No operational use made of these trials since the seaplane platform adversely affected E22's
              underwater performance. Sunk 25.4.16 by UB.18

HMS *ENDYMION*

Cruiser. Displacement 7350 tons. Armament 2 x 9.2'', 10 x 6'', 12 x 6-pounder.

Area of Operations: East Mediterranean 1916.

Type embarked:

Schneider (1916).   Example: 3788 (ex *Empress*)

Notes: Operated one Schneider off Bulgarian coast September 1916. Sold 16 March 1920.

HMS *ERIDGE*

Paddle Minesweeper. Displacement 810 tons. Armament 2 x 12-pounder.

Area of Operation: North Sea 1916.

Type embarked:

Schneider (1916).

Notes: Ascot class minesweeper fitted on completion to carry 2 Schneiders amidships. Trials were conducted, but
              there is no indication of operational use. Sold March 1922.

HMS *EURYALUS*

Armoured Cruiser. Displacement 12000 tons. Armament 2 x 9.2'', 12 x 6'', 14 x 12-pounder.

Area of Operation: East Mediterranean 1915.

Type embarked:

Short 184 (1915).   Example: 842 (ex *Ben-my-Chree*)

Notes: Short 184 embarked briefly October 1915. Converted to minelayer 1918. Sold 1 July 1920.

HMS *GENERAL CRAUFURD*

Monitor. Displacement 5900 tons. Armament 2 x 12'', 2 x 6'', 2 x 12-pounder.

Area of Operation: English Channel 1916.

Type embarked:

Short 184 (1916/17).   Examples: 8098, 8382, 9057, 9060

Notes: Served in Monitor Squadron based Dover for bombardment of Belgian coast. Two Short 184s embarked at intervals between July 1916 and April 1917.

HMS *GOLDEN EAGLE*

Paddle Air Service Transport. Gross tonnage 800.

Areas of Operation: British coastal waters, English Channel 1916.

Type embarked:

Wight Twin (1916).   Examples: 1450, 1451

Notes: Wight Twins, 1450 and 1451, transferred from Cowes to Felixstowe on 15 July 1916, were probably onboard *Golden Eagle*. Other seaplane Types were probably embarked on other dates. Reverted to ferry. Hired as AA Ship January 1940. Accommodation Ship January 1945. Returned to ferry service April 1945.

HMS *HALCYON*

Torpedo Gunboat. Displacement 1070 tons. Armament: 2 x 4.7'', 4 x 6-pounder, 5 x TT.

Area of Operation: North Sea 1916/17.

Type embarked:

Baby (1916/17).   Examples: 8133, 8149, 8150, N1066

Notes: Operated one Baby for anti-U-boat and anti-Zeppelin patrols, and for air-sea rescue. Sold 6 November 1919.

RIMS *HARDINGE*

Armed Merchant Cruiser. Displacement 6520 tons. Armament 6 x 4.7'', 6 x 3-pounder.

Area of Operation: Red Sea 1915.

Type embarked:

Nieuport VI (1915).   Examples: N16, N17, N18, N19

Notes: Formerly Troopship of Royal Indian Marine. Operated Nieuport VI's in the reconnaissance role along Red Sea coasts June 1915.

HMS *HERMES*

Cruiser. Displacement 5600 tons. Armament 8 x 6'' (3 removed), 9 x 12-pounder.

Areas of Operation: North Sea and English Channel 1913/14.

Types embarked:

Borel seaplane (1913).	Example:	48
Caudron GII (1913).	Examples:	55, 56
Short Folder (1913/14).	Examples:	81, 82, 119
Sopwith Seaplane (1914).	Example:	138
Short S80 (1914)	Example:	905

Notes: Parent Ship of Naval Wing RFC May 1913. Operated Caudron GII amphibian from fixed forecastle ramp and seaplanes from quarterdeck from July 1913. Sunk 30 October 1914 in English Channel by U27.

HMS *HIMALAYA*

Armed Merchant Cruiser. Gross tonnage 6919. Armament 8 x 6''.

Areas of Operations: East Africa 1916/17 and East Indies 1917.

Type embarked:

Short 827 (1916/17).	Examples:	3096, 3098, 8254 8641, 8642

Notes: Former P & O Liner, hired as AMC August 1914. Operated one Short 827 in support of ground forces in German East Africa 1916/17. Sold April 1922.

HMT *JERICO*

Trawler. Gross tonnage 351. Armament 1 x 12-pounder.

Area of Operations: North Sea 1915.

Types embarked:

Schneider (1915).	Examples:	3710, 3715, 3720, 3723
Baby (1915).	Example:	8120

Notes: Hired 1915-1919 and operated one Schneider or Baby on anti-Zeppelin patrols in North Sea 1915. As HMT *Kopanes* was sunk by air attack off Tyne 19 April 1941.

HMS *KILLINGHOLME*

Paddle Air Service Scout. Gross tonnage 508.

Area of Operations: North Sea 1916.

Types embarked:

Schneider (1916).	Example:	3801
Baby (1916).	Examples:	8131, 8141, 8142, 8147, 8148, 8154, 8155, 8174, 8207

Notes:　　Sister ship to HMS *Brocklesby*. Commissioned into RN 27 March 1916. Operated two Schneiders or Babies on anti- Zeppelin patrols in North Sea from April 1916. Served as Kite Balloon Depot Ship April 1941 - March 1945.

HMS *KINFAUNS CASTLE*

Armed Merchant Cruiser. Gross tonnage 9692. Armament 8 x 4.7''.

Area of Operation: East Africa 1915.

Type embarked:

Sopwith 807 (1915).	Examples:	920, 921

Notes:　　Former Union-Castle liner, hired as AMC August 1914-October 1915. Transported 2 Sopwith 807's (ex SS *Persia*) from Bombay to Niororo Island February 1915, where she served as seaplane Depot Ship for Rufiji Delta operations.

HMT *KINGFISHER*

Trawler. Gross tonnage 304. Armament: 1 x 12-pounder, 1 x 6-pounder.

Area of Operations: North Sea 1915/16.

Types embarked:

Schneider (1915).	Examples:	1446, 1558, 3710, 3715, 3720, 3723
Baby (1915/16).	Example:	8120, 8139, 8150, 8156, 8157, 8164, 8173

Notes:　　Purchased 1915 and operated one Schneider or Baby on anti-Zeppelin patrols in North Sea 1915/16. Renamed *Adele* 1918 and sold 1919.

HMS *LACONIA*

Armed Merchant Cruiser. Gross tonnage 18099.

Area of Operations: East Africa 1915/16.

Types embarked:

Short Folder (1915).   Examples: 119, 121, 122

Short 827 (1916).   Examples: 3096, 3097, 8218, 8641

Notes: Former Cunard Liner, hired as AMC 27 October 1914-2 August 1916. Transported 3 Short Folders to Durban March 1915 for Rufiji operations. Operated one Short 827 off German East Africa 1916.

HMS *LAURENTIC*

Armed Merchant Cruiser. Gross tonnage 14892.

Area of Operation: East Africa 1915.

Types embarked:

Henry Farman F27 (1915).   Examples: AS/8/HF, SA/9/HF (French c/n's. No RNAS serials allotted)

Caudron GIII (1915).

Notes: Former White Star Liner, hired as AMC 31 October 1914. Transported 2 Henry Farmans and 2 Caudrons to Mafia Island June 1915 for Rufiji Delta operations, but never operated aircraft. Sunk by mine off Northern Ireland 25 January 1917.

HMS *MANICA*

Seaplane Carrier. Gross tonnage 4120.

Area of Operations: East Africa 1916/17.

Types embarked:

Short 827 (1916/17).   Examples: 3096, 3097, 3098, 8218, 8254, 8641, 8642

Short 184 (1917).

Notes: Hired as Kite Balloon Ship 11 March 1915 and later purchased. Operated Short 827's and Short 184's off East Africa between May 1916 and May 1917 in addition to Kite Balloon. Sold 1920.

HMS *MANTUA*

Armed Merchant Cruiser. Gross tonnage 10946. Armament 8 x 4.7''.

Area of Operations: South Atlantic and Western Approaches 1918.

Type embarked:

Short 184 (1918).   Examples: N2816, N2817

Notes: Former P & O Liner, hired as AMC August 1914-December 1919. Operated one Short 184 as convoy
              escort from Dakar between September 1918 and November 1918.

HMS *MELTON*

Paddle Minesweeper. Displacement 810 tons. Armament 2 x 12-pounder.

Area of Operation: North Sea 1916.

Type embarked:

Schneider (1916).

Notes: Ascot class minesweeper fitted on completion to carry 2 Schneiders amidships. Trials were conducted, but
              there is no indication of operational use. Sold 25 November 1927 and renamed *Queen of Thanet*. Hired as
              minesweeper 12 September 1939. Accommodation Ship January 1944. Salvage duty 1945 to 7 June 1946.

HMS *MINERVA*

Cruiser. Displacement 5600 tons. Armament 11 x 6'', 9 x 12-pounder.

Areas of Operations: East Mediterranean and Red Sea 1914/15.

Types embarked:

Nieuport VI (1914).

Schneider (1915).   Example: 1438 (ex *Ark Royal*)

Sopwith 807 (1915).   Example: 922 (ex *Ark Royal*)

Notes: Operated one Nieuport VI in Gulf of Akaba December 1914, and one Schneider and later one Sopwith 807
              in East Mediterranean 1915. Sold 5 October 1920.

RIMS *NORTHBROOK*

Armed Merchant Cruiser. Displacement 5820 tons. Armament 6 x 4.7'', 6 x 3-pounder.

Areas of Operations: East Mediterranean and Red Sea 1916.

Type embarked:

Short 184 (1916).   Example: 8075

Notes: Formerly Royal Indian Marine troopship. Operated one Short 184 (ex *Anne*) off Hejaz coast 17 September 1916.

HMS *OROTAVA*

Armed Merchant Cruiser. Gross tonnage 5980. Armament 5 x 6'', 2 x 6-pounder.

Area of Operations: South Atlantic and Western Approaches 1918.

Type embarked:

Short 184 (1918).   Examples: N1774, N1790, N2816

Notes: Former Orient Liner, hired as AMC 19 November 1914. Operated one Short 184 on convoy escort duty from Dakar June 1918.

HMS *ORLIONOCH*

Seaplane Carrier. Gross tonnage 1406. Armament 2 x 4''.

Area of Operations: Caspian Sea 1919.

Type embarked:

Short 184 (1919).   Examples: N9078, N9081

Notes: Ex Russian tanker, captured at Baku 1 March 1919. Commissioned into RN as CMB Depot Ship until employment as Seaplane Carrier between 11 July 1919 and 26 August 1919. Operated 2 Short 184's of 266 Squadron RAF against Bolsheviks until transferred to White Russians.

HMS *PENELOPE*

Light Cruiser. Displacement 3500 tons. Armament 2 x 6'', 6 x 4''.

Area of Operations: North Sea 1915.

Type embarked:

Schneider (1915).   Examples: 1439, 1440, 1441, 1556, 1557

Notes: Fitted with fixed forecastle ramp 1915 for operation of aeroplane with wheeled under-carriage, but probably never used. One Schneider embarked May/June 1915 for anti-Zeppelin or anti-U-boat patrols. Sold October 1924.

SS *PENMORVAH*

Aircraft Repair Ship. Gross tonnage 4,323 tons

Notes: Allocated to HMS *Ark Royal* at Mudros in May 1915 for storing aviation spares and as an additional workshop. Two Sopwith 860s, 855 and 860, transferred from *Ark Royal* to *Penmorvah* for erection 8 May 1915. Schneider 1438 on board for overhaul and storage 3 June 1915 and 1437 for repair 8 June 1915. Returned to mercantile service by March 1917, when she survived attack by U-boat in English Channel.

HMS *PEONY*

Sloop. Displacement 1200 tons. Armament 2 x 12-pounder, 2 x 3-pounder.

Area of Operations: Aegean 1917/18.

Types embarked:

Schneider (1917).

Baby (1918).   Example: N1195, N1444, N2082

Notes: Operated nominally 3, but probably 2 Schneiders in search for suspected U-boat bases in Aegean from May 1917, and on anti-U-boat patrols. By 1 April 1918 she operated one Baby as part of 62 and 63 Wings RAF based on Mudros. Sold 20 August 1919 for conversion to cross-Channel ferry SS *Ardena*.

HMS *PRINCESS MARGARET*

Minelayer. Gross tonnage 5934. Armament 2 x 4.7'', 2 x 12-pounder, 2 x 6-pounder, 500 mines.

Area of Operations: North Sea 1917.

Types embarked:

Schneider (1917)

Baby (1917)   Examples: N1111, N1112

Notes: Former Canadian Pacific Liner, hired 26 December 1914. Two Schneiders or Babies embarked between June 1917 and September 1917. Purchased 14 June 1919. Sold 30 May 1929.

HMS *PRINCESS VICTORIA*

Air Service Transport. Gross tonnage 1687. Armament 1 x 3-pounder.

Area of Operations: North Sea 1915.

Types embarked:

Schneider ?(1915).

Wight Navyplane (1915).   Example: 894

Notes: Former Stranraer to Larne ferry, hired as Netlayer 1914. When the Seaplane Carrier *Empress* was refitted early 1915, *Princess Victoria* took the latter's place as Seaplane Tender until May 1915. Sold 12 May 1920.

HMS *RAGLAN*

Monitor. Displacement 6150 tons. Armament 2 x 14'', 2 x 6'', 2 x 12-pounder.

Area of Operations: East Mediterranean 1915/17.

Type embarked:

Short 184 (1915/17).   Examples: 8019, N1262, N1263

Notes: Operated one Short 184 (ex *Ark Royal*) October 1915 in Gulf of Xeros, and later another Short 184 (ex *City of Oxford*) off Palestinian coast October/November 1917. Sunk by SMS *Goeben* 20 January 1918 off Imbros.

HMS *RAVEN II*

Seaplane Carrier. Gross tonnage 4678. Armament 1 x 12-pounder.

Areas of Operation: East Mediterranean 1915/17, Indian Ocean and Red Sea 1917.

Types embarked:

Nieuport VI (1915/16).   Examples: N11, N15, N16, N17, N18, N19, N20,
                                              N22, N23

Schneider (1916).   Examples: 3721, 3722, 3727, 3770, 3774, 3775,
                                              3786, 3790

Baby (1917).   Examples: 8189, N1014

Short 184 (1916/17)   Examples: 850, 8004, 8018, 8019, 8021, 8022,
                                              8045, 8070, 8075, 8090, 8091, N1263

Notes: Ex German SS *Rabenfels* seized at Port Said 1914. Operated 2 Nieuport VI's from January 1915 as HMFA *Rabenfels*. Commissioned into RN as HMS *Raven II* June 1915. From early 1916 her Nieuport VI's were replaced by Short 184's and Schneiders or Babies. Paid off late 1917, and in 1918 became Collier *Ravenrock.*.

HMS *ROBERTS*

Monitor. Displacement 6150 tons. Armament 2 x 14'', 2 x 6'', 2 x 12-pounder.

Area of Operations: East Mediterranean 1915.

Types embarked:

Schneider (1915).	Example:	1437 (ex *Ark Royal*)
Short 166 (1915).	Example:	164 (ex *Ark Royal*)
Short 184 (1915).	Example:	184, 841 (ex *Ben-my-Chree*)

Notes: Operated one Short 166 during September 1915 against shore positions on Asiatic coast. Sold 9 May 1921 but retained until September 1936.

HMT *ST.GERMAIN*

Trawler. Gross tonnage 307. Armament 1 x 6-pounder

Type embarked:

Schneider (1915).	Example:	1447, 3708

Notes: Hired 1915-1919.

HMS *SEVERN*

Monitor. Displacement 1260 tons. Armament 2 x 6'', 2 x 4.7''.

Area of Operations: East Africa.

Type employed:

Short 827 (1916).

Notes: Ex-Brazilian *Solimoes* purchased 8 August 1914. Probably operated one of *Manica's* Short 827's against shore positions in German East Africa. Lacking the ability to hoist a seaplane in board, it was towed astern of the monitor. Sold 9 May 1921.

HMT *SIR JOHN FRENCH*

Trawler. Gross tonnage 351. Armament 1 x 12-pounder.

Area of Operations: North Sea 1915.

Type embarked:

Schneider (1915).	Examples:	1446, 1578, 3710, 3715, 3720, 3723

Notes: Hired 1915-1919, and operated one Schneider on anti- Zeppelin patrols in North Sea 1915.

HMS *SIR THOMAS PICTON*

Monitor. Displacement 5900 tons. Armament 2 x 12'', 2 x 6'', 2 x 12-pounder.

Area of Operations: East Mediterranean 1915/16.

Types embarked:

Short 166 (1915).

Short 184 (1916).

Notes: Operated one Short 184 transferred from *Empress* at Stavros September 1916. Sold 18 November 1921.

HMS *SLINGER*

Experimental Catapult Ship. Gross tonnage 875.

Type embarked:

Fairey F127 (1918).   Example: N9

Notes: Former steam hopper. Commissioned into Royal Navy for catapult trials at Isle of Grain. Armstrong catapult installed 1917 and first launch of catapult dummy (a Short 184) in October 1917. First successful launch of piloted Fairey F127 on 14 May 1918. Sold 16 October 1919.

HMS *UNDAUNTED*

Light Cruiser. Displacement 3500 tons. Armament 2 x 6'', 6 x 4''.

Areas of Operations: North Sea 1915.

Type embarked.

Schneider (1915).   Examples: 1440, 1557

Notes: Fitted with fixed forecastle ramp 1915 for operation of aeroplane with wheeled under-carriage, but probably never used. One Schneider embarked May/June 1915 for anti-Zeppelin or anti-U-Boat patrols. Sold 9 April 1923.

HMAS *AUSTRALIA*

Battle Cruiser. Displacement 18800 tons. Armament 8 x 12'', 16 x 4''.

Type embarked:

Avro 504L.   Example: H3034

Notes: Avro 504L embarked between July to September 1920, but not a success. Returned to Australian Air Corps 1921 and renumbered A3-46.

HMAS *MELBOURNE*

Cruiser. Displacement 5400 tons. Armament 8 x 6'', 4 x 3-pounder.

Type embarked:

Avro 504L.   Example: H3042

Notes: Avro 504L embarked September 1920, but not a success. Returned to Australian Air Corps and renumbered
                A3-47.

HMAS *GERANIUM*

Sloop. Displacement 1250 tons.

Area of Operation. Great Barrier Reef 1924.

Type embarked:

Fairey IIID (1924).   Example: A10-2

Notes: Transferred to R.A.N.1919. Joined Hydrographic Branch of R.A.N. in 1924 and embarked one Fairey IIID
                to assist in survey of Great Barrier Reef. Sunk as target 24 April 1935.

Footnote. The French Cruiser *Montcalm* operated one Nieuport VI seaplane in the Gulf of Akaba during May 1915, the
                only known example of a French Cruiser embarking a seaplane during World War I.
                The French seaplane carrier *Campinas,* when serving in EI & ESS, operated two Nieuport VIs, N19 and
                N23, in March 1916.

ADDENDUM

It was the intention to exclude from this account the activities of all the recognised seaplane carriers. However, the
operations involving the EI and ESS would be incomplete if the two carriers *Ben-my-Chree* between February 1916 and
January 1917, and *Empress* between February 1917 and January 1918 were left out of the story. Accordingly details of
these two ships, and of the seaplanes operated by them within those dates are given below:

HMS *BEN-my-CHREE*

Seaplane carrier. Gross tonnage 2,651.

Areas of Operation: East Mediterranean and Red Sea 1916/17.

Types embarked:

Short 184.   Examples: 846, 849, 850, 8035, 8054,
                                                            8070, 8075, 8076, 8080, 8082, 8087,
                                                            8090, 8091, 8372

Schneider.   Examples: 3721, 3727, 3770, 3771, 3773, 3774,
                                                            3777, 3778, 3779, 3786, 3789, 3790

Baby   Examples: 8135, 8188, 8189

HMS *EMPRESS*

Seaplane Carrier. Gross tonnage 2,540.

Areas of Operation: East Mediterranean 1917/18.

Types embarked:

Short 184	Examples:	8004, 8018, 8019, 8020, 8021, 8022, 8051, 8075, 8076, 8088, 8091, 8381, N1090, N1091, N1581, N1582, N1590
Baby	Examples:	N1028, N1036, N1038, N1129
Hamble Baby	Examples:	N1209, N1210

Additionally the following 4 ships were reported in September 1917 to be fitted to carry a seaplane, presumably a Sopwith Baby in the trawler and a Short 184 in the larger vessels.

HMY *ALBION III*

1346 tons. Armament 2 x 12-pounder, 1 x 6-pounder.

Hired as A/P Yacht 1915-1919. Based Loch Larne 1917.

HMS *ANGORA*

4300 tons. Armament 3 x 4.7'', 2 x 6-pounder, 320 mines.

Hired as M/L February 1915-April 1919.

HMY *BERYL*

1368 tons. Armament 1 x 3'', 1 x 12-pounder.

Hired as A/P Yacht January 1915-March 1919. Based Queenstown 1917.

HMT *LORDSHIP*

351 tons. Armament 1 x 12-pounder, 1 x 6-pounder.
Hired as A/S Trawler 1916-1919. Based Killingholme 1917.

Reports of RNAS pilots on board HM Drifter *Tarlair* between December 1917 and March 1918 suggest that she also operated a Baby. She was base ship of Hawkcraig Hydrophone Establishment in March 1918.

APPENDIX IIA

Short 184's operated from ships of EI and ESS and ships associated with them 1915-1918

SHORT 184	184	*Roberts* 8.15 (ex *Ben-my-Chree*)
	841	*Roberts* 8.15 (ex *Ben-my-Chree*)
	842	*Euryalus* 10.15 (ex *Ben-my-Chree*)
	846	*Ben-my-Chree* 3.16, 4.16. Lost 3.4.16
	849	*Ben-my-Chree* 2.16. Lost 11.2.16
	850	*Ben-my-Chree* 3.16, 5.16, 6.16;
		Raven II 3.16, 4.16
	8004	*Anne* 4.16, 9.16, 10.16, 1.17;
		Dufferin 9.16; *Raven II* 10.16, 12.16;
		Empress 5.17 - 8.17
	8018	*Raven II* 3.17 - 5.17;
		Empress 7.17 - 10.17. Lost 9.10.17
	8019	*Raven II* 3.17, 4.17, 6.17; *Empress* 6.17 -10.17;
		City of Oxford 10.17; *Raglan* 10.17
	8020	*Anne* 3.17; *Empress* 5.17 - 7.17;
		City of Oxford 12.17, 2.18, 3.18
	8021	*Anne* 2.17; *Raven II* 3.17, 4.17;
		Empress 6.17, 9.17, 10.17. Lost 11.10.17
	8022	*Anne* 2.17; *Empress* 8.17; *Raven* II 10.17,
		11.17; *City of Oxford* 2.18, 3.18
	8035	*Ben-my-Chree* 8.16
	8045	*Raven II* 8.16
	8051	*Empress* 4.16
	8054	*Anne* 4.16; *Ben-my-Chree* 5.16 - 8.16
	8070	*Raven II* 1916; *Ben-my-Chree* 12.16
	8075	*Anne* 1.16, 9.16, 1.17; *Ben-my-Chree* 5.16; *Empress*
		6.16, 5.17; *Northbrook* 9.16; *Raven II* 7.16, 8.16, 10.16, 12.16
	8076	*Ben-my-Chree* 5.16; *Empress* 6.17
	8080	*Ben-my-Chree* 5.16, 8.16, 9.16, 11.16 - 1.17. Lost 8.1.17
	8082	*Ben-my-Chree* 5.16, 6.16
	8084	*Anne* 4.16
	8087	*Ben-my-Chree* 5.16. Lost 23.5.16
	8088	*Empress* 4.16
	8090	*Anne* 8.16; *Ben-my-Chree* 11.16, 12.16;
		Raven II 5.16 - 7.16, 3.17. Lost 28.3.17
	8091	*Raven II* 5.16 - 8.16; *Anne* 8.16; *Ben-my-Chree*
		12.16; *Empress* 10.17
	8372	*Ben-my-Chree* 7.16 - 9.16; *Empress* 12.16. Lost 2.12.16
	8381	*Empress* 3.17
	N1090	*Empress* 9.17; *City of Oxford* 10.17, 11.17
	N1091	*Empress* 10.17; *City of Oxford* 11.17
	N1262	*City of Oxford* 10.17; *Raglan* 10.17. DBR 30.10.17
	N1263	*Raglan* 11.17; *Raven II* 11.17;
		City of Oxford 11.17, 2.18, 3.18
	N1581	*Empress* 1.18
	N1582	*Empress* 1.18. Lost 28.1.18
	N1590	*Empress* 1.18
	N1639	*City of Oxford* 2.18

Additionally, the following Short 184's were based at Port Said between 1915 and 1918, and some may have been embarked in ships of EI and ESS.

8043, 8046, 8047, 8083, 8095, N1597, N1649, N1679, N1749, N1784, N1827, N1838, N1839, N2648, N2791, N2792, N2812, N2822, N2823, N2824, N9066.

Schneiders and Babies operated from ships of EI and ESS and ships associated with them 1915 - 1918:

SOPWITH	1437	*Doris* 5.15 (ex *Ark Royal*);
SCHNEIDER		*Roberts* 9.15 (ex *Ark Royal*)
	1438	*Doris* 9.15 (ex *Ark Royal*), *Minerva* 1915
	3721	*Raven II* 3.16, 4.16; *Ben-my-Chree* 5.16, 6.16
	3722	*Raven II* 3.16
	3727	*Raven II* 3.16; *Ben-my-Chree* 4.16 - 6.16
	3770	*Ben-my-Chree* 4.16 - 6.16, 9.16, 12.16, 1.17; *Raven II* 12.16
	3771	*Ben-my-Chree* 4.16 - 7.16
	3772	*Empress* 3.16, 6.16
	3773	*Ben-my-Chree* 5.16
	3774	*Ben-my-Chree* 3.16, 4.16, 5.16; *Raven II* 3.16, 4.16
	3775	*Raven II* 4.16
	3777	*Anne* 8.16; *Ben-my-Chree* 4.16, 5.16, 9.16. Lost 19.9.16
	3778	*Ben-my-Chree* 4.16 - 6.16, 9.16, 12.16, 1.17
	3779	*Ben-my-Chree* 4,16, 9.16
	3786	*Ben-my-Chree* 4,16; *Raven II* 6.16, 7.16. Lost 2.7.16
	3788	*Endymion* 9.16 (ex *Empress*)
	3789	*Ben-my-Chree* 6.16, 9.16
	3790	*Raven II* 3.16; *Ben-my-Chree* 3.16 - 6.16
SOPWITH	8135	*Ben-my-Chree* 9.16. Lost 17.9.16
BABY	8188	*Ben-my-Chree* 5.16, 12.16, 1.17. Lost 8.1.17
	8189	*Ben-my-Chree* 5.16, 6.16; *Raven II* 6.16 - 8.16
	N1014	*Raven II* 3.17, 4.17;
		Brisbane 4.17, 5.17 (ex *Raven II*)
	N1016	*Anne* 3.17
	N1028	*Empress* 10.17, 11.17
	N1036	*Empress* 10.17, 11.17. Lost 2.11.17
	N1038	*Empress* 11.17. Lost 2.11.17
	N1126	*City of Oxford* 12.17
	N1129	*Empress* 11.17
FAIREY	N1209	*Empress* 11.17; *City of Oxford* 12.17, 1.18
HAMBLE BABY	N1210	*Empress* 11.17. Lost 2.11.17

Additionally the following Sopwith Babies based at Port Said between 1915 and 1918 may have been embarked in ships of EI and ESS: N1060, N1128, N2072, N2073

Nieuport VI's operated from ships of EI and ESS and ships associated with them 1915-1916:

NIEUPORT VI	N11	*Anne* 1.15, 8.15, 9.15, 11.15; *Raven II* 4.15
	N14	*Raven II* 8.15; *Anne* 10.15. Lost 10.10.15
	N15	*Anne* 1.15; *Raven II* 7.15
	N16	*Anne* 1.15, 9.15; *Raven II* 5.15; *Hardinge* 6.15
	N17	*Hardinge* 6.15; *Raven II* 6.15 - 8.15; *Anne* 9.15, 10.15, 12.15. Lost 22.12.15
	N18	*Anne* 1915; *Raven II* 4.15, 5.15; *Hardinge* 6.15
	N19	*Hardinge* 6.15; *Raven II* 6.15, 7.15; *Anne* 10.15, 12.15, 1.16; *Campinas* 3.16

N20	*Raven II* 4.15, 7.15, 12.15, 1.16;
	Anne 8.15 - 10.15
N21	*Anne* 1915
N22	*Raven II* 1916; *Anne* 11.15 - 1.16, 2.16, 4.16.
	Lost 16.4.16
N23	*Anne* 12.15, 2.16; *Raven II* 12.15, 1.16;
	Campinas 3.16
NB1	*Anne* 3.16
NB2	*Anne* 3.16, 4.16

Schneider 3772 on HMS Ark Royal's deck in 1915. This seaplane was not operated by El & ESS but is typical of the Schneiders employed by the Squadron. (FAAM)

Short 184, 184, here being hoisted by HMS Ben-my-Chree, was operated by HMS Roberts in August 1915. (GSL/JMB)

APPENDIX IIB

Aircrew of the East Indies and Egypt Seaplane Squadron, December 1914-January 1918

The following flew as pilots (P) or observers (O) in seaplanes of the Squadron operating from ships of the Squadron or ships associated with it. Against each pilot's or observer's name is given the ship in which he was borne and the months in which he flew operationally from that ship.

BANKES-PRICE, J. T. Lt. (P) RNAS
    Killed 17 September 1916

Raven II March 1916, April 1916
Ben-my-Chree May 1916, June 1916, July 1916, August 1916, September 1916

BARR, F. M. L. Flt. Lt. (P) RNAS

Empress June 1917

BAXTER, F. O. Lieut. (O)
    Cambridgeshire Regiment

Montcalm (French Cruiser) May 1915
Ben-my-Chree May 1916

BLANC, Jean Lt. (P) L'AMF

Anne March 1916

BOURGEOIS, Raymond, Ldg Seaman
    (P) L'AMF

Anne October 1915, December 1915, January 1916

BOURNE, C. A. 2nd Lieut. (O) RFA

Anne April 1916
Empress March 1917

BRONSON, C. G. Flt. Lt. (P) RNAS
    POW 28 January 1918

Raven II November 1917
Empress June 1917, August 1917, September 1917, November 1917, January 1918

BROOKE, J. C. Flt. Lt. (P) RNAS

Raven II June 1916, July 1916, August 1916
Anne August 1916, March 1917
Ben-my-Chree June 1916, December 1916
Empress May 1917

BROWN, J. W. Lieut. (O) RFA

Raven II July 1916

BURD, J. M. Lieut. (O) RFA

Campinas (French Seaplane Carrier) March 1916
Ben-my-Chree June 1916

BURLING, E. J. P. Flt. Lt. (P)
    RNAS

Anne January 1917
Raven II December 1916, March 1917, April 1917, May 1917, June 1917, November 1917
Empress July 1917, August 1917, September 1917, November 1917
City of Oxford October 1917, November 1917
Raglan October 1917, November 1917

BURNIER, Lt. (P) L'AMF

Raven II December 1915, January 1916

CHILDERS, R. E. Lt (O) RNVR

Ben-my-Chree January 1916, February 1916, March 1916

CHUTE, E. L. Capt. (O) Duke of
    Wellington's Regiment

Anne January 1916, February, 1916, March 1916

CINTRÉ, Alfred, Lt (P) L'AMF

Raven II April 1915
Hardinge June 1915

CLARKE, L. Lieut (O)   *Ben-my-Chree* June 1916
    Manchester Regiment

CLEMSON, A. W. Flt. Lt (P) RNAS   *Raven* II July 1916, August 1916, March 1917, April 1917, May 1917,
    Killed 11 October 1917   June 1917
                                              Anne September 1916, October 1916, February 1917, March 1917
                                              Ben-my-Chree December 1916
                                              Dufferin September 1916
                                              Brisbane May 1917
                                              Empress October 1917

CLIFFORD, R. M. F/S/L (P) RNAS   *Ben-my-Chree* February 1916
                                              Raven II March 1916, April 1916
                                              Empress February 1916

DACRE, G. B. Flt. Lt (P) RNAS   *Ben-my-Chree* January 1916, February 1916, April 1916
    POW 26 August 1916   *June* 1916, August 1916
                                              Raven II July 1916
                                              Anne August 1916

de SAIZIEU, Louis Lt (P) L'AMF   *Anne* January 1915, September 1915, October 1915, November 1915,
    POW 22 December 1915   December 1915
                                              Raven II June 1915, July 1915, August 1915

DESTREM, Antoine Lt. (P) L'AMF   *Anne* April 1915, August 1915, September 1915, October 1915, December
                                              1915, January 1916, February 1916
                                              Raven II July 1915, December 1915, January 1916
                                              Campinas (French Seaplane Carrier) March 1916

DOVER, M. G. F/S/L (P) RNAS   *Ben-my-Chree* August 1916, November 1916, December 1916

EDMONDS, C. H. K. Flt. Cdr (P)   *Ben-my-Chree* January 1916, February 1916, March 1916
    RNAS   *Raven II* March 1916, April 1916

ENGLAND, T. H. Flt. Cdr. (P) RNAS   *Raven II* March 1916, April 1916, March 1917, April 1917, May 1917,
                                              June 1917
                                              Ben-my-Chree May 1916, June 1916, July 1916, August 1916,
                                              September 1916, November 1916, December 1916

FERGUSON, A. D. 2nd Lieut (O) HLI   *Empress* April 1917, May 1917, June 1917, January 1918, February 1918
                                              City of Oxford October 1917, November 1917, February 1918, March 1918

FIELD, R. M. Flt. Lt. (P) RNAS   *Empress* March 1917

FINNEY, A. D. 2nd Lieut. (O) RFA   *Anne* March 1916, April 1916

FLETCHER, H. P. Major (O)   *Anne* August 1915, September 1915, October 1915, November 1915
    Middlesex Hussars   December 1915, January 1916, February 1916
                                              Raven II July 1915, December 1915, January 1916
                                              Hardinge June 1915

GOODWIN, H. F. Chief Petty   *City of Oxford* February 1918, March 1918
    Officer (O) RNAS

GRALL, Hervé Chief Petty Officer   *Anne* February 1915, April 1915, August 1915, September 1915
   (P) L'AMF   November 1915, December 1915, January 1916, February 1916, April 1916
                                     Raven II April 1915, July 1915
                                     Minerva December 1914

GRAMANT, Petty Officer (P) L'AMF   *Campinas* (French Seaplane Carrier) March 1916

GROUCOTT, E. Ldg. Mech. (O) RNAS   *Raven II* April 1917

HENDERSON, F. C. F/S/L (P) RNAS   *Ben-my-Chree* December 1916

HERBERT, J. R. Capt. (O) (Army)   *Anne* January 1915, August 1915
                                     Raven II June 1915
                                     Doris December 1914

HILLAS, N. Lieut (O) Duke of   *Anne* February 1915, September 1915
   Wellington's Regiment   *Hardinge* June 1915
                                     Raven II July 1915

HUGHES, T. V. Lieut. (O) RFA (TF)   *Anne* April 1916

KEMPSON, W. R. Capt. (O) RFA   *Empress* July 1917, September 1917, October 1917, January 1918,
                                     February 1918
                                     City of Oxford November 1917, December 1917
                                     Raven II March 1917, April 1917, May 1917, June 1917, November 1917

KENNEDY, R. C. Lieut. (O) (Army)   *City of Oxford* February 1918, March 1918

KERRY, J. L. Sub. Lt. (O) RNVR   *Ben-my-Chree* July 1916, August 1916, September 1916, December 1916
                                     Anne August 1916, February 1917, March 1917
                                     Raven II August 1916, March 1917, April 1917, May 1917, June 1917
                                     Empress July 1917

KING, E. M. Flt. Lt. (P) RNAS   *Raven II* December 1916
                                     Anne January 1917
                                     Empress May 1917, June 1917, August 1917, September 1917, November 1917
                                     City of Oxford November 1917, February 1918, March 1918
KING, 2nd Lieut. (O) KOSB   *Ben-my-Chree* June 1916, August 1916, September 1916
                                     Raven II July 1916

KNIGHT-BRUCE, R. E. C. Capt. (O)   *Raven II* March 1917, April 1917
   Royal 1st Devon Yeomanry

LEDGER, H. M. C. Lieut. (O) IAR   *Raven II* June 1915, July 1915, August 1915
   Killed 22 December 1915   *Anne* September 1915, October 1915, November 1915, December 1915
                                     Hardinge June 1915

LEIGH, H. de. V. Flt. Lt. (P)   *Raven II* August 1916
   RNAS   *Ben-my-Chree* September 1916
                                     Anne February 1917, March 1917
                                     Empress May 1917, July 1917, October 1917, November 1917, January 1918
                                     City of Oxford October 1917, November 1917, February 1918, March 1918

LEISH, D. J. O. Lt. (O) RNVR   *City of Oxford* March 1918

LEVASSEUR, Julien Ldg Seaman (P)   *Anne* January 1915
    L'AMF

LLOYD, Air Mech. (O) RNAS   *Ben-my-Chree* December 1916

LOW, L. Air Mech. (O) RNAS   *City of Oxford* February 1918, March 1918

MALONE, C. J. L'E. Lt. (O) RN   *Raven II* August 1916
                                        Anne September 1916, October 1916

MAN, W. F/S/L. (P) RNAS   *Ben-my-Chree* April 1916, May 1916, June 1916, September 1916
                                        Raven II June 1916, July 1916, December 1916
                                        Anne August 1916

MASKELL, A. S. Flt. Lt. (P) RNAS   *Ben-my-Chree* April 1916, July 1916, August 1916, September 1916,
                                        November 1916, December 1916

MILLARD, V. Capt. (O) Essex   *Raven II* March 1916, April 1916, July 1916, August 1916
    Regiment   *Anne* September 1916, October 1916, March 1917
                                        Empress May 1917, June 1917, July 1917, September 1917, January 1918
                                        City of Oxford October 1917, November 1917, February 1918, March 1918
                                        Dufferin September 1916

MEADE, W. C. A. Lt. (O) RNVR   *Ben-my-Chree* December 1916
                                        Raven II April 1917

NEWTON, E. A. Lt. (O) ASC   *Empress* September 1917, October 1917
    Killed 11 October 1917

NIGHTINGALE, A. G. F/S/L (P) RNAS   *Ben-my-Chree* September 1916, November 1916, December 1916
    Killed 2 December 1916

PAINE, L. P. F/S/L (P) RNAS   *Ben-my-Chree* June 1916, July 1916
                                        Raven II August 1916
                                        Anne January 1916, January 1917

PAKENHAM-WALSH, G. H. 2nd Lieut. *Empress* June 1917, July 1917, August 1917, September 1917, January 1918
    (O) Cheshire Regiment   *Anne* February 1917, March 1917
    POW 28 January 1918   *Raven II* November 1917
                                        City of Oxford November 1917

PAUL, Sir R. J. Lieut. (O)   *Anne* February 1915, April 1915, September 1915, October 1915
    Special List   *Raven II* April 1915
    POW 10 October 1915

PENNINGTON, G. A. A. F/S/L (P)   *City of Oxford* February 1918, March 1918
    RNAS

PERRY, A. Air Mech. (O) RNAS   *City of Oxford* February 1918, March 1918

PICARD, Lt. (O) L'AMF

Ben-my-Chree July 1916

POPHAM, A. E. Flt. Lt. (P) RNAS

Empress October 1917, November 1917
City of Oxford November 1917

PRINCE, Ldg. Mech. (O) RNAS

Empress October 1917

RAVENSCROFT, Lieut. (O) RFA

Ben-my-Chree June 1916
Raven II July 1916

RISK, C. E. Sqdn. Cdr. (O) RMLI

Empress June 1917, August 1917, September 1917

ROBERTSON, W. Ldg. Mech.
    (O) RNAS

City of Oxford February 1918, March 1918

ROUSSILLON, Henri Ldg Seaman (P)
    L'AMF

Anne March 1916, April 1916

SAMSON, C. R. Wg. Cdr. (P) RNAS

Ben-my-Chree May 1916, June 1916, July 1916, August 1916,
September 1916, December 1916
Raven II March 1917, April 1917, May 1917, June 1917

SAMSON, W. L. Lt. (O) RNVR

Ben-my-Chree December 1916

SITWELL, W. G. Flt. Cdr (P) RNAS

Empress March 1917

SMITH, A. K. Lieut. (O) HLI

Anne April 1916
Ben-my-Chree May 1916, July 1916
Raven II August 1916

SMITH, G. D. Flt. Lt. (P) RNAS

Raven II July 1916, August 1916, March 1917, April 1917, May 1917,
June 1917
Anne September 1916, October 1916, February 1917, March 1917
Ben-my-Chree December 1916
Northbrook September 1916
Empress July 1917, October 1917, November 1917
City of Oxford November 1917, December 1917, February 1918, March 1918

STEPHENS, T. G. M. Flt. Lt. (P)
    RNAS

Raven II March 1917, April 1917, May 1917, June 1917
Empress October 1917, November 1917

STEWART, N. W. Lieut. (O) RS
    Killed 23 January 1917

Raven II June 1916, December 1916
Ben-my-Chree July 1916, November 1916
Anne August 1916, January 1917

STIRLING, F. Capt. (O)
    Dublin Fusiliers

Minerva December 1914

TODD, R. E. Capt. (O) RAMC

Anne January 1915, April 1915
Raven II April 1915

TROUILLET Petty Officer (P) L'AMF
    POW 10 October 1915

Anne February 1915, September 1915,
October 1915
Raven II August 1915

WEDDERSPOON, J. H. B. Lieut (O)   *Minerva* December 1914
    RFA   *Campinas* (French Seaplane Carrier) March 1916
                                            Ben-my-Chree June 1916

WEDGWOOD BENN, J. Lieut. (O)   *Ben-my-Chree* May 1916, June 1916, July 1916, August 1916,
    Middlesex Yeomanry   September 1916, November 1916, December 1916

WELDON, L. B. Capt. (O)   *Anne* January 1915, April 1915
    Dublin Fusiliers

WILLIAMS, E. Lieut. (O)   *Empress* March 1917
    East Yorkshire Regiment

WILLIAMS, K. L. Lieut. (O)   *Anne* April 1915, December 1915, January 1916, August 1916,
    2nd Rajputs   September 1916, October 1916, January 1917
                                            Raven II December 1915, January 1916, July 1916, August 1916,
                                            December 1916
                                            Ben-my-Chree March 1916
                                            Northbrook September 1916

WOOD, M. C. Flt. Lt. (P) RNAS   *Empress* July 1917, September 1917, October 1917
    Killed 11 October 1917

WOODLAND, P. M. Lt. (O) RNVR   *Ben-my-Chree* August 1916, November 1916, December 1916

WORRALL, H. V. Flt. Lt. (P) RNAS   *Raven II* December 1916, November 1917
                                            Empress April 1917, June 1917, August 1917, September 1917, November
                                            1917, January 1918, February 1918

WRIGHT, M. E. A. Flt. Lt. (P)   *Ben-my-Chree* January 1916, March 1916, May 1916, June 1916
    RNAS   *Anne* April 1916
                                            Raven II March 1916, April 1916

For simplicity the ranks of French aircrew of the EI & ESS have been recorded in R.N. style. Out of respect to these men, however, their equivalent ranks in the French Navy are given below:

R.N.rank	**French equivalent**	**Abbreviation**
Lieutenant	Lieutenant de Vaisseau	LV
Petty Officer	Maître	Mt
Ldg. Seaman	Quartier-maître	QM

APPENDIX IIC

Summary of operations by seaplane carriers of East Indies and Egypt Seaplane Squadron

HMS *ANNE* January 1915-March 1917

1915	January 1	Reconnaissance of El Arish
	January 18-23	Reconnaissance of Kosseima, El Arish, Rafa, Khan Yunis, Gaza. Land and recover Agent.
	January 25-28	Reconnaissance of El Arish. Recovery of abandoned seaplane.
	February 1-8	Reconnaissance of El Auja, El Arish, Beersheba, Hebron. Land Agent. Drop propaganda leaflets.
	February 24-March 11	Reconnaissance of Beersheba, Jaffa. To Gulf of Smyrna to spot for bombardment of Smyrna. Damaged by torpedo attack 11 March 1915.
	March 12-May 16	In Mudros harbour.
	May 17-June 18	In dry dock at Alexandria.
	July 7	A/S patrol off Borollos, Aboukir Bay.
	July 8-24	A/S patrol Pegodia Bay, Delaman Chai. Makri bombed. A/S patrols Bay of Marmarice.
	August 12-21	Reconnaissance of El Arish, Haifa. Schooner captured. Tarsus and Adana bombed. Reconnaissance of Osmanieh, Bageh. Chicaldere bridge bombed. Reconnaissance of Beirut to Damascus railway.
	August 30-September 4	Reconnaissance of El Arish. 3 Agents landed near Haifa. Reconnaissance of Haifa, Shafa 'Amr, Nazareth. Reconnaissance of Acre Bay for mines. Reconnaissance of Wadi Burshein, Ramleh, Nahr Sukereir.
	September 19-27	Reconnaissance of El Arish, Khan Yunis, Ludd, Ramleh, Jaffa. Reconnaissance opposite Ruad Island.
	October 9-16	Reconnaissance of Beersheba, Tel el Sharia, Gaza, Tartus.
	October 19-24	Reconnaissance of El Arish, Kheima, Ramleh. Reconnaissance of railway north of Ramleh.
	November 5-13	Reconnaissance of Beersheba, El Auja, Gaza. Agent landed at Athlit.
	c.December 8-12	Reconnaissance of railway between Mersina and Adana. Factory west of Mersina bombed.
	December 20-24	Reconnaissance of Khan Yunis, Rafa, Beersheba.
1916	January 10-23	Reconnaissance for mines and submarines Beirut harbour, El Mina Roads. Reconnaissance of El Arish, and railway between Ramleh and Tul Keram.
	January 31	Reconnaissance of railway between Tarsus and Osmanieh.

February 11	Reconnaissance of railway between El Auja and Beersheba.
March 7	Reconnaissance of Gebel Libni, El Auja, El Sirr.
c.March 15	Reconnaissance of Kosseima, El Auja, Rafa.
March 31	Reconnaissance of Port Said inundations (for defensive purposes).
April 16	Reconnaissance of Beersheba, Shellal, Gaza, El Arish.
April 19-24	Reconnaissance of Makri, Levisi from harbours at Castelorizo and Tersana. Reconnaissance of possible submarine bases at Ikinjik Liman, Marmarice. Karagach and Marmarice bombed.
May 3-9	Passage Port Said to Malta to return all French seaplanes to seaplane carrier *Campinas*.
June 15-July 11	Red Sea. Employed as transport for operations on Hejaz coast, transporting Egyptian artillery, mules and gold.
August 5-6	Reconnaissance of Deir el Belah, El Maaden, Rafa.
August 6-12	Spotting for bombardment of Mersina. Railway station at Mersina bombed.
August 25-27	Railway station at El Afule bombed. Bombing attacks on viaduct at Wadi el Hessi and on railway at Nablus and Ramleh.
September 1-October 26	Red Sea. Reconnaissance of Yembo, Rabegh, Umlejj. Spotting for bombardment of Wej. Reconnaissance of road from Medina to Rabegh.
1917 January 11-26	Red Sea. Reconnaissance of Diba, Muweilah. Spotting for bombardment of Wej. Reconnaissance from Marduna Island to locate Arab army.
February 26-March 1	Reconnaissance of Haifa Valley, Carmel range. Reconnaissance of railway to Zahle and Rayak, also Damascus.
March 21-23	Reconnaissance of Tabaun, Jenin, Nazareth and railway east and south of El Afule.
August	Paid off at Port Said.

Summary of operations by seaplane carriers of East Indies and Egypt Seaplane Squadron

HMS *RAVEN II* April 1915-November 1917

1915 April 7-12	Reconnaissance of El Arish, Beersheba. Spotting for bombardment off Gaza.
April 15-19	Reconnaissance of Gaza, Ramleh, Ludd, Jaffa. Propaganda leaflets dropped. Spotting for bombardment off El Arish.
April 20-30	Reconnaissance of Mersina, Tarsus, Adana, Topra Kalle, Osmanieh, Port Ayas, Alexandretta, Hamidri, Chicaldere, Missis.
May 19-26	Reconnaissance of El Arish, Beersheba, Gaza, Jaffa, Ludd, Ramleh. Jaffa,

Ludd, Ramleh bombed.

June 29-July 10	Bombing and reconnaissance of El Arish. Schooner captured. Reconnaissance of Akir, Beirut. Agent landed. Reconnaissance of Ramleh, Abu Hareira, Gaza.
July 14-28	Reconnaissance of El Arish, Gaza. A/S patrol Aboukir Bay. Reconnaissance of Samaria, Tul Keram, Haifa, Acre, Beirut. Two Schooners captured. Reconnaissance of Latakia.
August 16-22	Tarsus and Adana bombed. Chicaldere bridge bombed. Reconnaissance of Jaffa.

1915/16

December 28- January 6	Reconnaissance of Nazareth. Bombing and reconnaissance of Ramleh, Ludd, Jaffa.

1916

March 28-April 5	Red Sea. Reconnaissance of Waht, Lahej, Subar, Fiyush. Bombing attacks on Waht, Subar, Fiyush. Propaganda leaflets dropped.
April 25	Reconnaissance of El Arish, Bir Mazar.
June 7	Reconnaissance of El Arish.
June 22	Bombing and reconnaissance of El Arish.
June 26	Reconnaissance of El Arish.
July 1-9	Reconnaissance of El Arish. From Castelorizo and Tersana Island bombing and reconnaissance of Volos Island, Kalmaki, Port Vathi, Fakdir, Makri.
July 26- August 7	Photo-reconnaissance Gulf of Akaba. Reconnaissance of Muweilah, Sherm Yahar, Sherm Jubba, Wej.
August 9-10	Spotting for bombardment of Bir El Mazar.
August 24-28	Bombing attack on railway south of El Afule, and camp at Bureir. Reconnaissance of Adalia, Fineka Bay, Jeronda Bay for mines or submarines. Factory bombed at Adalia.
August 31	Damaged by bomb at Port Said.
October 26- December 20	Arrived at Sherm Rabegh, Red Sea. Reconnaissance of Yembo, Mubarak. Fort bombed at Wej.
December 25-29	Bombing attack on railway bridge at Chicaldere.

1917

March 10-June 12	Red Sea. Reconnaissance of Lahej Delta. Indian Ocean. Reconnaissance of Laccadive and Maldive Islands to search for German raider. Escort for convoy routed Colombo to Red Sea. Further reconnaissance of Lahej Delta.
October 31 - November 2	Spotting for bombardment of railway at Wadi el Hesi, Deir Sineid.
c.November/December	Paid off at Port Said.

Summary of operations by seaplane carriers of East Indies and Egypt Seaplane Squadron

HMS *BEN-my-CHREE* February 1916-January 1917

1916	February 10-11	Reconnaissance of Sidi Barrani, Sollum.
	March 7	Reconnaissance of Beersheba, Khan Yunis, Gaza.
	May 17-18	Bombing and reconnaissance at Gaza. Propaganda leaflets dropped. Spotting for bombardment of El Arish. Kahn Yunis bombed.
	May 23-27	Bombing and reconnaissance of Jaffa, Ramleh, Gaza, El Arish.
	June 2-21	Red Sea. Reconnaissance and bombing of Lahej, Waht, Fiyush, Subar, Sheikh Said, Jeddah. Spotting for fire of ships' guns.
	July 6-11	Bombing and reconnaissance of El Arish, Beirut, Tel Keli, Tartus, Nahr el Kebir. Spotting for fire of ships' guns. Bombing and reconnaissance of Haifa, Acre.
	July 23-27	Reconnaissance of Gaza, El Shellal, Beersheba, Khan Yunis, El Arish. Reconnaissance of roads between Bir el Mazar and El Arish. Reconnaissance of Haifa, El Afule, Nablus, Jaffa, Ludd, Ramleh, Samaria, Falugeh. Railway at El Afule, Arak el Mensbiyeh bombed.
	August 14-15	Reconnaissance of Haifa Valley, El Afule, Ludd, Ramleh, Nahr Sukereir, Falugeh, Bureir, Shellal. Bombing attacks on El Afule railway junction, Tabaun, Jeida. Reconnaissance of roads between El Arish and Bir el Mazar.
	August 24-30	Bombing attacks on railway stations at El Afule and Homs, and viaduct over Wadi el Hesi. Reconnaissance of railway between Homs and Tripoli. Tel Keli bombed. Bombing attacks on Adana railway station and on dhows and lighters west of Karatash Burnu.
	September 13-14	Reconnaissance of Gaza, Beersheba, Shellal.
	September 16-17	Spotting for bombardment south of El Arish. Reconnaissance of El Arish.
	November 2-5	Reconnaissance of Turkish batteries at Adalia and opposite Castelorizo. Spotting for bombardment of batteries.
	December 1-3	Reconnaissance of Haifa, Tabaun, El Afule, Caesarea, Samaria, Jaffa, Ludd, Ramleh, Falugeh, Jenin, Gaza.
	December 21-23	Reconnaissance of Gaza, Falugeh, Jaffa, Haifa Valley. Tabaun bombed.
	December 26	Bombing attack on Chicaldere bridge.
1917	January 9	Shelled by Turkish batteries opposite Castelorizo and abandoned.

Summary of operations by seaplane carriers of East Indies and Egypt Seaplane Squadron

HMS *EMPRESS* March 1917-February 1918

1917	March 6-7	Reconnaissance of Tul Keram, Nablus, Ludd, Ramleh, Falugeh.
	April 17	A/S patrol off Deir el Belah.
	May 12-13	Bombing attack on Beirut harbour.
	June 22-23	Bombing attack on railway junction at Tul Keram.
	July 14-16	Bombing attack on factories north-west of Adana.
	August 16-18	Bombing attack on Beirut harbour.
	September 26-28	Spotting for bombardment of Beirut harbour. Bombing attack on Beirut harbour.
	October 8-12	Bombing attacks on Chicaldere railway bridge and locomotive sheds at Adana.
	November 1-3	Bombing attacks on Jaljulye railway bridge and oil refinery at Haifa.
1918	January 24-February 4	Bombing attacks at night on German battlecruiser *Goeben* aground off Nagara Point.

Summary of operations by seaplane carriers of East Indies and Egypt Seaplane Squadron

HMS *CITY OF OXFORD* October 1917-March 1918

1917	October 29-November 9	Spotting for bombardment of railway junction south of Deir Sineid, ammunition dump and bridge over Wadi el Hesi. Spotting for bombardment of batteries at El Nezele and roads through Deir Sineid. Spotting for bombardment of railway junction at Julis, trenches north-east of Askalon and railway at Bruberah.
1918	February 13-March 29	Red Sea. Bombing attacks on Jebel Al Milh, Beit Al Mokhay, Zohrah. Reconnaissance of Habil, Midi, Loheiya, Salif.

APPENDIX IID

Extracts from diary of Flt Lt (Later Flt Cdr) G. B. Dacre, DSO, RNAS, 1916

January 10   (HMS *Ben-my-Chree* at Mudros)
Coaled ship and received orders to proceed to sea at 1600 for Port Said. So we are about to start in a new theatre of war.

January 12   Arrived at Port Said about 0900. The place looks very much like Ostend from the sea.

A French Nieuport seaplane heralded our entry, but we evidently will have to show them how to fly.

January 18   We swung all the machines for compass corrections at the French seaplane base.

January 19   Left harbour at 2300 and steamed eastwards.

January 20   Arrived off El Arish. Here we could see a mosque, date palms and everywhere sand dunes. Edmonds was hoisted out with Childers for a reconnaissance over the desert 40 miles inland. This desert flying is no joke as it depends entirely on one's engine. There is just a chance that a seaplane of our type can be landed without doing in pilot and passenger.

Edmonds and Childers returned after one and three quarter hours bringing back valuable information and photographs. Very few troops are about so it looks as if the whole attack is a great big bluff. The whole show out here depends on our reconnaissance, and the only way to know what the Turks are up to is to find out by either unreliable agents or by our reconnaissance.

I then went up with Childers and a machine gun, and getting off a bad lop made for shore at 1000 feet. Here we saw several camels sitting down so I came down to 50 feet and Childers eased off the machine gun. The bullets hit up the sand all around but the camels got up. Two men came running up and started to run off at the double with the camels. I circled round again low and the men left the camels and ran. We eased off the machine gun again and the bullets spattered in the sand. One man dropped but no camels appeared to be hit. Jolly fine sport.

I then got into a squall and had a hard fight with the machine flying down to the agreed rendezvous, but no ship was there and I only had half an hour's petrol left. Anyhow I saw the ship 15 miles east of the agreed spot. The sea was very bad when I landed and I pushed an internal strut up through. Edmonds broke his chassis in the morning on landing. With great difficulty and much depreciation to the machine I got to the ship and broke my propeller alongside when a wave carried me on to it. Went back to Port Said at night.

January 23   Seaplane carrier *Empress* arrived this morning.

January 28   Bankes-Price 21 today so we had fizz for dinner.

January 29   Went to sea at 2300. The skipper was appointed an Acting Commander - more fizz.

January 30   Arrived off Gaza in the early morning in unsettled weather. Wright with Childers went off for a reconnaissance to Beersheba but got into clouds and had to return. However, they went off again at 1200 when the weather improved and returned safely at 1330 with valuable information.

January 31   At 0730 I ran my engine prior to an inland reconnaissance but found it dudd. After working on it until midday it improved and I was hoisted out 15 miles north of Jaffa, and getting off a bad sea went inland at 1500. Childers was with me and our object was to steer a compass course and strike the railway 12 miles inland at Tul Keram, and fly down it southwards to Ludd. We fetched up 8 miles in, over 2 villages north of our objective. Here my engine which was pretty dudd from the start started to develop trouble and drop revolutions. So not wanted to come to a sudden end by a forced descend on land I had to retrace my track to the sea and thence to the ship.

Edmonds and Childers went out later, and starting from where we finished off did a fine flight down the railway and struck the coast again a little north of Gaza after over 2 hours inland flying. We then packed up and returned to Port Said.

February 9   Taking 2 Army Sub's as observers aboard, we left Port Said for Alexandria at 2100.

February 10   After a very rolly passage we arrived in fine weather at Alexandria at 0900. We took aboard a General, a Commander and a Captain for our trip to the Gulf of Sollum, where the Senussis have given us trouble and driven us from our frontier outpost. We left Alex. in company with an Italian destroyer at 1700.

February 11   Arrived off the Gulf of Sollum at 0930 where a good wind was blowing and on the increase. However Edmonds and Childers were hoisted out and got off the water within 5 minutes. The General was awfully bucked. They were to be away one and a half to 2 hours. The wind was increasing and at the end of 2 hours we began to look out for them. After 3 hours we knew they must be down and feared the worst, as the sea by now was impossible for a seaplane to live in.

We steamed at full speed up and down the coast, but a sandstorm almost blotted out the coast. At 1400, much to our relief, a trawler hove in sight with Edmonds and Childers aboard in shirt sleeves. They had lost the ship in the mist and flew on until their petrol gave out, and after landing and smashing in the heavy sea they clung to the wreckage and could only have lasted 10 minutes longer when a trawler saw them and picked them up.

We went eastwards, and after inspecting an outpost station from the sea sailed for Alex. again. A trawler patrol challenged us but of course we didn't see it and they rightly put a shot across our bows. We turned and signalled to them "Who's your captain?" Their reply was "Jellicoe. Who's yours?" Some lads these trawler patrol fellows.

February 15   *Empress* started well by crashing a big Short. Pilot Clifford and observer unhurt. Wreckage towed back.

February 21   I busied myself at the new air base where we are getting things into order. Rigging masts for wireless, 2 aeroplane tents, one for men's mess, one for officers' mess, and 5 bell tents were erected. A dark room is being erected, galley, and a motor ambulance and a motor travelling workshop have been carted to the Island.

February 22   Got one new Short machine and 2 new Schneiders in several cases ashore at the base with the help of Arab labour. We also rigged up a fine field bakery by utilising old tipping trucks with one end biffed out. The existing Turkish Shed is having the entrance made bigger to house 4 big Shorts.

February 24   Busy at the shore station getting enormous crates full of seaplanes ashore with a small crane, removing parts of seaplanes and putting the crates aside for our living quarters.

February 29   We commissioned the shore station. Flt. Cdr. Crocker in command.

March 3   Two new machines in 6 cases arrived very badly damaged, about £10,000 damage. Later 2 more Schneiders arrived, so now we have 9 machines here. The new shed is rapidly being erected, and my hut (half a seaplane case) is rapidly becoming a palacial residence.

March 6   We learnt that Crocker had been fatally injured by a tram last night on his way back. He apparently got caught between shunting trams and got squeezed.

April 3   Did some instructional flying with Man. Man and Maskell did practice flights on 846. Maskell did a forced landing on the swell and crashed my old 846. Only the engine and a few fittings were recovered.

April 10   *Raven* party returned having done good work near Aden, where they dropped 90 bombs on Turkish camps. Edmonds had a narrow squeak by a bullet grazing his cheek, and all the others had shot holes through their machines.

[Ben-my-Chree, following her collision with SS *Uganda* on 19 February, had been in dry dock at Suez for repairs between 12 March-24 April, which explains the lack of operations during this period covered by the diary]

June 30   Left Depot for 10 days in *Raven II* with 2 Shorts and 2 Schneiders for a very interesting stunt. Pilots were Brooke and Man, observers Ravenscroft, Brown and King, Engineer Officer Fill, 25 air mechanics, armourers and photographer, myself in command. After a merry evening in Port Said we all repaired aboard.

July 1   Left Port Said in *Raven II* at 0630 and doing 9 knots in company with the armed tug *Laborieux* arrived at 1630 at a position 15 miles off El Arish - the Hun's nest which is the worst part of our work. I took up Brown as observer, and both of us were nearly sea sick before we left the water, spreading the planes of the old Short on a considerable swell.

                Brooke went out on a Schneider and skillfully got off the swell with his bombs.

                In the heat of the afternoon the Sunbeam boiled its water after 3 or 4 minutes in the air, and I had to throttle down and down until the 1000 feet which I had attained lessened to 900, the oil getting hot also.

                We got to 3 miles from the coast when it was necessary to return. We then got hoisted in, and Brooke returned soon after having made a good reconnaissance and dropped one of his bombs on the ammunition store. He was very heavily fired on by Archies and high explosive but managed to dodge them. No Huns came out after him or the ship as is the Hun's custom. We left this position about 1830.

July 2   Arrived off Haifa at 0600. I was hoisted out with Ravenscroft as observer, bombs and Lewis gun. We crashed into the atmosphere in company with Man in the Schneider and made a reconnaissance of Haifa district at 2000 feet. We dropped one small bomb on a road bridge and just missed it. We then went north and flew around Acre, the place from where my name is supposed to originate in the Crusader days. We dropped one small bomb on the railway bridge there and missed it.

                Flying back over Haifa I had to descend to 1800 feet to avoid black clouds. Here I let go a 112 lb bomb at a large shed on the railway pier. This large bomb went off within 15 yards in the water alongside the shed with a terrific explosion, chucking mud and water everywhere. We passed back close to the Convent on the high hill and waved in case there were any nice nuns there.

                On being hoisted in I learned that Man had not returned, so after a short while waiting it was certain he must be down somewhere. The ship closed to 8 miles from the coast and the escort went in closer. I ordered out the Short again, lightened with less fuel, taking Brown with me to use the Lewis gun if necessary and to render Man assistance if necessary. We discovered the Schneider in a sinking condition under the wall of Acre, and funnily enough no boat had gone out to him, nor were there many people on the beach. I landed alongside, and Man who was standing on the planes that were out of the water dived in and swam to the Short. We then eased off 47 rounds at the Schneider to make certain it would not fall into the enemy's hands. As Man was wet I packed him on the floor of the passenger seat out of the wind, while Brown sat astride the petrol tank to preserve the balance of the machine. This position was most cramped and uncomfortable, being just behind the hot air off the radiator. However Brown seemed to like it, and 3 up we flew back to the ship unmolested - rather like a cinema stunt, and Man lost his visit to Constantinople. Hoisting in, we packed up and left for Famagusta.

July 3   Arrived at Famagusta at dawn where we squeezed into the tiny harbour. The ship had all day been unloading coal on to the jetty for *Ben-my-Chree* to pick up when she arrives here.

July 4   Uncoaling went on until 1800. At 1830 we squeezed out of the harbour entrance again on our way to Castelorizo.

July 5   Still at sea on our way to Castelorizo doing our 9 knots.

July 6   Arrived at Castelorizo, now under French occupation, at daybreak. I went and saw the Governor and the Intelligence Officer who were both very affable. In the evening I went out on a Schneider and saw very little but mountains, but dropped my bombs on an outpost which caused a scrub fire. This fire spread rapidly and by night lit up the places for miles. A fine sight indeed and very impressive for the natives of Castelorizo.

              Next day a reconnaissance involving 3 hours had to be done, so knowing the unreliability of the Sunbeam I decided to form an advanced base at Tersana Island, an island a few hundred yards off the mainland, the inhabitants of which are friendly but treacherous. It was too dangerous to take *Raven II* to this submarine infested area, so I told off *Laborieux* with stores and mechanics to go to this island in advance. The Governor kindly told off trawler patrols on the journey there in case we came down.

July 7   I sent Man out in the Schneider to fly straight to Tersana at daybreak, while I went in the Short taking Ravenscroft as observer to do the journey and make a reconnaissance on the way. The engine boiled very quickly and I could only get to 500 feet. Mountains 3000 feet high went right down to the shore, so I dropped 3 of my bombs into the sea to lighten the machine and flying on got to 1800 feet over Makri district where important reconnaissance was to take place. We took photos, dropped bombs and got a few rifles fired at us in return. Then on and landed at Tersana, where I taxied into the creek and ran aground before reaching the shore. The astonished natives looked on in amazement, and offered coffee and got more in the way than anything in their efforts to assist. The Schneider had not turned up and I was beginning to wonder what had happened to Man again when he arrived, having struck the wrong island and found out his mistake. Soon after *Laborieux* arrived and we enjoyed a breakfast.

              During the afternoon we found the Short's float full of water. Several hours had to be spent pumping it out, but Man and his observer Brown were not able to get off with it as water got in again rapidly. I went off to Makri in the Schneider and dropped bombs on an important concrete works which had been constructed for submarines. One was a direct hit. I established a signal station on top of the hill to keep a look out on machines.

July 8   The Short was a nuisance, as it was not possible to get it back by flying. There were only rocky beaches, so it couldn't be hauled up, and it was dangerous to get *Raven II* up. I either had to burn it and leave it, or take it to bits on the water and get it somehow onto the tug. This was done by strengthening the boat davits and hauling the machine as high as possible, taking off one pair of wings, floating and hauling them aboard, then removing the floats and got many men onto them to sink them clear of the body. The body and left planes were then trussed up to the tug's side with the tail hauled up out of the water, and thus we rolled heavily back to Castelorizo. The wing tip dipped on every roll, but beyond one wing tip float being broken, no damage was done.

              At Castelorizo *Laborieux* was moored alongside *Raven II* and together the parts of the Short were transferred.

              We left at 1700 and July 10 saw us back in Port Said.

August 5   Left Port Said in *Anne* with one Short aboard to make a reconnaissance of Rafa and the coastal road. Hoisted out with Stewart as observer at 1530 and got off a swell. Rose to 2000 feet at the coast and went in over Khan Yunis where photos were taken. Engine went dud and we got beaten down by the bad bumps to 1000 feet. Got to Rafa with a struggle and after photographing it went out again to sea. We opened up the Lewis gun on a herd of pack camels and were glad to be over the sea again, and eventually hoisted aboard. No Huns came out.

August 6   Man with Kerry as observer went up near El Arish and Lake Bardawil to make a reconnaissance and returned reporting all clear. Returned to Port Said.

August 7   Hun came over Port Said and dropped bombs on the town. Two straddled the Island without hitting it.

Left once more in *Anne*, with one Short and a Schneider to be erected at sea, for Mersina for spotting operations with the French ships.

August 10   Arrived at dawn off Mersina where we picked up the French cruiser *Pothuau* and many patrol vessels. *Laborieux* led in towards Mersina sweeping for mines, *Pothuau* following with ourselves next. We anchored 2 miles off and hoisted out. I took up Stewart as observer, carrying wireless sending and receiving sets. Man did a submarine patrol in the Schneider.

[No further entries in Dacre's diary, and *Anne* returned to Port Said on 12 August. Dacre's Short 184 suffered engine failure on a flight to Bureir on 26 August and he was taken prisoner, spending many months as a POW]

Flt Cdr G. B. Dacre's diary commences in 1915, but only those entries concerned with EI and ESS operations have been quoted, by kind permission of the Fleet Air Arm Museum. Other entries concerned with the Dardanelles and with aspects of life ashore make informative and amusing reading.

HMS Ben-my-Chree, possibly at Famagusta. Bags piled on the quayside may contain coal. Famagusta was used as a coaling station by the seaplane carriers of the EI & ESS. GSL/JMB)

APPENDIX IIE

Administration of HM Ships *Anne* and *Raven II* from June 1915

The work in which the two ships were engaged, and the fact of providing them with armament necessitated the addition of naval ratings, and commissioning the ships under the White Ensign.

The naval ratings came under the Naval Discipline Act and were paid entirely by the Navy.

The Captain of *Anne* (J. Kerr) was granted a temporary commission as a Lt. RNR, his salary as such being £21.5.0 per month from the Navy, made up by the addition of £13.5.0 from the Ports and Lights Administration to his former salary.

For the sake of uniformity the salary of the Captain of *Raven II* (J. Jenkins), who was already a Lt. RNR, was augmented from the Ports and Lights Administration to the same figure.

Besides the two Captains, the complements of the two ships were as follows:

HMS *Anne*.	Executive Branch:	2 Sub. Lts's RNR, 1 Midshipman RNR, 1 CPO, 1 Ldg. Seaman, 1 Signalman all paid by the Navy. 15 AB's and 6 Syrian Boatmen (POW's) all paid by Ports and Lights.
	Engine Room Branch:	1 Lt. (E) RNR, 2nd, 3rd, and 4th Engineers all paid by the Navy. 1 Fitter, 2 Greasers, 8 Firemen, 3 Trimmers all paid by Ports and Lights.
	Daymen:	1 Chief Steward paid by the Navy. 3 Stewards, 1 Pantry Boy, 2 Cooks, 1 Crew's Cook all paid by Ports and Lights. 1 Wireless Operator lent from RE.
HMS *Raven II*.	Executive Branch:	2 Sub. Lt's RNR, 1 Midshipman RNR, 1 CPO, 1 PO, 2 Ldg. Seamen, 1 Signalman all paid by the Navy. 18 AB's and 7 Syrian Boatmen (POW's) all paid by Ports and Lights.
	Engine Room Branch:	1 Lt. (E) RNR, 1 Sub. Lt. (E) RNR, 3rd and 4th Engineers, 1 PO Stoker, 1 Stoker all paid by the Navy. 1 Fitter, 6 Greasers, 7 Firemen, 3 Trimmers all paid by Ports and Lights.
	Daymen:	1 Chinese Carpenter, 1 Chief Steward, 2 Stewards, 1 Mess Boy, 2 Pantry Boys, 1 Chief Cook, 2nd and 3rd Cooks, 1 Baker, all paid by Ports and Lights. 1 Wireless Operator lent from RE.

To place all personnel not in HM Service on a service footing, all such ratings signed on on Form T124. Victualling of the ships was paid for by the Ports and Lights Administration at between £200 and £230 per month.

APPENDIX IIF

Brief details of French warships operating in conjunction with EI and ESS 1915-1917

Amiral Charner	Armoured Cruiser. 4700 tons/completed 1895. $18^1/_2$ knots. 2 x 7.6'', 6 x 5.5'', 4 x 9-pounder.
Arbalette	Destroyer. 318/03. 31 knots. 1 x 65 mm, 6 x 47 mm, 2 TT.
Campinas	Seaplane Carrier. 3319/97. $11^1/_2$ knots. 2 hangars for 6 seaplanes.
Coutelas	Destroyer. 356/08. 29 knots. 1 x 9 pounder, 6 x 3-pounder, 2 TT.
Dard	Destroyer. 318/03. 31 knots. 1 x 65 mm, 6 x 47 mm, 2 TT.
D'Entrecasteaux	Protected Cruiser. 8114/98. $19^1/_2$ knots. 2 x 9.4'', 12 x 5.5'', 12 x 3-pounder.
D'Estrèes	3rd Class Cruiser. 2450/99. 21 knots. 2 x 5.5'', 4 x 3.9''
Dupleix	Armoured Cruiser. 7700/03. 21 knots 8 x 6.6'', 4 x 3.9'', 10 x 3-pounder
Foudre	Seaplane Carrier. 5971/96. 19 knots 8 x 3.9'', 4 x 9-pounder
Hache	Destroyer. 356/08. 29 knots 1 x 9 pounder, 6 x 3-pounder, 2 TT
Jauréguiberry	Battleship. 11900/96. 29 knots 2 x 12'', 2 x 10.8'', 8 x 5.5'', 4 x 9-pounder
Jeanne D'Arc	Armoured Cruiser. 11270/03. 23 knots 2 x 7.6'', 14 x 5.5'', 16 x 3-pounder
Laborieux	Armed Tug.
Montcalm	Armoured Cruiser. 9500/01. 21 knots 2 x 7.6'', 8 x 6.5'', 2 x 9-pounder
Nord Caper	Armed Trawler.
Paris II	Armed Trawler. 1 x 47 mm
Pierrier	Destroyer. 356/08. 29 knots 1 x 9 pounder, 6 x 3-pounder, 2 TT
Pothuau	Armoured Cruiser. 5365/96. 19 knots 2 x 7.6'', 10 x 5.5'', 12 x 3-pounder.

Requin	Coast Defence Ship. 7740/88. 12 knots
	2 x 10.8'', 6 x 3.9'', 10 x 3-pounder
St.Louis	Battleship. 11300/00. 18 knots
	4 x 12'', 10 x 5.5'', 8 x 3.9'', 20 x 3-pounder
Voltigeur	Destroyer. 450/10. 28 knots
	6 x 9-pounder, 3 TT

HMY Managem which besides providing escort for ships of the EI & ESS was mainly engaged in intelligence gathering and landing Agents along the Syrian Coast between February 1917 and October 1918. (via RCC)

Lt Cain RNR commanding HMY Managem is seated in the middle of the centre row with Capt L.B.Weldon, the Ship's Intelligence Officer on his left together with the rest of the ship's company. (via RCC)

APPENDIX IIG

Brief details of ships comprising the Caspian Flotilla 1919

Alader Youssanoff	Gross tonnage 2071. Built 1905. Tanker, converted to Seaplane Carrier. Armament: 2 x 6'', 2 seaplanes.
Asia	Gross tonnage 1331. Built 1898. Tanker, converted to AMC. Armament: 4 x 4 ''.
Bibi Eibat	Gross tonnage 1112. Built 1894. Tanker, converted to AMC. Armament: 3 x 4''.
Dublin Castle	Gross tonnage 1482. Built 1897. Tanker, converted to AMC. Armament: 2 x 6''.
Edinburgh Castle	Gross tonnage 1309. Built 1903. Tanker, converted to AMC. Armament: 1 x 4.7'', 2 x 4''
Emile Nobel	Displacement 5280 tons. Built 1909. Motor tanker, converted to AMC. Armament: 3 x 6'', 1 x 4.7''.
Orlionoch	Gross tonnage 1406. Built 1888. Tanker, converted to Seaplane Carrier. Armament: 1 x 4'', 1 x 3''. 2 seaplanes.
President Kruger	Gross tonnage 2177. Built 1902. Passenger vessel converted to AMC. Armament: 5 x 4''
Sergie	Gross tonnage 1642. Built 1894. Tanker, converted to CMB carrier. Armament: 1 x 3'', 2 CMB's.
Slava	Gross tonnage 1690. Built 1903. Tanker, converted to AMC. Armament: 1 x 6'', 1 x 4''.
Venture	Gross tonnage 1386. Built 1899. Tanker, converted to AMC. Armament: 3 x 4''.
Windsor Castle	Gross tonnage 1195. Built 1894. Tanker, converted to AMC. Armament: 4 x 4''.

Armament of these ships varied from time to time, but the above listing is typical for most of 1919. Six CMBs of 40 feet in length and six CMB's of 50 feet in length were also operated by the Caspian Flotilla during this period.

APPENDIX IIH

Summary of seaplanes and pilots embarked in HM ships engaged in anti-Zeppelin patrols in North Sea
June 1915 - July 1917.

SCHNEIDER

1446	*Kingfisher* 6.15, 7.15; *Sir John French* 7.15
1447	*St.Germain* 5.15, 6.15
3708	*St.Germain* 6.15
3710	*Jerico* 8.15, 9.15; *Kingfisher* 8.15; *Sir John French* 9.15
3715	*Kingfisher* 8.15, 9.15; *Jerico* 8.15, 10.15; *Sir John French* 10.15
3720	*Kingfisher* 9.15; *Sir John French* 9.15, 10.15; *Jerico* 10.15, 11.15
3723	*Sir John French* 9.15; *Kingfisher* 9.15, 12.15; *Jerico* 10.15
3736	*Brocklesby* 8.16
3776	*Brocklesby* 4.16
3801	*Killingholme* 9.16

BABY

8120	*Jerico* 10.15; *Kingfisher* 11.15, 1.16, 2.16; *Cantatrice* 2.16
8122	*Cantatrice* 3.16, 4.16
8131	*Killingholme* 10.16
8133	*Halcyon* 12.16, 1.17, 2.17, 3.17
8139	*Kingfisher* 3.16, 4.16
8140	*Cantatrice* 3.16, 3.16
8141	*Killingholme* 4.16, 5.16, 8.16, 9.16
8142	*Killingholme* 4.16, 5.16
8147	*Killingholme* 4.16; Wrecked 29.4.16
8148	*Killingholme* 4.16, 5.16, 8.16; *Brocklesby* 9.16
8149	*Christopher* 5.16; *Brocklesby* 8.16; *Halcyon* 4.17
8150	*Brocklesby* 4.16; *Kingfisher* 5.16; *Halcyon* 2.17; *Dryad* 3.17, 6.17
8154	*Killingholme* 4.16
8155	*Killingholme* 4.16
8156	*Cantatrice* 3.16
8157	*Kingfisher* 3.16
8159	*Dryad* 6.17
8160	*Brocklesby* 4.16
8163	*Cantatrice* 3.16
8164	*Brocklesby* 4.16; *Kingfisher* 4.16; *Killingholme* 5.16
8173	*Kingfisher* 4.16
8174	*Killingholme* 4.16
8207	*Killingholme* 9.16
N1066	*Dryad* 6.17; *Halcyon* 9.17
N1108	*Dryad* 7.17

PILOTS

Beare, S.C.	Flt Sub Lt	*Christopher* 5.16
Bittles, G.H.	Flt Sub Lt	*Kingfisher* 4.16, 5.16; *Brocklesby* 4.16, 8.16; *Halcyon* 2.17, 3.17; *Dryad* 7.17
Brenton, H.B.	Flt Sub Lt	*Dryad* 6.17
Cadbury, E.	Flt Sub Lt	*Kingfisher* 12.15, 1.16, 2.16, 3.16, 4.16
Davies, W.A.	Flt Sub Lt	*Brocklesby* 4.16
Halsted, F.N.	Flt Sub Lt	*Cantatrice* 3.16, 4.16
Hards, F.G.D.	Flt Lt	*Cantatrice* 3.16
Ireland, W.P.de C.	Flt Cdr	*Kingfisher* 6.15

Lister, T.V.	Flt Sub Lt	*St.Germain* 6.15
Marlowe, A.F.	Flt Sub Lt	*Brocklesby* 4.16; *Kingfisher* 4.16
Murray, L.E.R.	Flt Sub Lt	*Halcyon* 12.16
Nicholl, V.	Flt Lt	*Kingfisher* 6.15, 7.15, 8.15, 9.15, 11.15, 3.16; *Sir John French* 7.15, 9.15, 10.15; *Jerico* 10.15
Northrop, J.C.	Flt Sub Lt	*Brocklesby* 9.16
Smith, H.B.	Flt Sub Lt	*Kingfisher* 8.15, 9.15; *Jerico* 8.15, 9.15, 10.15; *Sir John French* 9.15; *Brocklesby* 8.16, 9.16; *Halcyon* 12.16, 1.17, 2.17, 4.17; *Dryad* 6.17
Wood, C.E.	Flt Lt	*Cantatrice* 2.16, 3.16

The Aberdeen trawler Norland was probably similar to HMS Cantatrice which operated a Baby on Anti-Zeppelin patrols in the North Sea during 1916, and for which no photograph is available. (S. Pulfrey)

PUBLISHED SOURCES

The following publications have been read and are useful:

Barnes, C H	Shorts Aircraft Since 1900. Putnam 1967
Blumberg, General Sir H E	Britain's Sea Soldiers 1914-1919. Swiss & Co 1927
Burns, I M	Cross and Cockade Vol 6/4, 7/1. 1975/76
Bruce, J M	British Aeroplanes 1914-1918. Putnam 1957
Colledge, J J	Ships of the Royal Navy Vols 1 and 2. David & Charles 1969/70

Conways All The World's Fighting Ships 1860-1905 and 1906-1921.
Conway Maritime Press 1979 and 1985

Corbett and Newbolt	Naval Operations, Various Vols. Longman's 1920-1931
Couhat, J L	French Warships of WWI. Ian Allen
Davies, R. Bell	Sailor in the Sky. Peter Davies 1967
Halpern, P G	The Naval War In The Mediterranean 1914-1918. Allen & Unwin 1987
Hughes, C E	Above And Beyond Palestine. Ernest Benn 1930
Jane's Fighting Ships	Various Vols between 1905-06 and 1919. Sampson Low Marston
Layman, R D	To Ascend From A Floating Base. Farleigh Dickson 1979
Melhorn, C M	Two Block Fox. US Naval Institute 1974
Moore, Major W G	Early Bird. Putnam 1963
Nowra, Robertson & Cooksley	Marine Aircraft Of The 1914-18 War. Harleyford 1966
The Naval Review	Vols 7 & 8

Raleigh and Jones   The War In The Air, Various Vols.
                                    HMSO

Robertson, B   Sopwith, The Man And His Aircraft.
                                    Harleyford 1970

Roskill, S W   Documents Relating to the Naval Air Service, Vol 1.
                                    Navy Records Society 1969

Samson, C R   Fights And Flights.
                                    Ernest Benn 1933

Snowden Gamble, C F   The Story Of A North Sea Air Station.
                                    Neville Spearman 1967 (reprint)

Temple Patterson, A   Tyrwhitt Of The Harwich Force.
                                    MacDonald 1973

Usborne, C V   Smoke On The Horizon.
                                    Hodder & Stoughton 1933

Wedgwood Benn, J   In The Sideshows.
                                    Hodder & Stoughton 1919

Weldon, L B   Hard Lying (Typescript).
                                    Cairo 1923

Young, D   Rutland Of Jutland.
                                    Cassell 1963

HMS Teazer towing a Lighter H2 with a Felixtowe F.2A on board. Teazer towed a similar flying boat into action on 11 June 1918 in Heligoland Bight. (NMM N11719)

UNPUBLISHED   SOURCES

AWMRC   Australian War Memorial Research Centre
FAAM   Fleet Air Arm Museum
IWM   Imperial War Museum
NMM   National Maritime Museum
PRO   Public Record Office
RAFM   Royal Air Force Museum

HMS *Alader Youssanoff*   ADM.137/1740. PRO
    Caspian 1919   ADM.137/1741. PRO
                        ADM.137/1742. PRO
                        ADM.137/2287 Paper No 489. PRO
                        CNH Bilney Papers. DS/MISC/86.CNB1. IWM
                        Naval Review Vol VII. NMM
                        Naval Review Vol VIII. NMM
                        Capt J A Sadler Log. DC/76/77/2. RAFM

HMY *Albion III*   ADM.53/33749. PRO
    1917   ADM.53/33750. PRO
                        AIR.1/304/15/226/153. PRO

HMS *Angora*   ADM.53/33749. PRO
    1917   ADM.53/33750. PRO
                        AIR.1/304/15/226/153. PRO

HMS *Anne*   AIR.1/271/15/226/119. PRO
    EI and ESS. 1915/17   AIR.1/361/15/228/50. PRO
                        AIR.1/648/17/122/391. PRO
                        AIR.1/654/17/122/503. PRO
                        AIR.1/667/17/122/736. PRO
                        AIR.1/1708/204/123/72. PRO
                        AIR.1/1708/204/123/73. PRO
                        AIR.1/1709/204/123/76. PRO
                        AIR.1/1709/204/123/77. PRO
                        AIR.1/1711/204/123/89. PRO
                        AIR.1/1719/204/123/182. PRO
                        AIR.1/2285/209/75/13. PRO
                        Capt L B Weldon Typescript

HMS *Arethusa*   AIR.1/189/15/226/6. PRO
    1915   AIR.1/190/15/226/7. PRO
                        AIR.1/193/15/226/10. PRO
                        AIR.1/194/15/226/11. PRO

HMS *Ark Royal*   ADM.53/34109. PRO
    January 1915 -   AIR.1/726/137/2. PRO
    January 1916,
    February 1919

HMS *Aurora*   AIR.1/189/15/226/6. PRO
    March - November 1915   AIR.1/193/15/226/10. PRO
                        AIR.1/194/15/226/11. PRO
                        AIR.1/202/15/226/19. PRO

HMAS *Australia* 1917/18	AIR.1/334/15/226/240. PRO AIR.1/335/15/226/242. PRO AIR.1/336/15/226/245. PRO *Australia*'s Signal Logs January/November 1918. AWMRC Flt Cdr D G Donald's Flying Logbook. FAAM
HMS *Ben-my-Chree* EI and ESS. 1916	ADM.53/35190. PRO ADM.53/35191. PRO ADM.53/35192. PRO ADM.116/1353. PRO AIR.1/361/15/228/50. PRO AIR.1/660/17/122/620. PRO AIR.1/665/17/122/714. PRO AIR.1/667/17/122/736. PRO AIR.1/1707/204/123/68. PRO AIR.1/1707/204/123/69. PRO AIR.1/1708/204/123/70. PRO AIR.1/1709/204/123/76. PRO AIR.1/1709/204/123/77. PRO AIR.1/2314/23/12. PRO Cross & Cockade Journal Vol 7 No 1 (I M Burns) Summary of Work 17 May - 29 December 1916, Cdr C R Samson. (via I.M.Burns)
HMY *Beryl* 1917	ADM.53/35316. PRO AIR.1/304/15/226/153. PRO
HMS *Birkenhead* 1918	AIR.1/336/15/226/245. PRO
HMS *Brocklesby* 1916	ADM.53/69478. PRO ADM.53/69479. PRO AIR.1/148/15/89. PRO AIR.1/213/15/226/30. PRO AIR.1/491/15/312/302. PRO AIR.1/632/15/122/59. PRO AIR.1/632/17/122/60. PRO Air Raids 1916, Intelligence Section GHQ Home Forces. FAAM
HMS *Caledon* Platform trials 1925	Busteed Papers. B1479. RAFM
HMS *Calliope* 1918	AIR.1/336/15/226/245. PRO
Campinas French seaplane carrier March 1916	AIR.1/665/17/122/722. PRO
HMS *Cantatrice* 1916	AIR.1/210/15/226/27. PRO AIR.1/212/15/226/29. PRO AIR.1/336/15/226/245. PRO AIR.1/414/15/243/4. PRO

HMS *Caroline* 1918	AIR.1/336/15/226/245. PRO
HMS *Cassandra* 1917/18	AIR.1/334/15/226/239. PRO AIR.1/334/15/226/240. PRO AIR.1/335/15/226/243. PRO AIR.1/436/15/282/2. PRO AIR.1/2103/66299. PRO AIR.1/2314/223/12. PRO
HMS *Chatham* 1918	AIR.1/335/15/226/242. PRO AIR.1/336/15/226/245. PRO
HMT *Christopher* 1916	AIR.1/215/15/226/32. PRO
HMS *City of Oxford* EI and ESS. 1917/18	ADM.53/37909. PRO ADM.53/37910. PRO AIR.1/1708/204/123/75. PRO AIR.1/1709/204/123/76. PRO AIR.1/1709/204/123/77. PRO AIR.1/1719/204/123/182. PRO AIR.1/1720/204/123/190. PRO AIR.1/2103/207/31. PRO AIR.1/2314/23/12. PRO
HMS *Comus* 1918	AIR.1/336/15/226/245. PRO
HMS *Courageous* 1916/18	AIR.1/150/15/106. PRO AIR.1/336/226/245. PRO
HMS *Diana* 1914	ADM.53/39817. PRO
HMS *Doris* 1915	ADM.53/40058. PRO ADM.53/40061. PRO AIR.1/726/137/2. PRO AIR.1/2066/204/412/1437. PRO
HMS *Dryad* 1917	AIR.1/415/243/5. PRO
HMS *Dublin* 1917/18	AIR.1/334/15/226/239. PRO AIR.1/334/15/226/240. PRO AIR.1/335/15/226/242. PRO AIR.1/336/15/226/245. PRO
RIMS *Dufferin* 1916	AIR.1/1708/204/123/73. PRO
HM. S/M. *E22* 1916	AIR.1/213/15/226/30. PRO

HMS *Emerald*	Busteed papers, platform trials 1926. B1490. RAFM
HMS *Empress* EI and ESS. 1916/18	ADM.53/40784. PRO ADM.53/40785. PRO ADM.116/1353. PRO AIR.1/361/15/228/50. PRO AIR.1/659/17/122/617. PRO AIR.1/662/17/122/678. PRO AIR.1/667/17/122/736. PRO AIR.1/667/17/122/741. PRO AIR.1/667/17/122/743. PRO AIR.1/1708/204/123/74. PRO AIR.1/1709/204/123/76. PRO AIR.1/1709/204/123/77. PRO AIR.1/1718/204/123/178. PRO AIR.1/2314/23/12. PRO
HMS *Endymion* September 1916	ADM.53/40875. PRO
HMS *Engadine* February 1919	ADM.53/40892. PRO
HMS *Eridge* 1916	AIR.1/148/15/89. PRO
HMS *Euryalus* October 1915	ADM.53/41219. PRO
HMS *Galatea* 1918	AIR.1/336/15/226/244. PRO AIR.1/336/15/226/245. PRO
HMS *General Craufurd* 1916/17	ADM.53/42546. PRO AIR.1/239/15/226/68. PRO AIR.1/311/15/226/197. PRO AIR.1/312/15/226/198. PRO AIR.1/492/15/312/304. PRO
HMS *Glorious* 1918	AIR.1/336/15/226/245. PRO
HMS *Halcyon* 1917	ADM.53/43661. PRO AIR.1/229/15/226/51. PRO AIR.1/231/15/226/53. PRO AIR.1/233/15/226/55. PRO AIR.1/239/15/116/68. PRO AIR.1/310/15/226/196. PRO AIR.1/311/15/226/197. PRO AIR.1/312/15/226/198. PRO AIR.1/415/15/243/5. PRO AIR.1/491/15/312/302. PRO
RIMS *Hardinge* June 1915	AIR.1/2285/209/75/13. PRO

HMS *Hermes* 1913	ADM.53/21931. PRO Longmore Papers Section 2. FAAM
HMS *Hibernia* April/May 1912	ADM.53/16757. PRO Lt C R Samson's Flying Log Book. IWM via FAAM
HMS *Himalaya* 1916	AIR.1/436/15/280/1. PRO
HMS *Indomitable* 1918	AIR.1/336/15/226/245. PRO
HMS *Inflexible* 1918	AIR.1/336/15/226/245. PRO
HMT *Jerico* October 1915	AIR.1/200/15/226/17. PRO AIR.1/201/15/226/18. PRO AIR.1/414/15/243/4. PRO
HMS *Killingholme* 1916	AIR.1/148/15/89. PRO AIR.1/212/15/226/29. PRO AIR.1/213/15/226/30. PRO AIR.1/215/15/226/32. PRO AIR.1/220/15/226/37. PRO AIR.1/224/15/226/42. PRO AIR.1/225/15/226/43. PRO AIR.1/632/17/122/60. PRO
HMS *Kinfauns Castle* February/March 1915	AIR.1/674/21/6/86. PRO
HMT *Kingfisher* 1915/16	AIR.1/193/15/226/10. PRO AIR.1/194/15/226/11. PRO AIR.1/195/15/226/12. PRO AIR.1/198/15/226/15. PRO AIR.1/199/15/226/16. PRO AIR.1/203/15/226/20. PRO AIR.1/207/15/226/24. PRO AIR.1/208/15/226/25. PRO AIR.1/210/15/226/27. PRO AIR.1/212/15/226/29. PRO AIR.1/213/15/226/30. PRO AIR.1/215/15/226/32. PRO AIR.1/414/15/243/4. PRO
HMS *Laconia* March/August 1915	ADM.53/45875. PRO AIR.1/674/21/6/86. PRO
HMS *Laurentic* June 1915	ADM.53/46282. PRO AIR.1/674/21/6/86. PRO
HMS *Lion* 1917/18	AIR.1/334/15/226/239. PRO AIR.1/334/15/226/240. PRO AIR.1/334/15/226/244. PRO AIR.1/336/15/226/245. PRO AIR.1/494/15/312/311. PRO

HMT *Lordship* 1917	ADM.53/47292. PRO AIR.1/304/15/226/153. PRO
HMS *Manica* 1916/17	ADM.53/48166. PRO ADM.53/48167. PRO ADM.53/48168. PRO ADM.53/48177. PRO ADM.53/48178. PRO AIR.1/436/15/280/1. PRO
HMS *Mantua* 1918	AIR.1/671/17/134/3. PRO
HMAS *Melbourne* 1918	AIR.1/336/15/226/245. PRO Sharwood Papers. FAAM *Melbourne*'s Signal Logs May/June 1918.AWMRC
HMS *Melton* 1916	AIR.1/148/15/89. PRO
HMS *Minerva* 1914/15	ADM.53/49449. PRO
Montcalm French Cruiser May 1915	AIR.1/2285/209/75/13. PRO
RIMS *Northbrook* September 1916	ADM/53/52878. PRO
HMS *Orlionoch*	ADM.137/1740. PRO ADM.137/1741. PRO ADM.137/1742. PRO ADM.137/2287, Paper No 489. PRO Naval Review Vol VII. NMM Naval Review Vol VIII. NMM Capt J A Sadler Log. DC/76/77/2. RAFM C N H Bilney Papers. DS/MISC/86. CNB1.IWM
HMS *Orotava* 1918	AIR.1/336/15/226/245. PRO AIR.1/671/17/134/3. PRO AIR.1/2111/207/49/9. PRO
HMS *Penelope* 1915	AIR.1/193/15/226/10. PRO AIR.1/194/15/226/11. PRO
SS *Penmorvah* 1915	AIR.1/2066/204/412/1437. PRO AIR.1/2066/204/412/1438. PRO
HMS *Peony* 1917/18	ADM.53/54978. PRO ADM.116/1353. PRO AIR.1/2111/207/49/9. PRO

HMS *Phaeton* 1918	AIR.1/334/15/226/240. PRO AIR.1/335/15/226/243. PRO AIR.1/336/15/226/245. PRO
HMS *Princess Margaret* 1917	AIR.1/323/15/226/217. PRO AIR.1/667/21/13/1908. PRO
HMS *Princess Royal* 1917/18	AIR.1/334/15/226/240. PRO AIR.1/335/15/226/243. PRO AIR.1/336/15/226/244. PRO AIR.1/336/15/226/245. PRO
HMS *Raglan* 1917	ADM.53/57130. PRO AIR.1/2314/23/12. PRO
HMS *Raven II* EI and ESS. 1915/17	ADM.53/57311. PRO ADM.53/57313. PRO ADM.53/57314. PRO ADM.53/57316. PRO ADM.116/1353. PRO AIR.1/361/15/228/50. PRO AIR.1/436/15/289/1. PRO AIR.1/654/17/122/503. PRO AIR.1/660/17/122/620. PRO AIR.1/667/17/122/736. PRO AIR.1/667/17/122/741. PRO AIR.1/667/17/122/743. PRO AIR.1/1706/204/123/64. PRO AIR.1/1706/204/123/65. PRO AIR.1/1707/204/123/67. PRO AIR.1/1709/204/123/76. PRO AIR.1/1709/204/123/77. PRO AIR.1/1711/204/123/89. PRO AIR.1/1719/204/123/182. PR AIR.1/2284/209/75/8. PRO AIR.1/2285/209/75/13. PRO AIR.1/2314/23/12. PRO
HMS *Renown* 1917	AIR.1/334/15/226/239. PRO AIR.1/334/15/226/240. PRO AIR.1/335/15/226/242. PRO AIR.1/336/15/226/244. PRO AIR.1/336/15/226/245. PRO AIR.1/677/21/13/1908. PRO
HMS *Repulse* 1917	AIR.1/334/15/226/239. PRO AIR.1/334/15/226/240. PRO AIR.1/335/15/226/242. PRO AIR.1/336/15/226/245. PRO AIR.1/641/17/122/218. PRO AIR.1/642/17/122/249. PRO Flt Cdr D G Donald's Flying Logbook. FAAM
HMS *Roberts*	ADM.53/58039. PRO

July 1915	AIR.1/726/137/2. PRO
HMS *Royalist* 1918	AIR.1/335/15/226/242. PRO AIR.1/335/15/226/243. PRO AIR.1/336/15/226/244. PRO AIR.1/336/15/226/245. PRO
HMT *St.Germain* 1915	AIR.1/193/15/226/10. PRO AIR.1/194/15/226/11. PRO
HMS *Severn* August 1916	ADM.53/59847. PRO
HMT *Sir John French* 1915	AIR.1/195/15/226/12. PRO AIR.1/198/15/226/15. PRO AIR.1/199/15/226/16. PRO AIR.1/200/15/226/17. PRO AIR.1/201/15/226/18. PRO AIR.1/414/15/243/4
HMS *Sir Thomas Picton* 1916	ADM.53/60273. PRO
HMS *Southampton* 1918	AIR.1/336/15/226/245. PRO
HMS *Suva* 1916	ADM.53/61878. PRO AIR.1/1706/204/123/65. PRO
HMAS *Sydney* 1918	AIR.1/334/15/226/240. PRO AIR.1/335/15/226/243. PRO AIR.1/335/15/226/243. PRO AIR.1/336/15/226/244. PRO AIR.1/336/15/226/245. PRO Sharwood Papers. FAAM Flt Lt A C Sharwood's Flying Logbook.AWMRC *Sydney*'s Signal Logs March/April 1918.AWMRC
HMS *Talbot* 1916	ADM.53/62199. PRO
HMD *Tarlair* 1917	AIR.1/2111/207/49/9. PRO Aux. Patrol Red List August 1917. NMM
HMS *Tiger* 1917/18	AIR.1/334/15/226/240. PRO AIR.1/335/15/226/242. PRO AIR.1/336/15/226/244. PRO AIR.1/336/15/226/245. PRO
HMS *Undaunted* 1915	AIR.1/193/15/226/10. PRO AIR.1/194/15/226/11. PRO
HMS *Vindictive* Catapult Trials 1924/25	Busteed Papers. B1472. RAFM Busteed Papers. B1480. RAFM

HMS *Yarmouth* 1917/18	ADM.53/69196. PRO AIR.1/304/15/226/153. PRO AIR.1/327/15/226/225. PRO AIR.1/334/15/226/239. PRO AIR.1/334/15/226/240. PRO AIR.1/335/15/226/242. PRO AIR.1/336/15/226/245. PRO AIR.1/677/21/13/1908. PRO Smart Papers. FAAM
Capt. J. S. Dumaresq's Report October 1917	AIR.1/641. PRO
Capt. A. V. Vyvyan's Memorandum August 1917	AIR.1/8436. PRO AIR.1/667. PRO
Disposition of Aircraft on Naval Duties January 1918- January 1919	AIR.1/670/17/124. PRO
Disposition of RNAS Officers 1918	AIR.1/2111/207/49/9. PRO
Flt. Lt. G. B. Dacre Diary January-August 1916	FAAM
Lighters for 2F.1 Camels 1918	AIR.1/287/15/226/137. PRO AIR.1/643/17/122/260. PRO AIR.1/643/17/122/274. PRO AIR.1/2103/207/31. PRO Samson's Memorandum. FAAM
Operation of Seaplanes from Light Cruisers 1915-1918	AIR.1/148/15/87. PRO
Proposed Beardmore Design	CID.172B Cab.38/23/11. PRO
Tail Guide Trestle and Quick Release Strop	AIR.1/733/187/4. PRO
Warship and Aircraft Distribution February 1916-June 1918	ADM.186/22 to 186/25. PRO ADM.186/33. PRO
Rufiji Delta Operations February/July 1915	AIR.1/674/21/6/86. PRO AIR.1/2064/204/412/920. PRO AIR.1/2065/204/412/921. PRO Research work by C G Mottram and I M Burns.

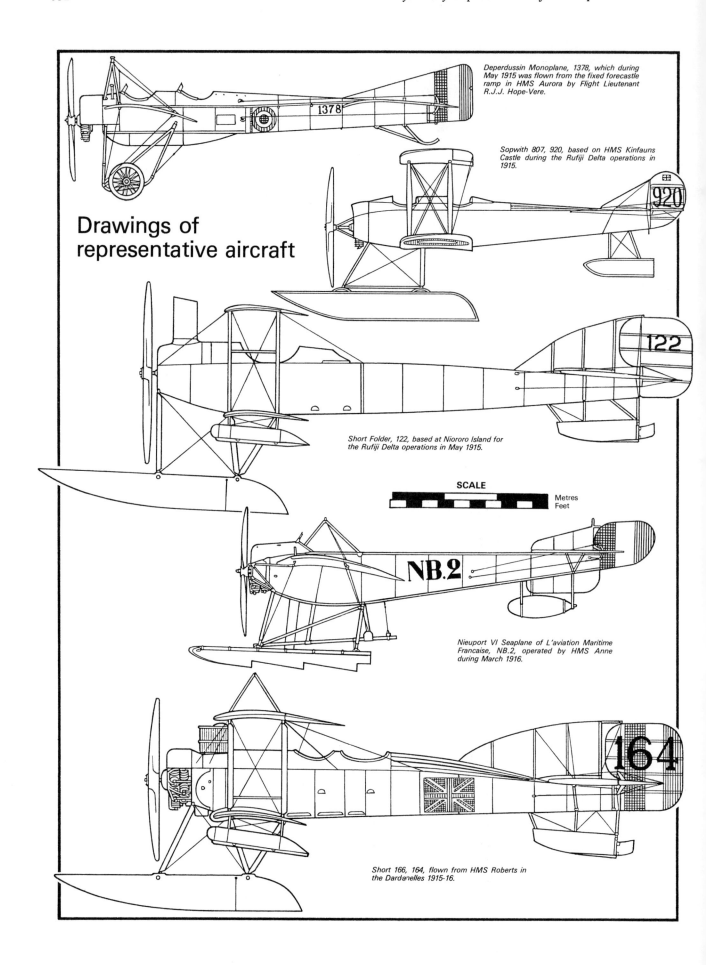

Deperdussin Monoplane, 1378, which during May 1915 was flown from the fixed forecastle ramp in HMS Aurora by Flight Lieutenant R.J.J. Hope-Vere.

Sopwith 807, 920, based on HMS Kinfauns Castle during the Rufiji Delta operations in 1915.

Drawings of representative aircraft

Short Folder, 122, based at Niororo Island for the Rufiji Delta operations in May 1915.

SCALE

Metres
Feet

Nieuport VI Seaplane of L'aviation Maritime Francaise, NB.2, operated by HMS Anne during March 1916.

Short 166, 164, flown from HMS Roberts in the Dardanelles 1915-16.

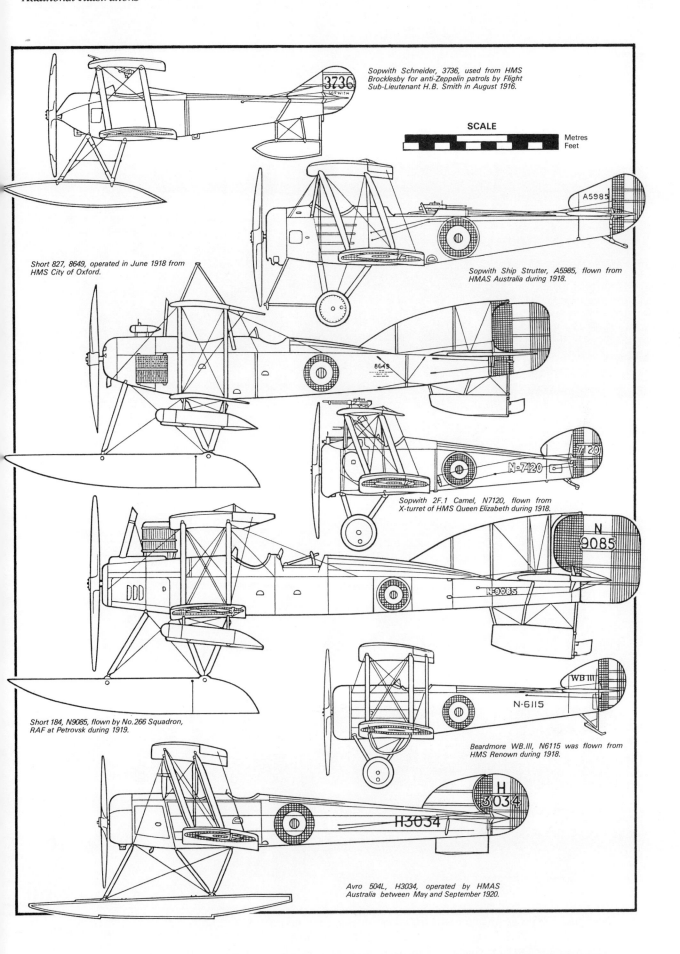

Sopwith Schneider, 3736, used from HMS Brocklesby for anti-Zeppelin patrols by Flight Sub-Lieutenant H.B. Smith in August 1916.

SCALE

Metres
Feet

Short 827, 8649, operated in June 1918 from HMS City of Oxford.

Sopwith Ship Strutter, A5985, flown from HMAS Australia during 1918.

Sopwith 2F.1 Camel, N7120, flown from X-turret of HMS Queen Elizabeth during 1918.

Short 184, N9085, flown by No.266 Squadron, RAF at Petrovsk during 1919.

Beardmore WB.III, N6115 was flown from HMS Renown during 1918.

Avro 504L, H3034, operated by HMAS Australia between May and September 1920.

HMS Endymion in 1915. She operated a Schneider transferred from HMS Empress off the Bulgarian coast in September 1916. (A.K.Vicary)

Schneider 3788 is hoisted on board HMS Endymion in September 1916. (G.S.Leslie/J.M.Bruce collection)

Four views of HM Submarine E.22 with a seaplane carrying platform on her after casing. She embarked two Schneiders, 3730 and 3743, at Felixstowe on 24th April 1916. Both seaplanes were launched with the submarine's stern partially submerged and flown back to Felixstowe by Flt Sub Lts Mackenzie and Helbert. This trial was not put to operational use because the platform adversely affected the submarine's underwater performance. (G.S.Leslie/ J.M.Bruce collection)

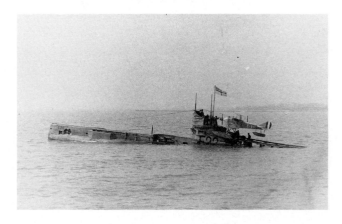

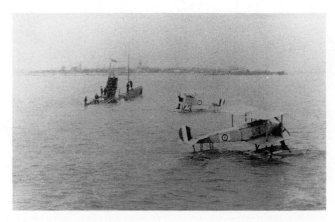

HMS General Craufurd embarked Short 184s during 1916/17 when bombarding the Belgian coast. (A.K.Vicary)

HMS Golden Eagle, probably on 15th July 1916 when she transported two Wight Twin Seaplanes 1450 and 1451 from Cowes to Felixstowe. (IWM SP3037)

HMS Sir Thomas Picton which operated a Short 184, transferred from HMS Empress, at Stavros September 1916.
(NMM N948)

A scene which illustrates the diversity of HM Ships associated with RNAS seaplanes in the Eastern Mediterranean during 1916. In the foreground a Short 184 taxies alongside the seaplane carrier HMS Empress. Astern of her is HMS Sir Thomas Picton, a monitor also operating a Short 184. Beyond her lies the cruiser HMS Endymion which embarked a Schneider during 1916. (IWM SP272)

Bristol Scout C, 1246, at Eastchurch on 7 October 1915 with Flt Cdr B.F.Fowler in the cockpit. This aeroplane was used for trials with the Tail Guide Trestle and Quick Release Strop for use in HM Ships. (IWM Q73707)

A view of Bristol Scout C, 1246, taken seconds after the above photograph. The Tail Guide Trestle has ensured that the aeroplane is already in a flying attitude - necessary for a short take off run on board a ship. (RAFM P10883)

Bristol Scout C, 1255, piloted by Flt Cdr B.F.Fowler, taking off from HMS Vindex on 3 November 1915, after using the Tail Guide Trestle and Quick Release Strop developed at Eastchurch. The Affirmative flag held by the rating repeats to the pilot a similar signal from the navigating bridge to indicate that the ship is head to wind with a wind speed over the deck of almost 25 knots. (via G.S.Leslie)

F.J.Rutland while still a Flight Lieutenant in 1915. Promoted to Flight Commander, by 1917 he pioneered many methods of launching aeroplanes from capital ships and cruisers. (FAAM)

Ship Strutter A599- is hoisted aboard HMS Renown using the 15-inch guns of B turret. (FAAM)

HMS Renown's Ship Strutter airborne from B turret ramp in 1918. (FAAM)

2F.1 Camel N6605 served aboard both Glorious and Repulse in 1918. The Admiralty overwing mounting for the Lewis gun is evident. (GSL/JMB)

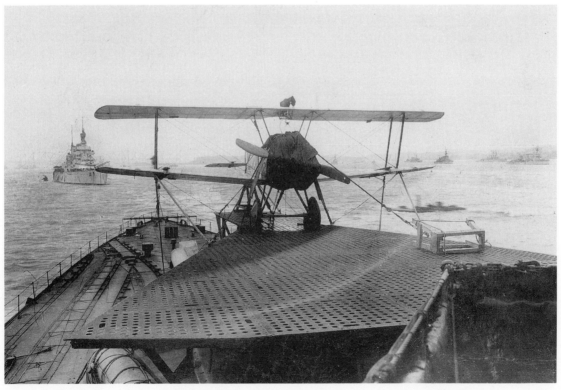

A 2F.1 Camel secured for sea on Y turret ramp of either Courageous or Glorious, possibly N6645 on Courageous. (RAFM)

Another view of Pup N6444 hoisted on board HMS Renown from the drifter alongside (see page 83). (GSL/JMB)

2F.2 Camel N7136 being hoisted on board HMS Barham 1918. (FAAM)

Murky but unusual views of HMS Ben-my-Chree in 1915 showing her forward launching ramp rigged for the operation of seaplanes, probably during May of that year for the abortive attacks on Norddeich before leaving for the Dardanelles and later service with EI & ESS. (FAAM)

HMS Ben-my-Chree at Mudros in 1915 before joining EI & ESS. The two Short 184s in her hangar are 841 operated by HMS Roberts in August 1915 and 842 operated by HMS Euryalis in October 1915. (FAAM)

HMS Ben-my-Chree probably in 1916 before joining EI & ESS. (IWM SP995)

HMS Anne while serving with EI & ESS in 1916. (FAAM)

HMS Empress at Port Said in 1917 with a Short 184 of EI & ESS on board. (FAAM)

HMT Veresis was employed as anti-submarine escort for HMS Raven II during 1917. (via RÇC)

HMY Managem also served as an escort for ships of EI & ESS during 1917. (via RCC)

Sopwith 860, 860, was one of HMS Ark Royal's seaplanes transferred to the Aircraft Repair Ship SS Penmorvah for erection at Mudros in May 1915. It is seen here on Ark Royal's deck after erection. (GSL/JMB)

One of HMS Ben-my-Chree's Short 184s undergoing maintenance at sea. (GSL/JMB)

HMS Engadine in June 1919. In February of that year she embarked No.266 Squadron RAF with its Short 184s at Mudros for service in the Caspian Sea. (RAFM P014757)

Short 184, N2823, at the base of the EI & ESS on No.3 Island, Port Said in 1917/18. (FAAM)

HMS Repulse, at Rosyth in 1918, ha a Ship Strutter on B turret ramp. Alongside her is HMS Pegasus with probably a Beardmore WB.III on the forward flying off deck. (S.C.Newton via R.D.Layman)

HMS Malaya with a Ship Strutter on B turret ramp and a 2F.1 Camel on X turret ramp. (IWM SP998)

ABBREVIATIONS

A.A.	Anti Aircraft	GHQ	General Headquarters	RCN	Royal Canadian Navy
ABS	Armed Boarding Steamer	GOC	General Officer Commanding	Regt	Regiment
Adm	Admiral	HD	Home-Dakar	RFA	Royal Fleet Auxiliary
Air Mech	Air Mechanic RNAS		(convoys)	RFA	Royal Field Artillery
AMC	Armed Merchant Cruiser	HE	High explosive	RFC	Royal Flying Corps
A/P	Auxiliary Patrol	HLI	Highland Light Infantry	RIMS	Royal Indian Marine Ship
A/S	Anti-submarine	HMAS	His Majesty's Australian Ship	R Gunboat	River Gunboat
ASC	Army Service Corps			RMLI	Royal Marine Light Infantry
BS	Battleship	HMFA	His Majesty's Fleet Auxiliary	RN	Royal Navy
BST	British Summer Time			RNAS	Royal Naval Air Service
B Cr	Battle Cruiser	HMS	His Majesty's Ship		
CAM-ship	Catapult Armed Merchant Ship	HMT	His Majesty's Trawler	RNAS	Royal Naval Air Station
Capt	Captain RN, or RMLI, or Army, or RAF	HQ	Headquarters	RNR	Royal Naval Reserve
		HMY	His Majesty's Yacht	RNVR	Royal Naval Volunteer Reserve
		IAR	Indian Army Reserve		
Capt D	Officer commanding destroyer flotilla	KOSB	King's Own Scottish Borderers	RP(A)	Revolving Platform (aft)
Cdr	Commander	L Cr	Light Cruiser	RP(F)	Revolving Platform (forward)
C in C	Commander in Chief	L'AMF	L'Aviation Maritime Française	rpm	Revolutions per minute
CMB	Coastal Motor Boat				
CPO	Chief Petty Officer	Ldg Mech	Leading Mechanic RNAS	2nd Lt	Second Lieutenant
Cr.	Cruiser			S/M	Submarine
D/F	Direction Finding	LH	Lighthouse	SNO	Senior Naval officer
DBR	Damaged Beyond Repair	Lt	Lieutenant RN, Army or RMLI	S/P	Carrier Seaplane Carrier
DNC	Director of Naval Construction	Lt Cruiser	Light Cruiser	Sqdn	Squadron
		LV	Light Vessel	Sqdn Cdr	Squadron Commander RNAS
DSC	Distinguished Service Cross	MAC-ship	Merchant Aircraft Carrier		
DSO	Distinguished Service Order	MAED	Marine Aircraft Experimental Depot	SS	Steam Ship
				Sub Lt	Sub Lieutenant
Dy	Dockyard	ML	Motor Launch	SWR	South Western Railway
EI and ESS	East Indies and Egypt Seaplane Squadron	M/L	Minelayer		
		MN	Merchant Navy	TBD	Torpedo Boat Destroyer
Exp	Experimental	M/S	Minesweeper		
FFR	Fixed Forecastle Ramp	NAED	Naval Aircraft Experimental Depot	TT	Torpedo Tube
				U/c	Undercarriage
Flt	Flight	NPL	National Physical Laboratory	UK	United Kingdom
Flt Cdr	Flight Commander RNAS			US	United States
		pdr	Pounder	USN	United States Navy
Flt Lt	Flight Lieutenant RNAS or RAF	POW	Prisoner of War	USS	United States Ship
		PS	Paddle Steamer	Wg Cdr	Wing Commander RNAS or RAF
FP	Fixed Platform	RAE	Royal Aircraft Establishment		
FP and BH	Fixed Platform and Bridge Hangar			W/T	Wireless Telegraphy
		RAMC	Royal Army Medical Corps	Yt	Yacht
F/S/L	Flight Sub-Lieutenant RNAS				

GENERAL INDEX

Aboukir Bay, 187, 189, 325, 327
Abu Hareira, 186, 327
Abu Zeminea, 184
Abu Zenima, 226
Acre, 187, 195, 212, 325, 327, 328, 332
Adalia, 224, 233, 327, 328
Adana, 182, 183, 190, 191, 195, 220, 224, 248, 249, 251, 252, 325-329
Aden, 135, 207, 209, 211, 242, 243, 332
Admiralty Committee on Deck Landing, 58
Aegean, 198, 284
Agra, 228
Aircraft Targets, 76
Akaba, 127, 128, 183, 184, 216, 238
Akir, 185, 327
Aleppo, 124, 234
Alexandretta, 124, 126, 182, 183, 190, 234, 326
Alexandria, 178, 188, 200, 325, 331
Aliya, 191
Allenby, EHH, General, 257, 261
Amiral Charner, French Armoured Cruiser, 336
Andifilo, 203
Anvers SS, Belgian cargo ship, 157
Arak El Mensbiyeh, 216, 328
Arballete, French Destroyer, 214, 220, 241, 242, 336
Ari Atoll, 243
Armstrong W G, 14
Armstrong Siddeley Lynx, 76
Armstrong Siddeley Ounce, 76
Armstrong Whitworth catapult, 73, 79
Armstrong Whitworth Ltd, 73
Arrester Hooks, 58
Arrester Wires, 58
Arsuf, 186, 197
Ashurada, 297
Askalon, 124, 185, 187, 194, 197, 224, 245, 259, 260, 329
Askaris, 138, 273
Askold, Russian Cruiser, 174
Astrakan, 292
Athlit, 194, 195, 197, 198, 241
A to K Line, 11
Ayas Bay, 191, 235
Baalbik, 241
Babington, J T, Sqdn Cdr RNAS, 159
Bagamoyo, 268, 269
Bageh, 191, 325

Baghdad, 289
Baku, 287, 289, 297, 309
Batum, 287, 289
Bay of Acre, 188, 190, 192
Bay of Ayas, 190
Bay of Marmarice, 190, 325
Bay of Tarsus, 190
Beardmore, Wm, 12
Beatty, Sir D, Admiral, 14, 32, 34
Beersheba, 124, 128, 172, 173, 174, 180, 183, 193-196, 200, 231, 257, 258, 325, 326, 328, 330
Beirut, 186, 187, 189-192, 198, 203, 214, 240, 241, 245, 249, 250, 250, 251, 251, 323, 325-327
Beit Al Mokhay, 264, 329
Belle Alliance, French Schooner, 185, 186, 214
Beryouzak, 289
Bethell, P, Cdr RN, 76
Bigsworth, A W, Sqdn Cdr RNAS, 159
Birch, Fitter RAF, 32, *47*
Bir El Abd, 172
Bir El Mazar, 209, 216, 327, 328
Bishop, Chief Engineer, 175, 178, 189, 226
Bizerta, 179
Black Sea, 287, 289
Bois, N M, Air Mech RNAS, 132, 133
Bolsheviks, 287, 289, 297, 298, 309
Bombay, 124, 133, 243, 276, 306
Borkum Riff, 37
Borollos, 189, 325
Bosphorous, 287
Bourg, 187
Brazier, Air Mech RNAS, 132, 133
Breslau, German Cruiser, 262
Brest Litovsk, Treaty of, 287
Bridge Hangars, 35
Bruberah, 260, 329
Budrum, 284
Bureika, 229
Bureir, 217, 224, 234, 327, 328, 334
Burgess, PO RNAS, 133
Buyuni Bay, 271
Caesarea, 187, 328
Calshot, 133, 135
Campinas, French Seaplane Carrier, 202, *202*, 203, 204, 314, 326, 336, 344
Canada, French Trawler, 233
Canvas Hangars, 61
Cape Andreas, 192
Cape Carmel, 197, 217, 220, 240

Cape of Good Hope Squadron, 129
Cape Orlok, 294
Cape Phuka, 284
Cape Pyrgo, 213
Carey, RF, 73, 74
Carmel Range, 326
Caspian Flotilla, 289, 290, 297
Caspian Sea, 287, 297, 298, 309, *368*
Castelorizo, 201-203, 212, 213, *218*, 233, 235, 326-328, 332, 333
Catapults, 70, 72, 74
Cephalonia, 204
Chakdara SS, 135
Chatham DY, 38
Chechen, 289, 290, 294-296
Chester, US Cruiser, 191
Chicaldere, 183, 190, 191, 231, *232*, 235, 251, 252, 325-329
Chukwani Bay, 266
Churchill, W S, 12
Chustan Island, 175, 177
Clan Macpherson SS, 266, *266*
Colombo, 243, 327
Convoys, 283
Cornelius, W H, Ldg Mech RNAS, 132-134
Coutelas, French Destroyer, 245, 258, 336
Cradock, Sir C, Rear Admiral, 12
Crampton, D B, Capt RN, 132
Cross Sand Buoy, 156
Cross Sand LV, 156
Curtiss A-3 flying boat, 72
Curtiss AB-2 flying boat, 72
Curtiss Model F flying boat, 131-133
Curtiss OX engine, 132
Curzon, Lt RNR, 153
Cuxhaven Raid, 135, 160

Daba, 238
Dabrouge, M, Agent, 186
Dago SS, 179
Dakar, 283, 306, 308
Damascus, 191, 241, 323, 324
Darb, 211
Dard, French Destroyer, 214, 233, 336
Dardanelles, 128, 178
Dar Es Salaam, 129, 139, 143, 268, 269
Dartige du Fournet, Vice Admiral French Navy, 190
Decauville Railway, 194, 196
Deir El Belah, 246, 257, 326, 329
Deir Sineid, 255, 257, 259, 327, 329

Delaman Chai, 189, 325
de Lapeyrère, B, Admiral French
    Navy, 170
Demir Hissar, Turkish TBD, 175,
    177
Denniken, Russian General, 287
D'Entrecasteaux, French Cruiser,
    182, 183, 185, 187, 188, 191,
    197, 336
Des Moines, US Cruiser, 189
de Spitz, Admiral French Navy,
    233
D'Estrées, French Cruiser, 182,
    183, 334
Détachment d'Aviation du
    Monténégro, 170
Deurt Yol, 126, 183
Dibbah, 184, 185, 326
Dinter, B, Oberleutnant Zur See, 30
Director of Navy Contracts, 14, 58
Djemel Pasha, 126
Dodoni, 269
Doggerbank Noord LV, 30, 35
Dolgoi Island, 296
Donibristle, 38
Dover, 304
Drury, BD, Cdr RN, *247*
Dumar, 241
Dumaresq, J S, Capt RN, 32, 34,
    38, 57, 277
Dunsterforce, 287
Dunsterville, L, Major General, 287
Dupleix, French Cruiser, 194, 336
Durban, 131, 135, 307

Eastchurch, 12, *358, 359*
Eastern Exchange Hotel, 189
East Indies and Egypt Seaplane
    Squadron (EI and ESS), 198,
    200, 201, 204, 220, 225, *236*,
    242, 245, 246, *254*, 255, *363-
    366*
El Afule, 214, *215*, 217, 220, 222,
    223, 224, 233, 240, 241, 326-
    328
El Arish, 124, 172, 173, 180, 183,
    185-187, 190, 192, 194, 198,
    200, 201, 205, 207, 209, 212,
    214, 231, 233, 251, 325-328,
    330, 332, 333
El Auja, 173, 194, 196, 198, 200,
    201, 325, 326
Elgood, P G, Lt Col, 170, 189
El Gralls, 172, 174
El Haram, 257
El Maadam, 214
El Mardan, 214
El Marden, 326
El Mina, 198, 203, 325
El Murra, 201
El Nezele, 258, 259, 329

El Sirr, 180, 326
Emir Feisal, 238
Ems Estuary, 37
Enzeli, 289
Escadrille Nieuport, Suez, 170

Fakdir, 213, 327
Falugeh, 214, 217, 234, 245, 328,
    329
Famagusta, 188, 190, 192, 198,
    212, 224, 238, 248, 252, 332,
    334
Fanny SS, Belgian Cargo Ship, 192
Fastnet, 283
Felixstowe, 302, 304, 307, *355, 356*
Fergusson, J A, Rear Adm, 32, 33
Fineka, 224, 327
Finn Class TBD, Russian, 293
Fixed Forecastle Ramps , 38, 39
Fixed Platforms, 14, 35, 38, 39
Fixed Quarterdeck Ramp, 14
Fiyush, 209, 211, 327, 328
Flechettes, 211
Flights, Fleet Air Arm, 41
Flights, Nos 437 and 438 RAF, 289
Folland, H P, 76
Fort Alexandrovsk, 289, 290, 292,
    292
Foudre, French Seaplane Carrier,
    124, 126, 170, 336
Friegs, von, Lt Cdr German Navy,
    175
Frienberg, M, Agent, 194
Fullerton, E J A, Capt RN, 142,
    144

Gallipoli Peninsula, 128, 179
Garcia, Lt Cdr RNA, 32
Gaskell, Capt M N, 170, *174*, 175,
    175, 178, 179
Gaza, 172-174, 180, 182, 183, 185,
    187, 193-195, 204, 207, 231,
    234, 255, 256, 258, 259, 325-
    328, 330, 331
Gebel Libni, 326
Gengeni Island, 139
Genoa, 245
German East Africa, 129, 266, 305,
    307, 312
Gilligan, A H H , Flt Lt RNAS,
    163
Gingwea, 268
Glasgow Yeomanry, 192
Gnôme Monosoupape engine, 133,
    183
Goeben, German Battle Cruiser,
    197, 262, 264, 311, 329
Goodier, H, Lt RN, *126*
Gowan, C H B, Cdr RN, 57
Grace, H E, Capt RN, 30, 31
Graffy, Mechanic RAF, 32, 34, *47*

Grain Island, 313
Grand Fleet, 14, 32, 153
Green, C H B, Lt Cdr RN, 57
Gregory, A H, Air Mech RNAS,
    132, 133
Gulf of Akaba, 126, 128, 183, 216,
    238, 301, 308, 312, 327
Gulf of Alexandretta, 190, 191,
    235, 251
Gulf of Kos, 284
Gulf of Scala Nuova, 285, 325
Gulf of Smyrna, 126, 174, 175
Gulf of Sollum, 200, 331
Guryev, 295, 297

Haaks LV, 153
Habil, 265, 329
Hache, French Destroyer, 246, 336
Hage, 160, 161
Haifa, 183, 187, 188, 192, 197, 198,
    212, 214, 217, 220, 224, 233,
    234, 240, 241, 257, 258, 325-
    329, 332
Halberstadt Scout, 255
Halsey, L, Rear Admiral RN, 14
Hamidri, 183, 326
Hansa Brandenburg W19, 37
Hartiya, 192
Harwich, 33, 299
Harwich Force, 14, 32, 33, 35, 37,
    153, 157, 159, 160, 161, 281
Hassani Island, 228, 229, 238, 240
Hatambura Island, 273
Hawkcraig Hydrophone
    Establishment, 315
HD Convoys, 283
Hebron, 172, 173, 174, 325
Hejaz, 214, 216, 226, 242, 307, 326
Hejaz Railway, 238
Heligoland Bight, 32, 35, 159
Helmuth, Armed tug, 133
Hendon, 73
High Seas Fleet, 31
Highland Queen, PS, 299
Holmes, G R A, Lt Cdr RNVR, 58
Homs, 224, 328
Hoyer, 161
Hudson, Mr Gerard, 131

Ibrahim Sayid, Agent, 182
Idrissi Troops, 264
Igoroff, Capt, Russian Naval Air
    Service, 297
Ikinjik Liman, 202, 326
Imbros, 262
Immingham, 154, 286
Inchkeith, 57
Invergordon, 13
Iraq, 76

Jackson, Mr, Sudan Civil Service, 182
Jaffa, 124, 174, 182, 185, 191, 192, 197, 198, 207, 214, 234, 260, 325-328
Jaljulye, 257, 329
Jauréguiberry, French Battleship, 190-192
Jeanne d'Arc, French Armoured Cruiser, 189-192, 336
Jebel Abs, 265
Jebel Akrabi, 211
Jebel Al Milh, 264, 265, 329
Jebel Malu, 211
Jeddah, 183, 184, 212, 214, 328
Jeida, 217, 328
Jeihan River, 234, 235
Jelameh, 241
Jenin, 241, 326, 328
Jenkins, J, Lt RNR, 172, 186, 187, 197
Jeronda Bay, 224, 327
Jerusalem, 261
Jonah's Pillar, 124, 126
Julis Junction, 260

Kalamaki, 203, 213, 327
Kalpeni, 242
Kamaran, 265
Kantara, 173
Karagach, 202, 326
Karatash Burnu, 224, 234, 249, 252, 328
Kaspy, Russian Icebreaker, 290, 291, 293
Kekova, 203
Keramus, 284
Kerr, J, Lt RNR, 172, 179, *189*, 190, 202, 214, 238
Khan Yunis, 172, 192, 195, 207, 251, 325, 328, 334
Kheima, 194, 325
Kheimel, 192
Khios Strait, 175, 177
Khor Ghorera, 211
Kikunja River, 133, 141, 143
Kikwale, 135, 269
Kilindi, 268
Killingholme, 155, 315
Kilwa, 268, 269
Kilwete, 271
Kingani River, 269
King-Hall, H G, Rear Admiral RN, 129, 131, 133
Kiombini Mundung, 269
Kis Il Ada, 202
Kissidyu, 271, 273
Kitope Hill, 269
Kiwale Island, 269
Knesovitch, M, Agent, 192
Kochak Creek, 296

Koma Island, 273, 273
Königsberg, German Cruiser, 129, 131-133, 135, 138, 139, 141-143, *143*, 266, 269
Kos, 285
Kosseima, 172, 325, 326
Krynovka, 296
Kulaly Island, 289, 290
Kurt Kulak, 252

Laborieux, French Armed Tug, 212, 213, 217, 332, 333, 336
Laccadive Islands, 242, 243, 327
Lacey, C V, CPO RNAS, 132, 133
Lagan, 295, 296
Lahej, 207, 209, 211, 243, 327, 328
Lake Bardawil, 173, 197, 209, 333
Lanchester, F W, Dr, 13
Lara, 233
Larken, F, Capt RN, 124, 126
Latakia, 188, 327
L'Aviation Maritime Française, 124, 170, 200
Law, T R, Air Mech RNAS, 132, 133, *149*
Lawrence, T E, Col, 238
Lemnos, 178
Leckie, R, Flt Lt RNAS, *163*
Leros, 285
Lettow-Vorbeck, von, General, 266
Levisi, 202, 213
Lifan, 172
Lighters, 35
Linberry, T J, Capt RN, 184, 214
Lindi, 129, 268-271, 276
List Naval Air Station, German, 30, 32
Loch Larne, 286, 315
Lodbjerg, 31
Lodmoor, 12
Loheiya, 264, 265, 329
Lokotemba Kijujani, 269
Loof, Capt Germany Navy, 133, 138, 143
Louis Fraissinet SS, French merchantman, 170
Lowestoft, 285
Ludd, 182, 192, 197, 214, 217, 245, 325-330

Ma'an, 127, 128, 183, 216
MacKenzie, C DSO, Capt RN, 271
Mafia Island, 131, 135, 138, 139, 141-143, 273, 307
Major, bull terrier, 202
Makri, 189, 201, 202, 212, 213, 325, 327333
Maktau, 143
Maldive Islands, 242, 243, 327
Male Island, 243
Malhalla, 209

Malta, 135, 203, 204, 326
Mange Reef, 273
Mangisani, 269
Marduna Island, 228, 240, 326
Marendego, 273
Marine Aircraft Experimental Depot, Grain, 72, 73
Marmarice, 201, 202, 326
Marriott, Cdr RN, 177
Marsh, L V, Lt RNR, 156, *165*
Mauritius, 129
Mawundja, 273
Maxwell, J, General Sir, 170, 204
Maybach Engines, 31
Mecca, 229, 230
Medina, 183, 216, 229, 326
Mendere River, 285
Merkez, 249
Mersa Matruh, 200
Mersina, 124, 182, 183, 188, 195, 217, 325, 326, 334
Midi, 265, 329
Mikendani, 268
Milo SS, 170
Mioreka, 271
Missis, 183, 191, 326
Mnasi Moja, 275
Mobsby, PO RNAS, 132, 133, *149*
Mohoro Bay, 273
Mombasa, 132, 134, 143, 266
Montcalm, French Armoured Cruiser, 183, 184, 314, 336, 348
Montenegro, 170
Mortalik Bay, 126
Mount Carmel, 124
Mozambique, 266
Mrweka, 270, 276
Mssala Channel, 135
Mtingi, 269
Mto Mbanja, 269
Mubarak, 231, 327
Mudros, 178, 179, 192, 262, 287, 310, 325, 330, *367, 368*
Munitions Department, 72
Munitions Inventions Department, 72
Mustin, H C Lt Cdr, USN, 72
Muweilah, 184, 216, 238, 326, 327

Nablus, 214, 216, 224, 245, 326, 328, 329
Nagara Point, 262, 329
Nahr Beirut, 246, *252*
Nahr Iskanderuneh, 224, 246
Nahr El Kebir, 188, 190, 214, 224, 328
Nahr Rubin, 224
Nahr Sukereir, 182, 192, 217, 325, 328
Namaan Island, 184
National Physical Laboratory, 41, 74

Nazareth, 188, 192, 197, 220, 241, 325, 326, 327
Nebi Rubin, 197
Nebi Yunis, 185, 186, 193, 194
Nekhl, 226
Nelson Island, 187
Newbridge SS, 131, 275
Newmarket SS, 284
Njemssati, 269
Niororo Island, 131-135, 275, 306
Noman Island, 240
Nord Caper, French Trawler, 201, 240, 336
Norddeich, 160, *363*
Norrington, H, ERA RNAS, 132, 133
Norris, D T, Commodore RN, 289, 291, 293, 295
North Carolina, US Cruiser, 72
North Hinder LV, 157
North Russia, 35
Novorossik, 287

Odessa SS, 126
Okusa Island, 132
Orfordness, 35
Osmaniah, 183, 191, 325, 326

Pangani, 268
Paris II, French Trawler, 336
Patterson, Surgeon Lt RN, 175
Payas, 126
Pegodia Bay, 189, 325
Peirse, R, Vice Admiral Sir, RN, 124, 174, 175, 177, *187*
Penmorvah SS, Aircraft Repair Ship, 310, 348, *367*
Perim Island, 207, 211
Persia SS, 133, *151*
Pertwee, H G, Lt RN, 291
Petrovsk, 289, 290, 294, 296, 297
Pierrier, French Destroyer, 245, 336
Pillar Buoy, 156
Plain of Esdraelon, 223
Plymouth, 283
Pongive, 268
Port Ayas, 183, 326
Port Beaver, 268
Porte, J C, Cdr RN, 35
Port Laki, 285
Portland, 12
Port Louis, Mauritius, 129
Port Nisus, 268
Porto di Smyrne SS, 124
Port Said, 124, 126, 170, 173, 174, 180, 183, 187-189, 191, 192, 194-198, 200, 209, 212-214, 216, 226, 230, 231, 233, 234, 238, 240, 245, 248, 254, 258, 260, 264, 311, 326, 327, 330, 331

Ports and Lights Administration, 170, 189
Port Sudan, 183, 211, 212, 214, 216, 230
Port Vathi, 213, 285, 331
Pothuau, French Cruiser, 217, 218, 242, 277, 334, 336
President SS, German Supply Vessel, 129, 270, 271
Proells, Korvettenkapitän, 37

Quarman, E, Air Mech RNAS, 132, 133
Queenstown, 286, 313
Quick Release Strop, 32, 35, 37, 58, *69, 358, 359*
Quirini, 268
Rabegh, 214, 229, 230, 238, 326
Radcliffe, Rigger RAF, 32, *47*
Radio Controlled Missiles, 76
RAE Catapult, 72, 73
RAE Farnborough, 72, 76
RAE 1921 Target, 76
RAE Larynx Drone, 76
Rafa, 195, 200, 201, 251, 325, 326, 333
Ramkine Island, 186
Ramleh, 182, 185, 189, 192, 194, 195, 198m 200m, 207, 214, 217, 224, 231, 234, 245, 246, 260, 325-329
Ramoth gilead, 291
Ranken Darts, 157
Ras Burun, 197
Ras Duleidela, 229
Ras El Tin, 189
Ras En Nakoura, 187
Ras Fungani, 273
Ras Mahrash, 184
Ras Malak, 228
Ras Simba Uranga, 139
Ras Wanga, 269
Rayak, 241, 324
Red Sea, 129, 216, 230, 302, 304, 309, 311, 327
Requin, French battleship, 257, 259, 260, 337
Revolving Platforms, 32, 34, 35, 38, 39, 41
Rhodes, 190, 285
Robinson, Cdr RN, 293
Romani, 216, 251
Roscalnikov, Sub Lt Bolshevik Navy, 295
Roscalnikov, Madame, 295
Rosetta, 187
Rosetta, L H, 187
Rosyth, 14, 30, 32, 34, 38, *369*
Royal Aircraft Factory, 76
Ruad Island, 183, 190, 192, 194, 198, 203, 325

Rubery Owen Quick Release Gear, 58
Rufiji River, 129, 131, 135, 139, *143*, 266, 269, 273, 275, 276, 306, 307
Rumpler C.I, 128

Sadani, 268
St.George's Bay, 191, 192
St.Louis, French Battleship, 180, 182, 337
Saint Salvy, Lt de Vaisseau, 212
Salif, 329
Salmon, P, 72
Salonika, 197
Samaria, 187, 234, 327, 328
Samos, 285
Samos Strait, 285
Sarari, 131, 216
Sayad Bey Ali, Egyptian Artillery, 214
Scala Nuova, 285
Scapa Flow, 38
Scarpanto Island, 189
Seal Island, 296
Seddon, J W, Sqdn Cdr RNAS, 157
Seihan Irmak, 195, 234
Senussi Tribesmen, 200
Shafa 'Amr, 192, 241, 325
Sh-Al-Khahrar, 229
Shaw, A W, Air Mech RNAS, 132, 133
Sheerness, 11, 12
Sheikh Hasan, 255, 258
Sheikh Nassir, 214
Sheikh Nebhan, 193
Sheikh Said, 328
Shellal, 201, 217, 231, 326, 328
Shemmune, *215*
Sherm Dumrigh, 240
Sherm Hanab, 238
Sherm Jubba, 216, 327
Sherm Murraiburra, 229
Sherm Rabegh, 228-230, 327
Sherm Yahar, 216, 327
Sherm Yembo, 228, 230
Shrimpton, Corporal RMLI, 177
Sidi Barrani, 200
Sidon, 124, 191
Simba Uranga, 131-133
Simonstown, 131
Sinai, 124, 220
Sloman, Boy Signaller, 175
Smoogroo, 38
Smyrna, 124, 325
Snepp, J W, Capt RMLI, 128
Sollum, 200, 328
Somali SS, 275
South Atlantic, 284
South Russia, 287, 297
Sprot, CPO RNAS, 132, 133

Squadrons, No 8 RNAS, 266, 271
Squadrons, No 14, RFC, 246, 248
Squadrons, Nos 220-223 RAF, 285
Squadrons, No 266 RAF, 289, *292*, 297
Stampalia, 285
Stavros, 311, *357*
Subar, 208, 209, 211, 243, 327, 328
Sueter, M, Capt RN, 70
Suez, 183, 184, 204, 214, 264, 265
Suez Canal, 124, 126, 183, 198, 214, 220, 234
Surada SS, 214
Sutcliffe, G W, Ldg Mech, 132, 133
Syra, 285

Tabaun, 217, 223, 234, 241, 326, 328
Tail Guide Trestle, 35, 58, *69*
Tanga, 268
Tarsus, 182, 183, 190, 191, 234, 327
Tartus, 194, 325, 326, 328
TBD No 250, French TBD, 201
Tel Busire, 203
Tel El Ajjul, 200
Tel El Sharia, 193, 325
Tel El Sharieh, 195
Tel Keli, 214, 224, 328
Tenedos, 175, 189
Tersana, 201, 202, 213, 326, 327, 333
Terschelling Bank, 38
Terschelling LV, 281
Texel, 38
Thermi, 284
Third Battle of Gaza, 257
Tiflis, 287, 289
Tilbury, 133
Tirene Bay, 135, 139, 141

Toll, G, Air Mech RNAS, 132, 133
Tondern, 30-32, 161
Topra Kalle, 183, 326
Trabaud, Lt, French Navy, 192
Tripoli, 188, 224, 328
Tubbs, C E, Air Mech RNAS, 132, 133
Tubeh, 245
Tul Keram, 187, 195, 198, 200, 216, 224, 234, 245, 246, *246*, 248, 325, 327, 329, 330
Turret Ramps, 38, 58, 61
Twakalet Al'Allah, Schooner, 185
Tyre, 183
Tyrwhitt, R, Commodore RN, 37, 159, 160

U-Boats, 283
Uganda SS, 204, 332
Ujret El Zol, 214
Umlejj, 228, 326
Ural River, 295
Utunda, 273

Vlieland, 37
Volos, 203, 213, 327
Voltigeur, French Destroyer, 205, 207, 217, 248, 337
Vyvyan, A V, Wing Capt RNAS, 15

Wadi Akaba, 128
Wadi Araban, 127
Wadi Burshein, 192, 325
Wadi El Arish, 190, 200
Wadi El Hesi, 180, 224, 255, 257-260, 326-329
Wadi Esh Sharia, 193, 194
Wadi Esh Sukereir, 194
Wadi Gaza, 174, 193-195, 201
Wadi Ithm, 216
Wadi Kabir, 208

Wadi Rubin, 194, 195
Wadi Yetham, 183
Waht, 208, 209, 211, 243, 327, 328
Warakini, *215*
Watts, Cdr RN, 296
Waygood-Otis Ltd, 73
Wej, 183, 216, 228, 229, 231, 238, 240, 326, 327
Western Frontier Force, 200
White Russians, 287, 309
Williams, T, Air Mech RNAS, 132, 133
Wilson, Sir Arthur, Adml of the Fleet RN, 12
Wilson, R A, Cdr RN, *144*
Wind Tunnel Models, 41, 74
Wings, Nos 62 and 63 RAF, 285, 289, 308
Wolf, German Raider, 242, 277, 299
Woolley, Capt RFA, 185, 186, 214
Yali Bay, 203
Yarmouth, 13, 37, 153, 154, 156, 157, 300, 301
Yembo, 183, 228, 230, 231, 238, 326, 327
Yemen, 207, 264
Zahle, 241, 326
Zanzibar, 129, 134, 266, 268, 271, 276
Zeppelins, 11, 30, 35, 36, 37. 57, 153, 156, 157, 159, 160
Zeppelin L5, 161
Zeppelin L13, 156
Zeppelin L17, 157
Zeppelin L23, 30, 31
Zeppelin L53, 37
Zeppelin L54, 161
Zeppelin L60, 161
Zimmarin, 241
Zohrah, 264, 329

INDEX OF HM SHIPS

ABERCROMBIE, Monitor, 128
ACTAEON, Destroyer, 11, *356*
AFRICA, Battleship, 11, 12, *356*
AGAMEMNON, Battleship, 287
AGINCOURT, Battleship, 64
AGNES DUNCAN, Collier, 32
AJAX, Battleship, 61, 90
ALADER YOUSSANOFF, Seaplane Carrier, *287*, 289-298, 338, 343
ALBION III, Armed Yacht, *285*, 286, 313, 343
ANGORA, Minelayer, 286, 313, 343

ANNE, Seaplane Carrier, 128, 170-179, *177-179*, 189-205, *201*, 214, 217-230, 238-242, 261, 298, 317-319, 321-326, 333, 334, 335, 343, *365*
ARETHUSA, Light Cruiser, 14, 157, 159, 160, 161, 299, 343
ARGUS, Aircraft Carrier, 41, 76
ARK ROYAL, Seaplane Carrier, 16, 76, 123, 129, 264, *284*, 285, 310, 317, *318*, 343, *367*
ASIA, Armed Merchant Cruiser, 289, 290, 291, 294, 338
ASTRAEA, 2nd Class Cruiser, 129

AURORA, Light Cruiser, 14, 39, 89, 90, 94, 157, 159, 299, 343
AUSTRALIA, Battlecruiser, 14, 61, *65*, 89-94, 278, 313, 344
BARHAM, Battleship, 61, *68*, 70, *73*, 88, 89, 91, 92, *362*
BELLEROPHON, Battleship, 61, 91
BENBOW, Battleship, 63
BEN-my-CHREE, Seaplane Carrier, 123, 160, *161*, 180, 198, 200, *203*, 204, 205, 207, 209, 212, 214, 216, 217, 220, 223-225, 231, 233-235, *236*, 238,

242, 314, 316, 317, *318*, 319-
324, 328, 330, 332, *334*, 344,
363, *364*, *367*
BERYL, Armed Yacht, *286*, 286,
315, 344
BIBI EIBAT, Armed Merchant
Cruiser, 290, 294, 297, 338
BIRKENHEAD, Cruiser, 39, 89-
91, 94, *100*, 344
BIRMINGHAM, Cruiser, 32, 33
BRISBANE, Cruiser, 243, *244*,
277, 299, 317, 320
BROCKLESBY, Paddle Air
Service Scout, 154-157, *156*,
300, 339, 340, 344
CALEDON, Light Cruiser, 14, 30,
31, 34, 39, 41, *53-54 64*, 88, 94,
344
CALLIOPE, Light Cruiser, 39, 88,
89, 344
CAMPANIA, Seaplane Carrier, 16,
38, 58, 123
CANADA, Battleship, 62, 91, *113*
CANTATRICE, Trawler, 153, 300,
339, 340, *340*, 344
CANTERBURY, Light Cruiser, 34
CARLISLE, Light Cruiser, 35, 39,
48
CAROLINE, Light Cruiser, 39, 88-
91, 94, 345
CASSANDRA, Light Cruiser, 14-
16, 34, 39, 41, *64*, 90-93, *95*,
345
CASTOR, Light Cruiser, 76
CEDAR TREE, Collier, 30
CENTAUR, Light Cruiser, 33
CENTURION, Battleship, 63, *114*
CHALLENGER, Cruiser, 268, 269
CHAMPION, Light Cruiser, 32
CHARLSIN, Trawler, 200
CHATHAM, Cruiser, 42, 39, 88-
90, 93, 94, *97*, 129, 131, 132,
139, 270, 345
CHRISTOPHER, Trawler, 153,
399, 345
CITY OF OXFORD, Seaplane
Carrier, 255-265, *263*, 301, 316,
317, 319-322, 329, 345
CLEETHORPES, Paddle Air
Service Scout, 154, *168*, 301
CMB 51, 297
CMB 60, 297
COLLINGWOOD, Battleship, 61,
63
COLOSSUS, Battleship, 64
COMUS, Light Cruiser, 39, 88-90,
94, 345
CONCORD, Light Cruiser, 37
CONQUEROR, Battleship, 63
CONSTANCE, Light Cruiser, 40
CORDELIA, Light Cruiser, 39, 89

COURAGEOUS, Battlecruiser, 14,
16, 32, 33, 62, 89-92, 94, *106*,
107, 345, *361*
COVENTRY, Light Cruiser, 37, 40
CURACOA, Light Cruiser, 37
DANAE, Cruiser, 37
DARTMOUTH, Cruiser, 131
DAUNTLESS, Cruiser, 35, 40
DELHI, Cruiser, 39, *47*, 41
DESPATCH, Cruiser, 41
DIANA, Cruiser, 126, 128, 277,
289, *301*, 345
DIOMEDE, Cruiser, 41
DORIS, Cruiser, *123*, 124, 126,
277, *301*, *302*, 317, 321, 345
DRAGON, Cruiser, 35, 40
DREADNOUGHT, Battleship, 64
DRYAD, Torpedo Gunboat, 154,
164, 302, 339, 340, 345
DUBLIN Cruiser, 14, 16, 32, 38,
39, 90-93, *98*, 345
DUBLIN CASTLE, Armed
Merchant Cruiser, 290, 338
DUFFERIN, Armed Merchant
Cruiser, 212, *229*, 229, 302,
316, 320, 322, 345
DUNEDIN, Cruiser, 40, 41
DURBAN, Cruiser, 41
E22, S/M, 303, 345, *355*
EDINBURGH CASTLE, Armed
Merchant Cruiser, 289, 290,
296, 338
EMERALD, Cruiser, 41, *55*, 74,
76, *82*, 346
EMILE NOBEL, Armed Merchant
Cruiser, 289-292, 296, 338
EMPEROR OF INDIA, Battleship,
62, 91, 92, *104*
EMPRESS, Seaplane Carrier, 16,
123, 160, 245-258, *245*, *254*,
262, 264, 310, 313-317, 319-
324, 328-330, 346, *354*, *357*,
365, *368*
ENCOUNTER, Cruiser, 277
ENDYMION, Cruiser, 303, 317,
346, *354*, *357*
ENGADINE, Seaplane Carrier, 16,
123, 135, 160, 289, 346, *368*
ENTERPRISE, Cruiser, 41, 76, *56*
ERIDGE, Paddle Minesweeeper,
155, *168*, 303, 346
ERIN, Battleship, 63
ESPIÈGLE, Sloop, 205, 229, 233,
238, 240
EURYALUS, Armoured Cruiser,
174, 175, 177-179, 207, 277,
278, 303, 346, *364*
EXMOUTH, Battleship, 243, 277
FORTH, Submarine Depot Ship,
154
FOX, Light Cruiser, 132, 212, 228,

229, 238, 240, 264
FURIOUS, Aircraft Carrier, 14, 32,
123
GALATEA, Light Cruiser, 40, 88-
91, 94, *99*, 346
GENERAL CRAUFURD, Monitor,
304, 346, *356*
GERANIUM, Sloop, *279*, 280, 314
GLORIOUS, Battlecruiser, 14, 32,
62, 88-92, 94, 346, *361*
GOLDEN EAGLE, Paddle Air
Service Transport, 304, *356*
GRAFTON, Cruiser, 250, 251, 258
HALCYON, Torpedo Gunboat,
154, *163*, *164*, 285, 286, 302,
304, 339, 340, 346
HARDINGE, Armed Merchant
Cruiser, 184, *185*, *186*, 212,
214, 228, 229, 238, 240, 304,
317, 319, 321, 346
HAZARD, Torpedo Gunboat, 204
HELMUTH, Armed Tug, 133
HERCULES, Battleship, 64
HERMES, Cruiser, 13, 14, 305,
347, *357*
HIBERNIA, Battleship, 12, *15*, 20,
21, *23*, 347, *357*, *383*
HIMALAYA, Armed Merchant
Cruiser, 266, 268-271, *271*, 275,
276, 305, 347
HOOD, Battlecruiser, 70, *71*
HYACINTH, Cruiser, 129, 131,
269
INCONSTANT, Light Cruiser, 40,
88, 90, 91, 94
INDOMITABLE, Battlecruiser, 61,
62, 88-92, 94, *114*, 347
INFLEXIBLE, Battlecruiser, 61,
62, 89, 90, 92, 94, 178, 347
IRON DUKE, Battleship, 62, 88-
91, *106*
JERICO, Trawler, 153, 305, 339,
340, 347
JUNO, Cruiser, 289
KILLINGHOLME, Paddle Air
Service Scout, 154, 155, *166*,
167, 306, 339, 347
KINFAUNS CASTLE, Armed
Merchant Cruiser, *128*, 131-134,
306, 347
KINGFISHER, Trawler, 153, *154*,
156, 306, 339, 340, 347
KING GEORGE V, Battleship, 63
LACONIA, Armed Merchant
Cruiser, 135, 139, *142*, 143,
143, 266, 276, 307, 347
LADYBIRD, River Gunboat, 260
LAURENTIC, Armed Merchant
Cruiser, *134*, 135, 139, 307, 347
LION, Battlecruiser, 32, 60, 62, *68*,
88-91, 93, 94, *112*, 347, 348
LONDON, Battleship, 12

LORDSHIP, Trawler, 286, 315, 348

M2, Submarine, 74

M15, Monitor, 205, 233, 259, 260

M21, Monitor, 216, 217

M23, Monitor, 205

M28, Monitor, 262

M29, Monitor, 260

M31, Monitor 231, 233, 260

MALAYA, Battleship, 62, 70, 91, 92, *119, 369*

MANAGEM, Armed Yacht, 257, *337, 366*

MANICA, Seaplane Carrier, 266, 268, *269*, 271, 273, 275, 276, 307, 310, 348

MANTUA, Armed Merchant Cruiser, *281*, 283, 308, 348

MANXMAN, Seaplane Carrier, 16, 123

MARLBOROUGH, Battleship, 63

MELBOURNE, Cruiser, 33, *33, 34*, 40, *44*, 89-91, 94, 278, 314, 348

MELTON, Paddle Minesweeper, 155, 308, 348

MERSEY, Monitor, 133, 135, 139, 141-143, 268, 269, 273

MINERVA, Cruiser, *124*, 126, 127, 128, 277, 308, 317, 321, 323, 324, 348

MONARCH, Battleship, 63, *115*

NAIRANA, Seaplane Carrier, 16, 123

NEPTUNE, Battleship, 61, 63

NEW ZEALAND, Battlecruiser, 61, 62, 88-92, 94, *103*

NORTHBROOK, Armed Merchant Cruiser, 229, 309, 316, 323, 324, 348

ORION, Battleship, 62, 90, 91

ORLIONOCH, Seaplane Carrier, 289, 296, *296*, 297, 309, 338, 348

OROTAVA, Armed Merchant Cruiser, *280*, 283, 309, 348

OSIRIS, Destroyer, 33

P32, Patrol Craft, 157

PARIS II, Trawler, 220

PEGASUS, Light Cruiser, 129

PEGASUS, Seaplane Carrier, 16, 123, *369*

PENELOPE, Light Cruiser, 14, 40, 89-91, *100*, 160, 309, 348

PEONY, Sloop, *283*, 284, 310, 348

PHAETON, Light Cruiser, 40, 88-90, 93, 94, 349

PHILOMEL, Cruiser, 173

PRINCE, Destroyer, 31, 32

PRESIDENT KRUGER, Armed Merchant Cruiser, 289-291, 338

PRINCESS ENA, Fleet Messenger, 289

PRINCESS MARGARET, Minelayer, 281, *282*, 310, 349

PRINCESS ROYAL, Battlecruiser, 60, 62, 88-94, *113*, 349

PRINCESS VICTORIA, Air Service Transport, *168*, 310

QUEEN ELIZABETH, Battleship, 62, 91, 92

RAGLAN, Monitor, 128, 255-260, *258*, 262, 311, 316, 348

RAMILLIES, Battleship, 63, 70

RAVEN II, Seaplane Carrier, 128, 170-191, *180*, 197, 205, 207, 208, 212-214, 216, *218*, 217, 220-224, 226, 230, 231, 235, 238, *238*, 242, 243, 255, 257, 261, 277, 311, 316-324, 326, 327, 332, 333, 335, 349, *366*

REDGAUNTLET, Destroyer, 32

REDOUBT, Destroyer, 35, 37, 38, *51*, 90

RELIANCE, Repair Ship, 179

RENOWN, Battlecruiser, 14, 60, 63, 70, *85*, 88, 90-94, 349, *360, 362*

REPULSE, Battlecruiser, 38, 57, 60, *60*, 61, 70, *71*, 88, 91-94, 349, *361, 369*

RESOLUTION, Battleship, 63, 74

RETRIEVER, Destroyer, 37

REVENGE, Battleship, 63, 70, *74, 109*

RINALDO, Sloop, 270, 271

RIVAL, Destroyer, 61

RIVER CLYDE, Landing Ship, 179

RIVIERA, Seaplane Carrier, 16, 123, 160

ROBERTS, Monitor, 128, 129, 312, 316, 317, 350, *364*

RONONIA, Trawler, 233

ROYALIST, Light Cruiser, 40, 88-94, *101*, 350

ROYAL OAK, Battleship, 63, 70, 90, *110*

ROYAL SOVEREIGN, Battleship, 63, 70, 89, 91, *111*

ST.GERMAIN, Trawler, 312, 339, 340, 350

ST.VINCENT, Battleship, 64

SALAMANDER, Torpedo Gunboat, 270

SENATOR, Destroyer, 35

SERGIE, Armed Merchant Cruiser, 289, 290, 292, 293, 338

SEVERN, Monitor, 133, *133*, 135, 139, 141-143, 269, 312, 350

SHARPSHOOTER, Destroyer, 34

SIR JOHN FRENCH, Trawler, 153, *162*, 312, 339, 340, 350

SIR THOMAS PICTON, Monitor, 128, 313, 350, *357*

SLAVA, Armed Merchant Cruiser, 290, 294, 338

SLINGER, Exp Catapult Ship, 73, 77, *78*, 313

SOUTHAMPTON, Cruiser, 32, 40, 88-91, 94, *99*, 350

SPENCER, Destroyer, 35

SPRINGBOK, Destroyer, *50*

STORK, Destroyer, 32

STRONGHOLD, Destroyer, 76, *83*

SUPERB, Battleship, 64

SUVA, Armed Boarding Steamer, 230, 231, 350

SWIFTSURE, Battleship, 124, 172, 174, 175, 177, 178

SYBILLE, Destroyer, 32

SYDNEY, Cruiser, 32, 33, *34*, 38, 40, 88-94, 350

TALBOT, Cruiser, 268, 350

TARLAIR, Drifter, *277*, 315, 320, 350

TEAZER, Destroyer, 37, *340*

TEMERAIRE, Battleship, 64

THANET, Destroyer, 76, *79*

THISBE, Destroyer, 37

THISTLE, Steel Gunboat, 276

THUNDERER, Battleship, 64

TIGER, Battlecruiser, 60, 63, 88, 90-94, *108*, 350

TRIUMPH, Battleship, 174

TRUCULENT, Destroyer, 35, 88, 90

UNDAUNTED, Light Cruiser, 14, 40, 88-91, *102*, 160, 161, 313, 350

VALIANT, Battleship, 63, 89, 90, 92, *116*

VENGEANCE, Battleship, 269

VENTURE, Armed Merchant Cruiser, 289-292, 294, 338

VERESIS, Trawler, 257, *366*

VINDEX, Seaplane Carrier, 16, 58, 123, 157, 161, *359*

VINDICTIVE, Aircraft Carrier, 74, *81*, 123, 350

WARSPITE, Battleship, 63, 91, *93, 116*

WELBECK, Trawler, *153*

WEYMOUTH, Cruiser, 40, *95*, 131

WINDSOR CASTLE, Armed Merchant Cruiser, 289, 290, 291, 294, 338

YARMOUTH, Cruiser, 14-16, 30, 32, 40, *44*, 57, 88, 92, 93, 351

INDEX OF AIRCREW

ARNOLD, H J, Flt Sub Lt, RNAS, 139, 141, *144*

BABINGTON, J T Sqdn Cdr RNAS, 159

BADGER, Asst Paymaster RN, 141

BANKES-PRICE, J T Lt RNAS, 207, 208, 212, 214, 217, 222, *223*, 231, 233, 319, 330

BARR, F M L Flt Lt RNAS, 246, 319

BAXTER, F O Lt, Cambridgeshire Regiment, 183, 319

BEARE, S C, Flt Sub Lt RNAS, 154, 339

BENNETT, W, Ldg Mech RNAS, *132*, 133

BICKNELL, F R, Lt RAF, 290, 293, 295

BILNEY, C N H, Capt RAF, 297

BISHOP, A G, Lt RMLI, 142, 143, *144*

BITTLES, G H, Flt Sub Lt RNAS, 154, *155*, 156, *157*, 339

BLACKBURN, V Gaskell, Flt Sub Lt RNAS, 139, 141, 143, *144*

BLANC, Jean, Lt L'AMF, 201, 319

BOGGIS, E H A, Air Mech RNAS, *132*, 135, 138

BOURGEOIS, R, Ldg Seaman L'AMF, 194, 195, 198, 319

BOWHILL, F W, Wg Cdr RAF, 289

BOURNE, C A, 2/Lt RFA, 245, 319

BOYLE, Capt The Hon A D E H RN (SNO Red Sea Patrol), 212, 240

BRENTON, H B, Flt Sub Lt RNAS, 339

BREWEN, Flt Sub Lt, *47*

BRIDGEMAN, Hon R, Cdr RN, 139, *274*, 275, 276

BRONSON, C G, Flt Lt RNAS, 246, 250, 257, 262, 264, 319

BROOKE, J C, Flt Lt RNAS, 212, 213, 216, 217, 222, 223, 224, 235, 241, 319, 332

BROWN, J W, Lt RFA, 212, 213, 319, 332, 333

BURD, J M, Lt RFA, 203, 319

BURLING, E J, Flt Lt RNAS, 230, 231, 235, 238, 240, 243, 249, 250, 255, 257- 260, 319

BURNIER, Lt L'AMF, 319

BUSTEED, H R, Lt Col RAF, 73

CADBURY, E, Flt Sub Lt RNAS, 154, *155*, 339

CAIN, Lt, *337*

CHILDERS, R Erskine, Lt RNVR, 200, 319, 330, 331

CHUTE, E L, Capt Duke of Wellington's Regiment, *197*, 198, 200, 201, 319

CINTRÉ, A, Lt L'AMF, 180, 182, 183, 184, *187*, 319

CLARKE, L, Lt Manchester Regiment, 320

CLEMSON, A W, Flt Lt RNAS, 216, 222-224, 228-230, 235, 241, 243, 252, 277, 320

CLIFFORD, R M, Flt Sub Lt RNAS, 208, 209, 320, 331

CORNELIUS, W H, Ldg Mech RNAS, 132-134

COVENEY, E W, Lt RAF, 285

CRAMPTON, D B, CAPT RN, 132, *150*

CULL, J T, Sqdn Cdr RNAS, *132*, 133-135, 138, 139, 141, 143, *144*, *149*, *150*, 268

CULLEY, S D, Lt RAF, 35-38, *37*

CUTLER, H D, Flt Sub Lt RNAS, 131-133

DACRE, G B, Flt Lt RNAS, 212, 213, *213*, 217, 218, 224, 320, 330-334

DAVIES, Flt Sub Lt RNAS, 339

DEANS, E E, Flt Sub Lt RNAS, 271, 273, 275, 276

de COURCY IRELAND, W P Flt Cdr RNAS, 154, 159, 340

de LESCAILLE, H, Lt L'AMF, 170, 179, *187*, *197*, 200, 204

de SAIZIEU, L, Capt L'AMF, 172, *175*, 185, 186, 189-193, 195, 196, 320

DESTREM, A, Lt L'AMF, 124, 174, 175, 186-192, 194, *194*, 197, 203, 204, 320

DONALD, D G, Flt Cdr RNAS, 60

DOVER, M G, Flt Sub Lt RNAS, 217, 222, 223, 320

EDMONDS, C H K, Flt Cdr RNAS, 207-209, 320, 330, 331

ENGLAND, T H, Flt Cdr RNAS, 207, 208, 212, 214, 216, 217, 222, 224, 233, 234, 320

EVANS, G W R, Capt RAF, 285

FANE, G W R, Capt RAF, 35

FERGUSON, A D, 2nd Lt HLI, 245, 246, 259, 260, 262, 264, 265, 320

FIELD, R M, Flt Lt RNAS, 245, 320

FINNEY, A D, 2nd Lt RFA, 200, *247*, 320

FITZHERBERT, C H, Sub Lt RN, 268, 271, 273

FLETCHER, H P, Major Middlesex Hussars, 184, 187, 188, 190, 192, 194, 195, 197, 320

FOWLER, B F, Flt Cdr RNAS, *358*, *359*

FOX, F M, Flt Lt RNAS, 14, 61

FREEMAN, C T, Flt Lt RNAS, 157

GALLEHAWK, A N, Flt Sub Lt RNAS, 131, *132*, 133, 134, 143, *150*, 268

GIBSON, L B, Flt Lt RAF, 33

GOODWIN, H F, Chief Petty Officer RNAS, 264, 320

GORDON, R, Sqdn Cdr RMLI, 139, 141, *144*

GRALL, H, Chief Petty Officer L'AMF, 127, 128, 172-174, *175*, 180, 182, 187, 188, 190, 192, 194-196, 198, 200, 321

GRAMANT, Petty Officer L'AMF, 203, 321

GROUCOTT, E, Ldg Mech RNAS, 243, 269, 321

HALSTED, F N, Flt Sub Lt RNAS, 154, 339

HARDS, F G D, Flt RNAS, 154, 339

HARRIS, W J, Chief Petty Officer RNAS, 276

HENDERSON, F C, Flt Sub Lt RNAS, 234, 235, 321

HERBERT, J R, Capt (Army), 124, 172, *175*, 189-192, 321

HILLAS, N, Lt Duke of Wellington's Regiment, 173, 186-189, 192, 321

HOPE-VERE, R J J, Flt Lt RNAS, 157

HUGHES, T V, Lt RFA (TF), 202, 321

KEMPSON, W R, Capt RFA, 249, 252, 254, 255, 257-260, 264, 321

KENNEDY, R C, Lt (Army), 264, 321

KERRY, J L, Sub Lt RNVR, 214, 217, 224, 233, 240, 241, 243, 249, 321

KING, 2/Lt KOSB, 213, 217, 224, 233, 321, 332

KING, E M, Flt Lt RNAS, 235, 240, 245, 246, 250, 257, 259, 264, 321

KINGHAM, F L, 2nd Lt RAF, 289, 290, 292, 293, 294

KNIGHT-BRUCE, R E C, Capt Royal 1st Devon Yeomanry, 242, 321

LACEY, Warrant Officer RNAS, 134, 143, *150*, 268

LEDGER, H M C, Lt Indian Army Reserve, 185, 186, 190-196, *195*, 321

LEIGH, H de V, Flt CdrRNAS, 231, 241, 245, *247*, 249, 252, 254, 257, 264, 265, 321

LEISH, D J O, Lt RNVR, 264, 322

LESLIE, FW, Flt Sub Lt RNAS, *155*

L'ESTRANGE MALONE, C J, Lt RN, 12, 124, 198, 200, 201, 204, 222, 223, 226, 228, 230, 322

LEVASSEUR, J, Lt L'AMF, 322

LISTER, T V, Flt Sub Lt RNAS, 340

LLOYD, Air Mech RNAS, 234, 322

LOW, L, Air Mech RNAS, 322

MACKENZIE, C, Capt RN, 271

MACLEAN, Flt Lt RNAS, 268, 269

MAN, W, Flt Sub Lt RNAS, 212-214, 217, 222-224, 231, 233, 322, 331-333

MARLOWE, Flt Sub Lt RNAS, 340

MASKELL, A S, Flt Lt RNAS, 214, 217, 233, 235, 322, 331

McCUGHEY, Lt RAF, 296, 297

MEADE, W C A, Lt RNVR, 243, 322

MILLARD, V, Capt Essex Regiment, 208, 209, 216, *217*, 222, 224, 228-230, 241, 245, 246, 249, 250, 259, 264, 322

MOON, E R, Flt Lt RNAS, 269-271, *274*, 275, 276

MORRISON, R G K, 2nd Lt RAF, 290, 293

MORRISON, F L, Lt RAF, 283

MURRAY, L E R , Flt Sub Lt RNAS, 340

NEWTON, E A, Lt ASC, 252, 322

NICHOLL, V, Flt Sub Lt RNAS, 154, *163*, 340

NIGHTINGALE, A G, Flt Sub Lt RNAS, 233, 234, 322

NORTHROP, J C, Flt Sub Lt RNAS, 340

PAIGE, C P, Major, Staff GOC Aden, 209, 243

PAINE, L P, Flt Sub Lt RNAS, 222-224, 322

PAKENHAM WALSH, G H, 2nd Lt Cheshire Regiment, 241, 246, 249, 250, 257, 259, 260, 262, 264, 322

PARTRIDGE, Lt Ceylon Rifles, 173

PAUL, Sir R J, Lt Special List, 173, 174, *178*, 180, 182, 183, 190-193, 322

PENNINGTON, G A A, Flt Sub Lt RNAS, 264, 322

PENNY, R E, Flt Cdr RNAS, 73

PERRY, A, Air Mech RNAS, 322

PICARD, Lt L'AMF, 323

POPHAM, A E, Flt Lt RNAS, 252, 257-260, 323

PRATT, H G, Lt RAF, 290, 293

PRINCE, Ldg Mech RNAS, 254, 323

PULLING, E L, Flt Lt RNAS, *165*

RAVENSCROFT, Lt RFA, 212, 213, 323, 332, 333

RISK, C E, Wg Cdr RNAS, 246, *247*, 248, 250, 251, 323

ROBERTSON, W, Ldg Mech RNAS, 323

ROSS, R P, Flt Lt RNAS, 13

ROUSSILLON, H, Lt L'AMF, 200, 323

RUTLAND, F J, Flt Cdr RNAS, 16, 35, 57, 60, *359*

SADLER, J A, Capt RAF, 283, 289, 290, 292, 293, 294, 296

SAMSON, C R, Wg Cdr RNAS, 11, 12, 35, *36*, 124, 205, 207, 212, 214, 217, 222, 223, 233, 235, 242, 243, 246, 323, *356*

SAMSON, W L, Lt RNVR, 235, 323

SEDDON, W J, Sqdn Cdr RNAS, 157

SHARWOOD, A C, Flt Lt RAF, 32-34, 38

SIMPSON, G H, Flt Sub Lt, *155*

SITWELL, W G, Flt Cdr RNAS, *208*, 245, 323

SMART, B A, Flt Sub Lt RNAS, 30, *30*, 32

SMITH, A K, Lt HLI, 201, 202, 207, 214, 216, 323

SMITH, G D, Flt Lt RNAS, 216, *216*, 222, 228, 229, 235, 240, 243, 249, 257, 259, 260, 264, 323

SMITH, H B, Flt Sub Lt RNAS, 154, *155*, 156, *162*, *164*, 340

STEPHENS, T G M, Flt Lt RNAS, 242, 252, 257, 258, 323

STEWART, N W, Lt 7th Royal Scots, 212, 214, 218, 230, 231, 235, 240, 323, 333

STIRLING, F, Capt Dublin Fusiliers, 127, 128, 323

THOMPSON, H G, 2nd Lt RAF, 290, 293, 295

TODD, R E, Capt RAMC, 172, 174, *175*, 180, 182, 183, 323

TROUILLET, Petty Officer L'AMF, 173, 189-193, 323

TURTON-JONES, J W, Lt RAF, 296

WAKE, Lt RAF, 296, 297

WALKER, Flt Sub Lt RNAS, *155*

WATKINS, H E M, Flt Lt RNAS, *132*, 133, 134, 139, 142, 143, *144*, *150*

WEDGWOOD BENN, J, Lt Middlesex Yeomanry, 207, *208*, 212, *213*, 214, 217, 222, 224, 233-235, 324

WELDON, L B, Capt Dublin Fusiliers, 170, *170*, 172, 174, 175, 179, 189, 190, 192-195, 200-202, 204, 205, 214, 226, 228, 238, 240, 324, *337*

WEDDERSPOON, J H B, Lt RFA, 203, 324

WILLIAMS, Flt Sub Lt RNAS, 32

WILLIAMS, E, Lt East Yorkshire Regiment, 195, 196, 198, 245, 324

WILLIAMS, K L, Lt 2nd Rajputs (formerly Ceylon Rifles), 174, 216, 222-224, 228-230, 235, 238, 240, 324

WILMSHURST, Air Mech RNAS, 269, 270

WOOD, C E, Flt Sub Lt RNAS, 340

WOOD, M C, Flt Lt RNAS, 249, 251, 324

WOOD, T G C, Flt Sub Lt RNAS, 154

WOODLAND, P M, Lt RNVR, 217, 222, 223, 234, 324

WORRALL, H V, Flt Lt RNAS, 230, *247*, 248-250, 257, 262, 264, 324

WRIGHT, M E A, Flt Lt RNAS, 201, 202, 207-209, 324, 330

INDEX OF AIRCRAFT

Armstrong Whitworth Siskin IIIA
J8390, 70, *72*
Avro 504H
N5261, 73
N5269, 73
N5270, 73
Avro 504L
H3034, 278, *280*, 313
H3042, 278, 314

Beardmore W.B.III
N6100, 39, *48,*
N6109, 63
N6115, 14, *27*, 62, 63
N6116, 63
N6123, 39
N6127, 40
N6128, 39
N6129, 40
N6686, 40

Borel Seaplane
48, *25*, 305

Bristol Scout C
1246, *69*, *358*
1255, 58, *359*

Bristol Scout D
8953, 157

Caudron G.II
55, 13, *13*, *24*, 305
56, 305

Curtiss H.12
8666, 285, 286

Deperdussin Monoplane
1378, 14, *26*, 39, 157

Fairey F.127
N9, 73, *80*, 313

Fairey Flycatcher
N9670, 41, *55*, 70
N9675, 70
N9679, 41, *54*
N9894, 41, *56*, 70
N9895, 70
N9902, 41, *56*
N9913, 70
N9917, 41
N9940, 41
S1063, 41, *55*

S1070, 70
S1277, 70, *75*
S1280, 70
S1292, *77*

Fairey Hamble Baby
N1209, 257, 301, 313, 315, 317
N1210, 257, 258, 315, 317

Fairey IIID
N9469, *81*
S1089, *82*
ANA-1, 278
A10-2, 280, 314

Farman, Henry, F.27(French c/n's)
AS/8/HF, *137*, 139, 307
SA/9/HF, *137*, 139, 141, 307

Friedrichshafen FF33E
874, 30, 242

Nieuport VI (French Serial
    Numbers)
N11, 172, 180, 182, 190-192, 194,
    195, 298, 311, 317
N14, 172, *173*, 190, 191, 193, 298,
    317
N15, 172, 174, 180, *184*, 186-188,
    298, 311, 317
N16, 172, *182*, 183, 184, 192, 298,
    304, 311, 317
N17, 172, 184-186, 190-196, 298,
    304, 311, 317
N18, 182-184, 298, 304, 311, 317
N19, 184-186, 194, 195, 198, 202,
    203, 298, 304, 311, 317
N20, 182, 186-188, 190-192, 194,
    197, 298, 311, 318
N21, *193*, 298, 318
N22, 195, 198, 200, 201, 298, 311,
    318
N23, 195, 197, 202, 203, 298, 311,
    318
NB1, 201, 298, 318
NB2, *176*, 200, 201, 298, 318

Parnall Panther
N92, 63
N7468, 63

Short Folder
81, *24*, *25*, 305
82, 305
119, *129*, 135, 139, 305, 307

121, 135, 143, *152*, 307
122, *129*, 135, 143, *143*, *151*, 307

Short S38
T2, 11, 12, *19*, *20*, 22, 23,

Short S41
H1, 12, *21*

Short S74
183, 299
818, *169*, 299

Short S80
905, 305

Short 166
164, *127*, 129, 312

Short 827
3096, 266, 271, 272, 305, 307
3097, 266, *268*, 271, 307
3098, 266, 269, *270*, 271, *272*, *273*,
    305, 307
8218, 266, 307
8253, 271
8254, 271, 273, *274*, 275, 305, 307
8641, 269, 271, 276, 307
8642, 269, 270, 271, 305, 307
8649, *262*, 301

Short 830
819, 299
821, 299

Short 184
184, 312, 316
841, 236, 312, 316, *364*
842, *278*, 303, 316, *364*
846, 204, *205*, 314, 316, 331
849, 200, 314, 316
850, 204, 207-209, 211, 311, 314,
    316
8004, 201, 226, 228-231, 235, 240,
    245, 248-250, 298, 302, 309,
    315, 314
8018, 242, *242*, 243, 249-251, 311,
    315, 316
8019, 242, 243, 246, 248-250, 252,
    255, 260, 301, 311, 315, 316
8020, 241, 245, 246, 248, 249, 264,
    301, 315, 316
8021, 240-242, 250, 252, 254, 298,
    311, 315, 316
8022, 240, 241, 250, 257, 264, 265,
    301, 311, 315, 316

8035, 222, 314, 316
8043, 317
8045, 222-224, 311, 316
8046, 317
8047, 317
8051, 315, 316
8054, 201, 202, 205, 209, 214, 217, 224, 298, 314, 316
8070, 311, 314, 316
8075, 216, 222-224, 228, 229, 231, 235, *240*, 245, 246, 298, 311, 314-316
8076, 248, *249*, 314-316
8080, 217, 222, 223, 233-235, 265, 314
8082, 209, 314, 316
8083, 317
8084, 298, 316
8087, 207, *209*, *213*, 314, 316
8088, 245, 315, 316
8090, 212, 213, 217, 218, *228*, 234, *241*, 242, 298, 311, 314, 316
8091, 212-214, 216, 222-224, 298, 311, 314-316
8095, 317
8098, 304
8372, 214, 216, 217, *220*, 222, 233, 234, 314, 316
8381, 245, 315, 316
8382, 304
9051, 303
9057, 304
9060, 304
N1090, 250, 257, 259, 301, 315, 316
N1091, 252, 254, 259, 260, *260*, 301, 315, 316
N1262, 255, 301, 311, 316
N1263, 257, 258, 260, 264, 265, 298, 300, 309, 316
N1581, 262, 264, 315, 316
N1582, 262, 264, 315, 316
N1590, 315, 316
N1597, 317
N1639, *261*, 264, 265, 301, 316
N1649, 317
N1679, 317
N1749, 317
N1774, *281*, 283, 309
N1784, 317
N1790, 309
N1827, 317
N1838, 317
N1839, 317
N2648, 317
N2791, 317
N2792, 317
N2812, 317
N2816, *282*, 308, 309
N2817, 283, 284, 308
N2822, 317

N2823, 317
N2824, 317
N9066, 317
N9078, *295*, 296, 309
N9079, 289, 290, *290*, 298
N9080, 289, 290, 292, 293, 298
N9081, 289, 296, 297, *297*, 309
N9082, 289, 295, 298
N9084, *291*

Sopwith Seaplane
138, 305

Sopwith 807
920, 133, 134, *146-149*, 306
921, 133, 134, *146*, *148*, 306
922, *126*, *145*, 302, 308

Sopwith 860
855, 310
860, 310, *367*

Sopwith Schneider
1437, *145*, 302, 312, 317
1438, *145*, 308, 310
1439, 299, 309
1440, 299, 309, 313
1441, 299, 309
1446, 306, 312, 339
1447, 312, 339
1556, 299, 308
1557, *157*, *160*, 299, 309, 313
1558, 306
1568, *162*
1578, 312
3708, 312, 339
3710, 305, 306, 312, 339
3715, 305, 306, 312, 339
3720, 305, 306, 312, 339
3721, 207, 208, 311, 314, 317
3722, *198*, 207, 208, 311, 317
3723, 305, 306, 312, 339
3727, 207, 208, 311, 314, 317
3730, 303, *355*,
3736, 156, *165*, 300, 339
3743, 303, *355*
3770, 233, 235, 311, 314, 317
3771, 214, 314, 317
3772, 317, *318*
3773, 314, 317
3774, 207-209, 311, 314, 317
3775, 311, 317
3776, 300, 339
3777, 217, 224, 233, 298, 314, 317
3778, *230*, 233, 235, 314, 317
3779, 231, 314, 317
3786, 212, 311, 314, 317
3788, 303, 317, *354*
3789, 209, *225*, 231, 233, 314, 317
3790, 207-209, 311, 314, 317
3801, 306, 339

Sopwith Baby
8120, 300, 305, 306, 339
8122, 300, 339
8131, 306, 339
8133, 304, 339
8135, 231, 233, *234*, 314, 317
8139, 306, 339
8140, *154*, 300, 339
8141, 155, 306, 339
8142, 306, 339
8147, 306, 339
8148, 155, 299, 306, 337
8149, 156, 300, 304, 339
8150, 300, 302, 304, 306, 339
8154, 306, 339
8155, 306, 339
8156, 300, 306, 339
8157, 306, 339
8159, 301, 339
8160, *166*, 300, 339
8163, 300, 339
8164, 300, 306, 339
8173, 306, 339
8174, 306, 339
8188, 205, *231*, 235, 314, 317
8189, 205, 207, 209, 212, 213, 222-224, 311, 314, 317
8207, 306, 339
N1014, 242, 243, *244*, 277, 299, 311, 317
N1016, 241, 298, 317
N1028, 258, *259*, 315, 317
N1036, 258, 315, 317
N1038, 257, 315, 317
N1060, 317
N1066, 302, 304, 339
N1108, 302, 339
N1111, 310
N1112, 310
N1126, 301, 317
N1128, 317
N1129, 258, 315, 317
N1195, 310
N1424, *284*
N1444, 310
N2072, 317
N2073, 317
N2082, 308

Sopwith Pup
9901, 40, *43*
9931, 39, 40
9932, 40
9934, 63,
9944, 40, 63,
9945, 63,
N6200, 39
N6430, 30, *31*, 32, 40
N6431, 39, 40
N6434, 63,
N6438, 63,

N6440, 62
N6443, 14, 28, 40, 62, 63
N6444, 63, 82, 84, 362
N6445, 62
N6446, 38, 40, 61, 63
N6448, 63,
N6449, 39, 40
N6453, 57-59, 63
N6455, 62, 63
N6456, 63,
N6458, 118
N6633, 62

Sopwith Ship Strutter
N5606, 61
N5644, 61, 62, 66
N6968, 65
A5981, 63
A5982, 63
A5984, 61
A5985, 61
A5987, 86
A5988, 62, 114
A5990, 62
A5994, 62
A5995, 87
A5998, 62
A6006, 62, 118
A6010, 62
A6905, 62
A6952, 62
A6966, 62
A6967, 62
A6968, 61
A6980, 62, 115
A6981, 62
A8224, 62
A8277, 62, 119
A8300, 63
B774, 62
F2210, 62
F2215, 61
F2216, 62
F2220, 62
F2221, 62
F2222, 62
F2224, 63
F2225, 63
F2227, 62
F2228, 61, 63
F7561, 62
F7562, 61, 67

Sopwith F.1 Camel
D9523, 63

Sopwith 2F.1 Camel
N6600, 40, 62
N6601, 63
N6602, 39, 52, 62
N6603, 40, 63

N6604, 62
N6605, 62, 63, 361
N6606, 63
N6607, 40, 62
N6611, 40, 63, 84, 85
N6614, 39, 62
N6616, 39, 40
N6617, 39, 62, 63
N6619, 62, 63
N6623, 35, 49, 50
N6625, 40
N6629, 39, 40, 62
N6630, 63
N6631, 40, 62
N6632, 39
N6633, 62, 63
N6635, 38, 40
N6636, 39
N6637, 39, 63
N6638, 40, 63
N6639, 40
N6640, 40
N6641, 63
N6642, 39, 62
N6643, 107
N6644, 40
N6645, 62, 361
N6646, 40
N6647, 62
N6648, 63
N6649, 40, 102
N6750, 61, 63, 120, 121
N6751, 40, 62, 63
N6752, 40, 62, 63, 111
N6753, 39
N6754, 40
N6755, 40
N6756, 33, 39, 40
N6757, 39, 62
N6758, 40, 62
N6759, 39, 62
N6760, 39
N6762, 40, 61
N6763, 62
N6764, 62, 112
N6766, 39, 40
N6767, 39
N6768, 39, 40, 62
N6769, 62
N6770, 39, 40, 62
N6772, 40
N6773, 39, 40, 62
N6774, 40
N6775, 39, 62
N6776, 62, 105
N6778, 40, 62
N6779, 29, 39
N6780, 39
N6782, 40
N6783, 32, 40
N6784, 40

N6785, 40
N6786, 61, 62
N6787, 40, 62
N6788, 62
N6789, 40, 62, 121
N6790, 39, 61, 62
N6791, 62
N6792, 62
N6793, 39, 62
N6794, 39, 40
N6795, 40, 63
N6797, 40, 63, 108
N6798, 40
N6799, 40, 63
N6800, 40
N6810, 39
N6811, 39
N6812, 33, 37, 51
N6813, 62
N6816, 39
N6817, 62
N6819, 62, 63, 110
N6820, 40, 61
N6821, 40
N6822, 40, 46, 61
N6824, 40
N6826, 61
N6828, 39, 61
N6829, 40
N6830, 62
N6831, 39, 40
N6832, 62
N6833, 39, 62
N6834, 61
N6835, 62, 63
N6838, 40, 63
N6839, 62
N6842, 40, 62
N6844, 39
N6845, 40
N6846, 39
N6847, 40
N6848, 39
N6849, 62
N7100, 40
N7101, 40, 63
N7103, 61, 63
N7104, 40
N7105, 63
N7106, 63
N7107, 40
N7108, 39, 63
N7109, 40, 62, 103
N7110, 39, 40
N7111, 39
N7112, 40
N7113, 40
N7114, 62
N7116, 40, 62
N7117, 40, 62
N7119, 40, 62

N7120, 62, 63, *117*

N7121, 39, 62

N7122, 39

N7123, 40

N7125, 62

N7126, 40, 62

N7128, 62

N7129, 62

N7134, 62

N7136, 40, 61, *362*

N7138, 39

N7139, 40

N7140, 62

N7146, 62

N7148, 62, *119*

Wight Navyplane

894, 310

Wight Twin

1450, 304, *356*

1451, 304, *356*

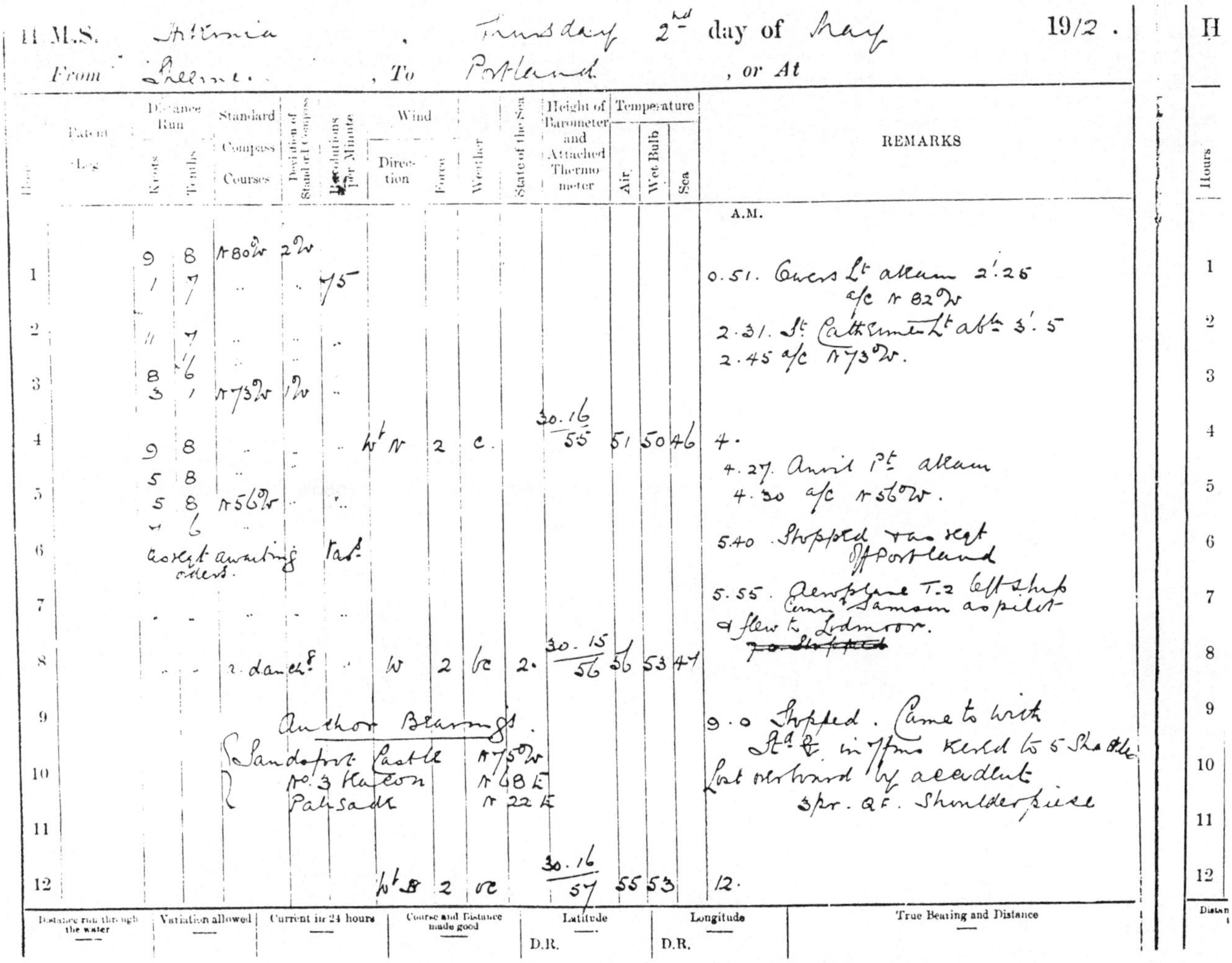

HMS *Hibernia's Ships Log for 2nd May 1912. (via PRO)*

AIR-BRITAIN - THE INTERNATIONAL ASSOCIATION OF AVIATION HISTORIANS - FOUNDED 1948

For forty-two years, Air-Britain has recorded aviation events as they have happened, because today's events are tomorrow's history. In addition, considerable research into the past has been undertaken to provide historians with the background to aviation history. Over 14,000 members have contributed to our aims and efforts in that time and many have become accepted authorities in their own fields.

Every month, AIR-BRITAIN NEWS covers the current civil and military scene.

Quarterly, each member receives AIR-BRITAIN DIGEST which is a fully-illustrated journal containing articles on aviation subjects, both past and present.

For those interested in military aviation history, there is the quarterly AEROMILITARIA which is designed to delve more deeply into the background of, mainly, British and Commonwealth military aviation than is possible in commercial publications and whose format permits it to be used as components of a filing system which suits the readers' requirements. This publication is responsible for the production of this volume and other monographs on military subjects. Also published quarterly is ARCHIVE, produced in a similar format to AEROMILITARIA but covering civil aviation history in depth on a world-wide basis. Both magazines are well illustrated by photogaphs and drawings.

In addition to these regular publications, there are monographs covering type histories, both military and civil, airline fleets, Royal Air Force registers, squadron histories and the civil registers of a large number of countries. Although our publications are available to non-members, prices are considerably lower to members who have priority over non-members when availablity is limited. Normally, the accumulated price discounts for which members qualify when buying monographs far exceed the annual subscription rates.

A large team of aviation experts is available to answer members' queries on most aspects of aviation. If you have made a study of any particular subject, you may be able to expand your knowledge by joining those with similar interests. Also available to members are libraries of colour slides and photographs which supply slides and prints at prices considerably lower than those charged by commercial firms.

There are local branches of the Association in Bournemouth, Gwent, Heston, Merseyside, Luton, Manchester, Rugby, Sheffield, Southampton, South-West Essex, Stansted and West Midlands. For visitors to London, the London Society of Air Britain arranges regular meetings and lectures on behalf of the Association.

If you would like to receive samples of Air-Britain magazines, please write to the following addresss enclosing 50p and stating your particular interests. If you would like only a brochure, please send a stamped self-addressed envelope to the same address (preferably 230 mm by 160 mm or over)

Air-Britain Membership Enquiries (BA), 1 Rose Cottages, 179 Penn Road, Hazlemere, Bucks, HP15 7NE

MILITARY AVIATION PUBLICATIONS

Royal Air Force Aircraft series: (prices are for members/non-members and are post-free)

J1-J9999	(£8.00/£12.00)	K1000-K9999	(£2.50/£3.75)*	L1000-L9999	(£2.50/£3.75)
N1000-N9999(R)	(£4.00/£6.00)	P1000-P9999	(£2.00/£3.00)	R1000-R9999	(£2.50/£3.75)
T1000-T9999	(£3.00/£4.50)*	V1000-W9999	(£4.00/£6.00)*	X1000-Z9999	(£4.00/£6.00)
AA100-AZ999	(£6.00/£9.00)	BA100-BZ999	(£6.00/£9.00)	DA100-DZ999	(£5.00/£7.50)
EA100-EZ999	(£5.00/£7.50)	FA100-FZ999	(£5.00/£7.50)	HA100-HZ999	(£6.00/£9.00)
JA100-JZ999	(£6.00/£9.00)	KA100-KZ999	(£6-00/£9.00)	SA100-VZ999	(£6.00/£9.00)
WA100-WZ999	(£5.00/£7.50)*				

* Currently out of print; (R) Reprinted in limited numbers with slightly reduced quality of photographic reproduction

Type Histories

The Halifax File	(£6.00/£9.00)*	The Lancaster File	(£8.00/£12.00)	The Washington File	(£2.00/£3.00)
The Whitley File	(£4.50/£6.75)	The Typhoon File	(£4.00/£6.00)*	The Stirling File	(£6.00/£9.00)
The Anson File	(£15.00/£22.50)	The Harvard File	(£7.00/£10.50)	The Hampden File	(£11.00/£16.50)

Hardbacks

The Squadrons of the Royal Air Force and Commonwealth (£18.00/£26.00)

The Squadrons of the Fleet Air Arm (£14.00/£21.00)

Both the above cover the histories of all squadrons with precise tables of movements and equipment. Squadron badges are included for all units and both are profusely illustrated.

Individual Squadron Histories

Strike True - The History of No.80 Squadron, Royal Air Force (£4.00/£6.00)

With Courage and Faith - The History of No.18 Squadron, Royal Air Force (£5.00/£7.50)

The above are available from Air-Britain Sales Department, 5 Bradley Road, Upper Norwood, London, SE19 3NT.